JAVA JUMP START

A Beginner's Guide to Internet Programming

Noel Enete

To join a Prentice Hall PTR Internet mailing list, point to
http://www.prenhall.com/register

Prentice Hall PTR
Upper Saddle River, New Jersey 07458
http://www.prenhall.com

Library of Congress Cataloging in Publication Data

Enete, Noel.
Java jump start : a beginner's guide to Internet programming / Noel Enete
p. cm..
Includes index.
ISBN 0-13-5658543
1. Java (Computer program language) 2. Internet programming I. Title.
QA76.73.J38E54 1997 96-38147
005.2'762—dc21 CIP

Editorial/production supervision: *Nicholas Radhuber*
Manufacturing manager: *Alexis Heydt*
Acquisitions editor: *Paul Becker*
Marketing manager: *Dan Rush*
Editorial assistant: *Maureen Diana*
Cover design: *Anthony Gemmellaro*
Cover design director: *Jerry Votta*

Prentice-Hall, Inc.
A Simon & Schuster Company
Upper Saddle River, New Jersey 07458

The Publisher offers discounts on this book when ordered in bulk quantities.
For more information, contact:

Corporate Sales Department
Prentice Hall PTR
1 Lake St.
Upper Saddle River, NJ 07458
Phone: 800-382-3419 Fax: 201-236-7141
E-mail: corpsales@prenhall.com

Printed in the United States of America
10 9 8 7 6 5 4 3 2

ISBN 0-13-565854-3

Prentice-Hall International (UK) Limited, *London*
Prentice-Hall of Australia Pty. Limited, *Sydney*
Prentice-Hall Canada Inc., *Toronto*
Prentice-Hall Hispanoamericana, S.A., *Mexico*
Prentice-Hall of India Private Limited, *New Delhi*
Prentice-Hall of Japan, Inc., *Tokyo*
Simon & Schuster Asia Pte. Ltd., *Singapore*
Editora Prenticre-Hall do Brasil, Ltda., *Rio de Janeiro*

To Denise,

. . . who is the love of my life for
the rest of my life. A wonderful, beautiful,
capable woman with a heart of gold.

Contents

Preface **xiii**

PART I GETTING ORIENTED TO JAVA

1 Introduction **1**
What Is Java? 1
What Are Java Enabled Browsers? 4
Where Does Java Fit? 6

2 Having Fun with Java **8**
Java Application — Launched from a Command Line 9
Java Applet — Launched from a Web Page 10
Summary 13

3 Having More Fun with Java **14**
Class — The Merging of Code and Data 15
Inheritance — The Extending of Code and Data 18
Responsibility — The Duties of a Class 24
Language Issues 25

4 Passing Data to Programs **26**
Passing Command Line Parameters 27
Passing Applet Parameters 30
ParmApplet — Rendering a Message in a Font and Color 31
stringToColor() — Parsing a Color String 34
Font Selection 35
Language Issues 37

5 Exploring System Capabilities **38**

Array — A Fixed Collection of One Object Type 39
Enumeration — A Consumable Collection of Multiple Object Types 41
ArrayApplication — Surfacing System Information 44
ArrayApplet — Displaying System Fonts 48
Language Issues 53
Summary 55

6 Launching Java Services **56**

Vector — A Variable Collection of Multiple Object Types 57
Hashtable — A Collection of Key/Value Pairs 59
Properties — A Persistent Collection of Key/Value Pairs 62
StringTokenizer — A Service for Parsing Through a String 66

7 Touching Java Windows **70**

Mouse Messages 71
Click and Drag 75
Dragging a Picture 82

8 Animation **88**

Triggering Each Picture 89
Displaying Each Picture 93
Loading the Pictures 97

PART II GETTING COMFORTABLE WITH JAVA

9 User Input **104**

How to Receive Input from the Command Line (stdin) 105
How to Receive Input from a Window (events) 107
How to Receive Input from Other Objects (Event Triggering) 118

10 Buttons and Things **130**

Button — A One-State Input Control 131
Checkbox — A Two-State Input Control 133
CheckboxGroup — A Single Choice Input Control 135
Label — A Text Output Control 138
TextField — A Scrolling Area for Single Line Text Editing 140
TextArea—A Scrolling Area for Multiple Line Text Editing 142

List — A Selectable Collection of Text Items 145
Choice — A Drop Down Collection of Text Items 147
Scrollbar — A Representation of a Range of Values 149
An Applet with Controls and No Layout Manager (LoanApplet) 152

11 Layout Managers **160**

FlowLayout — Controls in Rows 161
GridLayout — Controls in Checkerboard Cells 165
BorderLayout — One Control Flanked by the Others 167
Panel — A Component with its Own Layout Manager 170
CardLayout — A Notebook of Controls 173
GridBagLayout — Controls in Irregular Checkerboard Cells 175
GridBag Constraints.fill 179
GridBag Constraints.weightx and weighty 179
GridBag Constraints.gridwidth and gridheight 179
GridBag Constraints.gridx and gridy 180

12 Standalone Windows **186**

Frame — A Standalone Window 187
Applet — An Addable Component 194
Dialog and (Popup) Window — Dependent Windows 198
Menu — A Specialized Dependent Window 204
FileDialog — Dependent Window for File Access 210

13 Sound **216**

PCM — How to Represent Sound as Data 217
AU — How to Format a Sound File for Java 219
Play( ) — How to Render a Sound File 219

14 File I/O **224**

File — Name and Location 225
RandomAccessFile — Direct File System Access 228
Stream — Sequential Access 231
ByteArrayInputStream, ByteArrayOutputStream and StringBufferInputStream 231
FileInputStream and FileOutputStream 233
SequenceInputStream 235
FilterStream — Smart Sequential Access 237
DataInputStream and DataOutputStream 237
PrintStream 240

LineNumberInputStream 241
BufferedInputStream and BufferedOutputStream 241
PushbackInputStream 242
PipedInputStream and PipedOutputStream 242

PART III IMPLEMENTING CLIENT/SERVER IN JAVA

15 Sockets and a Simple Server 246
What is a Socket? 247
ServerSocket — The Starting Point of a Conversation 249
Sockets — The End Points of a Conversation 253

16 A Simple Web Server 260
HTTP — The Format of Web Requests and Web Responses 261
WebServer — Responds to a Web Browser Request 262
WebClient — Generates a Web Browser Request 268
URL — A Convenient WebClient Class 271

17 A Web Server for Client/Server Programming 276
How to Open Up the Web 277
Attaching a Client to the Web Browser 279
Attaching a Server to the Web Server 285
CGI — Extending traditional web servers 285
ExtendableWebServer — A Web server that launches Java classes 286
ServerExtension — A class that extends the Web server 299
FormServerExtension — A class to process an HTML form 300
Implementing a Client/Server Application 304
SqlQuery — A Look at JDBC Syntax 305
TimeClient/TimeServer — A client/server application to fetch the current time 308

18 The CaffeineCafe 316
Try It Out — How to Run CaffeineCafe 318
Extend It — How to Code Drippers 321

How to code a simple dripper 321
How to Code a Forms Processing Dripper 322
How to code a Client/Server application 329
Packages — How CaffeineCafe is Organized 341
JavaDoc — How CaffeineCafe is Documented 344
Source — How CaffeineCafe Works 349
Design — Enhances the ExtendableWebServer 349
CaffeineCafe — Listens for new connections 350
SConnection — Handles Communications between Client and Dripper 353
Dripper — Implements default dripper behavior 364
EchoDripper — Presents an "About Box" for the server 369
FileDripper — Fetches files for the server 370
CaffeineCafeDefaults — Maintains system-wide defaults 373

APPENDICES

Appendix A How Do I . . . 380
String and Array 381
How do I concatenate strings? 381
How do I parse through a string? 382
How do I dimension and load an array at the same time? 383
How do I append one array with another array? 384
Loop 385
How do I code a for() loop? 385
How do I code a while() loop? 386
How do I code a do/while() loop? 387
How do I abruptly exit a loop (break)? 388
How do I skip some statements and return to the top of the loop (continue)? 390
How do I process an Enumeration? 391
How do I create an Enumeration? 392
Flow of Control 393
How do I code if/then/else logic? 393
How do I perform case logic (switch)? 394
How do I force a program exit with a return code (exit)? 395
How do I code bitwise AND/OR logic? 396
Conversion 397
How do I convert a String into an int, float, or double? 397
How do I convert an int, float, or double to a String? 398
How do I convert a String to an array and back? 399

How do I convert a Boolean/Integer/Double to a boolean/int/double? *400*

File 402

How do I code basic file I/O? *402*

How do I read from stdin and write to stdout and stderr? *403*

Math 404

How do I code arithmetic? *404*

How do I round a number or get its ceiling or floor? *405*

How do I truncate a number? *406*

How do I calculate a division remainder? *407*

How do I raise a number to a power? *408*

How do I specify the constant "Pi" or the constant "e"? *409*

How do I invoke sin, cos, and tan functions? *410*

Language 411

How do I code literals? *411*

How do I create a variable? *412*

How do I create a single variable that all instances of a class can access? *413*

How do I call a method? *414*

How do I call a method that throws an Exception? *415*

How do I explicitly call a method in a super class? *416*

How do I use an Interface? *417*

How do I see if an object is an instance of a particular class? *418*

User Interface 419

How do I cut, copy, and paste inside a TextField or TextArea? *419*

How do I receive keyboard input? *419*

How do I pass parameters to a command line Java application? *419*

How do I pass parameters to an applet? *420*

How do I write text on an Applet window? *422*

How do I get FontMetrics for a Font? *423*

How do I place a button at a particular (x, y) spot? *425*

How do I draw lines, circles, and rectangles on the face of an applet? *426*

How do I copy pixels from one spot in the window to another? *427*

How do I draw in one cell of a Layout Manager? *428*

How do I place an independent window at a particular (x, y) spot? *432*

How do I get an independent window to close? *433*

Client/Server 434

How do I get Netscape to release the applet? *434*

System 435
How do I get the IP number of this machine? 435
How do I find the font face names that are available? 436
How do I find out how much memory is available? 437
How do I launch a thread? 438
How do I dynamically load a class? 439
Special Services 441
How do I create a bit coded variable? 441
Utilities 443
How do I generate documentation? 443
How do I list the Class Hierarchy of Java classes? 443

Appendix B Introduction to the World Wide Web 444

How Did the Internet Start? 445
How Does the Internet Work? 446
How is Internet Software Structured? 449
How Does a Program Use the Internet? 450
How Does a Web Browser Use the Internet? 451
How are Web Pages Connected to One Other? 452
How Do Web Pages Support Multimedia? 452
How are Java Programs Shared Across the Internet? 452

Appendix C Introduction to Java's Virtual Machine 454

How does the Virtual Machine Work? 455
What is a Virtual Machine? 455
How do you use the Virtual Machine? 455
What does the VM do when it runs? 457
What instructions does the VM interpret? 458
Is the Virtual Machine an interpreter? 460
Java's VM Opens Up Distributed Processing 461

Appendix D How to Parse a Java Class File 462

A Class File Is a Collection of Fields 463
The Fields Are Organized into Groups 465
Inspecting the Class File Can Suggest Optimizations 468
Inspecting the Class File Can Locate Errors 469

Appendix E Enete Utilities 470

Imaging Scanning Utilities 471

Implementers — All the methods that implement the requested method 471
Passers — All the methods that pass the requested class 472
Returners — All the methods that return the requested class 473
General Utilities 474
GenApplet — Generate a skeleton Java applet 474
GenApplication — Generate a skeleton Java application 475
MakeNugget — Create a self-extracting archive of files 476
Dumpclass — A display of the constant pool 478

Appendix F Java Resources **480**
Primary 481
Gamelan <http://www.gamelan.com/> 481
Java World <http://www.javaworld.com> 481
JARS <http://www.jars.com> 481
Cafe Au Lait <http://sunsite.unc.edu/javafaq/> 482
The Java Developer <http://www.digitalfocus.com/faq> 482
Secondary 482
Rapid Systems Solutions' Java Resource List <http://www.rssi.com/info/java-info.html> 482
Performance Java <http://www.preemptive.com/lectures/Optimization.html> 483
Java Optimization <http://www.cs.cmu.edu/~jch/java/optimization.html> 483
Kaffe <http://web.soi.city.ac.uk/homes/tim/Kaffe/kaffe.html> 483
Usenet <news:comp.lang.java> 483
Borland's Internet Tools <http://www.borland.com> 483
Symantec Cafe <http://cafe.symantec.com> 483

Index **485**

Preface

This book is centered around the learning process. Any material that would detract from learning is removed. Any concept that would overload the learning process is postponed until a later chapter. The examples are simple and the concepts are central.

This book will help the reader over the "hump" in learning Java. After working through this book, the reader will be ready to use standard reference documentation and follow advanced techniques.

The chapters in Part I offer a mix of topics that help to orient and motivate programmers who are new to Java. At the end of Part I, the reader has been exposed to all of the core techniques in the Java environment.

Part II presents more systematic treatments of core Java topics.

Part III is an extended treatment of one advanced topic — how to use a Web server to implement a Client/Server application. The reader explores the internals of a Web server written in Java — the *CaffeineCafe.*

This Web server is constructed so that it launches other Java classes in the same way that a Web client launches Java applets. Examples demonstrate how to use this technique to write complete Client/Server applications or to use Java to write CGI like back-end programs.

As the reader watches a Web browser in one window make requests to a Web server in another window, it will be easy to gain a perspective for Web processing that is difficult to acquire in any other way.

Audience

This book is intended for individuals who have exposure to at least one other programming language.

Development Environment

Although a number of development environments enhance the experience of programming Java (Symantec Café, Java Workshop, Visual J++, etc.), this book does not assume any such environment. In order to focus on the task of learning Java, this book avoids the use of productivity aids. These can be added as the need arises.

The CaffeineCafe

The *CaffeineCafe* is the Web server that is developed in Part III of the book. The reader can use it to start their own Web site or use it to learn how a Web server works. Readers that want to build their own server for a custom application can use this working server as a springboard for developing their own.

This system was written to be complete enough to use as a server, but to be simple enough to read and understand. The reader is encouraged to send fixes or enhancements to *noel@enete.com.* As new versions of the program are available, they can be downloaded from *http://www.enete.com.*

Installing the CD

The files in the CD are stored in three separate directories—one for each platform. The reader should look in the directory that corresponds to their platform (Windows, Mac, or Sun) and load its ReadMe.txt file into a text editor. The steps for copying the JDK and Jump Start archive files to the hard disk and unpacking them are described in the ReadMe.txt file.

CD Web Page

When the CD data is installed, the file *index.html* is installed into the *JumpStrt* directory. This is a Web page that gives quick access to all of the examples in the book. By clicking on the links of this page, the reader can go directly to the program source or directly execute the applet examples.

The *index* page also provides links to the Java API documentation and is the quickest way to find all the methods a particular class implements.

To access the *index* file, the reader should open the Web browser and choose the option in the *File* menu for opening a file. In the file selection dialog, choose the file *c:\JumpStrt\index.html.* Once the page is found, it can be added as a bookmark in the Web browser.

Enete Utilities

I have included several classes that I have found helpful when doing Java development. They are described in the *Enete Utilities* appendix. These are command level applications that are installed from the CD into the Java CLASSES directory so they can be available from any command line prompt.

Feedback

With the readers' help, future editions of this work can be of greater benefit to those who are learning Java. If anyone has suggestions or simply enjoys this work, they can drop me a note. Unfortunately, I probably won't be able to reply. But I would love to hear from my readers.

If one is not able to find the answer to a Java question, they should write me with the explanation of the question and the index entries used to search for the answer.

As the software in this book evolves and the operating systems for which it is prepared expand, the newest versions of the code will be available for download from *http://www.enete.com*.

Acknowledgments

I would like to thank my four teenagers — Charis, Shane, Shannon, and John for their support of this project. I would also like to thank John Gladfelter, Bruce Boyer, and my parents for encouraging me to write. Deborah Bayles and Alan Evans of NeTouch Communications were instrumental in providing extended support for this project.

Thanks to Leonard Megliola for porting the examples in the book to Solaris and to Stephen Franklin for freeing up Leonard for the task.

I hope the reader will find Java as fun to learn as it was to explain.

Noel Enete (*eee NET*)
January 17, 1997
noel@enete.com
http://www.enete.com

CHAPTER 1

Introduction

A new technology is expanding across the fabric of the computer industry. It promises to enable the transparent execution of programs across the Internet.

Some people call the technology *Java*, others call it *HotJava*. Some say it is a new script language. Others say it is a new Internet service.

Let's begin by clarifying what this new technology is and how it works.

What is Java?

Java is a programming language.

It is a programming language in the same way that C is a programming language and COBOL is a programming language and BASIC is a programming language. People write programs in Java.

Do the letters 'J' 'A' 'V' 'A' stand for anything?—No.

The name was chosen purely on the value of its connotation. The language was not always called Java. When the creator of the language, James Gosling, came to the moment of giving it a name, he looked up from his computer and saw a large oak tree standing outside his window. This being sufficient inspiration, he named the language *Oak*. The language was known as Oak from 1991 to 1994. Then in 1994, the name did not survive a trademark search and was dropped in favor of the name *Java*.

James was not looking to create a new language when his project began. He was simply trying to find a way for programs to run unchanged on a wide variety of computers.

He set out to create a compiler and environment that would enable C++ programs to run on incompatible computer platforms without having to be recompiled. As he progressed, he found that his task would be much easier if he could modify some of the C++ conventions. As he made modifications to C++, the Java language was born.

Although it is considered a new language, Java syntax is close to the syntax of C++. Notice the similarity of conventions between the Java program on the left and the C++ program on the right.

```
/*******************************************

    Greeter — Java Code

*******************************************/

    class Greeter
      {
      void offerGreeting ()
        {
        System.out.println ("Hello World!");
        }



      public static void main (String args[])
        {
        Greeter Ralph;

        Ralph = new Greeter ();
        Ralph.offerGreeting ();
        }
      };

/*===========(  End of Source  )============*/


C:\> java Greeter

Hello World!
```

```
#include <iostream.h>

/*******************************************

    Greeter — C++ Code

*******************************************/

    class Greeter
      {
      public:
        void offerGreeting ()
          {
          cout << "Hello World!\n";
          }
      };

    void main (int argc, char* argv[])
      {
      Greeter *pRalph;

      pRalph = new Greeter ();
      pRalph->offerGreeting ();
      delete pRalph;
      }

/*===========(  End of Source  )============*/


C:\> Greeter

Hello World!
```

The primary difference between the two programs is that the Java program defines the *main()* function within the *class* definition, whereas the C++ program defines it outside the class. Another difference is that Java variables are not declared as pointers, but are allocated with the *new* operator. Notice the code below.

```
Greeter Ralph;
Ralph = new Greeter ();
Ralph.offerGreeting ();
```

The most distinctive feature of the new language is the way a Java program runs on a computer.

When a conventional program runs, it provides the computer's chip with a sequence of instructions to perform. When a Java program runs, it does not have direct contact with the chip. Instead, its instructions are made available to another program that is *pretending* to be the computer's chip. The *pretending* program relays the instructions to the real chip and the task is executed.

This intermediate program is part of the Java system. Some people call it a *Virtual Machine (VM) program* because it stands in the place of the real machine. Other people call it a *Java Interpreter* because it translates the instructions of a Java program into instructions that the real chip can understand (Fig. 1–1).

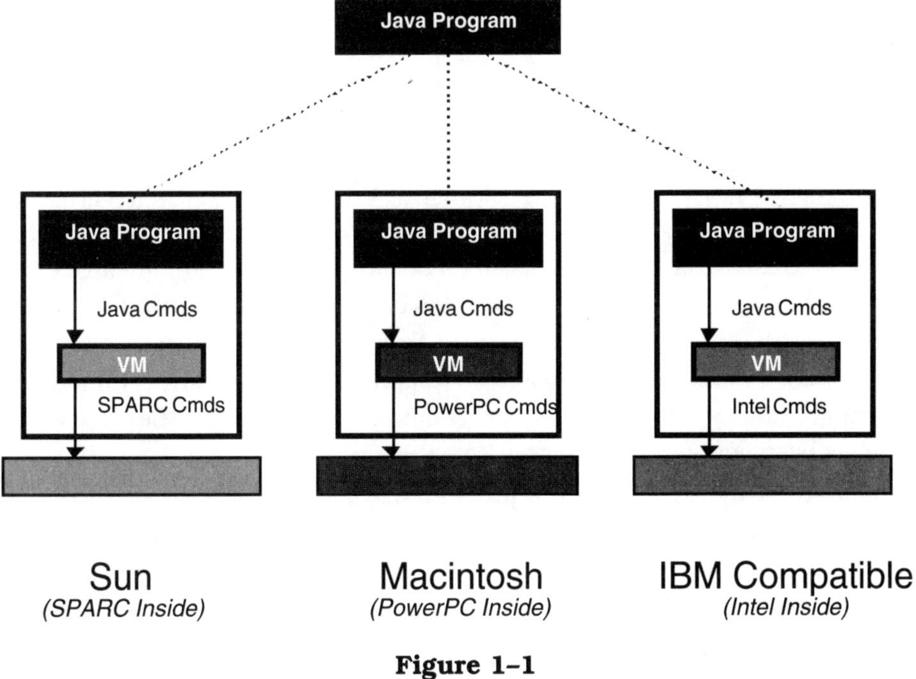

Figure 1–1

One might wonder, at this point, why the Java system has placed this translation step between their programs and the computer's processor. Wouldn't it be more efficient to have the programs talk directly to the chip? Yes, it would.

Why does the Java system include this extra step? This layer is added to provide a way for Java programs to move from computer to computer and run as well on the first computer as on the next. This means that a compiled Java program can be copied to a Sun workstation, to an IBM compatible PC, and to a PowerPC Macintosh, and it will run on each platform without modification.

This is possible because Java programs are only in contact with the Java Virtual Machine—not with the real machine. When a Java program runs on a Sun computer, the VM program translates the Java instructions into instructions for the SPARC chip. When the program runs on a PC, the VM translates them into Intel commands, and when the program runs on the Mac it translates them into PowerPC commands. On each platform, the commands reach the real computer and are carried out. But the Java program does not need to be recompiled.

So, Java is just a programming language. What makes it special is the way it runs on a computer. As a Java program runs, its commands are being interpreted and passed along to the computer's processor. This extra step allows Java programs to run unchanged on a wide variety of computers.

What are Java Enabled Browsers?

As the Java language was taking shape, the popularity of the Internet was exploding.

Leading the charge was the very popular World Wide Web mechanism for sharing documents. Web documents (also known as Web pages) made reference to other Web pages by specifying a special tag within the document; it included the Internet address and the name of the target document. This type of linking between Web pages created a Web of interrelated text documents across the globe.

The Java team wanted to leverage the Web mechanism for passing text documents between computers. Since Java programs could run on many computers without needing modifications, Java programs could be shared in the same way that text documents are shared on the Web.

To demonstrate the potential of this program sharing, the Java team decided to write a new Web browser program, which they called *HotJava*. Although this Web browser was written in Java, that is *not* what made it special. HotJava was special because it implemented a new *tag* so that when Web pages fetched a Java program across the Web, they included the Java Virtual Machine as part of the browser. This allowed Java programs to run once they arrived.

These features cause a Web browser to become a fetcher of Web pages and a fetcher of Java programs. When a Web page arrives, the browser checks to see if the new *applet* tag has been specified. If it has, the browser fetches the requested Java program (applet). When the Java applet arrives, the browser uses its Virtual Machine to run the applet and dedicates a section of the Web page to be a window within which the applet can draw and accept key strokes.

This adds a new dimension to distributed processing. Now graphic intensive services can be requested across the World Wide Web. This has become very popular. A common use of this capability is to request an animation program that flashes several pictures on the screen in rapid succession which together create the sense of motion. By creating links to programs like these, Web pages come alive with cartoon figures waving, horses running, and text dancing. Figure 1–2 demonstrates an animated Web page.

HotJava was the first *Java Enabled* Web browser. After HotJava established the potential of communicating Java programs across the Web infrastructure, other Web browser companies decided to make their browsers Java Enabled.

The two early leaders to apply this technology to their browsers were Netscape and Microsoft. Netscape was the earliest adopter of Java technology with their *Navigator* browser. They also provided most of the funding that allowed the Java team to bring this new technology to the mainstream. When Microsoft saw the

Figure 1–2

potential of Java, they made a number of adjustments in their product strategy that allowed them to create a Java Enabled browser called the *Internet Explorer* (or *IE*).

Now it is a consumer requirement for Web browsers to include Java technology. Licensing fees from companies that build Java into their browsers continue to make it possible for Sun Computers to offer the *Java Developer Kit (JDK)* at no charge to the general public.

As browser companies embraced Java technology, Sun Computers decided to place HotJava on hold and rely on other companies to build Java Enabled browsers. This move enabled Sun to focus on bringing Java to its first production release.

The HotJava project was placed on hold when it was at the Alpha 3 release level. But after Java was produced for Solaris, Windows, and Macintosh, HotJava was revived. A new team is seeking to demonstrate how the generalized Java classes in HotJava can be used to construct full applications that are Internet centered. HotJava is still available from Sun (free of charge) at *http://www.javasoft.com/products/index.html.*

Java is a new language and Java Enabled browsers provide a way to share Java programs across the World Wide Web.

Where does Java Fit?

Java is a programming language that blends the strengths of several programming languages.

Programming in this new environment is simpler in many ways than programming in other languages. Beginners find Java easier to learn than C. This is probably because they do not need to learn to use pointers. Yet the Java syntax is close enough to C that it seems familiar to most programmers.

Java has the object-oriented benefits of C++, yet it has removed some of the more awkward rules.

Java makes use of a dynamic memory area of classes and objects and runs on a Virtual Machine like Smalltalk. Yet Java syntax can be grasped more quickly than Smalltalk syntax.

With Java, the programmer enjoys the stability of a Virtual Machine and the familiarity of a C/C++ programming syntax.

The following chapters take the reader through progressive examples that provide a safe and comfortable passage on the journey to becoming a proficient Java programmer.

The first step is to put together one's first Java program.

CHAPTER 2

Having Fun with Java

If Java is a programming language, is it possible to write a program in Java that is *not* related to the Internet?

Yes. Java provides a full-featured environment that will sustain a wide range of development activity. Programs that are not launched from a Web browser are called Java *applications*. The following text explains how to write, compile, and run a Java *application*.

Java Application—Launched from a Command Line

To write a Java application, open a new file and code a *class* structure. The name of the *class* and the name of the file must be the same (including upper and lower case). The maximum length of the name is determined by the maximum length of a filename in the local file system.

Here is the famous "Hello world" program as a Java application.

```
class HelloApplication
  {
  public static void main (String argv[])
    {
    System.out.println ("Hello world!");
    }
  }
```

The name of the file for this program is *HelloApplication.java*.

If the CD examples were loaded into the *\JumpStrt* directory, one could find this file in the directory *\JumpStrt\examples\HelloApplication*. The directory *\JumpStrt* also contains the file *index.html,* which is a Web page that provides links to the examples in each chapter. This file can be opened by a Web browser and used like a local Web site.

There is a single function inside the *HelloApplication* class. It is called *main*() and it accepts an array of String parameters and does not return any value (void). This function is the entry point to the application. The function contains a single call to the *println*() function to print the string *"Hello world*!"

To compile this program, switch to its directory and invoke the compiler with a source file name.

```
javac HelloApplication.java
```

Every Java class compiles down to a *.class* file. The output of this compile is the executable *HelloApplication.class* file that contains instructions for the Java Virtual Machine.

To run this program, invoke Java's Virtual Machine and pass it the name of the class.

```
java HelloApplication
```

```
C:\JumpStrt\examples\HelloApplication>javac HelloApplication.java

C:\JumpStrt\examples\HelloApplication>java HelloApplication
Hello world!
```

The *java.exe* and *javac.exe* programs are located in Java's BIN directory. The *java.exe* program invokes Virtual Machine routines to load and run the HelloApplication.class. As the class runs, the *main*() function is called and the *"Hello world!"* string is sent to the standard output device.

To construct a general purpose Java application, a person simply needs to construct a *class* with a *main*() function. This kind of program runs independent of a Web browser and can generate complete GUI windows, perform file I/O, and access Internet resources.

Java Applet—Launched from a Web Page

If that is how to construct a *regular* Java program, how does one construct the special kind of Java program that is launched from a Web page? The steps are very similar.

One opens a new file and codes a class structure in it. The name of the file and the name of the class must be the same. But now, the class statement must also say that it *extends Applet*.

```
import java.applet.Applet;
import java.awt.Graphics;

    public class HelloApplet extends Applet
      {
      public void paint (Graphics g)
        {
        g.drawString ("Hello world!", 50, 25);
        }
      }
```

Applet is the name of the Java class that can ride in a Web page. When a class *extends* the Applet class, the new class becomes an extension of the Web riding class and can be launched by a Web page. Since this kind of Java program works so closely with the Applet class, the Java program is called a Java *applet*.

The second difference is that an applet has a *paint*() function rather than a *main*() function. The *paint*() function gets called each time the applet's region on the Web page needs to be refreshed. A *Graphics* object is passed to the *paint*() function and nothing (void) is returned.

The Graphics object is responsible for marking on the display surface. In the example above, the Graphics object is given the name *g*. Then the *drawString*() function is called to print the string *"Hello world!"* on the display surface.

The parameters *50* and *25* identify the (*x*, *y*) position at which to place the string. This is precisely the lower left corner of the baseline upon which the string characters are drawn; it is measured in pixels from the upper left corner of the window.

Notice that there are two new classes referenced in this program—the Applet class and the Graphics class. Whenever a class outside of the current source file is referenced, an *import* statement must be coded to tell the compiler where to find the external class.

Related classes are stored together in a unit called a *package*. The Applet class is part of the *java.applet* package and the Graphics class is part of the *java.awt* package. By coding the package name with the class name in the import statement, the programmer gives the compiler all the information that is necessary to include the class in the compilation.

The last way an applet differs from an application is that it must be launched from a Web page rather than from a command line. The special *<APPLET>* tag must be added to a Web page to identify the applet to launch. Here is the *HelloApplet.html* Web page that launches the HelloApplet class above.

```
<HTML>
<HEAD>
<TITLE> The Hello Applet </TITLE>
</HEAD>

<BODY>
Here is the output of my program:
<HR>
<APPLET CODE="HelloApplet" WIDTH-150 HEIGHT=50>
</APPLET>
</BODY>
</HTML>
```

The *<APPLET CODE= ____ > . . . </APPLET>* tag identifies the Java applet to launch. When the browser loads the Web page, it sees that the page requires an applet and submits a separate request to the server to fetch the *HelloApplet.class*. The browser knows the directory from which it loaded the Web page. By default, it looks to that same directory to find the Java class files. When the class is received, the browser loads it and runs it.

The phrase *WIDTH=150 HEIGHT=50* in the *<APPLET>* tag defines the size of the region on the Web page that the applet owns. The browser places that rectangle on the Web page in the same way that it places a rectangular image on the Web page. It is treated as a tall word in a flow of HTML text.

Although it is always possible to display an applet in a Web browser, during development, it is desirable to test the applet with the *appletviewer*. The appletviewer (*appletviewer.exe*) is a program in Java's BIN directory that interprets the *<APPLET>* tag in a Web page and runs an applet in a simulated Web browser window. It is more forgiving than a full Web browser and provides a friendlier test environment.

The following sequence compiles the HelloApplet and launches the appletviewer to run it. Figure 2–1 demonstrates the results.

Figure 2–1

```
C:\JumpStrt\examples\HelloApplet>javac HelloApplet.java

C:\JumpStrt\examples\HelloApplet>appletviewer HelloApplet.html
```

Summary

The Java programming language can be used to write programs that execute separately from a Web browser. These programs are called Java *applications* and can serve a wide variety of programming needs.

The special kind of Java program that is attached to a Web page is called a Java *applet*. It can be communicated across the Internet in the same way that a Web page is communicated. When a Web page and applet arrive at a Web browser, the applet is launched by the browser and begins drawing on a section of the Web page.

Very simple Java programs that consist of a single class and a single function can be constructed. But the power of the language does not emerge until one adjusts to its object-oriented structure.

Chapter 3

Having More Fun with Java

The reader has probably heard that Java is object-oriented. So where are all the *objects?* Where are the program code and program data being wed together into a single *object?* Where can one piece of code gain the services of another piece of code by simply inheriting them?

Class—The Merging of Code and Data

Each time a Java class is built, an *object* maker is created.

Objects can be created from a class by asking for a *new* instance of the class. In the code fragment below, a new instance of the class *MyClass* is created with the phrase *new MyClass*(). The new object is placed in the variable *mc*.

```
MyClass mc;

mc = new MyClass ();


class MyClass
  {
  }
```

When coding a class for a Java application, one is coding potential objects. When coding a class for a Java applet, one is coding potential objects.

But how is the code and the data put together in the class structure?

The program code is written into small functions that live inside the class structure. To highlight the object-oriented nature of this code, the function structure is given a new name—a *method*. This conforms to the Smalltalk convention.

The following example creates the classes *NewObject* and *MyClass*. In the *main*() method, one instance of the class *MyClass* is created. The new object is stored in the variable *mc*.

```
class MethodInClass
  {
  public static void main (String argv[])
    {
    MyClass mc;

    mc = new MyClass ();

    mc.printMyMessage();
    }
  }

  class MyClass
    {
    void printMyMessage ()
      {
      System.out.println ("Surf's Up");
      }
    }
```

Remember that in object-oriented programming, the code is in the variables. The variable *mc* is used to call the method *printMyMessage*(). The variable is associated with a class and the class holds the methods. So, a variable is used to call a method.

All code in Java is associated with an object by placing the code inside a class structure. Data is also associated with the object by placing it in the class structure. Notice the variable *sTitle* in MyClass below.

```
class DataInClass
  {
  public static void main (String argv[])
    {
    MyClass mc1;
    MyClass mc2;

    mc1 = new MyClass ();
    mc1.printMyMessage ();

    mc1.sTitle = "Testing";
    mc1.printMyMessage ();

    mc2 = new MyClass ("Yo Dude");
    mc2.printMyMessage ();
    }
  }

  class MyClass
    {
    String sTitle;

   MyClass ()
     {
     sTitle = "Attention";
     }

   MyClass (String s)
     {
     sTitle = s;
     }

   void printMyMessage ()
     {
     System.out.println (sTitle + ": Surf's Up");
     }
}
```

```
1.0 C:\JumpStrt\examples\DataInClass>java DataInClass
Attention: Surf's Up
Testing: Surf's Up
Yo Dude: Surf's Up
```

The variable *sTitle* has been defined inside the class *MyClass*. When an instance of MyClass is created and placed in *mc1*, the *MyClass*() constructor method is called and places the string *"Attention"* in *sTitle*.

At that point, the variable *mc1* holds all of MyClass's methods and it holds the string *"Attention"* in its *sTitle* instance variable. A call to mc1's *printMyMessage*() method sends the string *"Attention: Surf's Up"* to the standard output device.

Then the statement *mc1.sTitle = "Testing"* uses *mc1* to access the data portion of the object. In this case, the new string *"Testing"* is placed into mc1's *sTitle* variable. Then, when *mc1.printMyMessage*() is called, the string *"Testing: Surf's Up"* is printed.

If the programmer wants to pass data to the new object *as* it is being created, then the data should be placed in the *new* statement and a special constructing method should be created to receive the data. In the example above, the string *"Yo Dude"* is passed in the *new* statement that creates *mc2*. The *MyClass*(*String*) constructor method catches the string and assigns it to *sTitle* as the object is being created.

Constructors are special methods. Most method names begin with lowercase characters. Constructors must match the name of the class exactly so they usually begin with uppercase characters.

A constructor method definition does not include a return type. If a return type is specified, the compiler assumes that the method is a normal method and may return an error message that says it cannot find the constructor.

Java uses the class structure to bring together code and data into the *object* construct, but how does it implement the object-oriented concept of *inheritance*?

Inheritance—The Extending of Code and Data

Each time a Java class is built, code is inherited from another Java class.

When a Java applet class *extends* the Applet class, it inherits all the public methods and instance variables in the Applet class. It is as though, with the addition of a single phrase, a wealth of method code was added to the applet under construction.

When one class *inherits* the functionality of another class, it is faced with a decision. It can either make use of the functionality as it was coded by the other class or it can override the functionality of selected methods.

The work of developing a Java applet centers around choosing applet methods to override and selectively coding those methods. Most of the work for maintaining an applet has already been coded in the Applet class. The programmer only needs to override certain methods, like *paint*(), to construct the program.

In the example below, each of the common Applet methods are overridden. A print statement is included in the methods so one can watch the applet run and figure out what conditions cause the Web browser or appletviewer to call each method. Figure 3–1 shows the results of the example.

```
import java.applet.Applet;
import java.awt.Graphics;
import java.awt.Event;

    public class HelloApplet2 extends Applet
      {
      MyLog log;

      public HelloApplet2 ()
        {
        super ();
        log = new MyLog ();
        displayQuietly ("constructing... ");
        }

      public void init ()
        {
        displayQuietly ("initializing... ");
        }

      public void start ()
        {
        displayQuietly ("starting... ");
        }

      public void stop ()
        {
        display ("stopping... ");
        }

      public void destroy ()
        {
        display ("destroying... ");
        }

      public void update (Graphics g)
        {
        displayQuietly ("updating... ");
        super.update (g);
        }
```

```
public void paint (Graphics g)
  {
  displayQuietly ("painting... ");
  g.drawString (log.toString (), 5, 15);
  }

public boolean mouseDown (Event evt, int x, int y)
  {
  display ("down.. ");
  return (true);
  }

public boolean mouseUp (Event evt, int x, int y)
  {
  display ("up.. ");
  return (true);
  }

public boolean mouseDrag (Event evt, int x, int y)
  {
  display ("dragging... ");
  repaint ();
  return (true);
  }

void display (String s)
  {
  log.writeLine (s);
  repaint ();
  }

void displayQuietly (String s)
  {
  log.writeLine (s);
  }
}


class MyLog
  {
  StringBuffer sbContents;

MyLog ()
  {
  sbContents = new StringBuffer ();
  }
```

```
    void writeLine (String s)
      {
      sbContents.append (s);
      System.out.println (s);
      }

    public String toString ()
      {
      return (sbContents.toString ());
      }
    }
```

```
<HTML>
<HEAD>
<TITLE> A Slightly Fuller Program </TITLE>
</HEAD>
<BODY>

Here is the output of my program:
<HR>
<APPLET CODE="HelloApplet2" WIDTH=500 HEIGHT=100>
</APPLET>
</BODY>
</HTML>
```

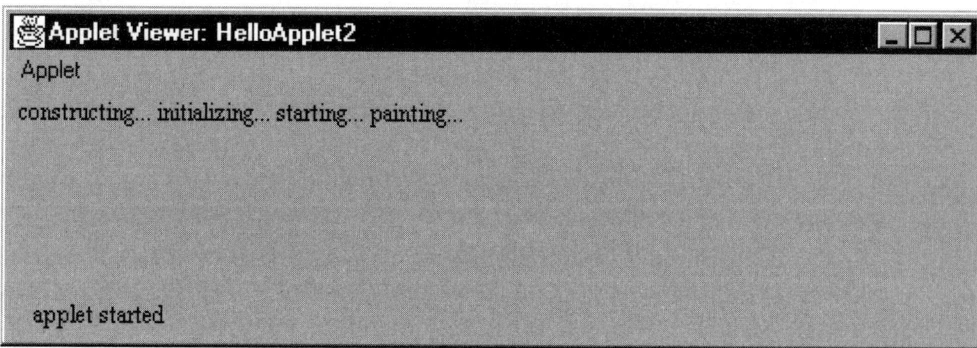

Figure 3–1

There is one instance variable in the *HelloApplet2* class. It is given the name *log* and it is an *instance* of the *MyLog* class defined later in the source.

```
public class HelloApplet2 extends Applet
{

MyLog log;

log = new MyLog ();

}

class MyLog
{
}
```

The first statement defines the object *log* and allocates enough storage to hold the address of the object when it is brought to life. The second statement creates a new instance of the class *MyLog* and assigns its address to *log*. The last structure defines the class *MyLog*.

Nine of the methods in HelloApplet2 override Applet methods and are coded with the *public* attribute. The rest of the methods are service methods that are called from other methods within the class.

The most common Applet methods to override are *init*() and *paint*(). The *init*() method is called after the applet is started and before anything is displayed on the screen. Most people initialize objects and fetch parameters in this method.

The *paint*() method is called each time the screen needs to be redrawn. To avoid recursive *paint*() calls, HelloApplet2 outputs the log message for *paint*() with the *displayQuietly*() method, which only sends the string to the standard output device and not back to the window.

The *paint*() method receives a Graphics object as a parameter. A Graphics object represents a graphical display surface that knows how to draw on itself. One can use the methods in this object to get and set the font, draw text, and draw various geometric shapes on the surface of the window.

The *destroy*() method is sent to the applet just before the class is removed from the image. This is the method where any resources that need explicit releasing should be closed. If an applet called this method directly, the browser would first call a *stop*() method and then call the *destroy*() code.

The *start*() method is called when the applet's Web page is displayed. The *stop*() method is called when the user goes on to the next Web page. If the applet spawns a continuous process in the *start*() method, then it should stop the process in the *stop*() method. This is a matter of courtesy to the user so the CPU is only taxed when the user is viewing the applet's page.

The mouse methods are not actually implemented in the Applet class. Just as HelloApplet2 extends the Applet class, the Applet class extends the Panel class which extends Container which extends Component which extends Object (see Figure 3–2).

Because of this tree, the HelloApplet2 inherits methods from all of the classes above it. The mouse methods *mouseDown*(), *mouseUp*(), and *mouseDrag*() are implemented in the Component class. By coding them in HelloApplet2, one is overriding the behavior of a class three levels up.

When executing this applet, try clicking and dragging on the window. It is interesting to notice when the *update*() method is called and when it is not called. By observing the applet run, one can get a sense for the order in which applet methods are called.

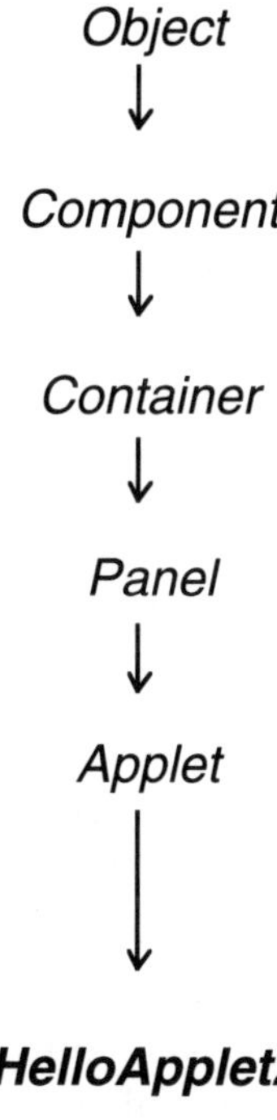

Figure 3–2

Applets are not the only classes that inherit functionality. If a class does not include the *extends* clause, the compiler assumes that the class is extending the Object class. So, every class in the Java system is ultimately an extension of the class *Object.*

Responsibility—The Duties of a Class

To accomplish programming tasks in Java, one must enlist the services of a number of other Java classes.

Each class has been designed to perform a specialized responsibility. When the Java system runs, it consists of many small objects that collaborate with one another to accomplish the processing tasks.

HelloApplet2 uses several classes to accomplish its processing task. The *writeLine*() method in the *MyLog* class uses *System.out* to print its messages to the standard output device.

```
String s;

System.out.println (s);
```

System.out is an object that is defined and instantiated when the Java system is launched. It is an instance of the *PrintStream* class. To determine the class of an object, one can ask the object to get the class and ask the class to get its name:

```
System.out.println
   (
   " System.out is "
   + System.out.getClass().getName()
   + " class"
   );
```

The special job of the *PrintStream* class is to attach itself to a certain output stream and provide services to move data to that stream. A *String* object is passed to the *println*() method. Notice that Java provides the ability to concatenate String objects by coding a "+" operator between them.

Since each class in the Java system has a specialized responsibility, one should look for ways to specialize the responsibilities of the classes that are created. HelloApplet2 created the *MyLog* class to meet the specialized need of shipping strings to a log destination. A successful object-oriented program is one that has factored all of the processing code into a number of highly specialized and widely reusable classes.

Language Issues

Occasionally, one would like to explicitly invoke a method in the class directly above it (in the super class). Java provides the pseudo object, *super*, for this purpose. In the *update*() method in HelloApplet2, *super* is used to call the *update*() method in the Applet class.

Super can be used in several ways.

```
super ();

super.init();

super.update (g);
```

In the first statement, there is no method name specified. In this case, the constructor for the super class is called. This construction is only legal to call from within another constructor method.

In the second use of *super*, the *init*() method is being called in the super class. In the last, the *update*() method is being called and the object *g* is being passed to it.

When writing source code in Java, it is helpful to know the convention concerning the capitalization of the names of identifiers.

This convention is not a requirement, but is helpful and is followed by most Java coders. It follows the convention that is used when coding Smalltalk source code. It says that class names should begin with a capital letter, and method names and object names should begin with a lowercase letter.

Names that are long can be made more readable by capitalizing selected letters in the identifier. Sometimes this causes an identifier to begin with a lowercase character and be followed by one or more uppercase characters. This looks unusual at first, but the convention is widely used and is helpful.

The Java programming language gives the programmer a fully object-oriented development paradigm. Seasoned object-oriented programmers will instinctively be able to plan ways to use Java to implement their application programs.

But for most people, the OO paradigm is less than intuitive. Until one adjusts to the new paradigm, it can be surprisingly difficult to accomplish the simplest of tasks. So, the next chapter will bridge the gap by explaining how to solve a common programming requirement—the passing of startup parameters.

CHAPTER 4

Passing Data to Programs

Passing Command Line Parameters

When a Java application is launched from the command line, any additional parameters typed on the line are passed along to the *main*() method as an array of strings.

```
java ParmApplication abc xyz 32
```

This statement launches the Java Virtual Machine and the *ParmApplication* class. The characters "abc", "xyz", and "32" would be instantiated as an array of strings.

This array is the parameter that is passed to the *main*() method and is often called *argv*[] for argument vector array. The "abc", "xyz", and "32" strings are considered *argv*[*0*], *argv*[*1*], and *argv*[2], respectively.

The ParmApplication demonstrates how to receive command line parameters:

```
    class ParmApplication
/**************************************************************************

    ParmApplication--Demonstrates How to Pass Command Line Parameters

    This program accepts command line parameters on the line that invokes
    the Virtual Machine.  The parameters are converted to String objects
    and passed to the program as the array of Strings, argv.

    Format:

      c:\> java ParmApplication Parm0 Parm1 Parm2 [...]
```

```
*********************************************************************/
    {

    public static void main (String argv[])
      {
      int i;

      if (argv.length == 0)
        {
        System.out.println ("");
        System.out.println ("  Put parameters on the command line.  "
          + "Here is the syntax:");
        System.out.println ("");
        System.out.println ("      java ParmApplication Parm0 Parm1 "
          + "Parm2 [...]");
        System.out.println ("");
        System.exit (1);
        }

      System.out.println ("");
      System.out.println ("  " + argv.length
        + " string parameter(s) entered:");

      for (i = 0; i < argv.length; i++)
        {
        System.out.println
          (
          "      Parm #"
          + i
          + ": --->"
          + argv[i]
          + "<---"
          );
        }

      System.out.println ("");
      }

    }

/*============================(  End of Source )========================*/
```

```
1.0 C:\ProgJava\examples\ParmApplication>java ParmApplication abc xyz 32

  3 string parameter(s) entered:
      Parm #0: --->abc<---
      Parm #1: --->xyz<---
      Parm #2: --->32<---
```

The *argv* is considered an Array object. To discover the number of elements in the *argv* array, one uses the construction *argv.length*.

It might take a little thinking to figure out what this is doing. Notice that there are no parentheses following the construction. So, it is not invoking one of the class's methods. But it seems to be fetching something from the object since it is attached with a period.

This is a reference to a variable called *length* in the Array object. It holds an integer that identifies the maximum length of the array.

Any variable that is defined in a class can be referenced in this way. This kind of variable is known as an *instance variable,* because with each new instance of the class comes a new instance of the variable.

The practice of making direct reference to instance variables is discouraged in object-oriented programming. The preferred way to make a variable like this accessible to outside objects is to code a *getLength*() method that simply returns the value of *length.*

Instance variables are *public* by default, but they can be made *private* by placing the *private* attribute at the beginning of the variable definition.

There is a clear movement, as the Java API matures, to hide more variables. But sometimes it can be handy to allow direct access to an instance variable.

In the ParmApplication, there is an example of a long concatenated string. Here is one portion of it:

```
"       Parm #"
+ i
```

In this statement, a string is being concatenated with an *int*. The Java compiler converts this into the following statement:

```
new StringBuffer().append("      Parm #").append(i).toString();
```

On the far left of this statement, a new *StringBuffer* object is created. On the far right, the StringBuffer method *toString*() is called to convert it back to a String object. The compiler has chosen to convert the statement from a string (which cannot grow) to a StringBuffer (which can grow). After all the concatenations are performed, it is converted back to a string because the user is expecting a string.

After the *StringBuffer* object is instantiated, an *append*() method is invoked to add the string *"   Parm #"* to the object. The return value from the *append*() is the *StringBuffer* object. This StringBuffer receives another *append*() method with the *int* parameter *i*. As it happens, the *StringBuffer* class has several *append*() methods—one for each data type. In the *append*() method for *int* parameters, the StringBuffer converts the *int* to a string, then appends it.

The exact *StringBuffer* object that was created at the far left of the statement is the return value for each of the *append*() methods. The method *toString*() is the final call to the *StringBuffer* object which returns the object's value as a string.

This kind of syntax is known as a *cascading method send*. The return from one method becomes the object to which the next method is sent. This is a common programming technique in object-oriented programming. For reasons of style, the number of cascades should be kept low. It is much easier to read one or two cascades than to read six method sends in one statement.

Passing Applet Parameters

Java applications are launched from the command line and their startup parameters are specified on the command line.

Java applets are launched from a Web page and their startup parameters are specified in the Web page.

Here is the portion of a Web page that launches the ParmApplet with some startup parameters.

```
<APPLET CODE="ParmApplet" WIDTH=500 HEIGHT=100>
<PARAM NAME=Message VALUE="Java World">;
<PARAM NAME="Font Size" VALUE="48">
<PARAM NAME=BackgroundColor VALUE="#008000">
<PARAM NAME="ForegroundColor" VALUE="#FFFFFF">
</APPLET>
```

Inside the <*APPLET*> . . . </*APPLET*> tag are several <*PARAM*> subtags. Each <*PARAM*> subtag identifies the name and value for one parameter to be passed to the applet. Each parameter name and value are treated as strings. If there is a space in the name, then the optional double quote characters are needed.

The applet receives these parameters by calling the applet's *getParameter*() method. The parameter name is passed as a parameter and the string value is returned.

```
sMessage = getParameter ("Message");

sFontSize = getParameter ("Font Size");
if (sFontSize == null)
  {
  sFontSize = "22";
  }
```

If the *getParameter*() method is unable to find the parameter name, it returns a *null*. The keyword *null* is a predefined object in the Java system and represents "no object" or "no instance." It can be used anywhere to check for the absence of an object.

ParmApplet—Rendering a Message in a Font and Color

This applet accepts several parameters from the Web page and then uses them to write a message to the applet window in a certain font and color. Figure 4–1 demonstrates the results of this applet.

```
import java.applet.*;
import java.awt.*;

    public class ParmApplet extends Applet
/*************************************************************************

    ParmApplet -- Java Applet that Demonstrates Passing Web Page
    Parameters

/*************************************************************************/

    {

    int iFontSize;                  /* Point size of the font.          */
    String sMessage;                /* Message to write to the screen.   */
```

```
/**********************************************************************/


  public String getAppletInfo ()
    {
    return ("ParmApplet v1.0, (c) Noel Enete, 1996");
    }


  public void init ()
    {
    Color cForeground;
    Color cBackground;
    String sFontSize;

    sMessage = getParameter ("Message");

    sFontSize = getParameter ("Font Size");
    if (sFontSize == null)
      {
      sFontSize = "22";
      }
    iFontSize = Integer.valueOf(sFontSize).intValue();

    cBackground = stringToColor
     (
     getParameter ("BackgroundColor"),
     getBackground ()
     );
    cForeground = stringToColor
     (
     getParameter ("ForegroundColor"),
     Color.black
     );

    setBackground (cBackground);
    setForeground (cForeground);
    }


  public Color stringToColor (String sColor, Color cDefault)
    {
    Integer iRgb;
```

```
  if ((sColor == null)
  || (sColor.charAt (0) != '#')
  || (sColor.length () != 7 ))
    {
    return (cDefault);
    }

  try
    {
    iRgb = Integer.valueOf (sColor.substring (1, 7), 16);
    return (new Color (iRgb.intValue ()));
    }
  catch (Exception e)
    {
    return (cDefault);
    }
  }


 public void paint (Graphics g)
   {
   Font fFont;          /* Selected font.                     */
   int x, y;            /* Point at which to write string.    */
   FontMetrics fm;      /* Metrics of current font.           */

   fFont = new Font
    (
    "TimesRoman",
    Font.BOLD,
    iFontSize
    );
   g.setFont (fFont);
   fm = g.getFontMetrics ();

   x = 5;
   y = fm.getHeight ();
   g.drawString (sMessage, x, y);
   }

 }


/*========================( End of Source )========================*/
```

Figure 4–1

```
<HTML>
<HEAD>
<TITLE> ParmApplet -- How to Pass Parameters to an Applet </TITLE>
</HEAD>
<BODY>

Here is the output of my program:
<HR>
<APPLET CODE="ParmApplet" WIDTH=500 HEIGHT=100>
<PARAM NAME=Message VALUE="Java World">;
<PARAM NAME="Font Size" VALUE="48">
<PARAM NAME=BackgroundColor VALUE="#008000">
<PARAM NAME="ForegroundColor" VALUE="#FFFFFF">
</APPLET>
</BODY>
</HTML>
```

stringToColor()—Parsing a Color String

The method *stringToColor*(), which is in the ParmApplet, converts a hexadecimal string into a Color object. The hex string represents a three byte number. The value of each byte can range from *00* to *FF*. The bytes indicate the amount of red, green, and blue to include in the color.

```
"#FF0000"   Red
"#00FF00"   Green
"#0000FF"   Blue
"#808080"   Gray
"#FFFFFF"   White
"#000000"   Black
```

If the color string is improperly formatted or if there is an error converting the string, the *stringToColor*() method returns the default color.

In this method, one will notice the *try . . . catch*() structure. This is a mechanism borrowed from C++ to channel the processing of error conditions. If an error occurs during the execution of the *try* code, an Exception object is created and control is passed to the *catch*() section.

There can be multiple *catch*() sections for a single *try*. Each *catch*() section is constructed to handle a different Exception class. Java will transfer control to the *catch*() section whose parameter most closely matches the Exception class that is being thrown.

In the case of the *stringToColor*() method, all Exception classes that are thrown are subclasses of the Exception object. Thus, they are channeled to a single *catch*() method that returns the default color.

Font Selection

Fonts are selected by specifying the face name, the font style, and the point size. The ArrayApplication, in the next chapter, will enumerate all the face names that are installed in a particular Java environment.

The Font class includes some static variables that specify font style codes: Font.PLAIN, Font.BOLD, and Font.ITALIC. Static variables are like global variables for a class. All instances of the class can access and modify a single copy of the class's static variables.

Static variables are defined inside the class, like instance variables, but the *static* attribute is added to the definition. The class name is used to reference them rather than the name of an instantiated object.

```
class StaticVars
  {
  static int iStatic;

  public static void main (String args[])
    {
    StaticVars sv;

    sv = new StaticVars ();

    StaticVars.iStatic = 3;

    System.out.println ("StaticVars.iStatic = " + StaticVars.iStatic);
    }
   }
```

The ParmApplet instantiates a new font by passing the face name, the font style (using a provided static variable), and the point size to the *Font*() constructor. The method *setFont*() is sent to the Graphics object to establish this new font as the default font for the applet's window surface.

```
fFont = new Font
  (
  "TimesRoman",
  Font.BOLD,
  iFontSize
  );
g.setFont (fFont);
fm = g.getFontMetrics ();

x = 5;
y = fm.getHeight ();
g.drawString (sMessage, x, y);
```

Once the new font is in place, the *FontMetrics* object is obtained from the Graphics object. FontMetrics is the keeper of the current dimensions of the current font. The only dimension that is needed by the ParmApplet is the total height of the font from baseline to baseline (*getHeight*()). This is used to position the left edge of the baseline for the call to *drawString*().

Language Issues

Although objects can be defined anywhere within the definition of a class or a method, it is better to define them at the top of the structure and instantiate them at the proper place during the code.

The alternative is to define the objects at the point of use. This approach can make the code harder to read and hide inconsistencies in naming conventions. Placing all definitions at the beginning of a method is a technique that makes source code easier to read and maintain.

Sometimes it is necessary to force an immediate program exit to the operating system with a return code. This is accomplished in the ParmApplication with a call to the *System.exit*() static method. The return code is passed as a parameter to the System.exit() method.

```
public static void main (String argv[])
   {
   if (argv.length == 0)
      {
      System.exit (1);
      }
```

The *stringToColor*() method makes use of another interesting aspect of object-oriented programming. Newly instantiated objects do not need to be assigned to any particular variable to be useful. Notice how a Color object is instantiated to be returned to the caller and does not need to be assigned to any local variable in the *stringToColor*() method.

```
public Color stringToColor (String sColor, Color cDefault)
   {

   return (new Color (iRgb.intValue ()));
   }
```

CHAPTER 5

Exploring System Capabilities

Most variables are defined so that they hold a single object of a class. Many times, however, there is a need to create several instances of a class and to reference each of them.

If a method creates three new Color objects, it could keep track of them by assigning them to three instance variables like color1, color2, and color3. However, if the number of occurrences gets large, this technique can become awkward.

Most programming languages solve this problem by providing a mechanism for storing multiple occurrences of a type of data. The most common way to accomplish this in Java is to use the Array or Enumeration class.

Array—A Fixed Collection of One Object Type

An array is one variable that can reference a number of objects by position number.

If the variable *colors* was defined to be an array, one could reference its first object as *colors[0]*, its second object as *colors[1]*, and its ninth object as *colors[8]*. Although *colors* is a single variable, it can store a number of objects because it is an array.

The position number that is used to retrieve an individual object is called an *array index* and the number of positions available within an array is called an *array dimension*.

In Java, an array is a class that has one instance variable—*length*. The *length* identifies how many slots are available within the array to store objects. The *length* does not indicate how many objects are actually stored in the array, just how many *could* be stored in it.

The array is an unusual class within the Java system. No methods can be sent to it and it cannot be explicitly *extended*. The Array class is implemented entirely within the compiler and Virtual Machine and is more of a convention than an independent class.

Although it cannot be explicitly extended, it is *implicitly* extended each time an array is created.

```
int aiSizes[];                    // Declaring an array variable
aiSizes = new int[14];            // Allocating an array variable

int aiSizes[] = new int[14];      // Declaring and Allocating on same line

aiSizes[0] = 24;                  // Assigning values to array positions
aiSizes[1] = 12;
```

In the example above, the first two lines are equivalent to the third line. The first line identifies *aiSizes* as an *array of int's* (*ai*...), because the square brackets are present. In the second line, an array object with a *dimension* of 14 is created and assigned to *aiSizes*. This is a little different from the way normal constructors appear, but it makes sense.

The class name of the object that is being instantiated in the above example is *int*[] (name includes the square brackets). The class *int*[] extends the class Array implicitly. The compiler looks at what follows *new* and how the variable is defined; and it knows to create a new class as an extension to array; and it knows to construct the name from the object type.

Since the class name includes the square brackets, the array could be defined directly with the bracketed class name. The following statements are identical:

```
int[] aiSizes;

int aiSizes[];
```

Any time an object is defined as an array and instantiated, a special Array class that matches the object's type is implicitly created as an extension to array and is given a name that matches the object's type.

The array positions are assigned values individually as shown below.

```
class ArrayPositions
  {
  public static void main (String argv[])
    {
    int i;
    int[] aiEvens = new int[4];
    for (i = 0; i < aiEvens.length; i++)
    {
    aiEvens[i] = i * 2;
    System.out.println (i + ": = " + aiEvens[i]);
    }
  }
 }
```

The Array class and all of its implicit subclasses have a fixed dimension. They cannot grow. If one desires an object that works like an array but can grow, one should use the *Vector* class in the *java.util* package.

Enumeration—A Consumable Collection of Multiple Object Types

There is another mechanism for collecting similar objects together in Java—an *Enumeration*. Although this mechanism is unfamiliar to most programmers, it is a very simple concept and has several benefits over other techniques.

Let's begin with an example. Java stores its system-wide information in a structure that is much like the environment variable pool of many operating systems. An environment variable has a name and a value. A Java property has a key and a value. The Java class that holds a collection of these key/value pairs is called the *Properties* class.

One must use an Enumeration object to examine the key/value pairs in a Properties object. The following Java application fetches the system-wide properties and displays them back to the standard output device.

```
import java.util.*;

    class SystemProperties
      {
      public static void main (String argv[])
        {
        Properties prSystem;
        Enumeration enPropNames;
        String sPropName;

        prSystem = System.getProperties ();
        enPropNames = prSystem.propertyNames();

        while (enPropNames.hasMoreElements ())
        {
        sPropName = (String) enPropNames.nextElement ();
        System.out.print (sPropName + " = ");
        System.out.println (prSystem.getProperty (sPropName));
        }
       }
      }
```

To itemize the system properties, this application does three things. It sends the static method *getProperties*() to the System class to get the system-wide Properties object. Then it asks the Properties object for a list of the keys that it is holding. Then it iterates through the keys and fetches the value that is associated with each key and prints it to the standard output device.

When the Properties object returns the keys it is holding, it does not return an array of strings. It returns an Enumeration object. In the example, the variable *enPropNames* stores the returned Enumeration object.

It may be helpful to think of an enumeration as a behavior that chains together several objects into a linked list. The Enumeration object knows how to say if there are more elements in the list (*hasMoreElements*()) and how to get the next object in the list (*nextElement*()).

In a sense, an enumeration represents a position in a chain of objects. It can return the object that is next on the chain and indicate if there are any more objects on the chain.

The *propertyNames*() method constructed the chain of objects and instantiated the Enumeration object to allow the caller to walk the chain.

An enumeration is list-oriented, whereas an array is buffer-oriented. Because array dimensions are fixed, they can be more difficult to build and modify on the fly. Since enumerations are focused on a spot on a chain and on the spot next to it, enumerations are unaware of the dimension of the chain. Elements could be added to the end of the chain while the enumeration is moving from point to point.

An enumeration can also manage a list of multiple object types, whereas arrays must store objects of the same type. The variable that is returned from the *nextElement*() method is an instance of the Object class. The caller should either know what class to expect from the enumeration or figure out what class it is by using the comparison operator *instanceof*.

```
import java.util.*;

    class InstanceOf
      {
      public static void main (String args[])
        {
        Properties prSystem;
        Enumeration enPropNames;
        Object obj;

        prSystem = System.getProperties ();
        enPropNames = prSystem.propertyNames();

        while (enPropNames.hasMoreElements ())
          {
          obj = enPropNames.nextElement ();

          if (obj instanceof Integer)
            {
            System.out.println ("key is an Integer");
            }
          else if (obj instanceof StringBuffer)
            {
          System.out.println ("key is a StringBuffer");
            }
          else if (obj instanceof String)
            {
          System.out.println ("key is a String");
          }
        }
      }
    }
```

Objects are created directly from a class. Enumerations are created indirectly. They are usually created by calling a method that returns an enumeration. To create an Enumeration object that links together one's own objects is very simple and involves the use of the Vector class in the next chapter. One creates a Vector, adds the objects to the Vector, then asks the Vector for its elements. The *elements*() method returns an Enumeration object.

An enumeration is a dynamic collection of multiple object types. An array is a static collection of one object type.

Array Application—Surfacing System Information

This Java application uses arrays and enumerations to fetch system information from a running Java image. It lists the face names for the fonts that are installed in the Java system, it enumerates the default system properties, and it reports on the current total memory and current free memory available.

```
import java.util.*;
import java.awt.Toolkit;

    class ArrayApplication
/**************************************************************************

    ARRAYAPPLICATION -- This Demonstrates Arrays in Java

**************************************************************************/

      {

    String sTag = "ArrayApplication v1.0, (c) Noel Enete, 1996";

/*************************************************************************/


    void displayFaceNames ()
      {
      int i;
      String[] asFaceName;

      System.out.println
        (
        "\n*===================( FONT FACES )===================*\n"
        );
```

```
asFaceName = Toolkit.getDefaultToolkit().getFontList();

for (i = 0; i < asFaceName.length; i++)
{
System.out.println (asFaceName[i]);
}
}


void displayProperties ()
{
Properties prSystem;
Enumeration enPropNames;
String sPropName;

System.out.println
(
"\n*============( CURRENT SYSTEM PROPERTIES )==============*\n"
);

prSystem = System.getProperties ();
enPropNames = prSystem.propertyNames();

while (enPropNames.hasMoreElements ())
{
sPropName = (String) enPropNames.nextElement ();
System.out.print (sPropName + " = ");
System.out.println (prSystem.getProperty (sPropName));
}
}


void displayRuntime ()
{
Runtime rt;

System.out.println
(
"\n*===========( CURRENT RUNTIME STATISTICS )==============*\n"
);

rt = Runtime.getRuntime ();

System.out.println ("Total Memory = " + rt.totalMemory ());
System.out.println ("Free Memory = " + rt.freeMemory ());
}
```

```
   void displayTrailer ()
      {
      System.out.println
         (
         "\n*=====================================================*\n"
         );
      }


   public static void main (String argv[])
      {
      ArrayApplication app;

      app = new ArrayApplication ();

      app.displayFaceNames ();
      app.displayProperties ();
      app.displayRuntime ();
      app.displayTrailer ();

      System.exit (0);
      }

   }


/*=======================( End of Source )=============================*/
```

```
1.0 C:\JumpStrt\examples\ArrayApplication>java ArrayApplication

*====================( FONT FACES )=====================*

Dialog
Helvetica
TimesRoman
Courier
Symbol

*============( CURRENT SYSTEM PROPERTIES )==============*
java.home = C:\JAVA\JAVA\BIN\..
awt.toolkit = sun.awt.win32.MToolkit
java.version = 1.0
file.separator = \
line.separator =

java.vendor = Sun Microsystems Inc.
user.name = unknown
os.arch = x86
os.name = Windows 95
java.vendor.url = http://www.sun.com/
user.dir = C:\java\examples\ArrayApplication
java.class.path =
.;C:\JAVA\JAVA\BIN\..\classes;C:\JAVA\JAVA\BIN\..\lib\classes
.zip
java.class.version = 45.3
os.version = 4.0
path.separator = ;
user.home = C:\JAVA\JAVA\BIN\..

*===========( CURRENT RUNTIME STATISTICS )==============*

Total Memory = 3145720
Free Memory = 3129000

*=======================================================*
```

The next applet enumerates the font faces of a system and then displays them.

ArrayApplet—Displaying System Fonts

This Java applet accepts a point size parameter from the Web page. It then draws a string in all of the font faces in the current Java system using the point size parameter.

It uses an array to store the font face names in the Java system. An array is also used to store the option code and string description for each Font style. Figure 5–1 displays the results of this applet.

```
import java.applet.*;
import java.awt.*;

    public class ArrayApplet extends Applet
/*************************************************************************

    ArrayApplet -- Displays Strings in all the System Fonts

*************************************************************************/

    {

    final int[] aiStyle =       /* Font style codes.                    */
      {
      Font.PLAIN,
      Font.BOLD,
      Font.ITALIC,
      Font.ITALIC | Font.BOLD
      };
    final String[] asStyle =   /* Desc of each Font Style.              */
      {
      " Plain",
      " Bold",
      " Italic",
      " Italic Bold"
      };
    int iFontSize;            /* Point size of the font.              */

    /*******************************************************************/


    public String getAppletInfo ()
   {
   return ("ArrayApplet v1.0, (c) Noel Enete, 1996");
   }
```

Applet Viewer: ArrayApplet
Applet
Dialog Plain, 22pt
Dialog Bold, 22pt
Dialog Italic, 22pt
Dialog Italic Bold, 22pt
Helvetica Plain, 22pt
Helvetica Bold, 22pt
Helvetica Italic, 22pt
Helvetica Italic Bold, 22pt
TimesRoman Plain, 22pt
TimesRoman Bold, 22pt
TimesRoman Italic, 22pt
TimesRoman Italic Bold, 22pt
Courier Plain, 22pt
Courier Bold, 22pt
Courier Italic, 22pt
Courier Italic Bold, 22pt
Symbol Plain, 22pt
Symbol Bold, 22pt
Symbol Italic, 22pt
Symbol Italic Bold, 22pt
applet started

Figure 5–1

```
public void init ()
  {
  Color cForeground;
  Color cBackground;
  String sFontSize;

  cBackground = stringToColor
    (
    getParameter ("BackgroundColor"),
    Color.lightGray
    );
  cForeground = stringToColor
    (
    getParameter ("ForegroundColor"),
    Color.black
    );

  setBackground (cBackground);
  setForeground (cForeground);

  sFontSize = getParameter ("FontSize");
  if (sFontSize == null)
    {
    sFontSize = "22";
    }

  iFontSize = Integer.valueOf(sFontSize).intValue();
  }


public Color stringToColor (String sColor, Color cDefault)
  {
  Integer iRgb;

  if ((sColor == null) || (sColor.charAt (0) != '#')
  || (sColor.length () != 7 ))
    {
    return (cDefault);
    }

  try
    {
    iRgb = Integer.valueOf (sColor.substring(1, 7), 16);
    return (new Color (iRgb.intValue ()));
    }
  catch (Exception e)
```

```
      {
      return (cDefault);
      }
    }


  public void paint (Graphics g)
    {
    Font fFont;             /* Selected font.                          */
    int i, j;               /* Counters.                               */
    int x, y;               /* Point at which to write string.         */
    String[] asFontName;    /* Array of font face names.               */
    FontMetrics fm;         /* Metrics of current font.                */

    asFontName = Toolkit.getDefaultToolkit().getFontList();
    x = 5;
    y = 0;

    for (i = 0; i < asFontName.length; i++)
      {
      for (j = 0; j < aiStyle.length; j++)
        {
        fFont = new Font
          (
          asFontName[i],
          aiStyle[j],
          iFontSize
          );
        g.setFont (fFont);
        fm = g.getFontMetrics ();
        y += fm.getHeight ();

        g.drawString (asFontName[i] + asStyle[j] + ", "
          + iFontSize + "pt", x, y);
        }
      }
    }
  }


/*=========================( End of Source )==========================*/
```

```
<HTML>
<HEAD>
<TITLE> ArrayApplet </TITLE>
</HEAD>
<BODY>
ArrayApplet
<HR>
<APPLET CODE="ArrayApplet" WIDTH=340 HEIGHT=525>
</APPLET>
</BODY>
</HTML>
```

The font is selected in the *paint*() method. An new font is chosen for each line that is written to the window.

A font name is selected in the outer loop. The inner loop selects and draws a line of text in each of the styles that are available —PLAIN, BOLD, ITALIC, and ITALIC-BOLD.

At the beginning of the class, the instance variable *aiStyle* is an array of integers that stores the numbers that the Font class uses to identify each Font style.

Notice the keyword *final* on the variable *aiStyle*. This is how Java indicates a constant. Remember that there are no *#define's* in Java. Constants are specially designated variables that are stored with the class itself and are instantiated and never changed. They are much like a *literal pool* in other languages. They are stored in the compiled *.class* file in its *constant pool*.

The font face names are received from the current Toolkit as an array of strings at the beginning of the *paint*() method. Each of the nested output loops complete when they reach the dimension of the array as identified in the array instance variable *length*.

Once the font is selected, it is placed into the Graphics object as the default font for the applet's window surface. Then the Graphics object is asked for the *Font-Metrics* object that identifies all of the dimensions of the current font. The *get Height*() method returns the overall height of a line of text from the baseline of one line to the baseline of the next line. This is used to calculate the vertical displacement from one line to the next.

Finally, the Graphics method, *drawString*(), is used to write a concatenated string of text to the display surface in the default font.

Language Issues

This example program demonstrates an important new concept in the Java language. The following construction appears in the *init*() method.

```
Integer.valueOf(sFontSize).intValue();
```

When a method is sent, it is usually sent to an object that is a new instance of a class. But in the construction above, the identifier on the left is not the name of an object. It is the name of a class.

When one defines a method, it can either be an *instance* method or a *static* method. All methods are assumed to be instance methods unless the static attribute is added to the method definition.

The method *valueOf*() is a static method. This method is not being sent to an instance of Integer. It is being sent to the *Integer* class itself.

The *valueOf*() method receives an object, like a String and returns a corresponding integer. Why is this a static method rather than an instance method?

Suppose one creates the new *Integer x* as follows:

```
Integer x;
 x = new Integer (3);
```

Now, suppose one needs to convert the string "7" into an integer. If *valueOf*() was sent to *x* like

```
x.valueOf("7"),
```

the return value would be a new integer with a value of "7". The value "3", in *x*, did not play any role in returning the value "7". If *x* was instantiated with a value of "5",

```
x.valueOf("7"),
```

would still return an integer with a value of "7".

Since *valueOf*() does not rely upon the data within an Integer object to perform its work, it is associated with a class rather that with an instance. In Java terms, this is known as a static method and the attribute *static* is attached to the method declaration of *valueOf*() in the Integer class.

Whenever a *static* method is called, it must be sent to the class name (which is normally capitalized) rather than to the instance name.

After *valueOf*() is sent to the Integer class, the *intValue*() method is sent to the resulting integer to convert the number to an *int*.

Now, this probably seems a little odd. What could possibly be the difference between an Integer object and an *int*?

This is one of the special things about the Java language. While it is an object-oriented language and provides the Integer object to encapsulate the integer services that are available to a run-time Java program, it also permits the use of non-class data types like *int*.

Java refers to an *int* as a *simple type*. It refers to a class as a *composite type*. The simple types are listed below with their widths:

byte	8	bit
short	16	bit
int	32	bit
long	64	bit
float	32	bit
double	64	bit
character	16	bit unicode character

The only behaviors that can be performed on a simple type are arithmetic and comparisons. The rest of the behavior for a simple type is available in the corresponding composite type. The Integer class was created to wrap behavior around an *int*. The *Double* class was created to wrap behavior around a *double*, and so on.

Classes like Integer are known as *wrappers* because they wrap procedural resources in object-oriented clothes.

Summary

The simplest way to store a small number of objects of the same data type is to place them in an array. The enumeration concept brings the flexibility of linked list processing to an object collection.

Now that collection objects have been introduced, it is time to demonstrate how to make use of the powerful collection classes in Java.

CHAPTER 6

Launching Java Services

One of the joys of an object-oriented environment is to discover high functioning classes. The following classes belong to the *java.util* package and bring significant functionality to any program that instantiates them.

Vector—A Variable Collection of Multiple Object Types

A vector can be viewed as a *growable* array. When an array is created, the number of elements that it can hold is identified. If there is a need to hold more elements later, a new array must be created with a greater capacity; then the elements must be copied.

The Vector class maintains an ordered collection of objects, like an array; but when more space is needed, the vector automatically performs the allocation. It is not as simple to use as an array and it carries slightly more processing overhead, but a vector can be very handy.

```
import java.util.*;

    class Vectors
      {
      public static void main (String argv[])
        {
        Vector v;
        Enumeration enum;
        Object object;
```

```
        v = new Vector ();
        v.addElement (new Double (5.0));
        v.addElement ("Second Element is a String");
        v.addElement (new Integer (7));
        v.addElement (new StringBuffer ("Fourth Element is a String" +
          "Buffer"));
        v.addElement ("Last Element");

        enum = v.elements ();
        while (enum.hasMoreElements ())
          {
          object = enum.nextElement ();
          System.out.print ("Class = " + object.getClass().getName() +
           ",\t");
          System.out.println ("Value = " + object);
          }
        }
    }
```

```
1.0 C:\JumpStrt\examples\Vectors>java Vectors
Class = java.lang.Double,       Value = 5
Class = java.lang.String,       Value = Second Element is a String
Class = java.lang.Integer,      Value = 7
Class = java.lang.StringBuffer, Value = Fourth Element is a StringBuffer
Class = java.lang.String,       Value = Last Element
```

In the example above, a vector is allocated and five objects are added to it. Then the class name and value of each element of the vector are displayed to the standard output device. To iterate a vector, one must call its *elements*() method and step through the Enumeration object that is returned.

One will notice that more steps are required to use a Vector object than to use an array. However, a vector is more flexible. The objects in an array must be instances of the same class (or super class). The objects in a vector can be instances of many different classes.

In the example above, vector *v* holds five objects. The objects are instances of the classes Double, String, Integer, and StringBuffer. The vector collection has no trouble storing and traversing this diversity of object types. This ability can be very important in object-oriented programming.

Possibly the hardest thing about a vector is to understand how the term *vector* describes this ordered collection.

A vector is a mathematical arrow that contains direction and magnitude. The Vector class preserves the order in which the objects are added to it. This may carry a vague sense of the directional component of a vector. The Vector class also has a size, or number of elements. This size may be analogous to the magnitude of a mathematical vector.

So, the vector class could be viewed as a directive sequencing of a certain magnitude of objects. Perhaps is should have been named an OrderedCollection.

Hashtable—A Collection of Key/Value Pairs

The Array and Vector classes hold a collection of individual objects. The Hashtable holds a collection of pairs of objects. Each element in a Hashtable consists of a key and a value. The key is what is used to find the correct element in the table. The value is the content that is associated with the key.

The key objects in a Hashtable might be strings like "name", "phone", and "zip". The value for the "name" key might be the string "George". The value for "phone" might be "555-1212" and the value for "zip" might be "90210".

If a Hashtable contained key/value pairs like these, the table would be representing attributes of a person. The Hashtable would probably be an instance variable for a Person object.

Notice, in the example below, that elements are added to a Hashtable by sending a *put*() method to it. The first parameter of the *put*() is the key object; the second is the value object. Individual values are retrieved from a Hashtable by sending the *get*() method and passing the key that identifies which value to return. Elements are removed by sending the *remove*() method and passing the appropriate key.

```
import java.util.*;

    class Person
      {
      Hashtable htAttributes;

      public Person ()
        {
        Enumeration enum;

        htAttributes = new Hashtable ();
        htAttributes.put ("name", "George");
        htAttributes.put ("phone", "555-1212");
        htAttributes.put ("zip", "90210");

        System.out.println ("*------------Display Hashtable------------*");
        System.out.println (htAttributes);

        System.out.println ("*---------Display Individual Fields-------*");
        System.out.println ("name  = " + htAttributes.get ("name"));
        System.out.println ("phone = " + htAttributes.get ("phone"));
        System.out.println ("zip   = " + htAttributes.get ("zip"));

        System.out.println ("*-------------Display Values--------------*");
        displayElements (htAttributes.elements ());

        System.out.println ("*---------------Display Keys--------------*");
        displayElements (htAttributes.keys ());

        System.out.println ("*----------Display After Removal----------*");
        htAttributes.remove ("zip");
        System.out.println (htAttributes);

        System.out.println ("*-----------------------------------------*");
        }


      void displayElements (Enumeration enum)
        {
        Object object;

        while (enum.hasMoreElements ())
          {
          object = enum.nextElement ();
          System.out.print ("Class = " + object.getClass().getName() +
             ",\t");
```

```
            System.out.println ("Value = " + object);
            }
          }


        public static void main (String argv[])
          {
          new Person ();
          }
        }
```

```
1.0 C:\JumpStrt\examples\Person>java Person
*----------------Display Hashtable----------------*
{phone=555-1212, name=George, zip=90210}
*------------Display Individual Fields------------*
name  = George
phone = 555-1212
zip   = 90210
*-----------------Display Values------------------*
Class = java.lang.String,       Value = 555-1212
Class = java.lang.String,       Value = George
Class = java.lang.String,       Value = 90210
*------------------Display Keys-------------------*
Class = java.lang.String,       Value = phone
Class = java.lang.String,       Value = name
Class = java.lang.String,       Value = zip
*--------------Display After Removal--------------*
{phone=555-1212, name=George}
*-------------------------------------------------*
```

To iterate through a Hashtable, one calls either *elements*() or *keys*() and processes the enumeration that is returned. The enumeration that is returned from *elements*() is a chain of value objects. The enumeration from the *keys*() method is a chain of key objects.

Notice the unusual order in which the Hashtable stores the key/value pairs.

This is because a Hashtable stores its keys as hash codes. Since the order of a hash code bears little resemblance to the uncoded data, the order of the Hashtable keys appears haphazard.

When the *get*() method is called, the key that is passed with the method is converted to a hash code and the hash code identifies a specific location in the table.

Since the location can be determined mathematically, the search for the value data can be very fast.

The actual storage order is neither input order nor sorted order. In fact, there are many (internal) slots within the table that are allocated but empty. A Hashtable is a sequence of slots that are directly addressable by a hash code.

Practically speaking, a Hashtable is a mechanism to provide *keyed* access to objects.

Although String objects were used in the discussion above, a Hashtable allows the programmer to use any kind of object as the key and any kind of object as the value.

For example, instead of storing an element whose key is a person's name and whose value is a Person object, one could use the Person object itself as the key object. The value object might be a vector of objects that represent all contacts that this person has made with a company.

This concept of storing higher functioning objects in collection classes, like the Hashtable, begins to demonstrate the added value that the object-oriented approach brings to programming.

Properties—A Persistent Collection of Key/Value Pairs

A Hashtable would be a good class to use to store system default information. The key could be the name of a system default like "BackgroundColor", "ForegroundColor", or "FontSize", and the value could be the color or size to use in the application.

However, a Hashtable is not persistent and it goes away when the program exits.

The Properties class was designed to be a persistent Hashtable. The key/value pairs are added to a Properties class in the same way as a Hashtable, and then the whole object can be saved to a text file. When the application starts up again, the text file can be read and the key/value pairs can be reconstructed.

The following example creates a Properties object to store system defaults.

```
import java.util.*;
import java.io.*;

    class Defaults1                          // Creates a Property and Saves it
      {
      public static void main (String argv[])
        {
        String RED   = "#FF0000";
        String GREEN = "#00FF00";
        String BLUE  = "#0000FF";
        String BLACK = "#000000";
        String WHITE = "#FFFFFF";
        Properties prDefaults;
        Properties prop;
        FileOutputStream fos;

        System.out.println ("*-----------Display Defaults-----------*");
        prDefaults = new Properties ();
        prDefaults.put ("BackgroundColor", GREEN);
        prDefaults.put ("ForegroundColor", WHITE);
        prDefaults.list (System.out);

        System.out.println ("*--------Properties After Creation--------*");
        prop = new Properties (prDefaults);
        prop.list (System.out);

        System.out.println ("*--------Properties After Additions-------*");
        prop.put ("BackgroundColor", BLACK);
        prop.put ("ForegroundColor", RED);
        prop.put ("FontSize", "12");
        prop.list (System.out);
        try
          {
          fos = new FileOutputStream ("DefaultProperties");
          prop.save (fos, "The Default Properties for My System");
          }
        catch (Exception e)
          {
          System.out.println ("Unable to open FileOutputStream");
          }

        System.out.println ("*----------------------------------------*");
        }
      }
```

```
1.0 C:\JumpStrt\examples\Defaults1>java Defaults1
*------------Display Defaults-------------*
-- listing properties --
BackgroundColor=#00FF00
ForegroundColor=#FFFFFF
*--------Properties After Creation--------*
-- listing properties --
BackgroundColor=#00FF00
ForegroundColor=#FFFFFF
*--------Properties After Additions-------*
-- listing properties --
FontSize=12
BackgroundColor=#000000
ForegroundColor=#FF0000
*-----------------------------------------*
```

Actually two Properties objects are being used. The first one is used to hold initial values for the second one. This allows a program to hard code default values for certain keys in the first Properties object, then load them into the second object that reads the rest of the values from the saved text file.

After the *prop* object is created, several elements are added to it. Some of them override previous values and one creates a new element. The syntax is the same as for the Hashtable.

The Properties class includes a *list*() method. This accepts a *PrintStream* object parameter and displays a list of the objects in the collection to that stream.

When all of the activity has been completed, the Properties object is saved to an OutputStream by passing the OutputStream to the *save*() method. The string parameter is a comment that is placed in the text file.

The FileOutputStream in this example, and the FileInputStream in the next example, perform the I/O to the text file.

After the *save*() method completes, the *DefaultProperties* file is created:

```
#The Default Properties for My System
#Wed Apr 24 12:14:41  1996
FontSize=12
BackgroundColor=#000000
ForegroundColor=#FF0000
```

The second step in using persistent properties is to retrieve the properties from the text file. The next example accomplishes that.

It begins like the previous example. Then it loads the values from the previous session by calling the *load*() method and passing a *FileInputStream* object. Further activity occurs with the *prop* object and its values are displayed at each step.

```
import java.util.*;
import java.io.*;

    class Defaults2                         // Retrieves Property and Adds to it
      {
      public static void main (String argv[])
        {
        String RED   = "#FF0000";
        String GREEN = "#00FF00";
        String BLUE  = "#0000FF";
        String BLACK = "#000000";
        String WHITE = "#FFFFFF";
        Properties prDefaults;
        Properties prop;
        FileInputStream fis;

        System.out.println ("*------------Display Defaults------------*");
        prDefaults = new Properties ();
        prDefaults.put ("BackgroundColor", GREEN);
        prDefaults.put ("ForegroundColor", WHITE);
        prDefaults.list (System.out);

        System.out.println ("*--------Properties After Creation--------*");
        prop = new Properties (prDefaults);
        prop.list (System.out);

        System.out.println ("*----------Properties After Load----------*");
        try
          {
          fis = new FileInputStream ("DefaultProperties");
          prop.load (fis);
          }
        catch (Exception e)
          {
          System.out.println ("Unable to open FileInputStream");
          }
```

```
        prop.list (System.out);

        System.out.println ("*-------Properties After Additions--------*");
        prop.put ("ForegroundColor", BLUE);
        prop.put ("FontSize", "25");
        prop.list (System.out);

        System.out.println ("*-----------------------------------------*");
        }
    }
```

```
1.0 C:\JumpStrt\examples\Defaults2>java Defaults2
*------------Display Defaults-------------*
-- listing properties --
BackgroundColor=#00FF00
ForegroundColor=#FFFFFF
*--------Properties After Creation--------*
-- listing properties --
BackgroundColor=#00FF00
ForegroundColor=#FFFFFF
*----------Properties After Load----------*
-- listing properties --
FontSize=12
BackgroundColor=#000000
ForegroundColor=#FF0000
*-------Properties After Additions--------*
-- listing properties --
FontSize=25
BackgroundColor=#000000
ForegroundColor=#0000FF
*-----------------------------------------*
```

As the values from the saved file are loaded, they override several of the default values. Further processing activity in the method overlay the values of some other keys. To save the new state of the Properties object, one should add the code from the Defaults1 example.

The Properties class provides a way to make Hashtables persistent.

StringTokenizer—A Service for Parsing Through a String

In every programming language, one is faced with the job of picking through the characters of a string and extracting meaningful substrings. Java has implemented a generalized class to free the programmer from the tedium of this chore. It is called the StringTokenizer.

One instantiates a StringTokenizer with the String object upon which parsing must be performed. Then repeated calls to the method *nextToken*() return one substring for each call. The default character that identifies the end of a token is the space character.

```
import java.util.*;

    class SpaceTokens
      {
      public static void main (String argv[])
        {
        StringTokenizer st;
        String sIn;

        sIn = "Many waters cannot quench love, "
            + "neither can the floods drown it. (Songs8:7)";

        st = new StringTokenizer (sIn);

        while (st.hasMoreTokens ())
          {
          System.out.println ("-->" + st.nextToken () + "<--");
          }
        }
      }
```

```
1.0 C:\JumpStrt\examples\SpaceTokens>java SpaceTokens
-->Many<--
-->waters<--
-->cannot<--
-->quench<--
-->love,<--
-->neither<--
-->can<--
-->the<--
-->floods<--
-->drown<--
-->it.<--
-->(Songs8:7)<--
```

To accommodate more complex parsing tasks, token delimiters can be specified at the time a StringTokenizer is constructed or at the time the next token is received. To specify special delimiters, one passes a string that includes each of the potential delimiting characters.

The next example shows how to use the StringTokenizer to parse a string of Web page parameters. The *sIn* variable holds a typical string that an HTML form might generate. The key/value pairs are separated by "&"s and the key is separated from the value by an equals "=" sign.

```
import java.util.*;

    class SpecifiedTokens
      {
      public static void main (String argv[])
        {
        StringTokenizer st;
        String sIn;

        sIn = "Item=Book&Cost=$39.95&Qnty=3&Date=09/01/96";

        st = new StringTokenizer (sIn, "\r\n ", false);

        while (st.hasMoreElements ())
          {
          System.out.print ("Key-->" + st.nextToken ("=\r\n ") + "<--\t");
          System.out.print ("Value-->" + st.nextToken ("&\r\n ") + "<--\n");
          }
        }
      }
```

```
1.0 C:\JumpStrt\examples\SpecifiedTokens>java SpecifiedTokens
Key -->Item<--  Value -->=Book<--
Key -->Cost<--  Value -->=$39.95<--
Key -->Qnty<--  Value -->=3<--
Key -->Date<--  Value -->=09/01/96<--
```

In this example, the StringTokenizer was initialized with three delimiting characters: a carriage return, a line feed, and a space character. When the tokenizer encounters any of these characters, it detects the end of a token.

The last parameter in the constructor is a boolean that tells the tokenizer how to handle the delimiting character. A value of *true* instructs the tokenizer to include the delimiter as part of the token and *false* instructs it to discard the delimiter.

This example specifies a new set of delimiters every time it calls *nextToken*(). Each time a new set is specified, the new set replaces the original set and remains in force for subsequent calls to *nextToken*().

In only three statements, this Web Form was parsed using the StringTokenizer.

CHAPTER 7

Touching Java Windows

Mouse Messages

Users pass visual signals to a program by moving and clicking a mouse on the window's surface. The most convenient mechanism for picking up these signals is to implement mouse methods within the applet.

Mouse messages are methods that get called when the user operates the mouse over the applet's window. There are methods that indicate when the user has clicked the mouse button down or up, methods that indicate that the mouse is moving or dragging over the window, and methods that signal when the mouse enters and leaves the applet rectangle.

Here is an example that identifies when each of these methods is called. Figure 7–1 demonstrates the results of this example.

```
import java.applet.Applet;
import java.awt.*;

    public class MouseMessages extends Applet
/************************************************************************

    MouseMessages - Demonstrates Mouse Methods


************************************************************************/

    {

/************************************************************************/
```

```
public String getAppletInfo ()
  {
  return ("Copyright (c) Noel Enete, 1996");
  }


public void init ()
  {
  setBackground (Color.lightGray);
  }


public boolean mouseEnter (Event evt, int x, int y)
  {
  messageOut ("x=" + x + "y=" + y + ":  mouseEnter()");
  return (true);
  }


public boolean mouseExit (Event evt, int x, int y)
  {
  messageOut ("x=" + x + "y=" + y + ":  mouseExit()");
  return (true);
  }


public boolean mouseDown (Event evt, int x, int y)
  {
  messageOut ("x=" + x + "y=" + y + ":  mouseDown()");
  return (true);
  }


public boolean mouseUp (Event evt, int x, int y)
  {
  messageOut ("x=" + x + "y=" + y + ":  mouseUp()");
  return (true);
  }


public boolean mouseDrag (Event evt, int x, int y)
  {
  messageOut ("x=" + x + "y=" + y + ":  mouseDrag()");
  return (true);
  }
```

```
    public boolean mouseMove (Event evt, int x, int y)
      {
      messageOut ("x=" + x + "y=" + y + ":  mouseMove()");
      return (true);
      }


    void messageOut (String s)
      {
      System.out.println (s);
      showStatus (s);
      }


    public void paint (Graphics g)
      {
      int x, y;
      FontMetrics fm;
      String sMessage = "Move & click the mouse and watch the command "
      + "line.";

      fm = g.getFontMetrics ();
      x = (size().width / 2) - (fm.stringWidth (sMessage) / 2);
      y = (size().height / 2) - (fm.getHeight () / 2);
      g.drawString (sMessage, x, y);
      }

    }

/*=========================(  End of Source  )========================*/
```

```
<HTML>
<HEAD>
<TITLE> MouseMessages — Demonstrate Mouse Messages </TITLE>
</HEAD>
<BODY>

Move the mouse around within the screen and watch the messages on the
command line.
<HR>
<APPLET CODE="MouseMessages" WIDTH=300 HEIGHT=200>
</APPLET>
</BODY>
</HTML>
```

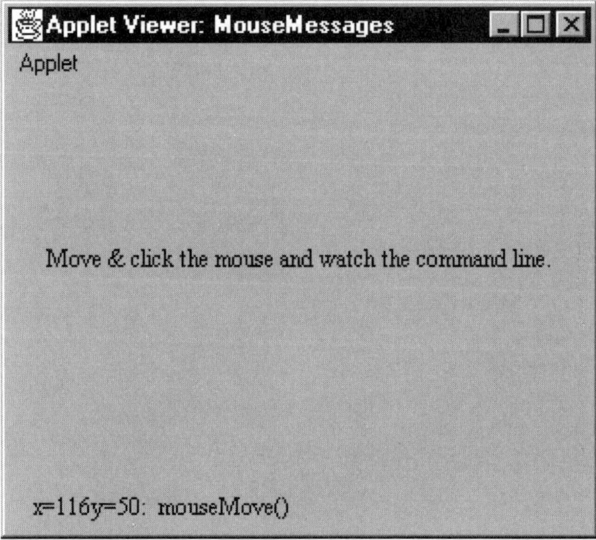

Figure 7–1

```
1.0 C:\JumpStrt\examples\MouseMessages>appletviewer MouseMessages.html
thread applet-MouseMessages find class MouseMessages
Opening stream to: file:/C:/JumpStrt/examples/MouseMessages/MouseMessages.
class to get MouseMessages
x=176y=158:  mouseEnter()
x=176y=158:  mouseMove()
x=176y=150:  mouseMove()
x=176y=146:  mouseMove()
x=176y=146:  mouseDown()
x=176y=146:  mouseDrag()
x=176y=146:  mouseUp()
x=176y=146:  mouseMove()
x=176y=146:  mouseDown()
x=177y=146:  mouseDrag()
x=178y=146:  mouseDrag()
x=179y=146:  mouseDrag()
x=179y=146:  mouseDrag()
x=179y=146:  mouseUp()
x=179y=146:  mouseMove()
x=187y=152:  mouseMove()
x=301y=182:  mouseExit()
```

Each mouse method is passed an Event object and the *x* and *y* coordinates of the mouse when the input occurred. The Event object carries more information about the current state of the input devices (like shift-key states).

Each method expects a boolean return value. If the mouse method returns *true,* the caller assumes that the mouse event has been completely handled and it takes no further action. If *false* is returned, then the caller also sends the message to the next higher class in the applet's hierarchy (which would normally be the Applet class) for further processing.

Since Java is targeting a number of computer platforms, some of which do not have multiple mouse buttons, the methods do not distinguish right or left mouse buttons. On systems with multiple buttons, the *mouseDown()* method is called whenever any of the buttons is pressed.

Click and Drag

The most common use for these messages is to provide a way for the user to move things on the window surface by clicking them, dragging them, then releasing them.

The behavior is implemented by adding code to the *mouseDown(), mouseDrag(),* and *mouseUp()* methods. When the method *mouseDown()* is called, the user has just pressed the mouse button down. This is the time to capture the starting position for the drag operations.

Each time the *mouseDrag()* message is called, the user has moved the mouse with the button pressed down. To show the illusion of motion, the screen should be repainted and the mouse position should be updated each time the *mouseDrag()* method is called. The *mouseUp()* method is available to reinitialize any drag state variables that were set in the *mouseDown()* method.

In the following example, the user can click and drag anywhere on the screen, and a sparkler will suddenly appear and follow the mouse pointer around the window. The sparkler is implemented in the *drawSparkler()* method as a series of lines having random direction, length, and color.

```
import java.applet.Applet;
import java.awt.*;
import java.util.*;

    public class MouseApplet extends Applet
/*************************************************************************

    MouseApplet - Demonstrates Mouse Methods


*************************************************************************/

    {

    int xMouse, yMouse;                /* Current position of the mouse.    */
    int xMouseDown, yMouseDown;        /* Mouse positn when it was clicked .*/
    int xWindow, yWindow;              /* Window width and height.          */
    boolean bClear = true;             /* Reinitialization flag.            */
    boolean bFlicker = false;          /* T = erase bkground between paints.*/

/*************************************************************************/


    public void init ()
      {
      if (getParameter ("Flicker") != null)
        {
        bFlicker = true;
        }
      xMouse = 0;
      yMouse = 0;
      xWindow = size().width;
      yWindow = size().height;
      setBackground (Color.lightGray);
      }

    public boolean mouseDown (Event evt, int x, int y)
      {
      xMouse = x;
      yMouse = y;
      xMouseDown = x;
      yMouseDown = y;
      return (true);
      }
```

```
public boolean mouseUp (Event evt, int x, int y)
  {
  if ((x == xMouseDown) && (y == yMouseDown))
    {
    xMouse = 0;
    yMouse = 0;
    bClear = true;
    repaint ();
    }
  return (true);
  }


public boolean mouseDrag (Event evt, int x, int y)
  {
  if ((x != xMouse) || (y != yMouse))
    {
    repaint ();
    xMouse = x;
    yMouse = y;
    }
  return (true);
  }


public void update (Graphics g)
  {
  if (bFlicker)
    {
    super.update (g);
    }
  else
    {
    paint (g);
    }
  }


public void paint (Graphics g)
  {
  int i;
  int x, y;
  Color c;
  FontMetrics fm;
  String sMessage = "Click and Drag on a Spot. To reinitialize, "
    + "Click without a Drag";
```

```
        if (bClear)
          {
          g.clearRect (0, 0, xWindow, yWindow);
          bClear = false;
          }

        drawSparkler (g, 25);

        g.setColor (new Color (0, 0, 0));
        fm = g.getFontMetrics ();
        x = (xWindow / 2) - (fm.stringWidth (sMessage) / 2);
        y = (yWindow / 2) - (fm.getHeight () / 2);
        g.drawString (sMessage, x, y);
        }


      void drawSparkler (Graphics g, int iNumSpokes)
        {
        int i;
        Color c;

        for (i = 0; i < iNumSpokes; i++)
          {
          c = new Color
            (
            (int) (255 * Math.random ()),
            (int) (255 * Math.random ()),
            (int) (255 * Math.random ())
            );
          g.setColor (c);
          g.drawLine
            (
            xMouse,
            yMouse,
            (int) (xWindow * Math.random ()),
            (int) (yWindow * Math.random ())
            );
          }
        }

      }

/*=========================(  End of Source  )==========================*/
```

```
<HTML>
<HEAD>
<TITLE> MouseApplet -- Demonstrate Mouse Messages </TITLE>
</HEAD>
<BODY>

Click and drag on this applet then try the same on the next one.
Single click to clear the rectangle.
<HR>
<APPLET CODE="MouseApplet" WIDTH=500 HEIGHT=500>
<PARAM NAME=Flicker VALUE=>;
</APPLET>
<HR>
<APPLET CODE="MouseApplet" WIDTH=500 HEIGHT=500>
</APPLET>
</BODY>
</HTML>
```

In this example, two applets are launched with different techniques for repainting the window. One of them, Figure 7–2, clears the screen before every paint method. This gives the sense of clean motion across the window, but it has a slight flickering side effect.

The other applet, Figure 7–3, disables the clearing of the screen and just draws the new picture on top of the old one. This effect is noticeably faster and works well with many bitmap applications. In this particular application, it leaves an intriguing trail of lines as the sparkler crawls across the window.

These two techniques represent two different ways of managing the applet's *repaint()* method. In the *mouseDrag()* method, *repaint()* is called to update the screen each time the mouse is moved. *Repaint()* calls the methods *update()* and *paint()* to redraw the window.

If the MouseApplet had not coded an *update()* method, the *update()* message would be sent to one of the super classes for processing. The default implementation of *update()* clears the window and then calls the *paint()* method. When an *update()* method is coded, this applet steps in and selectively clears the screen.

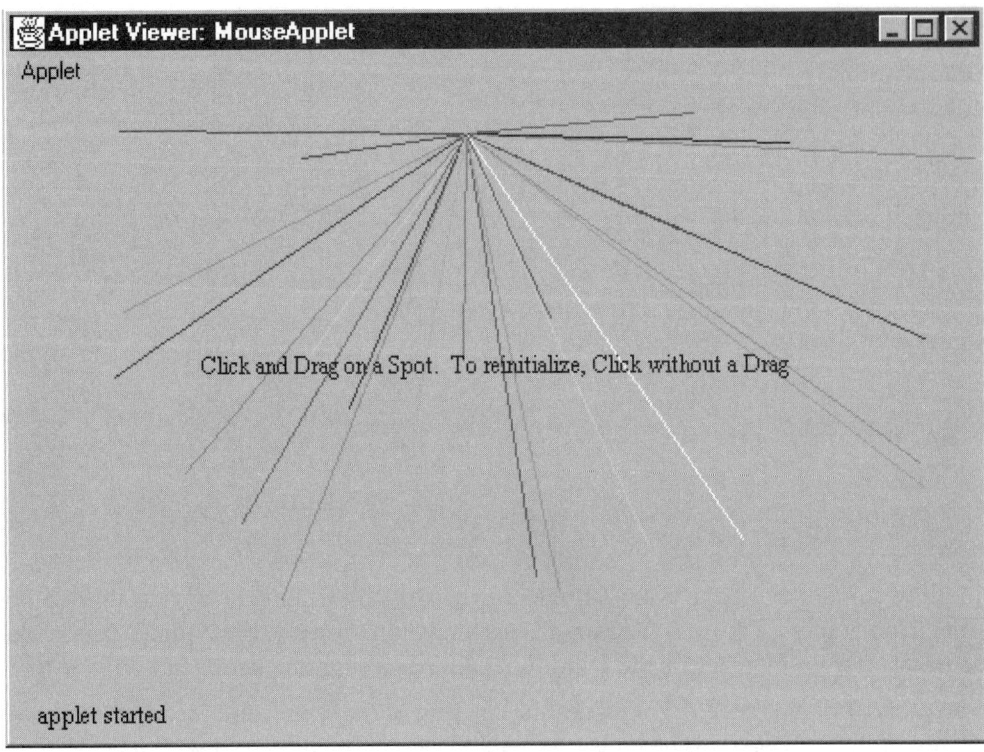

Figure 7–2

The *update()* method determines when to clear the screen by using the value of the boolean *bFlicker* variable, which was set in the *init()* method from parameters passed to the applet. If flicker is set, the *update()* method in the next higher super class is called; this will clear the screen, then call *paint()*. If flicker is not set, the *paint()* method is called directly.

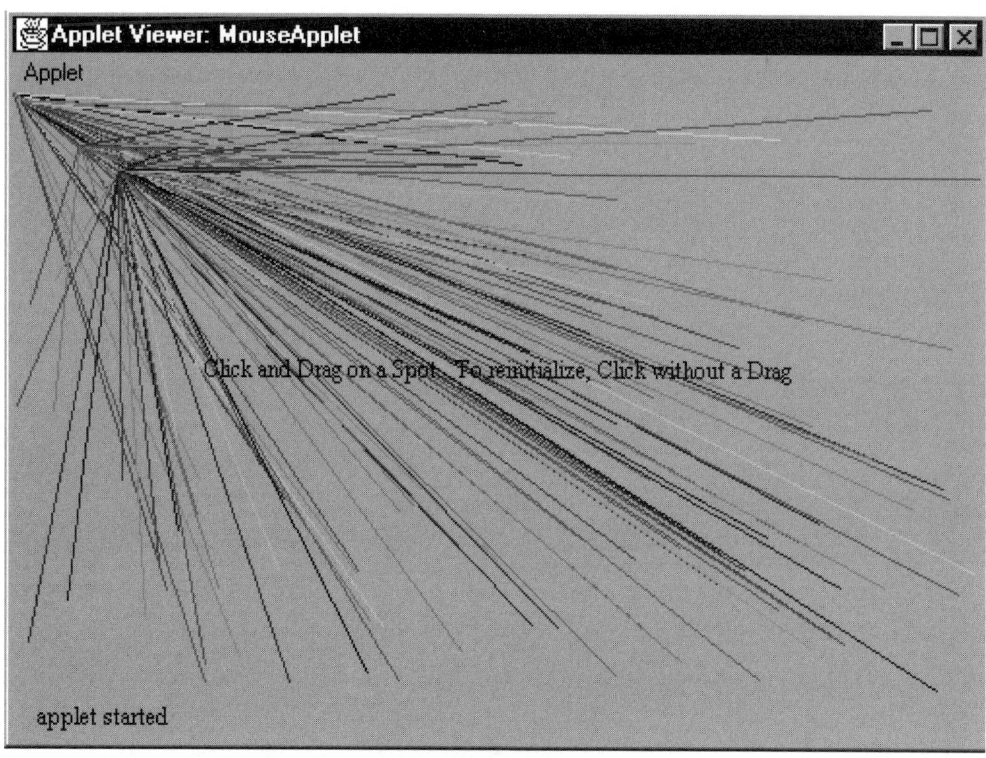

Figure 7–3

```
if (bFlicker)
  {
  super.update (g);
  }
else
  {
  paint (g);
  }
```

Dragging a Picture

To extend the previous example to allow a user to drag a picture across the screen with the mouse, one can follow the same basic steps: capture the mouse position in *mouseDown()*, repaint and reposition in *mouseDrag()*, and clean up in *mouseUp()*.

But, instead of painting the window with lines, one paints it with an image. The techniques for achieving motion and position are exactly the same. But, the object to paint is different.

The following example allows the user to drag an image around the screen.

```
import java.applet.*;
import java.awt.*;

    public class ImageApplet extends Applet
/*************************************************************************

    ImageApplet -- Allows a Mouse to Drag a GIF Image around in a Window


*************************************************************************/

    {

    Image imPicture;                  /* The loaded GIF picture.           */
    int xMouse, yMouse;               /* Current position of the mouse.    */
    int xMouseDown, yMouseDown;       /* Mouse positn when it was clicked.  */
    int xImage, yImage;               /* Current position of the image.    */
    int xImageWidth, yImageHeight;    /* Image size.                       */
    boolean bClear = true;            /* Reinitialization flag.            */
    boolean bFlicker = false;         /* T = erase bkground between paints. */
    boolean bCapturing = false;       /* T = dragging icon.                */

/************************************************************************/
    public void init ()
      {
      String sImage;

      sImage = getParameter ("Image");
      if (sImage == null)
        {
        sImage = "ImageApplet.gif";
        }
      imPicture = getImage (getDocumentBase (), sImage);
```

```
      if (getParameter ("Flicker") != null)
        {
        bFlicker = true;
        }

      xImage = 0;
      yImage = 0;
      setBackground (Color.lightGray);
      }


   public void update (Graphics g)
      {
      if (bFlicker)
        {
        super.update (g);
        }
      else
        {
        drawImg (g);
        }
      }


   public void paint (Graphics g)
      {
      drawImg (g);
      }


   private void drawImg (Graphics g)
      {
      if (bClear)
        {
        g.clearRect (0, 0, size().width, size().height);
        bClear = false;
        }

      g.drawImage (imPicture, xImage, yImage, this);
      }


   public boolean mouseDown (Event evt, int x, int y)
      {
      if (xImageWidth == 0) xImageWidth = imPicture.getWidth (this);
```

```
    if (yImageHeight == 0) yImageHeight = imPicture.getHeight (this);

    xMouse = x;
    yMouse = y;
    xMouseDown = x;
    yMouseDown = y;

    if ((x >= xImage) && (x <= xImage + xImageWidth)     // Targeting
    && (y >= yImage) && (y <= yImage + yImageHeight))    // code.
      {
      bCapturing = true;
      }
    else
      {
      bCapturing = false;
      }
    return (true);
    }


  public boolean mouseUp (Event evt, int x, int y)
    {
    if ((x == xMouseDown) && (y == yMouseDown))
      {
      xImage = 0;
      yImage = 0;
      bClear = true;
      repaint ();                        /* Cause Applet to send a paint.   */
      }
    return (true);
    }

  public boolean mouseDrag (Event evt, int x, int y)
    {
    int xImageNew = xImage;
    int yImageNew = yImage;

    if (!bCapturing) return (true);

    xImageNew += (x - xMouse);
    yImageNew += (y - yMouse);
    xMouse = x;
    yMouse = y;
```

```
      if ((xImageNew != xImage) || (yImageNew != yImage))
        {
        repaint ();                          /* Cause Applet to send a paint.   */
        xImage = xImageNew;
        yImage = yImageNew;
        }
      return (true);
      }

    }

/*=========================(  End of Source  )============================*/
```

```
<HTML>
<HEAD>
<TITLE> ImageApplet -- Display and Slide an Image </TITLE>
</HEAD>
<BODY>

Click on this image or the next one and slide it around.
Single click to clear the rectangle.
<HR>
<APPLET CODE="ImageApplet" WIDTH=500 HEIGHT=200>
<PARAM NAME=Image VALUE="ImageApplet.gif">;
</APPLET>
<HR>
<APPLET CODE="ImageApplet" WIDTH=500 HEIGHT=200>
<PARAM NAME=Image VALUE="ImageApplet.gif">;
<PARAM NAME=Flicker VALUE=>;
</APPLET>
</BODY>
</HTML>
```

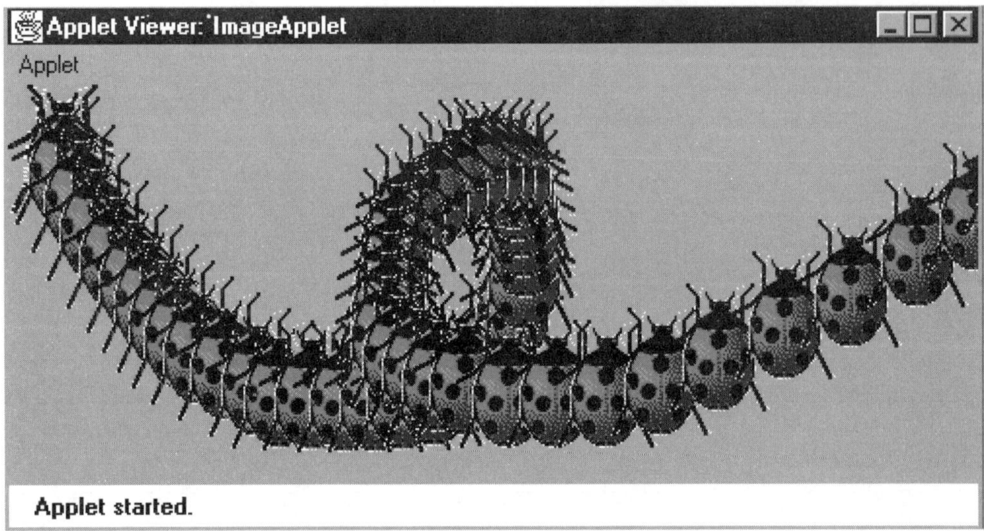

Figure 7–4

Figure 7–5

In this example, the "Flicker" parameter selects a refresh technique that erases the screen in between each movement of the mouse. Figure 7–4 shows the ImageApplet running with "Flicker" set to false. When "Flicker" is set to true the image follows the mouse without leaving a trail (Figure 7–5).

The image is drawn by calling the Graphics method *drawImage()*. The drawImage() parameters, which identify the placement of the picture, identify a point on the window that is the upper left corner of the image rectangle.

```
g.drawImage (imPicture, xImage, yImage, this);
```

In the *mouseDown()* method, image targeting is accomplished by comparing the current position of the mouse *(x, y)* with the current position of the upper left corner of the image *(xImage, yImage)*.

```
if ((x >= xImage) && (x <= xImage + xImageWidth)     // Targeting
&& (y >= yImage) && (y <= yImage + yImageHeight))    // code.
   {
   bCapturing = true;
   }
else
   {
   bCapturing = false;
   }
```

Image movement is accomplished by repainting the image in the *mouseDrag()* method. This only occurs if the mouse's coordinates have changed since the last time the image was drawn.

The image is released in the *mouseUp()* method. All dragging variables are reinitialized and the screen is repainted one last time.

By trapping the activity of the mouse, the programmer can give the users the sense that they have *touched* the screen and manipulated one of the visual images.

CHAPTER 8

Animation

Another way to make output dynamic is to establish a repeating pattern in which the screen gets repainted every so-many seconds. By changing the location or look of the output, the program can create the sense of motion or animation.

What makes this technique special is that the program is not repainting the screen in response to a user request. The program is repainting the screen on its own. Instead of the program servicing the user, it is performing *for* the user.

Triggering Each Picture

To establish this automated behavior, one must write a routine whose only purpose is to wake up at regular intervals and ask for the screen to be repainted.

The processing code could look something like this:

```
while (true)
  {
  repaint ();
  try {Thread.sleep (iWaitMilliseconds);}
  catch (Exception e) {break;}
  }
```

This code establishes a repeating pattern. The screen is repainted. The thread goes to sleep for a certain number of milliseconds, then the pattern is repeated.

This code establishes the kind of controlled update that is desired, but there is a problem. When this code is waiting, it has put the entire thread to sleep. Most programs run in a single thread of execution. If this single thread is put to sleep, the program is completely unresponsive to any user input while it is waiting for the next repaint request. This is normally unacceptable.

The simplest way around this problem is to cause the prompting code to run in its own separate thread of execution. Then the program will be running in two threads, one to control the repaint interval and the other to allow the program to respond to the user.

There are two methods to cause a chunk of code to run in its own thread. First, one can create a new class that is an extension of the Thread class, and the code can be placed into this new class. This technique is normally suited to extensive programming chores that involve multiple processing steps.

The code above is very short and simple. It would be nice if the prompting code could live in the same class that is being repainted. But the program that is getting repainted is not in the Thread class. It is in another class that has its own special responsibilities. How can one class take on the responsibilities of another class without losing its own identity?

By implementing some of the methods of the other class.

Many classes have identified methods that other classes can implement to gain specific behavior without losing the class's original identity. In order to communicate which methods should be implemented to gain the behavior, the method definitions are collected into a class-like structure called an *interface*.

```
public interface Runnable
  {
  public abstract void run();
  }
```

The Thread class has defined the Runnable Interface above to communicate how other classes can assume thread-like behavior. All the other class has to do is implement the *run*() method.

So, to implement a repeating pattern and independent thread, implement a *run*() method and put the prompting code in it. The following example implements this technique and identifies the basic building blocks of all time-oriented update programs.

```
class ThreadApplication implements Runnable
  {
  int iCount;
  int iWaitMilliseconds;
  Thread thUpdatePrompter;

  ThreadApplication ()
    {
    iCount = 0;
    iWaitMilliseconds = 1000;

    thUpdatePrompter = new Thread (this);
    thUpdatePrompter.start ();
    }

  public void run ()
    {
    while (true)
      {
      repaint ();
      try {Thread.sleep (iWaitMilliseconds);}
      catch (Exception e) {break;}
      }
    }

  void repaint ()
    {
    System.out.println ("The Update Prompter has signaled repaint #"
      + iCount);
    iCount++;
    }

  public static void main (String args[])
    {
    new ThreadApplication ();
    }
  }
```

```
1.0 C:\JumpStrt\examples\ThreadApplication>java ThreadApplication
The Update Prompter has signaled repaint #0
The Update Prompter has signaled repaint #1
The Update Prompter has signaled repaint #2
The Update Prompter has signaled repaint #3
     .
     .
     .
^C
```

First, the class must let everyone know that it is implementing methods that will allow it to behave like a thread:

```
class ThreadApplication implements Runnable
```

Remember that an interface like *Runnable* is a communication technique that allows the Thread class to specify what methods other classes need to implement to be able to act like a thread.

Then, the class must implement the method *run*(). The *run*() method holds all the code that will be running in the separate thread. This is the code that identifies when to request a repaint of the screen.

The last step is to create the new thread.

```
thUpdatePrompter = new Thread (this);
thUpdatePrompter.start ();
```

When the object creates the new thread, it passes itself (*this*) as a parameter. From then on, the new Thread object is able to send messages back to the launching object.

When the calling object sends the *start*() message to the newly created thread, its normal behavior is to send a *run*() message to itself. But the newly created thread knows about the *Runnable* object and chooses to call that object's *run*() method instead. When it does, the new thread begins execution.

As the separate thread runs, it waits for an established interval, then sends a request to update the screen. This thread becomes the main driver of a program that controls screen output with a timer. The rest of the code is concerned with the changes in position or content between screen updates or with drawing the screen update itself.

Displaying Each Picture

Once the regular update interval has been established, one's attention can be turned to the actual screen update. The screen update technique that is chosen depends on how short the wait interval is and on how long it takes to repaint each screen.

Often the wait interval is very short to present the user with the illusion of continuous motion. For the visual effect to work, each frame must be presented to the user completely drawn. If the user is allowed to see the incremental drawing of each frame, the illusion of motion is defeated.

If drawing is performed on the Graphics object that is passed to the *paint()* method, the user will often be able to perceive the incremental progress of drawing and will loose the desired visual effect of motion.

To allow the necessary time to render the object and still present the user with completely drawn frames, a copy of the screen is created in memory. All drawing is performed out of the user's view on the screen in memory. When the drawing has been completed, the real screen is updated from the screen in memory (a very fast process).

The example below implements this double buffering scheme without the timing loop. To get a sense of the unified refresh of this screen, click on the screen. This will redraw the pattern in the background buffer and present the completed drawing to the user at one time. Figure 8–1 shows the image produced by this example.

Figure 8–1

```
import java.applet.Applet;
import java.awt.*;

    public class FlickerFree extends Applet
      {
      int iTextIndex;
      Image imBackground;
      Graphics gBackground;

      public void init ()
        {
        iTextIndex = 0;
        imBackground = createImage (size().width, size().height);
        gBackground = imBackground.getGraphics ();

        gBackground.setColor (Color.lightGray);
        gBackground.fillRect (0, 0, size().width, size().height);
        gBackground.setColor (Color.black);
        gBackground.setFont (getFont ());
        }

      public boolean mouseDown (Event e, int x, int y)
        {
        repaint ();
        return (true);
        }
```

```
public void update (Graphics g)
  {
  gBackground.setColor (Color.lightGray);
  gBackground.fillRect (0, 0, size().width, size().height);
  gBackground.setColor (Color.black);
  paint (g);
  }

public void paint (Graphics g)
  {
  String [] as = {"Java", "Applet", "Web", "Server"};
  FontMetrics fm;
  int i, j;
  int x, y;
  int iInitialX;

  fm = g.getFontMetrics ();
  y = fm.getHeight ();
  iInitialX = 0;
  showStatus ("Click in the Window...");

  for (i = 0; i < 12; i++)
    {
    x = iInitialX;
    iInitialX -= 6;
    for (j = 0; j < 16; j++)
      {
      gBackground.drawString (as[iTextIndex], x, y);
      x += fm.stringWidth (as[iTextIndex]) + 4;
      }
    y += fm.getHeight ();
    }

  g.drawImage (imBackground, 0, 0, this);

  if (++iTextIndex > 3)
    {
    iTextIndex = 0;
    }
  }
}
```

```
<HTML>
<HEAD>
<TITLE> FlickerFree </TITLE>
</HEAD>
<BODY>
FlickerFree
<HR>
<APPLET CODE="FlickerFree" WIDTH=300 HEIGHT=200>
</APPLET>
</BODY>
</HTML>
```

In the *paint*() method, the drawing occurs first to the Graphics context of the memory copy of the screen image. Then the background image is drawn to the visible Graphics screen.

```
gBackground.drawString (as[iTextIndex], x, y);
g.drawImage (imBackground, 0, 0, this);
```

In the *init*() method, the hidden copy of the screen is created and its Graphics context is secured. Then there is some initialization that is required to get its attributes to match those of the visible screen.

```
imBackground = createImage (size().width, size().height);
gBackground = imBackground.getGraphics ();

gBackground.setColor (getBackground ());
gBackground.fillRect (0, 0, size().width, size().height);
gBackground.setColor (Color.black);
gBackground.setFont (getFont ());
```

As one clicks on the screen, a completely drawn frame is presented. All of the incremental drawing delays are hidden from the user.

This double buffering technique accomplishes the uniform presentation of each output display even when the drawing takes a while to accomplish. This hides the effects of long output drawing time from the user's perception.

Loading the Pictures

The uniform presentation of frames of visual output can be disrupted by another kind of delay. If the loading time for the presentation data is noticeably long, one should delay the presentation of the first frame until enough data is available for repaints to continue smoothly.

In the case of images being loaded from computers across the network, this can take a significant amount of time. When asking for an image to be loaded, the Applet method *getImage*() is used. When it is called, it returns a handle to the image immediately even if the image data has not been loaded into memory yet. This helps to avoid unnecessary delays in processing while waiting on the network to load the resource.

For both of these reasons, the programmer must find a way to identify when the requested output resources have actually arrived. The Java environment provides the MediaTracker class for this purpose.

To use the MediaTracker, one creates a new instance, then adds each media object handle to the tracker. Then the program can ask the MediaTracker for the status of any of the objects at any time.

```
mtTracker = new MediaTracker (this);

for (i = 0; i < iNumImages; i++)
  {
  aimImages[i] = getImage (getDocumentBase(), sBaseFilename + (i + 1)
    + ".gif");
  mtTracker.addImage (aimImages[i], 1);
  }
```

The final example of this chapter incorporates each of these techniques to load 12 images into memory and display each of them in rapid succession. The images that are shown are three-dimensional drawings of a surfboard. The colors represent relative volume displacements at each point in the board. The drawings are selected so that the surfboard appears to be rotating horizontally.

The images were generated using an excellent CAD tool for surfboard design called D.A.T. Designer, which is available at *http://www.windsurfer.com/DATDesigner*.

The code at the beginning of the *run*() method uses the MediaTracker to wait until all of the images known by the group ID of 1 have been loaded. In this case, all of the images were added with the single group ID of 1.

```
try
  {
  mtTracker.waitForID (1);
  }
catch (InterruptedException e)
  {
  return;
  }
```

As a courtesy to the user, some controls are placed on the thread that establishes the update pattern. It is launched when the applet is started and stopped when the applet is stopped. While the applet is active, some animations can become tiresome. So this applet has implemented the *mouseDown*() method to stop and start the thread in response to a click on the applet.

When viewing this applet through a Web browser like *Netscape,* the animation may not begin immediately. Because of a browser bug, the user might need to press the reload button on the tool bar, or exit and re-enter the page several times before the animation begins. As shown in Figure 8–2, the *appletviewer* renders the animation without error.

```
import java.applet.Applet;
import java.awt.*;

    public class AnimateApplet extends Applet implements Runnable
/*************************************************************************

    AnimateApplet -- Displays Images in Rapid Succession

 ************************************************************************/
```

```
   {
   MediaTracker mtTracker;      /* The store of images                  */
   Image[] aimImages;           /* Images that have arrived.            */
   int iImageIndex = 0;         /* Current image number to paint.       */
   Thread thAnimation;          /* The thread that does the animatn.    */
   String sBaseFilename;        /* Filename upto numbers and extn.      */
   int iNumImages;              /* Total number of images.              */
   int iPauseInMS;              /* Num milliseconds between images.     */
   Image imBackground;          /* Double buffered background image.    */
   Graphics gBackground;        /* Background Graphics context.         */

/**********************************************************************/


   public String getAppletInfo ()
     {
     return ("Copyright (c) Noel Enete, 1996");
     }
```

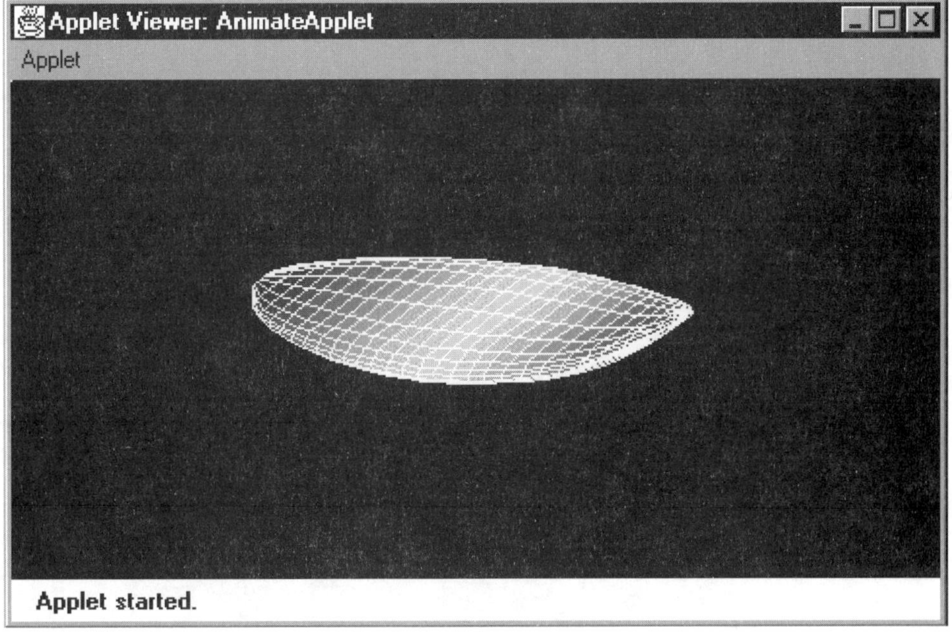

Figure 8–2

```
public void init ()
  {
  int i;
  String[][] aasParms;
  Object o = null;

  sBaseFilename = "images/T";
  iNumImages    = 10;
  aimImages     = new Image[iNumImages];
  iPauseInMS    = 175;

  mtTracker = new MediaTracker (this);

  for (i = 0; i < iNumImages; i++)
    {
    aimImages[i] = getImage (getDocumentBase(), sBaseFilename + (i + 1)
      + ".gif");
    mtTracker.addImage (aimImages[i], 1);
    }

  imBackground = createImage (size().width, size().height);
  gBackground = imBackground.getGraphics ();
  gBackground.setColor (Color.lightGray);
  gBackground.fillRect (0, 0, size().width, size().height);
  }

public void start ()
  {
  thAnimation = new Thread (this);
  thAnimation.start ();
  }


public void stop ()
  {
  iImageIndex = 0;
  repaint ();
  if (thAnimation != null)
    {
    thAnimation.stop ();
    thAnimation = null;
    }
  }
```

```
public void run ()
  {
  try
    {
    mtTracker.waitForID (1);
    }
  catch (InterruptedException e)
    {
    return;
    }

  Thread tSelf = Thread.currentThread();

  while (thAnimation == tSelf)
    {
    try {Thread.sleep (iPauseInMS);}
    catch (InterruptedException e) {break;}

    synchronized (this)
      {
      iImageIndex++;
      if (iImageIndex >= aimImages.length)
        {
        iImageIndex = 0;
        }
      }

    repaint();
    }
  }


public void update (Graphics g)
  {
  gBackground.setColor (Color.lightGray);
  gBackground.fillRect (0, 0, size().width, size().height);
  paint (g);
  }
```

```
    public void paint (Graphics g)
      {
      if (mtTracker.isErrorAny ())
        {
        g.setColor (Color.magenta);
        g.fillRect (0, 0, size().width, size().height);
        return;
        }
      gBackground.drawImage (aimImages[iImageIndex], 0, 0, this);
      g.drawImage (imBackground, 0, 0, this);
      }


    public boolean mouseDown (Event evt, int x, int y)
      {
      if (thAnimation != null)
        {
        thAnimation.stop ();
        thAnimation = null;
        }
      else
        {
        thAnimation = new Thread (this);
        thAnimation.start();
        }
      iImageIndex = 0;
      repaint();

      return (true);
      }

    }

/*========================(  End of Source  )==========================*/
```

```
<HTML>
<HEAD>
<TITLE> AnimateApplet -- Display Images in Rapid Succession </TITLE>
</HEAD>
<BODY>

Here is the program:
<HR>
<APPLET CODE="AnimateApplet" WIDTH=480 HEIGHT=250>
</APPLET>
</BODY>
</HTML>
```

CHAPTER 9

User Input

After a Java program has begun executing, there is still a way for a program to receive input from the user.

Command line programs must pause and query the command line for user input. When the user enters some input, the program can receive it and process it.

Java applets or other graphical applications receive input as events. Each time the mouse moves across the interface, an event is sent to the program. Each time a key is pressed or a mouse button is clicked, an event is sent to the applet.

The two techniques are quite different. The first deals with file streams and the second processes Event objects.

How to Receive Input from the Command Line (stdin)

A command line Java program must read user input from the operating system's standard input device. So where is the standard input device in Java?

Every time programmers use the phrase *System.out.println()*, they are making use of the standard output device. Recall that *out* is an instance variable of the System class. This variable holds an object that implements the behavior for writing output to the standard output device. In many ways, System.out *is* the standard output device in the Java environment.

In the documentation for the System class (in the *java.lang* package), one will notice two other instance variables: *in* and *err*. These hold objects that represent the operating system's standard input and standard error devices respectively. The instance variables for the System class are defined as follows:

```
public static InputStream in;
public static PrintStream out;
public static PrintStream err;
```

The *static* attribute connects these variables with the class, rather than with an instance of the class.

When the *System.out.println*() call is made, the *println*() method is sent to the *PrintStream* object that is stored in the *out* variable. To read input, one would need to send something like a *readLine*() method to the *InputStream* object that is stored in the *in* variable.

Unfortunately, the *InputStream* object only implements very low-functioning input behavior. The *readLine*() method that understands line boundaries is not in the InputStream. It is in the *DataInputStream* class.

In Java, when one has a lower-functioning object and wants to make use of a higher-functioning service, there is usually a way to use the lower object to instantiate the higher-functioning object.

```
DataInputStream dis = new DataInputStream (System.in);
```

Simply use the *InputStream* object when creating a new DataInputStream. Then every reference to the new *dis* object will use *System.in* to perform the processing.

The example below reads command line input and echo's it back to the command line.

```
import java.io.*;

    class InputApplication
      {
      InputApplication ()
        {
        DataInputStream dis = new DataInputStream (System.in);
        String sIn = " ";

        System.out.println ("*-----------------------------------*");

        while ((sIn.length () != 0)
        && (sIn.compareTo ("quit") != 0)
        && (sIn.compareTo ("exit") != 0))
          {
          System.out.print ("Enter Something Here: ");
          System.out.flush ();
```

```
            try {sIn = dis.readLine ();}
            catch (Exception e) {break;}

            System.out.print ("       You entered  -->");
            System.out.print (sIn);
            System.out.println ("<--");
            }

          System.out.println ("*-------------------------------------*");
          }


        public static void main (String args[])
          {
          new InputApplication ();
          }
        }
```

```
1.0 C:\JumpStrt\examples\InputApplication>java InputApplication
*---------------------------------------*
Enter Something Here: Hello
      You entered  -->Hello<--
Enter Something Here: Java World
      You entered  -->Java World<--
Enter Something Here: Fans
      You entered  -->Fans<--
Enter Something Here: quit
      You entered  -->quit<--
*---------------------------------------*
```

How to Receive Input from a Window (events)

Graphical programs do not need to explicitly request user input. User input is always sent to a graphical Java program. The input can be ignored and allowed to be handled by default behavior, or it can be processed.

To process user input, the graphical program class needs to implement a *handleEvent*() method. This method passes an Event object to the program and expects a boolean return value.

```
public boolean handleEvent (Event evt)
  {

  return (super.handleEvent (evt));
  }
```

If default processing is desired, the event is passed to the *handleEvent*() method of the next higher class. The return from that call is passed back as the return from this method.

Often, the default processing of an event is to call a helper method like *mouseDown*(), *mouseMove*(), or *keyDown*(). These are more convenient methods for processing the MOUSE_DOWN, MOUSE_MOVE, and KEY_PRESS events.

To keep the complexity of the code to a minimum, a class should either implement the helper methods or implement a *handleEvent*() method, but not both. The helper functions are listed in the documentation under *java.awt.Component.handleEvent*() and are listed here for convenience:

mouseEnter()

mouseExit()

mouseMove()

mouseDown()

mouseDrag()

mouseUp()

keyDown()

action()

Everything that is needed to quantify the user input is in the Event object.

There are a wide variety of events that can come to a Java GUI program. To get a feel for the range of input possibilities, launch the example below, run the mouse across it, and send key strokes to it. Each event that the program receives is parsed and displayed in a list box.

The value on the far left is the *event id*. This is the broad event type that identifies the event's main category. In the applet's *init*() method, each possible event *id* is added to the Hashtable object *htEventIds.* There are keyboard events, scroll events, window events, and mouse events.

This field holds a coded integer to identify the event type. To decode the event type, compare the value in the *id* field with one of the event constants. The following code identifies and processes the MOUSE_DOWN event:

```
public boolean handleEvent (Event evt)
  {
  if (evt.id == Event.MOUSE_DOWN)
    {
    // Process MouseDown event

    return (true);
    }
  return (super.handleEvent (evt));
  }
```

After identifying the main category of the event from the *id* field, more specific information is available from other variables in the Event object.

The event *key* field provides further information for keyboard events. If the event *id* field holds a KEY_PRESS event, the *key* field holds the ASCII value of the key that was pressed. If the event *id* holds a KEY_ACTION event, then the *key* field holds a coded integer that identifies one of the keys for which there is no ASCII value.

The following code identifies and processes the pressing of the F1 key or the Enter key:

```
public boolean handleEvent (Event evt)
  {
  if (evt.id == Event.KEY_ACTION)
    {
    if (evt.key == Event.F1)
      {
      // Process the F1 key event
      return (true);
      }
    }
```

```
if (evt.id == Event.KEY_PRESS)
   {
   if (evt.key == 10)
      {
      // Process the Enter (ASCII linefeed) key event
      return (true);
      }
   }
return (super.handleEvent (evt));
}
```

The *x* and *y* variables of the Event object hold the (x, y) location of the mouse on the screen when the event was generated.

The *clickCount* variable helps to identify a MOUSE_DOWN event that is actually a double click on the mouse. If the value is a "1", then this event is the first mouse click. If the value is a "2", this is the second MOUSE_DOWN event within the double click interval. If the value is a "3", the mouse has been clicked three times in rapid succession.

If the user rapidly clicked the mouse seven times, then seven MOUSE_DOWN events would be sent to the application with incrementing values in the *click-Count* variable (from "1" to "7").

Shift states are stored in the bit coded variable called *modifiers*. To detect the presence of a shift state, one performs a bit-wise AND between the *modifiers* variable and one of the event constants. In the *init*() method of the example program below, each shift state is trapped as follows:

```
public boolean handleEvent (Event evt)
  {
  if ((evt.modifiers & Event.SHIFT_MASK) != 0)
     {
     // Process the Shift key down state
     }
```

```
    if ((evt.modifiers & Event.CTRL_MASK) != 0)
      {
      // Process the Control key down state
      }  if ((evt.modifiers & Event.META_MASK) != 0)
      {
      // Process the Meta key down state
      }
    if ((evt.modifiers & Event.ALT_MASK) != 0)
      {
      // Process the Alt key down state
      }
    return (super.handleEvent (evt));
    }
```

The META_MASK is the operating system GUI event that identifies a visual object on a desktop. In the Intel world, this corresponds to the clicking of the right mouse button.

The *arg* variable in the Event object holds additional parameters for specific events. For example, the LIST_SELECT event puts the item number of the item that was selected in this *arg* variable.

The following example allows the user to view their input as it is being generated. It is recommended to perform the mouse interaction over the lower one-third of the screen. The event generation is not as uniform when events are generated in the List object and then forwarded to the applet.

```
import java.applet.Applet;
import java.awt.*;
import java.util.*;

    public class EventApplet extends Applet
/**************************************************************************

    EventApplet -- Displays Applet Events

**************************************************************************/
```

```
    {

    int iCount;                /* Current number of scrollg lines.         */
    int iMaxCount;             /* Maximum number of scrollg lines.         */
    List l;                    /* List control.                            */
    Scrollbar s;               /* Scrollbar control.                       */
    Button b;                  /* Button control.                          */
    TextField t;               /* Text field control.                      */
    Checkbox c;                /* Checkbox control.                        */
    CheckboxGroup cg;          /* Checkbox group.                          */
    Hashtable htEventIds;      /* Event handles and a string desc.         */
    Hashtable htKeyIds;        /* Key handles and a string desc.           */
    int xCurr, yCurr;          /* Current applet dimensions x & y.         */
    int yBottomOrigin;         /* Origin of the bottom panel, y dim        */
    int yBottomSize;           /* Height of the bottom panel.              */

/***************************************************************************/


    public String getAppletInfo ()
      {
      return ("Copyright (c) Noel Enete, 1996");
      }


    public void init ()
      {
      iCount = 0;
      iMaxCount = 10;

      setBackground (Color.lightGray);
      setLayout (null);
      l = new List ();
      add (l);
      xCurr = size().width;
      yCurr = size().height;
      yBottomOrigin = (yCurr * 2) / 3;
      yBottomSize = yCurr / 3;
      l.reshape (0, 0, xCurr, yBottomOrigin);
      l.setFont (new Font ("Courier", Font.PLAIN, 12));

      s = new Scrollbar (Scrollbar.VERTICAL, 1, 0, 1, 200);
      s.reshape (0, yBottomOrigin, 40, yBottomSize);
      add (s);

      b = new Button ("Bttn");
      b.reshape (40, yBottomOrigin, 40, yBottomSize);
      add (b);
```

```
t = new TextField ("Txt");
t.reshape (80, yBottomOrigin, 40, yBottomSize);
add (t);

cg = new CheckboxGroup ();

c = new Checkbox ("Ck");
c.reshape (120, yBottomOrigin, 40, yBottomSize);
add (c);
c = new Checkbox ("Ck1", cg, true);
c.reshape (160, yBottomOrigin, 40, yBottomSize / 2);
add (c);
c = new Checkbox ("Ck2", cg, false);
c.reshape (160, yBottomOrigin + (yBottomSize / 2), 40, yBottomSize / 2);
add (c);

htEventIds = new Hashtable ();
htEventIds.put (new Integer (Event.ACTION_EVENT),       "ACTION_EVENT        ");
htEventIds.put (new Integer (Event.GOT_FOCUS),          "GOT_FOCUS           ");
htEventIds.put (new Integer (Event.KEY_ACTION),         "KEY_ACTION          ");
htEventIds.put (new Integer (Event.KEY_ACTION_RELEASE), "KEY_ACTION_RELEASE  ");
htEventIds.put (new Integer (Event.KEY_PRESS),          "KEY_PRESS           ");
htEventIds.put (new Integer (Event.KEY_RELEASE),        "KEY_RELEASE         ");
htEventIds.put (new Integer (Event.LIST_SELECT),        "LIST_SELECT         ");
htEventIds.put (new Integer (Event.LIST_DESELECT),      "LIST_DESELECT       ");
htEventIds.put (new Integer (Event.LOAD_FILE),          "LOAD_FILE           ");
htEventIds.put (new Integer (Event.LOST_FOCUS),         "LOST_FOCUS          ");
htEventIds.put (new Integer (Event.META_MASK),          "META_MASK           ");
htEventIds.put (new Integer (Event.SAVE_FILE),          "SAVE_FILE           ");
htEventIds.put (new Integer (Event.SCROLL_ABSOLUTE),    "SCROLL_ABSOLUTE     ");
htEventIds.put (new Integer (Event.SCROLL_LINE_UP),     "SCROLL_LINE_UP      ");
htEventIds.put (new Integer (Event.SCROLL_LINE_DOWN),   "SCROLL_LINE_DOWN    ");
htEventIds.put (new Integer (Event.SCROLL_PAGE_UP),     "SCROLL_PAGE_UP      ");
htEventIds.put (new Integer (Event.SCROLL_PAGE_DOWN),   "SCROLL_PAGE_DOWN    ");
htEventIds.put (new Integer (Event.WINDOW_DEICONIFY),   "WINDOW_DEICONIFY    ");
htEventIds.put (new Integer (Event.WINDOW_DESTROY),     "WINDOW_DESTROY      ");
htEventIds.put (new Integer (Event.WINDOW_EXPOSE),      "WINDOW_EXPOSE       ");
htEventIds.put (new Integer (Event.WINDOW_ICONIFY),     "WINDOW_ICONIFY      ");
htEventIds.put (new Integer (Event.WINDOW_MOVED),       "WINDOW_MOVED        ");
htEventIds.put (new Integer (Event.MOUSE_UP),           "MOUSE_UP            ");
htEventIds.put (new Integer (Event.MOUSE_DOWN),         "MOUSE_DOWN          ");
htEventIds.put (new Integer (Event.MOUSE_DRAG),         "MOUSE_DRAG          ");
htEventIds.put (new Integer (Event.MOUSE_MOVE),         "MOUSE_MOVE          ");
htEventIds.put (new Integer (Event.MOUSE_ENTER),        "MOUSE_ENTER         ");
htEventIds.put (new Integer (Event.MOUSE_EXIT),         "MOUSE_EXIT          ");
```

```
    htKeyIds = new Hashtable ();
    htKeyIds.put (new Integer (Event.LEFT),      " LEFT");
    htKeyIds.put (new Integer (Event.RIGHT),     "RIGHT");
    htKeyIds.put (new Integer (Event.UP),        "   UP");
    htKeyIds.put (new Integer (Event.DOWN),      " DOWN");
    htKeyIds.put (new Integer (Event.HOME),      " HOME");
    htKeyIds.put (new Integer (Event.END),       "  END");
    htKeyIds.put (new Integer (Event.PGDN),      " PGDN");
    htKeyIds.put (new Integer (Event.PGUP),      " PGUP");
    htKeyIds.put (new Integer (Event.F1),        "   F1");
    htKeyIds.put (new Integer (Event.F2),        "   F2");
    htKeyIds.put (new Integer (Event.F3),        "   F3");
    htKeyIds.put (new Integer (Event.F4),        "   F4");
    htKeyIds.put (new Integer (Event.F5),        "   F5");
    htKeyIds.put (new Integer (Event.F6),        "   F6");
    htKeyIds.put (new Integer (Event.F7),        "   F7");
    htKeyIds.put (new Integer (Event.F8),        "   F8");
    htKeyIds.put (new Integer (Event.F9),        "   F9");
    htKeyIds.put (new Integer (Event.F10),       "  F10");
    htKeyIds.put (new Integer (Event.F11),       "  F11");
    htKeyIds.put (new Integer (Event.F12),       "  F12");

    logMessage ("     Id           Shf Ctl Met Alt   X    Y     "
      + "Key Cnt Parms");
    }


  public boolean handleEvent (Event evt)
    {
    Integer nEventId;
    Integer nKeyId;
    StringBuffer sbEventDesc;
    String sEventDesc;
    String sYes = " Y ";
    String sNo  = "   ";
    String sWk;

    sbEventDesc = new StringBuffer ();

    nEventId = new Integer (evt.id);                        // Event Id
    sEventDesc = (String) htEventIds.get (nEventId);
    if (sEventDesc == null) sEventDesc =
      "Unknown Evt " + toDecimalWidth (evt.id, 6, ' ');
    sbEventDesc.append (sEventDesc);
```

```
if ((evt.modifiers & Event.SHIFT_MASK) != 0)         // Modifiers
  {
  sbEventDesc.append (sYes);
  }
else
  {
  sbEventDesc.append (sNo);
  }
sbEventDesc.append (" ");
if ((evt.modifiers & Event.CTRL_MASK) != 0)
  {
  sbEventDesc.append (sYes);
  }
else
  {
  sbEventDesc.append (sNo);
  }
sbEventDesc.append (" ");
if ((evt.modifiers & Event.META_MASK) != 0)
  {
  sbEventDesc.append (sYes);
  }
else
  {
  sbEventDesc.append (sNo);
  }
sbEventDesc.append (" ");
if ((evt.modifiers & Event.ALT_MASK) != 0)
  {
  sbEventDesc.append (sYes);
  }
else
  {
  sbEventDesc.append (sNo);
  }

sbEventDesc.append (toDecimalWidth (evt.x, 5, ' ')); // X
sbEventDesc.append (toDecimalWidth (evt.y, 5, ' ')); // Y

nKeyId = new Integer (evt.key);                      // Key
sWk = (String) htKeyIds.get (nKeyId);
if (sWk == null) sWk = toDecimalWidth (evt.key, 5, ' ');
sbEventDesc.append ("  " + sWk);
sbEventDesc.append                                   // Click Count
  (
  toDecimalWidth (evt.clickCount, 3, ' ')
  );
```

```
    sbEventDesc.append ("  " + evt.arg);                    // Parameters

    logMessage (sbEventDesc.toString ());

    return (super.handleEvent (evt));
    }


  void logMessage (String s)
    {
    if (iCount > iMaxCount)
      {
      l.delItem (1);
      }
    else
      {
      iCount++;
      }
    l.addItem (s);
    l.makeVisible (l.countItems () - 1);
    System.out.println (s);
    }


  public static String toDecimalWidth (int iIn, int iWidth, char cPad)
    {
    StringBuffer sbAnswer;
    int iPadSize;
    int i;

    sbAnswer = new StringBuffer (String.valueOf (iIn));
    iPadSize = iWidth sbAnswer.length ();
    if (iPadSize <= 0)
      {
      return (sbAnswer.toString ());
      }
    for (i = 0; i < iPadSize; i++)
      {
      sbAnswer.insert (0, cPad);
      }
    return (sbAnswer.toString ());
    }
  public void paint (Graphics g)
    {
    int x, y;
    FontMetrics fm;
    String sMessage = "Experiment with Keyboard and Mouse.";
```

```
        if ((xCurr != size().width) || (yCurr != size().height))
          {
          xCurr = size().width;
          yCurr = size().height;
          yBottomOrigin = (yCurr * 2) / 3;
          yBottomSize = yCurr / 3;
          l.reshape (0, 0, xCurr, yBottomOrigin);
          s.reshape (0, yBottomOrigin, 40, yBottomSize);
          b.reshape (40, yBottomOrigin, 40, yBottomSize);
          c.reshape (80, yBottomOrigin, 40, yBottomSize);
          }

        fm = g.getFontMetrics ();
        x = ((size().width * 2) / 3) - (fm.stringWidth (sMessage) / 2);
        y = yBottomOrigin + (yBottomSize / 2);
        g.drawString (sMessage, x, y);
        }

    }


/*========================(  End of Source  )==========================*/
```

```
<HTML>
<HEAD>
<TITLE> EventApplet </TITLE>
</HEAD>
<BODY>
EventApplet
<HR>
<APPLET CODE="EventApplet" WIDTH=550 HEIGHT=300>
</APPLET>
</BODY>
</HTML>
<HR>
```

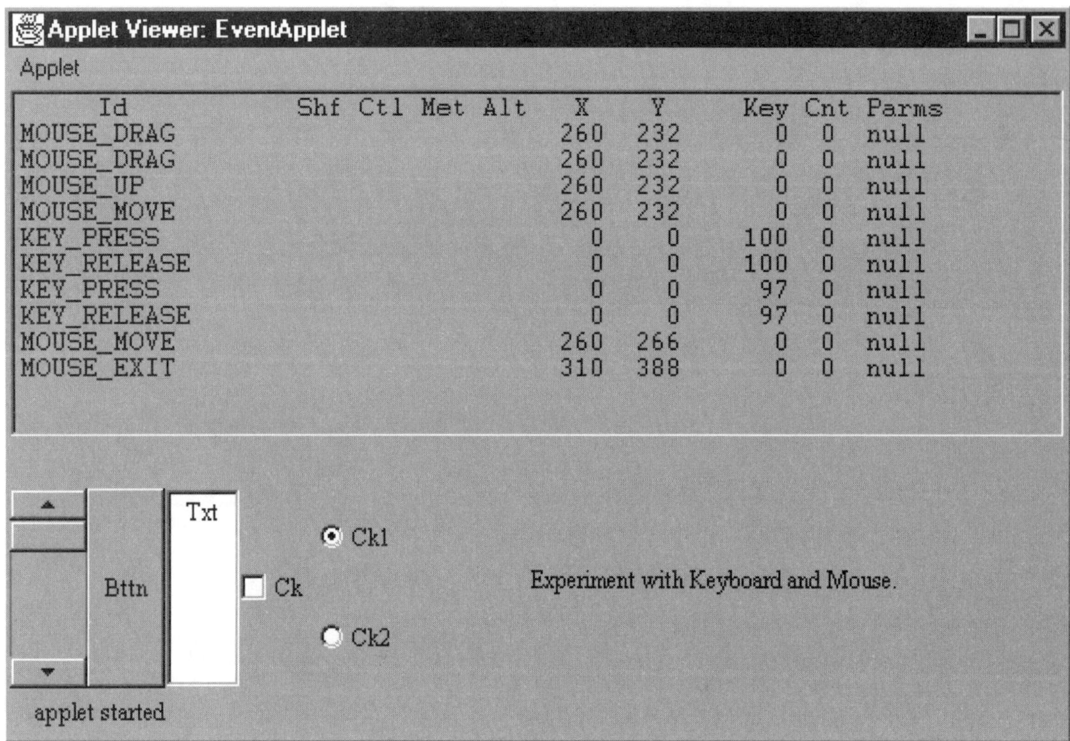

As the user clicks on the screen in Figure 9–1, the events are intercepted and written to the scrolling list box in the upper portion of the window.

How to Receive Input from Other Objects (Event Triggering)

Each event that comes to a program conveys the fact that something important has happened to the class from which the event was sent.

When a user clicks a mouse button or types a key, the Java graphical classes take note that something significant has occurred within their environment. To let all interested classes know what has occurred, they create an Event object and send it to the applets on the desktop.

This Event mechanism is not restricted to representing occurrences of user input. It can represent any occurrence inside an object that might be of interest to other classes. Any class can create and send Events to communicate what is occurring inside itself. The sending of events between objects is the chief method of communication in other object-oriented environments.

To create a user-defined event in Java, pass the destination object, the event identifying integer, and an optional parameter object to the *Event*() constructor.

```
MyObject oTarget = new MyObject ();
Event myEvent = new Event (oTarget, 175, "A B C");
oTarget.handleEvent (myEvent);
```

To pass the event to the receiving object, construct a method in the target object that accepts an Event object. Since there is already a convention for sending events from the GUI system, one should probably pattern their method after *handleEvent*() to keep things easy to read. Inside the method, the event is examined to determine what event was received and to respond appropriately.

```
class MyObject
  {
  public boolean handleEvent (Event evt)
    {
    if (evt.id == 175)
      {
      // Process event 175
      sParameters = (String) evt.arg;
      }
    return (true);
    }
  }
```

This unilateral publishing of state changes to all who are interested is a very powerful technique in object-oriented programming. This technique is able to simplify object interactions that quickly become complex.

For this reason, an example of generalized event sending has been included below. To implement it, one must add a *Wirer* object to their class and must implement the *Wireable* interface.

The Wirer class provides the event connecting behavior as well as the storage to track objects that want to be notified. The Wireable interface ensures that there is a method to receive the event when it is sent.

```
class Wirer
  {
  public void addTrigger (String s)
    {
    }
  public boolean registerEvent (String sEventName, Event evt)
    {
    }
  public boolean triggerEvent (String sEventName)
    {
    }
  public boolean triggerEvent (String sEventName, Object oParm)
    {
    }
  }


interface Wireable
  {
  public abstract boolean handleEvent (Event evt);
  public abstract Wirer getWirer ();
  }
```

Setting up the links between two communicating objects can be called *wiring* the objects together. A link (or *wire*) is established when one object *registers* to receive a specific event from another object. This registration is performed with a call to the *registerEvent*() method in the Wirer class.

```
w.registerEvent ("setText", new Event (this, SETTEXT, null));
w.registerEvent ("setSize", new Event (this, SETSIZE, null));
w.registerEvent ("setStyle", new Event (this, SETSTYLE, null));
```

When an object's state has changed and a particular event should be sent to the interested objects, a call is made to the *triggerEvent*() method in the Wirer class. This method passes the event to the *handleEvent*() method in each of the interested objects.

```
getWirer().triggerEvent ("setText", asTextParm[iTextParmCount]);
getWirer().triggerEvent ("setSize", aiSizeParm[iSizeParmCount]);
getWirer().triggerEvent ("setStyle", aiStyleParm[iStyleParmCount]);
```

When an event sending object is initialized, it must notify its Wirer instance variable of the events that it will be triggering. This allows the Wirer to refuse registration requests for events that are not supported.

The two classes below establish a link between an applet and a Runnable object. The applet instantiates the Runnable object and registers interest in three Events: "setText", "setSize", and "setStyle". The Runnable object launches a timer thread and cycles through a predictable pattern of triggering those events. The Wirer behavior sends the events from the Runnable object to the applet.

The *handleEvent*() method in the applet receives the events and performs appropriate processing to update the size, style, and text of their large display message. Figure 9–2 displays the results of this applet.

```
import java.applet.Applet;
import java.awt.*;
import java.util.*;

    public class DependentApplet extends Applet implements Wireable
      {
      int iFontSize;
      int iFontStyle;
      String sFontFace;
      String sMessage;
      Wirer wires = new Wirer ();
      final int SETTEXT = 2000;
      final int SETSIZE = 2001;
      final int SETSTYLE = 2002;
      static DisplayServer svr;


      public String getAppletInfo ()
        {
        return ("Copyright (c) Noel Enete, 1996");
        }


      public void init ()
        {
        Color cForeground;
        Color cBackground;
        String sFontSize;
        Wirer w;
```

```
    if (DependentApplet.svr == null)
      {
      DependentApplet.svr = new DisplayServer ();
      }

    w = DependentApplet.svr.getWirer ();
    w.registerEvent ("setText", new Event (this, SETTEXT, null));
    w.registerEvent ("setSize", new Event (this, SETSIZE, null));
    w.registerEvent ("setStyle", new Event (this, SETSTYLE, null));

    sMessage = getParameter ("Message");
    sFontSize = getParameter ("FontSize");
    iFontSize = Integer.valueOf(sFontSize).intValue();
    sFontFace = getParameter ("FontFace");
    cBackground = stringToColor
      (
      getParameter ("BackgroundColor"),
      Color.lightGray
      );
    cForeground = stringToColor
      (
      getParameter ("ForegroundColor"),
      Color.black
      );
    setBackground (cBackground);
    setForeground (cForeground);
    iFontStyle = Font.BOLD;
    }


  public boolean handleEvent (Event evt)
    {
    switch (evt.id)
      {
      case SETTEXT:
        sMessage = (String) evt.arg;
        return (true);

      case SETSIZE:
        iFontSize = ((Integer) evt.arg).intValue ();
        return (true);

      case SETSTYLE:
        iFontStyle = ((Integer) evt.arg).intValue ();
        repaint ();
        return (true);
      }
```

```
    return (super.handleEvent (evt));
    }


  public Wirer getWirer ()
    {
    return (wires);
    }


  public Color stringToColor (String sColor, Color cDefault)
    {
    Integer iRgb;

    if ((sColor == null)
    || (sColor.charAt (0) != '#')
    || (sColor.length () != 7 ))
      {
      return (cDefault);
      }

    try
      {
      iRgb = Integer.valueOf (sColor.substring (1, 7), 16);
      return (new Color (iRgb.intValue ()));
      }
    catch (Exception e)
      {
      return (cDefault);
      }
    }


  public void paint (Graphics g)
    {
    Font fFont;
    FontMetrics fm;

    fFont = new Font (sFontFace, iFontStyle, iFontSize);
    g.setFont (fFont);
    fm = g.getFontMetrics ();
    g.drawString (sMessage, 5, fm.getHeight ());
    }

}
```

```
class DisplayServer implements Wireable, Runnable
  {
  String sTag = "Copyright (c) Noel Enete, 1996";
  Wirer wires;
  Thread thInterval;
  int iTextParmCount;
  int iSizeParmCount;
  int iStyleParmCount;
  String[] asTextParm =
    {
    "Life",
    "Liberty",
    "Happiness"
    };
  Integer[] aiStyleParm =
    {
    new Integer (Font.PLAIN),
    new Integer (Font.BOLD),
    new Integer (Font.ITALIC)
    };
  Integer[] aiSizeParm =
    {
    new Integer (24),
    new Integer (36),
    new Integer (54)
    };


  public DisplayServer ()
    {
    wires = new Wirer ();
    wires.addTrigger ("setText");
    wires.addTrigger ("setSize");
    wires.addTrigger ("setStyle");

    thInterval = new Thread (this);
    thInterval.start ();
    }


  public boolean handleEvent (Event evt)
    {
    return (true);
    }
```

```
public Wirer getWirer ()
  {
  return (wires);
  }


public void run ()
  {
  Thread thSelf;

  thSelf = Thread.currentThread();
  iTextParmCount = 2;
  iSizeParmCount = 2;
  iStyleParmCount = 2;

  while (thInterval == thSelf)
    {
    try {Thread.sleep (1000);}
    catch (InterruptedException e) {break;}

    iStyleParmCount++;
    if (iStyleParmCount > 2)
      {
      iStyleParmCount = 0;
      iSizeParmCount++;
      if (iSizeParmCount > 2)
        {
        iSizeParmCount = 0;
        iTextParmCount++;
        if (iTextParmCount > 2)
          {
          iTextParmCount = 0;
          }
        getWirer().triggerEvent ("setText",
          iTextParmCount]);
        }
      getWirer().triggerEvent ("setSize",
        [iSizeParmCount]);
      }
    getWirer().triggerEvent ("setStyle",
      [iStyleParmCount]);
    }
  }

}
```

```
class Wirer
  {
  String sTag = "Copyright (c) Noel Enete, 1996";
  Hashtable htTriggers;


  public Wirer ()
    {
    htTriggers = new Hashtable ();
    }


  public void addTrigger (String s)
    {
    htTriggers.put (s, new Vector ());
    }


  public boolean registerEvent (String sEventName, Event evt)
    {
    Vector v;

    v = (Vector) htTriggers.get (sEventName);
    if (v == null) return (false);
    v.addElement (evt);
    return (true);
    }


  public boolean triggerEvent (String sEventName)
    {
    return (triggerEvent (sEventName, null));
    }


  public boolean triggerEvent (String sEventName, Object oParm)
    {
    Vector v;
    Event evt;
    Enumeration e;

    v = (Vector) htTriggers.get (sEventName);
    if (v == null) return (false);
    System.out.print ("Triggering " + sEventName + " to: ");
```

```
        for (e = v.elements (); e.hasMoreElements (); )
          {
          evt = (Event) e.nextElement ();
          evt.arg = oParm;
          System.out.print (evt.target.getClass().getName() + " ");
          ((Wireable) evt.target).handleEvent (evt);
          }

        System.out.println ("");
        return (true);
        }

      }


    interface Wireable
      {
      public abstract boolean handleEvent (Event evt);
      public abstract Wirer getWirer ();
      }


/*======================(  End of Source  )============================*/
```

```
<HTML>
<HEAD>
<TITLE> DependentApplet </TITLE>
</HEAD>
<BODY>
DependentApplet
<HR>
<APPLET CODE="DependentApplet" WIDTH=300 HEIGHT=100>
<PARAM NAME=Message VALUE="Java">;
<PARAM NAME="FontSize" VALUE="64">
<PARAM NAME="FontFace" VALUE="TimesRoman">
<PARAM NAME=BackgroundColor VALUE="#008000">
<PARAM NAME="ForegroundColor" VALUE="#FFFFFF">
</APPLET>
<HR>
<APPLET CODE="DependentApplet" WIDTH=300 HEIGHT=100>
<PARAM NAME=Message VALUE="New">;
<PARAM NAME="FontSize" VALUE="48">
<PARAM NAME="FontFace" VALUE="Courier">
<PARAM NAME=BackgroundColor VALUE="#000080">
<PARAM NAME="ForegroundColor" VALUE=""#FFFFFF">
</APPLET>
<HR>
<APPLET CODE="DependentApplet" WIDTH=300 HEIGHT=100>
<PARAM NAME=Message VALUE="World">;
<PARAM NAME="FontSize" VALUE="36">
<PARAM NAME="FontFace" VALUE="Helvetica">
<PARAM NAME=BackgroundColor VALUE="#800000">
<PARAM NAME="ForegroundColor" VALUE="#FFFFFF">
</APPLET>
<HR>
</BODY>
</HTML>
```

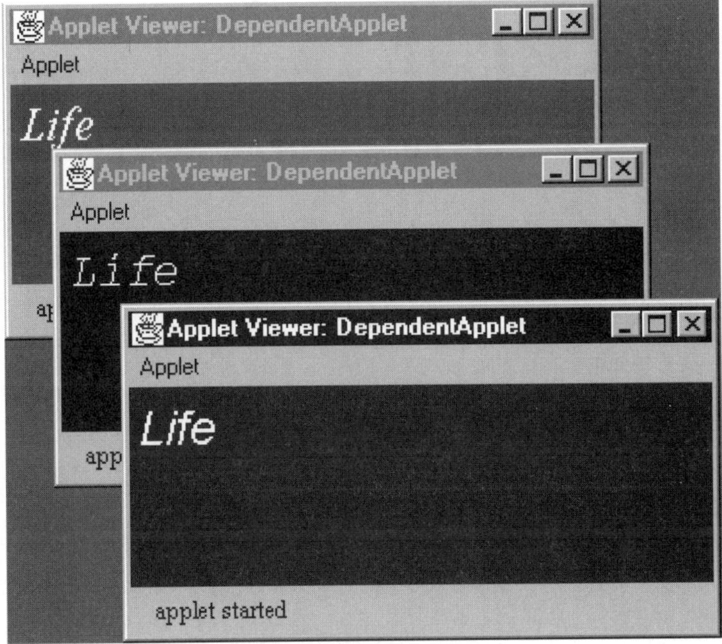

Figure 9–2

Three applets are launched from the browser and each register to receive the same event from the runnable object. Since each applet was launched with a different font face name, the interpretation of the events as they arrive is different.

This event triggering example provides a starting point for the development of a full-featured mechanism for communication between Java objects. It also provides a peak into the dependency mechanism used in other object-oriented environments.

The three input techniques discussed in this chapter allow Java classes to be continually responsive to the changing environment within which they run.

CHAPTER 10

Buttons and Things

Visual techniques like buttons, scrollbars, and listboxes have become common in graphical applications. Most graphical environments call these techniques *controls* because they carefully manage the way users can input data and selections to a program.

Java implements a number of controls as extensions to the Component class. Each control has its own class (e.g., *Button* class, *List* class, and *Checkbox* class) and each class extends the Component class. In Java terminology, a control is also known as a *component* because each control inherits behavior from the Component class.

Each control communicates with the applet by sending events to the applet. To use these controls, a Java applet must instantiate the control, add it to the window, then prepare the *handleEvent*() method to process events that the control may send back.

The Event Applet from the previous chapter displays the events that are sent to the applet from several controls. It may be helpful to experiment with that example while studying these controls to get a sense of the how the controls use the events.

Button—A One-State Input Control

Java implements a push button control in a class called *Button*. It is a single state button that pops back out after it is pressed.

To create a button, one passes the text that should appear on the face of the button to the *Button*() constructor. To add the button control to the applet, one calls the *add*() method, passing the newly created button as a parameter. The *add*()

method asks the default Layout Manager to position the button in a spot that makes sense on the surface of the applet window.

Each time the button is pressed, it sends an event to the applet's *handleEvent()* method. If the applet has not coded a *handleEvent()* method, control is passed to the component's *handleEvent()* method for default processing.

When the button is pressed, it sends an event to the applet with an event *id* of *Event.ACTION_EVENT* and an event *arg* value that matches the text on the face of the button. The example below creates a button and adds it to the applet. Each time the button is pressed, a message is written to the standard output device. Figure 10–1 displays the button created by this example.

```
import java.applet.Applet;
import java.awt.*;

    public class ButtonControl extends Applet
      {
      final String sButtonText = "Java Now";

      public void init ()
        {
        Button b;
        b = new Button (sButtonText);
        add (b);
        }

      public boolean handleEvent (Event evt)
        {
        if ((evt.id == Event.ACTION_EVENT) && (evt.arg == sButtonText))
          {
          System.out.println ("Button '" + sButtonText + "' was pressed");
          }
        return (super.handleEvent (evt));
        }
      }
```

Figure 10–1

```
<HTML>
<HEAD>
<TITLE> ButtonControl </TITLE>
</HEAD>
<BODY>
ButtonControl
<HR>
<APPLET CODE="ButtonControl" WIDTH=300 HEIGHT=200>
</APPLET>
<HR>
</BODY>
</HTML>
```

Checkbox—A Two-State Input Control

A Checkbox is a control that presents some text next to a small box. When the user clicks on the text or the box, a small checkmark is drawn in the box. When the user clicks again, the check is removed.

To create a Checkbox, pass the text that should appear next to the box as a parameter to the *Checkbox*() constructor. Then call the *add*() method, passing the newly created Checkbox to have it positioned and drawn on the window.

Checkboxes will send an event back to the applet every time the users click on them. The *arg* field of the event object contains the boolean state of the Checkbox after the click. So, repeated clicks to the Checkbox send repeated events with *arg* fields that alternate between *true* and *false*.

The *handleEvent*() method in the applet usually processes a number of events. To identify the events that a particular Checkbox is sending, one must examine the *x* and *y* fields of the event. If the *x* and *y* fields match the current (x, y) position of the upper left hand corner of the Checkbox control, then the event was sent from that Checkbox.

In the example below, the *handleEvent*() code sends a *bounds*() method to the Checkbox to determine its current position on the window. Then the *x* and *y* coordinates of the event are compared against the position of the Checkbox to identify its events. The event *id* field always contains *Event.ACTION_EVENT* for events sent from Checkboxes. Figure 10–2 demonstrates a Checkbox with a small checkmark.

```
import java.applet.Applet;
import java.awt.*;

    public class CheckboxControl extends Applet
      {
      Checkbox c;

      public void init ()
        {
        c = new Checkbox ("Java Now");
        add (c);
        }

      public boolean handleEvent (Event evt)
        {
        Rectangle rect;
        Boolean bbState;

        rect = c.bounds ();

        if ((evt.id == Event.ACTION_EVENT)
        && (evt.x == rect.x)
        && (evt.y == rect.y))
          {
          bbState = (Boolean) evt.arg;
```

```
        System.out.println ("Checkbox was pressed and is now "
          + bbState);
        }

      return (super.handleEvent (evt));
      }
    }
```

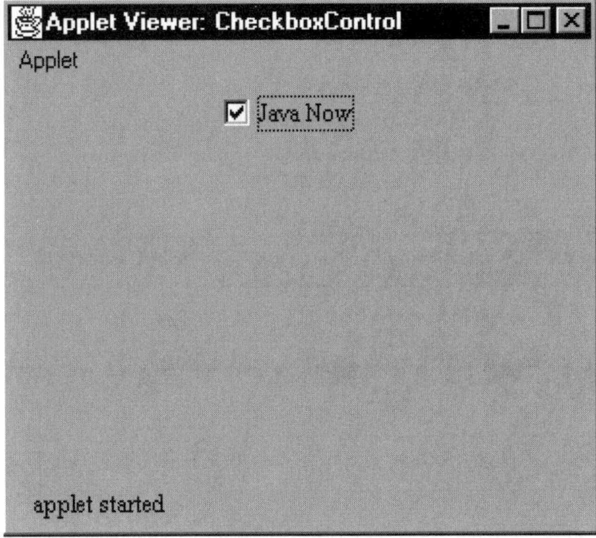

Figure 10–2

CheckboxGroup—A Single Choice Input Control

The CheckboxGroup class collects several Checkboxes into a single group. When the users check one of the Checkboxes, the group unchecks all of the other boxes in the group. This enforces a single selection input technique.

Since the Checkboxes in a CheckboxGroup function differently than when Checkboxes appear alone, they render themselves differently on the screen. Instead of having a small box next to the text, Checkboxes that are in a group have a small circle next to the text. This is similar to the radial button controls of some graphical environments.

The easiest way to create a group of Checkboxes is to create the CheckboxGroup first, then use it as a parameter when creating each of the Checkboxes. The third parameter on this type of *Checkbox()* constructor identifies the initial state of the checkbox as either checked (true) or unchecked (false).

A Checkbox in a CheckboxGroup will only send an event to an applet when the users click on it. There is no notification that the previous Checkbox has been unchecked. The event identifies the Checkbox that sent it, by placing its current coordinates in the event *x* and *y* variables.

The program can check the state of a Checkbox at any time by calling its *getState()* method.

In the *handleEvent()* method below, a *point* is constructed from the *x* and *y* variables of the Event object and it is compared against the current *bounds()* rectangle of the Checkbox. If the coordinates are the same, then the Checkbox has just been checked and the others in the group have just been unchecked. Figure 10–3 shows a CheckboxGroup that offers three choices to users.

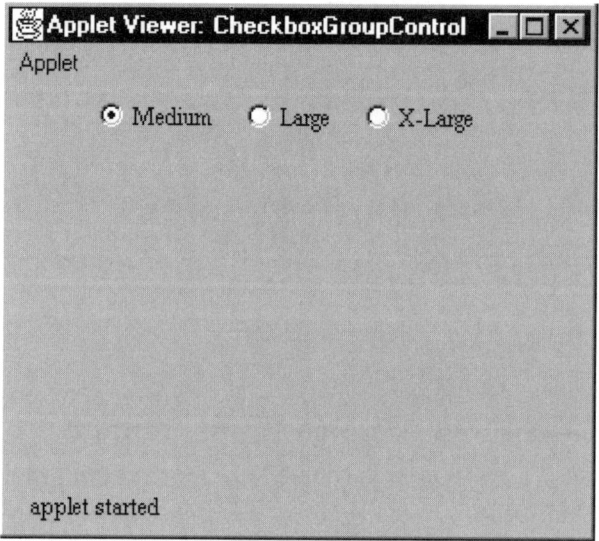

Figure 10–3

```
import java.applet.Applet;
import java.awt.*;

    public class CheckboxGroupControl extends Applet
      {
      Checkbox ckMedium;
      Checkbox ckLarge;
      Checkbox ckXLarge;

      public void init ()
        {
        CheckboxGroup cg;

        cg = new CheckboxGroup ();

        ckMedium = new Checkbox ("Medium", cg, true);
        add (ckMedium);
        ckLarge = new Checkbox ("Large", cg, false);
        add (ckLarge);
        ckXLarge = new Checkbox ("X-Large", cg, false);
        add (ckXLarge);
        }

      public boolean handleEvent (Event evt)
        {
        Point point;

        if (evt.id == Event.ACTION_EVENT)
          {
          point = new Point (evt.x, evt.y);
          if (originMatches (point, ckMedium.bounds ()))
            {
            System.out.println ("The user has selected Medium");
            }
          else if (originMatches (point, ckLarge.bounds ()))
            {
            System.out.println ("The user has selected Large");
            }
          else if (originMatches (point, ckXLarge.bounds ()))
            {
            System.out.println ("The user has selected X-Large");
            }
          }
        return (super.handleEvent (evt));
        }
```

```
boolean originMatches (Point p, Rectangle r)
  {
  if ((p.x == r.x)
  && (p.y == r.y))
    {
    return (true);
    }
  return (false);
  }
}
```

Label—A Text Output Control

A Text control is a read-only component that displays static text on the surface of the applet window. The users cannot interact with it an any meaningful way and it does not send any events back to the applet.

It provides the ability to center or justify text within the control. It also allows the text to be updated as the program runs.

To create a Label object, pass the initial text to the *Label*() constructor and optionally pass a code to specify whether the text should be left justified (*Label.LEFT*), centered (*Label.CENTER*), or right justified (*Label.RIGHT*). Then add the label to the applet's surface by using the *add*() method.

In the example below, each time the users click on the applet, a count is incremented and a new text string is given to the Label control. Each new text string remains centered in the Label control because the *Label.CENTER* style was selected when creating it. Figure 10–4 shows the initial screen display for this applet.

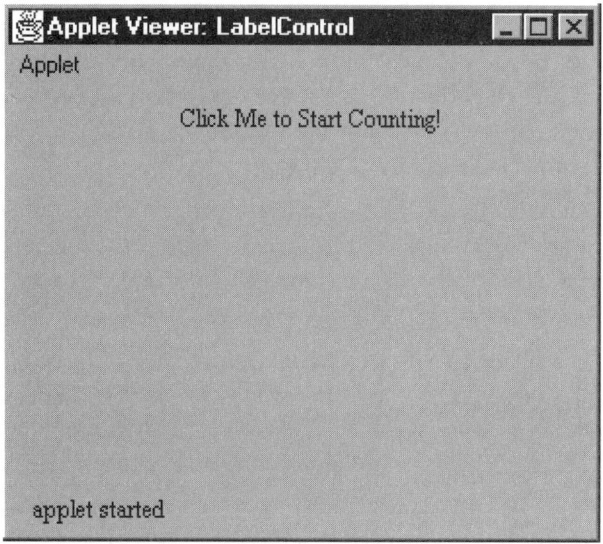

Figure 10–4

```
import java.applet.Applet;
import java.awt.*;

    public class LabelControl extends Applet
      {
      Label l;
      int iCount = 1;

      public void init ()
        {
        l = new Label ("Click Me to Start Counting!", Label.CENTER);
        add (l);
        }

      public boolean mouseDown (Event evt, int x, int y)
        {
        l.setText ("Click Count = " + iCount);
        iCount++;
        return (true);
        }
      }
```

TextField—A Scrolling Area for Single Line Text Editing

The TextField component is a single line text edit control. Users can enter and edit text with it. In Windows95, a cut-copy-paste menu pops up when the users click on a TextField with the right mouse button. Text that does not fit into the control will scroll horizontally.

Methods within the TextField class allow a program to get the current text, *getText*(), get the current selected text, *getSelectedText*(), select text directly, *select*(*beginningOffset*, *endingOffset*), and echo a single character for each keystroke, *setEchoCharacter*(), for password entry fields.

Like other Java controls, a TextField communicates with the applet by sending events to it. When the users press the enter key, the TextField sends an event with an event *id* of *Event.ACTION_EVENT*. This is the primary TextField event. The *arg* field carries the current value of the text string at the time the enter key was pressed.

In addition to this event, TextField sends KEY_PRESS and KEY_RELEASE events to the applet each time the users press a key in the TextField control. By handling these events, the program can gain more detailed control over the component's editing behavior.

In the following example, a TextField and a button are created and added to the applet in the *init*() method. The *handleEvent*() method watches for events that contain either *(x, y)* coordinates that correspond to the TextField or events whose *arg* field matches the text on the face of the button.

Events sent from the TextField are displayed on the standard output device, as shown in Figure 10–5. In response to Button events, the applet sends a *selectAll*() method to the TextField to illustrate how to manipulate the TextField directly.

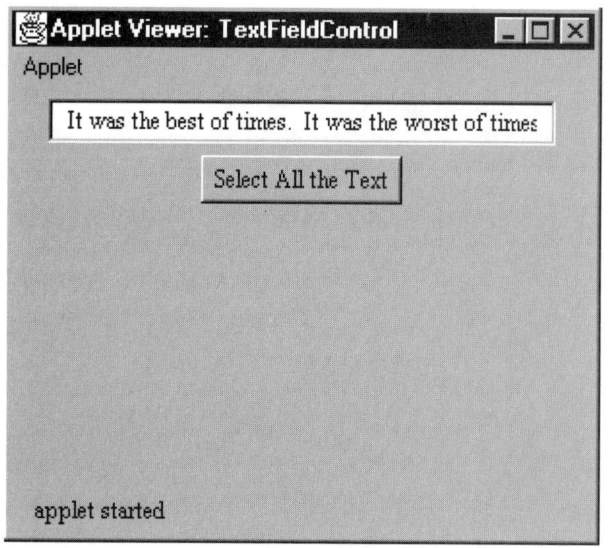

Figure 10–5

```
import java.applet.Applet;
import java.awt.*;

    public class TextFieldControl extends Applet
      {
      TextField tf;
      final String sButtonText = "Select All the Text";

      public void init ()
        {
        Button b;

        tf = new TextField
          (
          "It was the best of times. It was the worst of times."
          );
        add (tf);
        b = new Button (sButtonText);
        add (b);
        }

      public boolean handleEvent (Event evt)
        {
        Rectangle rect;
```

```
        rect = tf.bounds ();

        if ((evt.x == rect.x) && (evt.y == rect.y))
          {
          if (evt.id == Event.ACTION_EVENT)
            {
            System.out.println ("ACTION EVENT:   " + evt.arg + "\n");
            }
          else
            {
            System.out.println ("GENERAL EVENT: " + evt + "\n");
            }
          }

        if (evt.arg == sButtonText)
          {
          tf.selectAll ();
          tf.requestFocus ();
          }

        return (super.handleEvent (evt));
        }
      }
```

TextArea—A Scrolling Area for Multiple Line Text Editing

A TextArea is a multiple line text editing control. It works very much like the TextField class. In Windows95, a cut-copy-paste menu pops up when the user clicks on the TextArea with the right mouse button. TextAreas scroll horizontally and vertically as needed.

TextAreas can be manipulated by sending methods directly to them. Since TextFields and TextAreas extend the TextComponent class, services for setting and retrieving selected text are available to both classes. In addition, TextAreas can *appendText*(), *insertText*(), and *replaceText*().

The big distinction between a TextField and a TextArea is how they communicate with the applet. When the users press an enter key in a TextField, an ACTION_EVENT is sent to the applet with the current text string in the *arg* field. When the users press an enter key in a TextArea, the cursor goes to the next line in the edit area.

A TextArea does not include any single action for the users to perform that will initiate processing. Instead, every key stroke sends a KEY_PRESS and KEY_RE-

LEASE event to the applet with the current text string of the control in the *arg* variable. It is up to the programmer to include a Button or another control to initiate the processing of the data in the TextArea.

The following example creates a TextArea and a Button in the *init*() method. The TextArea constructor accepts an initial string and initial size in rows by columns. The TextArea events are identified in the *handleEvent*() method by the current position of the control on the applet window. The Button events are identified by the text that is on the face of the Button.

When the users press the button, a string of text "<*Waldo*>" is inserted into the TextArea at a random position (see Figure 10–6). When it is pressed again, the previous text is replaced with an empty string and the text is inserted at another random position.

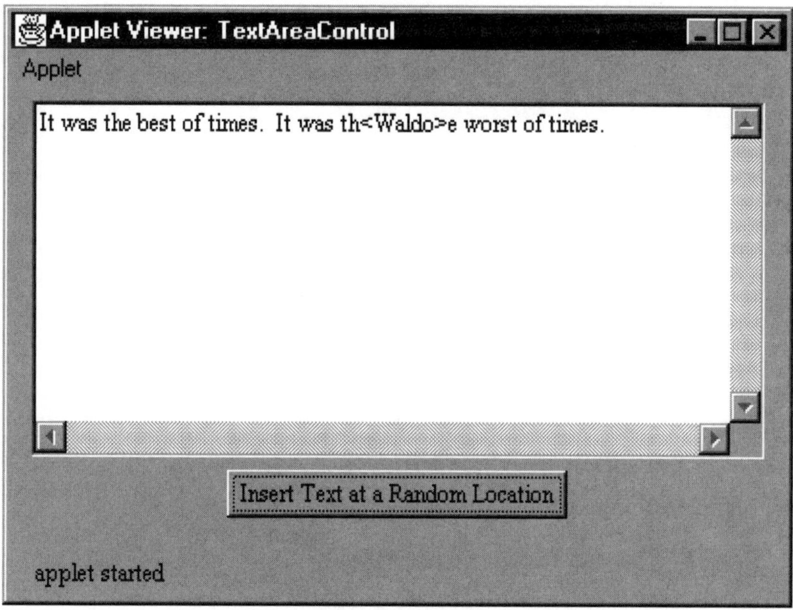

Figure 10–6

```
import java.applet.Applet;
import java.awt.*;

    public class TextAreaControl extends Applet
      {
      TextArea ta;
      final String sButtonText = "Insert Text at a Random Location";
      int iPosition;

      public void init ()
        {
        Button b;

        ta = new TextArea
          (
          "It was the best of times. It was the worst of times. ",
          10, 40
          );
        add (ta);
        b = new Button (sButtonText);
        add (b);
        }

      public boolean handleEvent (Event evt)
        {
        Rectangle rect;
        String s;

        rect = ta.bounds ();

        if ((evt.x == rect.x) && (evt.y == rect.y))
          {
          if (evt.id == Event.ACTION_EVENT)
            {
            //-------- This should not ever get called --------//
            System.out.println ("ACTION EVENT:  " + evt.arg + "\n");
            }
          else
            {
            System.out.println ("GENERAL EVENT: " + evt + "\n");
            }
          }

        if (evt.arg == sButtonText)
          {
          s = ta.getText ();
```

```
        if ("<Waldo>".equals (s.substring (iPosition, iPosition + 7)))
          {
          ta.replaceText ("", iPosition, iPosition + 7);
          s = ta.getText ();
          }
        iPosition = (int) (s.length () * Math.random ());
        ta.insertText ("<Waldo>", iPosition);
        }

      return (super.handleEvent (evt));
      }
    }
```

List—A Selectable Collection of Text Items

The List class implements a scrolling list box control. Items can be added (*addItem*()), removed (*delItem*()), selected (*select*()), and scrolled (*makeVisible*()).

In the *init*() method below, a List component is created and a number of items are added to it. Then it is added to the layout manager to size and position it on the applet screen.

When the users make a selection in the List control, an event is sent to the applet with the value *Event.LIST_SELECT* in the event *id* field. To identify which item was selected, the item number (zero based) is instantiated as an Integer object in the event's *arg* field.

This is not the only event that the List component sends to the applet. When the List control has the input focus, and a key is pressed on the keyboard, the applet generates KEY_PRESS and KEY_RELEASE events that are also sent to the applet.

In the *handleEvent*() method below, the item number in a LIST_SELECT event is used to get the item string from the list and display it on the standard output device (see Figure 10–7). All other events are displayed on the standard output device as they occur.

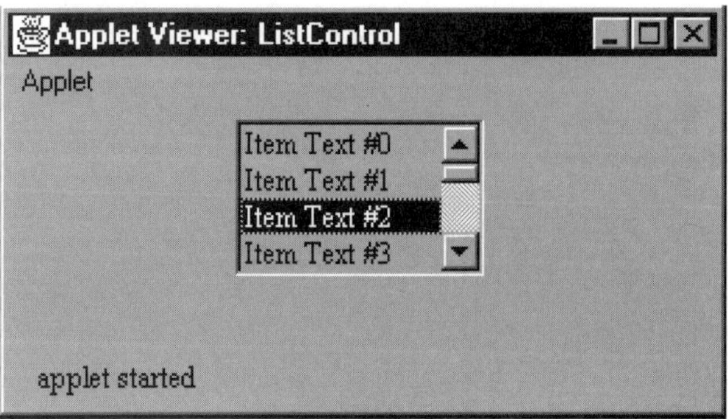

Figure 10–7

```
import java.applet.Applet;
import java.awt.*;

    public class ListControl extends Applet
      {
      List l;

      public void init ()
        {
        int i;

        l = new List ();
        for (i = 0; i < 30; i++)
          {
          l.addItem ("Item Text #" + i);
          }
        add (l);
        }

      public boolean handleEvent (Event evt)
        {
        int iListItem;
        Rectangle rect;

        rect = l.bounds ();
```

```
        if ((evt.x == rect.x) && (evt.y == rect.y))
          {
          iListItem = ((Integer) evt.arg).intValue ();

          if (evt.id == Event.LIST_SELECT)
            {
            System.out.println
              (
              "Item " + iListItem + " selected ->"
                + l.getItem (iListItem)
                + "<-\n"
              );
            }
          else
            {
            System.out.println ("GENERAL EVENT: " + evt + "\n");
            }
          }

        return (super.handleEvent (evt));
        }
    }
```

Choice—A Drop Down Collection of Text Items

A Java Choice class implements a drop down list control. It is a more static version of a List control and takes up much less room on the page. When the items are pulled down and do not all fit in the space available, the control allows the users to scroll the items even though the screen does not display a scroll bar. To scroll the list, the users drag the mouse in the list area.

When a selection is made, the control sends an event to the applet with the value *Event.ACTION_EVENT* in the *id* field. The *arg* field holds the text string of the selected item in the Choice control (see Figure 10–8). As with the List control, key strokes are also passed to the applet as KEY_PRESS and KEY_RELEASE events.

```
import java.applet.Applet;
import java.awt.*;

    public class ChoiceControl extends Applet
      {
      Choice c;

      public void init ()
        {
        int i;

        c = new Choice ();
        for (i = 0; i < 30; i++)
          {
          c.addItem ("Item Text #" + i);
          }
        add (c);
        }

      public boolean handleEvent (Event evt)
        {
        Rectangle rect;

        rect = c.bounds ();

        if ((evt.x == rect.x) && (evt.y == rect.y))
          {
          if (evt.id == Event.ACTION_EVENT)
            {
            System.out.println
              (
              "Item selected -->" + evt.arg + "<--\n"
              );
            }
          else
            {
            System.out.println ("GENERAL EVENT: " + evt + "\n");
            }
          }

        return (super.handleEvent (evt));
        }
      }
```

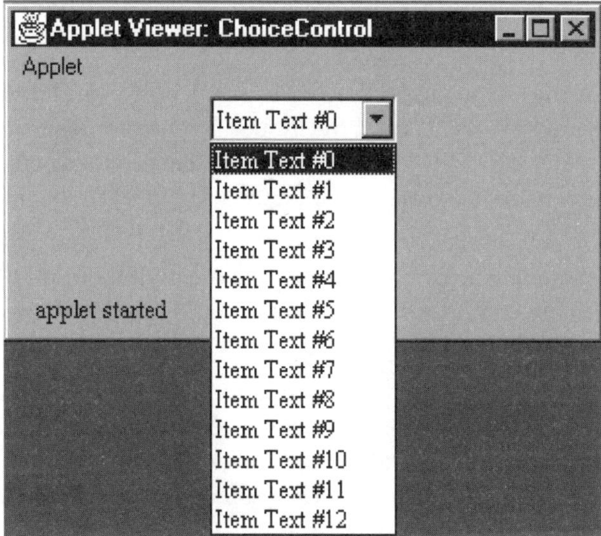

Figure 10–8

Scrollbar—A Representation of a Range of Values

The Scrollbar class implements a platform-independent scrollbar control.

Remember that a Scrollbar is a visual way to represent an integer. When the bar is all the way to the top or to the left, it represents a minimum value. When it is at the other extreme, it represents a maximum value. When the integer is a reference to a line number in a scrolling document, there are several lines that are visible on the page, which take away from the total number of lines that the Scrollbar needs to represent.

The values that are passed to the *Scrollbar*() constructor are in this order: the desired orientation (HORIZONTAL or VERTICAL), the initial value, the page size, and the minimum and maximum values.

When the users click on various parts of the Scrollbar, it sends a SCROLL event to the applet. The Scrollbar's current numerical value is passed as an Integer in the event's *arg* field.

The exact events that are sent are listed in the *handleEvent*() method below. Notice that there are no MOUSE_DOWN or MOUSE_UP events. Also, the initial versions of Java only sent Scrollbar events when the mouse was released.

This means that if the users click on the down arrow of a Scrollbar and hold it down, the Scrollbar would not send any events to the applet until the arrow is released. When it is released, only one event is sent—the SCROLL_LINE_DOWN event.

It also means that if the users click on the scroll button and drag it, the Scrollbar would not send any events until the mouse is released. Instead, the Scrollbar records the potential SCROLL_ABSOLUTE events as the users drag the button and play them back to the applet when the users release the mouse button.

This behavior is in transition in Java version 1.0.2. The new code is in place to give more immediate notification of scrollbar activity, but it is "buggy". To observe predictable Scrollbar behavior, one should use a Web browser like *Netscape* to test applets with Scrollbars.

To circumvent problems with Java Scrollbar behavior, one can create a new class that implements custom Scrollbar behavior. This class could extend the Canvas class. Arrow buttons, scroll buttons, and elevator shafts would all need to be rendered. The MOUSE_DRAG messages would need to be managed in detail.

If one is interested in this kind of work, there are several classes available on the network. Adam Doppelt has written a Slider class that implements this scheme. It is available from *http://www.cs.brown.edu/people/amd/* (his Brown University account).

The example below adds a new Scrollbar and Label to the applet, then listens for the Scrollbar events (see Figure 10–9). When a Scrollbar event is received, the current numerical value is extracted from the event's *arg* field and displayed in a Label control. All other events are displayed on the standard output device.

Figure 10–9

```
import java.applet.Applet;
import java.awt.*;

    public class ScrollbarControl extends Applet
      {
      Scrollbar sb;
      Label l;

      public void init ()
        {
        sb = new Scrollbar (Scrollbar.HORIZONTAL, 1, 0, 1, 20);
        add (sb);
        l = new Label ("Move the Scrollbar", Label.CENTER);
        add (l);
        }

      public boolean handleEvent (Event evt)
        {
        Rectangle rect;

        rect = sb.bounds ();

        if ((evt.x == rect.x) && (evt.y == rect.y))
          {
          if ((evt.id == Event.SCROLL_LINE_UP)
          || (evt.id == Event.SCROLL_LINE_DOWN)
          || (evt.id == Event.SCROLL_PAGE_UP)
          || (evt.id == Event.SCROLL_PAGE_DOWN)
          || (evt.id == Event.SCROLL_ABSOLUTE))
            {
            l.setText (String.valueOf (evt.arg));
            }
          else
            {
            System.out.println ("GENERAL EVENT: " + evt + "\n");
            }
          }

        return (super.handleEvent (evt));
        }
      }
```

An Applet with Controls and no Layout Manager (LoanApplet)

There are times that it is convenient to position and size the controls in an applet without the use of a Layout Manager.

Since there is a default Layout Manager with each applet, and it is in charge of the position and size of each control, any direct change to a control's position or size will be quickly overlayed by the Layout Manager. One must explicitly remove the Layout Manager to gain control over the control's size and position.

To remove the Layout Manager, pass *null* to the *setLayout*() method.

```
setLayout (null);

myComponent.reshape (15, 10, 100, 80);
```

To change the position and size of the component, send the *reshape*() method to the component. The first two parameters are the (x, y) position of the upper left corner of the component. The next two parameters are the width and height of the component in pixels.

The following applet uses this technique to build an applet that calculates the monthly payment for a loan of a certain amount over a number of years using a selectable interest rate (see Figure 10–10). The idiosyncrasies of the Java components, especially the Scrollbar, are easy to grasp by playing with this applet. A study of the source will reveal the way the sizes and positions are managed.

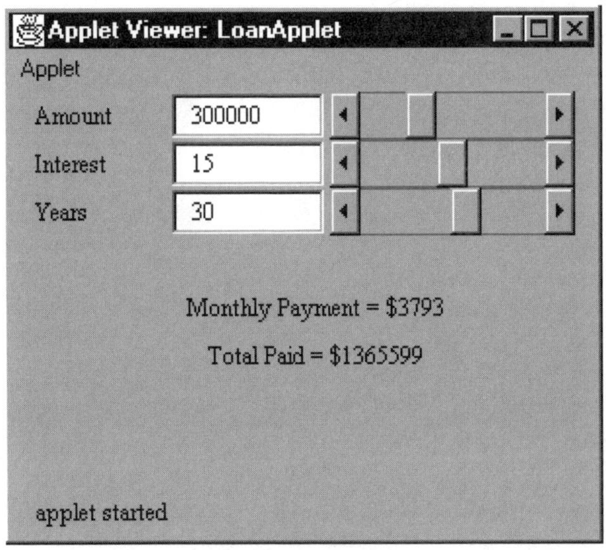

Figure 10–10

```
import java.applet.Applet;
import java.awt.*;

    public class LoanApplet extends Applet
      {
      double dAmount;
      double dAnnualInterest;
      int iYears;
      int xAmountScroll, yAmountScroll;
      int xAnnualInterestScroll, yAnnualInterestScroll;
      int xYearsScroll, yYearsScroll;
      TextField tfAmount;
      TextField tfAnnualInterest;
      TextField tfYears;
      Scrollbar sbrAmount;
      Scrollbar sbrAnnualInterest;
      Scrollbar sbrYears;
      Label lMessage;
      Label lMonthlyPayment;
      Label lTotal;
```

```
    public String getAppletInfo ()
      {
      return ("Copyright (c) Noel Enete, 1996");
      }


    public void init ()
      {
      int iWk;
      int xCellSize, yCellSize;
      int xCurr, yCurr;
      Label lAmountTitle;
      Label lAnnualInterestTitle;
      Label lYearsTitle;
      FontMetrics fm;

      setBackground (Color.lightGray);
      setLayout (null);
      xCurr = size().width;
      yCurr = size().height;
      xCellSize = 40;
      fm = getFontMetrics (getFont ());
      yCellSize = (fm.getHeight () * 3) / 2;
      dAmount = 300000;
      dAnnualInterest = 15.0;
      iYears = 30;


/*    Create and place controls for the 'Amount' line.
      ===============================================  */

      xAmountScroll = 0;
      yAmountScroll = 2;
      lAmountTitle = new Label ("Amount");
      lAmountTitle.reshape (xAmountScroll, yAmountScroll,
        xCellSize * 2, yCellSize);
      add (lAmountTitle);

      xAmountScroll += (xCellSize * 2) + 2;
      tfAmount = new TextField (String.valueOf (dAmount));
      tfAmount.reshape (xAmountScroll, yAmountScroll,
        xCellSize * 2, yCellSize);
      add (tfAmount);

      xAmountScroll += (xCellSize * 2) + 2;
      iWk = (int) dAmount / 1000;
```

```
        sbrAmount = new Scrollbar (Scrollbar.HORIZONTAL, iWk, 0, 1, 1000);
        sbrAmount.reshape (xAmountScroll, yAmountScroll,
          xCurr - xAmountScroll - 10, yCellSize);
        add (sbrAmount);


/*      Create and place controls for the 'Interest' line.
        ==================================================  */

        xAnnualInterestScroll = 0;
        yAnnualInterestScroll = yAmountScroll + yCellSize;
        lAnnualInterestTitle = new Label ("Interest");
        lAnnualInterestTitle.reshape (xAnnualInterestScroll,
          yAnnualInterestScroll, xCellSize * 2, yCellSize);
        add (lAnnualInterestTitle);

        xAnnualInterestScroll += (xCellSize * 2) + 2;
        tfAnnualInterest = new TextField (String.valueOf
          (dAnnualInterest));
        tfAnnualInterest.reshape (xAnnualInterestScroll,
          yAnnualInterestScroll, xCellSize * 2, yCellSize);
        add (tfAnnualInterest);

        xAnnualInterestScroll += (xCellSize * 2) + 2;
        iWk = (int) dAnnualInterest * 10;
        sbrAnnualInterest =
          new Scrollbar (Scrollbar.HORIZONTAL, iWk, 0, 1, 300);
        sbrAnnualInterest.reshape (xAnnualInterestScroll,
          yAnnualInterestScroll, xCurr - xAnnualInterestScroll - 10,
          yCellSize);
        add (sbrAnnualInterest);


/*      Create and place controls for the 'Years' line.
        ===============================================  */

        xYearsScroll = 0;
        yYearsScroll = yAnnualInterestScroll + yCellSize;
        lYearsTitle = new Label ("Years");
        lYearsTitle.reshape (xYearsScroll, yYearsScroll,
          xCellSize * 2, yCellSize);
        add (lYearsTitle);

        xYearsScroll += (xCellSize * 2) + 2;
        tfYears = new TextField (String.valueOf (iYears));
```

```
        tfYears.reshape (xYearsScroll, yYearsScroll,
          xCellSize * 2, yCellSize);
        add (tfYears);

        xYearsScroll += (xCellSize * 2) + 2;
        sbrYears = new Scrollbar (Scrollbar.HORIZONTAL, iYears, 0, 1, 50);
        sbrYears.reshape (xYearsScroll, yYearsScroll,
          xCurr - xYearsScroll - 10, yCellSize);
        add (sbrYears);


/*      Create and place labels for the monthly payment and total lines.
        ================================================================= */

        lMessage = new Label (" ", Label.CENTER);
        lMessage.reshape (0, yYearsScroll + (yCellSize * 1),
          xCurr, yCellSize);
        add (lMessage);

        lMonthlyPayment = new Label
          (
          "Monthly Payment = $" + String.valueOf ((int) monthlyPayment
            (dAmount, dAnnualInterest, (double) iYears)),
          Label.CENTER
          );
        lMonthlyPayment.reshape (0, yYearsScroll + (yCellSize * 2),
          xCurr, yCellSize);
        add (lMonthlyPayment);

        lTotal = new Label
          (
          "Total Paid = $" + String.valueOf ((int) totalPaid
            (dAmount, dAnnualInterest, (double) iYears)),
          Label.CENTER
          );
        lTotal.reshape (0, yYearsScroll + (yCellSize * 3),
          xCurr, yCellSize);
        add (lTotal);

        }


      public boolean handleEvent (Event evt)
        {
        int iWk;
        double dWk;
        String sWk;
```

```
switch (evt.id)
  {
  case (Event.SCROLL_LINE_UP):
  case (Event.SCROLL_LINE_DOWN):
  case (Event.SCROLL_PAGE_UP):
  case (Event.SCROLL_PAGE_DOWN):
  case (Event.SCROLL_ABSOLUTE):
    iWk = ((Integer) evt.arg).intValue();      // Scroll value

    if ((evt.x == xAmountScroll)               // Amount scrollbar
    && (evt.y == yAmountScroll))
      {
      iWk *= 1000;
      tfAmount.setText (String.valueOf (iWk));
      dAmount = (double) iWk;
      }
    else if ((evt.x == xAnnualInterestScroll) // Interest scrollbar
    && (evt.y == yAnnualInterestScroll))
      {
      dWk = iWk / 10.0;
      tfAnnualInterest.setText (String.valueOf (dWk));
      dAnnualInterest = dWk;
      }
    else if ((evt.x == xYearsScroll)           // Years scrollbar
    && (evt.y == yYearsScroll))
      {
      tfYears.setText (String.valueOf (iWk));
      iYears = iWk;
      }
    updateTotals ();                           // Calc new Totals
    break;

  case (Event.ACTION_EVENT):
    try
      {
      sWk = tfAmount.getText ();
      dAmount = (new Double(sWk)).doubleValue ();
      sbrAmount.setValue (((int) dAmount) / 1000);

      sWk = tfAnnualInterest.getText ();
      dAnnualInterest = (new Double(sWk)).doubleValue ();
      sbrAnnualInterest.setValue ((int) (dAnnualInterest * 10));

      sWk = tfYears.getText ();
      iYears = (int) (new Double(sWk)).doubleValue ();
```

```
          sbrYears.setValue (iYears);
          updateTotals ();                              // Calc new Totals
          }
        catch (Exception e)
          {
          lMessage.setText ("Error in number format");
          System.out.println ("Error in number format");
          }
        break;
      }

    return (super.handleEvent (evt));
    }


  void updateTotals ()
    {
    lMessage.setText (" ");
    lMonthlyPayment.setText
      (
      "Monthly Payment = $" +
      String.valueOf ((int)
        monthlyPayment (dAmount, dAnnualInterest, (double) iYears))
      );
    lTotal.setText
      (
      "Total Paid = $" +
      String.valueOf ((int)
        totalPaid (dAmount, dAnnualInterest, (double) iYears))
      );
    }


  double monthlyPayment (double dAmount, double dAnnualInterest,
    double dYears)
    {
    double dMonths;
    double dMonthlyInterest;
    double dPF;

    dMonths = dYears * 12.0;
    dMonthlyInterest = dAnnualInterest / 1200.0;
    dPF = paymentFactor (1.0, dMonthlyInterest, dMonths);
    return (dPF * dAmount);
    }
```

```
    double totalPaid (double dAmount, double dAnnualInterest,
      double dYears)
      {
      return (monthlyPayment (dAmount, dAnnualInterest, dYears)
        * dYears * 12.0);
      }


    double paymentFactor (double dAmortizationFactor,
      double dMonthlyInterest, double dMonths)
      {
      try
        {
        return (dAmortizationFactor *
          (
                                   dMonthlyInterest /
          /*-----------------------------------------------------*/
          (1.0 - (1.0 / Math.pow (1.0 + dMonthlyInterest, dMonths)))
          ));
        }
      catch (Exception e)
        {
        System.out.println ("Math exception " + e);
        return (1.0);
        }
      }

  }

/*==========================(  End of Source  )==========================*/
```

```
<HTML>
<HEAD>
<TITLE> LoanApplet </TITLE>
</HEAD>
<BODY>
LoanApplet
<APPLET CODE="LoanApplet" WIDTH=300 HEIGHT=200>
</APPLET>
</BODY>
</HTML>
```

CHAPTER 11

Layout Managers

The placement of controls can be a tedious process for application programs.

Java has constructed a series of classes to remove much of this tedium. The theory is, if the programmer can pick the right Layout Manager for each application, the control placement task can be automated and the program can be free to concentrate on application processing.

Every Applet, Window, Dialog, Frame, and Panel object has a default Layout Manager. As each control is added to the window surface, the default Layout Manager takes over responsibility for setting the control's size and position.

If a program attempts to directly set the size or position of a component that is being controlled by a Layout Manager, the new values will not stick. At the first opportunity, the Layout Manager will change them back.

Each of the three main Layout Manager classes has a unique approach to managing the arrangement of controls on the window surface. One places controls into rows (*FlowLayout*), one places them into a checkerboard (*GridLayout*), and one brings a single control to center stage and flanks it with the other controls (*BorderLayout*).

FlowLayout—Controls in Rows

The FlowLayout is the default Layout Manager for most window surfaces.

It organizes controls into horizontal rows. A FlowLayout organizes controls in the same way that a word processor organizes characters—the items are collected into a flow of wrapping horizontal lines. Since any component can be added to a FlowLayout, the rows can end up looking quite uneven.

Every layout manager must determine how to dimension the grid into which the controls are placed and how large to make each control.

The rows of a FlowLayout grid are tall enough to accommodate the tallest component in each row. There are no columns in the grid. Any vertical alignment is incidental.

To determine the size of each component, the FlowLayout asks the component for the optimal rectangle into which the control can be easily drawn. This is done by calling its *preferredSize*() method. Then it sets the component's size to that value. In the case of a Button control, the preferred size is usually the size that is large enough to fit the button's text and border shading.

If one wants the control to be sized differently, a new class that overrides the *preferredSize*() method can be created. In the example below, the classes *BigButton* and *TinyButton* extend the Button class. Button's *preferredSize*() method is overridden and hard-coded dimensions are returned to illustrate how to control the size of a component within the FlowLayout (see Figure 11–1).

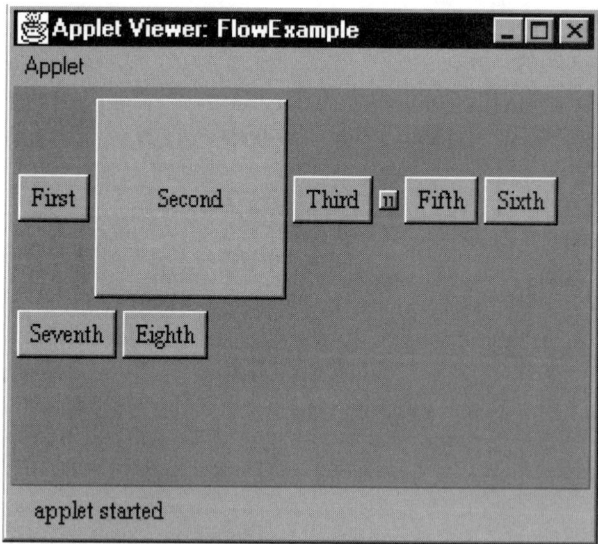

Figure 11–1

```
import java.applet.Applet;
import java.awt.*;

    public class FlowExample extends Applet
      {
      public void init()
        {
        Button b;

        setLayout (new FlowLayout (FlowLayout.LEFT, 3, 6));
        b = new Button ("First");
        add (b);
        b = new BigButton ("Second");
        add (b);
        b = new Button ("Third");
        add (b);
        b = new TinyButton ("Fourth");
        add (b);
        b = new Button ("Fifth");
        add (b);
        b = new Button ("Sixth");
        add (b);
        b = new Button ("Seventh");
        add (b);
        b = new Button ("Eighth");
        add (b);
        }

      public void paint (Graphics g)
        {
        g.setColor (Color.green);
        g.fill3DRect (0, 0, size().width, size().height, true);
        }

      }


    class BigButton extends Button
      {
      BigButton (String s)
        {
        super (s);
        }
      public Dimension preferredSize ()
        {
```

```
        return (new Dimension (100, 100));
        }
      }


    class TinyButton extends Button
      {
      TinyButton (String s)
        {
        super (s);
        }
      public Dimension preferredSize ()
        {
        return (new Dimension (10, 10));
        }
      }
```

```
<HTML>
<HEAD>
<TITLE> FlowExample </TITLE>
</HEAD>
<BODY>
FlowExample
<HR>
<APPLET CODE="FlowExample" WIDTH=300 HEIGHT=200>
</APPLET>
<HR>
</BODY>
</HTML>
```

The FlowLayout gives one the ability to set the amount of gap to leave between components (horizontally and vertically). The following constructor specifies that each row is to be left justified, the horizontal gap is to be 3 pixels, and the vertical gap is to be 6 pixels (gaps of 0 pixels are acceptable).

```
FlowLayout f = new FlowLayout (FlowLayout.LEFT, 3, 6);
```

The rows can also be set to be centered (with *FlowLayout.CENTER*) or to be right justified (with *FlowLayout.RIGHT*).

This FlowLayout is the default Layout Manager for many window surfaces. This is probably because it is so simple to use. But the Layout Managers that are the most useful are the GridLayout and the BorderLayout.

GridLayout—Controls in Checkerboard Cells

The GridLayout makes its decisions about where a control should be placed and how large the control should be based on an imaginary grid of cells that it constructs on the surface of the display area.

The cells in the grid are all the same size. The position of a new control is set to the upper left coordinate of the next open cell in the grid. The size of each control is set to the size of its cell. Any extension of the Component class can be placed in a grid cell.

If the display area is resized, the grid maintains its number of rows and columns and either expands or contracts to accommodate the new size. The cells are filled one row at a time from left to right.

The number of rows in the grid is determined by a parameter passed to the GridLayout constructor. The following statement creates a new GridLayout with a grid of 2 rows by 4 columns, a horizontal gap of 3 pixels, and a vertical gap of 6 pixels (gaps of 0 pixels are acceptable):

```
GridLayout g = new GridLayout (2, 4, 3, 6);
```

If there are not enough controls to populate the 2 x 4 grid, the number of columns will be reduced to minimize wasted space in the display area. If too many controls are added to fit within the 2 x 4 grid, columns are added to make room for each control. The overall display size does not change. So when columns are removed or added, the grid expands or contracts to maintain coverage over the entire display region.

```
import java.applet.Applet;
import java.awt.*;

    public class GridExample extends Applet
      {
      public void init()
        {
        int i;
        Button b;
        List l;
        Choice c;
        Scrollbar sb;

        setLayout (new GridLayout (2, 3, 3, 6));
```

```
        b = new Button ("First");
        add (b);

        l = new List ();
        for (i = 0; i < 30; i++)
          {
          l.addItem ("Second Text #" + i);
          }
        add (l);

        b = new Button ("Third");
        add (b);

        sb = new Scrollbar (Scrollbar.VERTICAL, 1, 0, 1, 20);
        add (sb);

        b = new Button ("Fifth");
        add (b);

        c = new Choice ();
        for (i = 0; i < 30; i++)
          {
          c.addItem ("Sixth Text #" + i);
          }
        add (c);
        }

    public void paint (Graphics g)
        {
        g.setColor (Color.green);
        g.fill3DRect (0, 0, size().width, size().height, true);
        }

    }
```

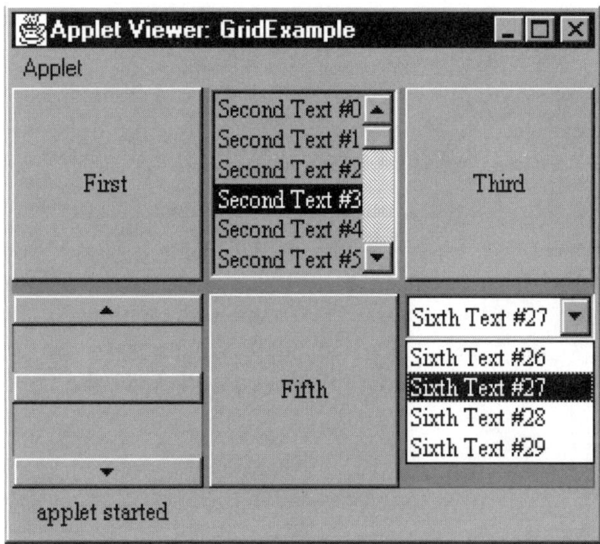

Figure 11–2 Notice in this example that the controls are placed into the grid horizontally from left to right. Also notice that the GridLayout has resized each component to fit into the cells. The horizontal gap between the cells is 3 pixels and the vertical gap is 6 pixels as specified when creating the GridLayout.

BorderLayout—One Control Flanked by the Others

The BorderLayout positions its controls in a way that causes one of the controls to take up most of the room in the display area. This helps to establish one of the controls as the primary panel in an interface. The other controls are assigned positions on the border of the display area.

The grid that a BorderLayout constructs does not consist of rows or columns. It consists of five possible cells that are named by their relative positions: *Center*, *North*, *South*, *East*, and *West*. A parameter on the *add*() method identifies the cell into which the new control should be placed.

The size of the cells on the border is determined by calling the *preferredSize*() method of the control that is placed there. If no control has been placed into one of the border cells, then the size is set to 0.

The size and location of the center cell is set so that it takes up all of the remaining space in the display area. If none of the cells around the border of the display area have components in them, then the *Center* cell takes over the entire display area.

The most common way to use this Layout Manager is to use the center cell and one or two of the border cells. This gives one the opportunity to construct a main display area and a status bar on the bottom, or an option panel on the side.

If the sizing of the controls in the border cells does not give the desired effect, one can control the size specifically by creating a subclass of the control and implementing the *preferredSize*() method. The *TinyButton* class in the following example demonstrates this technique in the *South* cell of the BorderLayout. It returns a hard-coded size of 10 x 10, which causes the BorderLayout to create a much smaller button (see Figures 11–3 and 11–4).

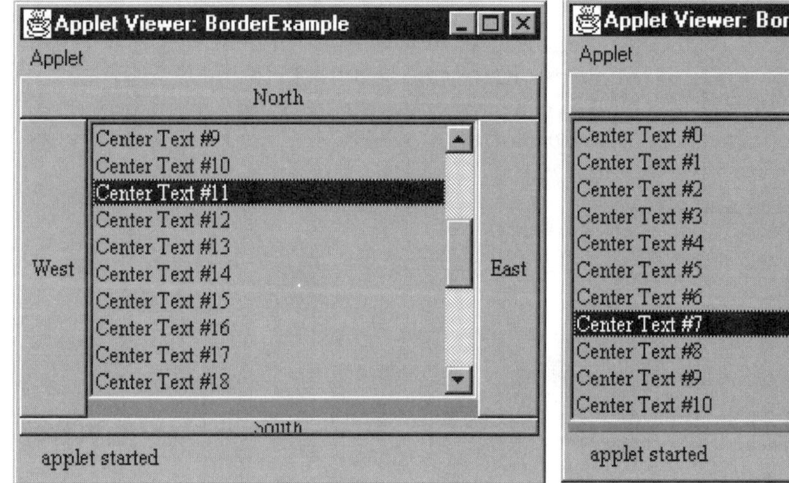

Figure 11–3

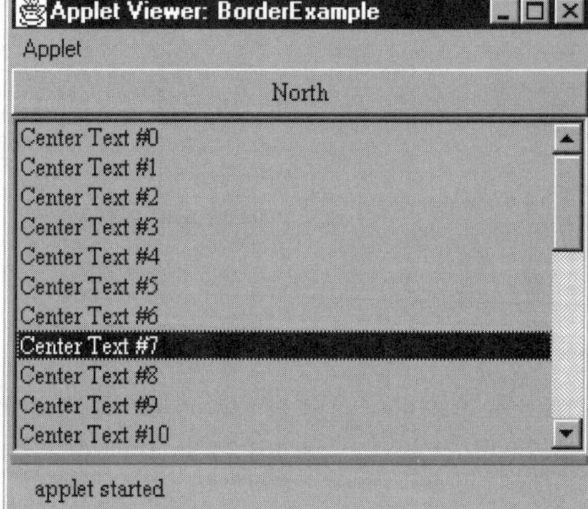

Figure 11–4

```
import java.applet.Applet;
import java.awt.*;

    public class BorderExample extends Applet
      {
      public void init()
        {
        int i;
        Button b;
        List l;

        setLayout (new BorderLayout (0, 0));

        l = new List ();
        for (i = 0; i < 30; i++)
          {
          l.addItem ("Center Text #" + i);
          }
        add ("Center", l);

        b = new Button ("North");
        add ("North", b);

        b = new TinyButton ("South");
        add ("South", b);

        b = new Button ("East");
        add ("East", b);

        b = new Button ("West");
        add ("West", b);

        }

      public void paint (Graphics g)
        {
        g.setColor (Color.green);
        g.fill3DRect (0, 0, size().width, size().height, true);
        }

      }
```

```
class TinyButton extends Button
  {
  TinyButton (String s)
    {
    super (s);
    }
  public Dimension preferredSize ()
    {
    return (new Dimension (10, 10));
    }
  }
```

The display on the left (Figure 11–3) is a picture of the program as is. The *East*, *West*, and *South* buttons have been removed in the display on the right (Figure 11–4).

The following syntax was used in this example to create a BorderLayout with horizontal and vertical gaps of 0 pixels. Other values could have been choosen.

```
setLayout (new BorderLayout (0, 0));
```

The space at the bottom of the *Center* cell is caused by the way List and Choice objects set their vertical height. The BorderLayout set the List object to the same height as the *West* button, but the List object will only allow its vertical size to display complete lines of text. So it changed the size request to a value that was as close to the requested size as possible, but would show complete lines of text.

The FlowLayout, GridLayout, and BorderLayout are the building blocks of most user interfaces in Java.

The easiest way to achieve a more complex layout is to combine these basic layouts. Panels and CardLayouts allow a single user interface to be built from combinations of these basic layouts.

Panel—A Component with its Own Layout Manager

A *Panel* object is a component just like a Button object is a component or a Scrollbar object is a component. When a Panel object is added to an applet, it takes up a cell in the grid, just like other components. But a Panel does not draw anything in its cell.

Instead, other components can be added to a Panel and the Panel will arrange the new components within its cell. What is visible within a Panel component are all the controls that have been added to it. To manage the layout of these controls, each Panel object has its own Layout Manager.

So, Panel components are positioned within the applet area, according to the applet's Layout Manager and the components within the Panel are positioned within the Panel's cell according to the Panel's Layout Manager. This makes it possible to have Layout Managers within Layout Managers.

In the example below, the applet has a BorderLayout. A Panel component is added to the South cell. The layout within the Panel is set to a GridLayout. Then a number of buttons are added to the Panel (see Figure 11–5).

This nesting of Layout Managers can continue. Panels can receive additional components including other Panels. So, one could construct a display area that consists of Layout Managers within Layout Managers within Layout Managers.

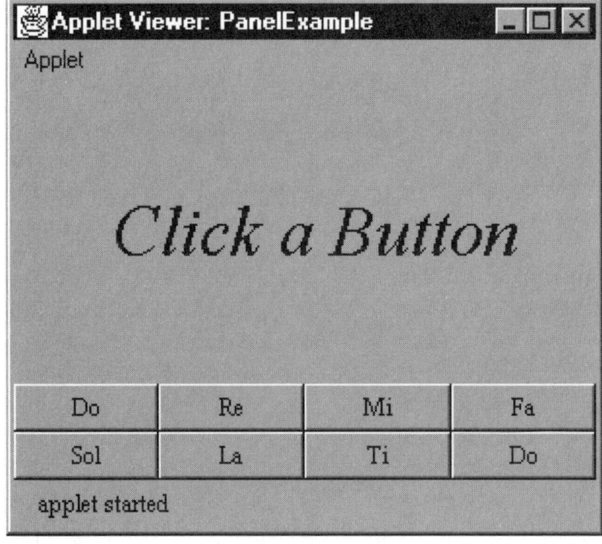

Figure 11–5

```
import java.applet.Applet;
import java.awt.*;

    public class PanelExample extends Applet
      {
      Label lCenterLabel;

      public void init()
        {
        Panel p;

        setLayout (new BorderLayout (0, 0));

        lCenterLabel = new Label ("Click a Button", Label.CENTER);
        lCenterLabel.setFont (new Font ("TimesRoman", Font.ITALIC, 36));
        add ("Center", lCenterLabel);

        p = new Panel ();
        p.setLayout (new GridLayout (2, 4, 0, 0));
        p.add (new Button ("Do"));
        p.add (new Button ("Re"));
        p.add (new Button ("Mi"));
        p.add (new Button ("Fa"));
        p.add (new Button ("Sol"));
        p.add (new Button ("La"));
        p.add (new Button ("Ti"));
        p.add (new Button ("Do"));
        add ("South", p);
        }

      public boolean handleEvent (Event evt)
        {
        if (evt.id == Event.ACTION_EVENT)
          {
          lCenterLabel.setText ((String) evt.arg.toString ());
          }
        return (super.handleEvent (evt));
        }
      }
```

CardLayout—A Notebook of Controls

Each control that is added to a CardLayout occupies the entire display area. The position of each new control is set to the upper left corner (0, 0) and the size is set to the width and height of the display area. As additional components are added, they are placed on top of the previous components.

The main task of the CardLayout is to make a particular control visible when the program requests it. The program has two ways to ask the CardLayout to make a different component visible.

Since the CardLayout remembers the order in which the components were added, the program can send the *next*() or *previous*() methods to the CardLayout and the next or previous control will be made visible. Other relative selection methods include *first*() and *last*(). The order of the components is not altered by sending these methods.

When a new component is added to an applet managed by a CardLayout, a string is included to give the component a name. Later, the applet can pass that name with the *show*() method to the CardLayout and the component will be made visible.

```
setLayout (new CardLayout (0, 0));

add ("Process It", new Button ("OK"));

((CardLayout) getLayout()).show (this, "Process It");
```

The first statement above creates a CardLayout with a horizontal gap of 0 pixels and a vertical gap of 0 pixels, and makes it the default layout of the applet. The second statement adds a new Button control to the layout and gives it the name *"Process It."*

The last statement retrieves the *CardLayout* object from the applet and sends it a *show*() method, which identifies the component to send by the name *Process It*. The first parameter is the parent object that owns the Layout Manager, which is the applet in this case.

In the example below, a new CardLayout with no horizontal or vertical gap is installed as the default Layout Manager. Then three buttons are added to the CardLayout. Each time a button is pressed, the *next*() method is sent to the Layout Manager, so that the next button is made visible. In Figure 11–6, the *Alpha* button is displayed.

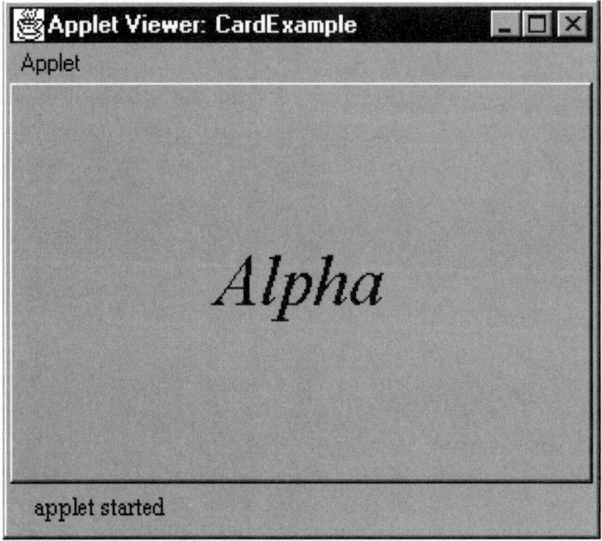

Figure 11–6

```
import java.applet.Applet;
import java.awt.*;

    public class CardExample extends Applet
      {
      public void init()
        {
        Button b;

        setLayout (new CardLayout (0, 0));

        b = new Button ("Alpha");
        b.setFont (new Font ("TimesRoman", Font.ITALIC, 36));
        add ("Greek Alpha", b);

        b = new Button ("Beta");
        b.setFont (new Font ("Courier", Font.ITALIC, 36));
        add ("Greek Beta", b);

        b = new Button ("Gamma");
        b.setFont (new Font ("Helvetica", Font.ITALIC, 36));
        add ("Greek Gamma", b);
        }
```

```
    public boolean handleEvent (Event evt)
      {
      if (evt.id == Event.ACTION_EVENT)    // A button is pressed
        {
        ((CardLayout) getLayout()).next (this);
        }
      return (super.handleEvent (evt));
      }
    }
```

CardLayouts can be very useful. Remember that any component can be added to a CardLayout. One could add several Panel objects to the CardLayout and assign them different Layout Managers. Then, as the program rotates through the panels, the display area paints a different layout of components for each Panel.

Also, keep in mind that a CardLayout can be installed into a panel, and the panel can be placed in one of the cells of a BorderLayout.

There is one more way to build a complex interface. One can use the GridBagLayout to construct an irregular grid of cells and place the controls over these cells.

GridBagLayout—Controls in Irregular Checkerboard Cells

The GridBagLayout is similar to a GridLayout in that it places its controls into a checkerboard grid. But the rows and columns in the grid do not have to be the same size.

The following drawing, Figure 11–7, illustrates the kind of grid that a GridBagLayout constructs. Notice that there are still distinct rows and columns. Every cell in a row has the same height and every cell in a column has the same width. But one row may not conform to the height of the other rows and the columns may not be the same width.

This is the grid into which a GridBagLayout places its components. The overall size of the grid does not usually snap to the size of the display area. Rather, the grid size is determined from the size of each of the components.

To construct the grid, the GridBagLayout places components into cells left-to-right, row-by-row. Then the Layout Manager goes back through each row and sets the row height to a value that has enough room for the tallest component of the row. A similar process occurs with the columns, so that each column is wide enough to accommodate its widest component.

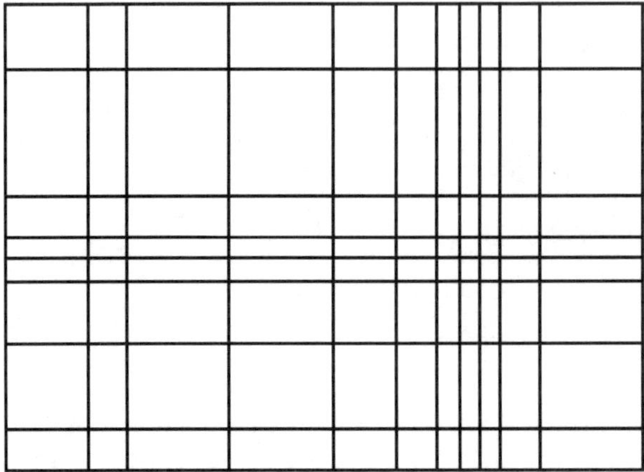

Figure 11–7 The Grid in a GridBagLayout is a variable sized checkerboard.

The size of each component is determined by calling the component's *minimumSize*() method. Notice that this is using a different method to determine the size of a component. The FlowLayout and the BorderLayout call the component's *preferredSize*() method to determine its size.

The following example installs a GridBagLayout as the default applet Layout Manager and adds a number of buttons. Some of the buttons have intercepted the *minimumSize*() method to force a different size cell.

```
import java.applet.Applet;
import java.awt.*;

    public class GridBagExample1 extends Applet
      {
      public void init()
        {
        GridBagLayout gridBag;
        GridBagConstraints constraints;
        Button b;

        gridBag = new GridBagLayout ();
        setLayout (gridBag);
        constraints = new GridBagConstraints ();
        constraints.fill = GridBagConstraints.BOTH;
//      constraints.weightx = 1.0;      // Uncomment these to snap...
//      constraints.weighty = 1.0;      //...grid size to display area size.
```

```
    b = new Button ("One");
    gridBag.setConstraints (b, constraints);
    add (b);

    b = new Button ("Two");
    gridBag.setConstraints (b, constraints);
    add (b);

    b = new Button ("Three");
    constraints.gridwidth = GridBagConstraints.REMAINDER;
    gridBag.setConstraints (b, constraints);
    constraints.gridwidth = 1;
    add (b);

    b = new Button ("Four");
    gridBag.setConstraints (b, constraints);
    add (b);

    b = new MyButton ("Five", 100, 50);
    gridBag.setConstraints (b, constraints);
    add (b);

    b = new Button ("Six");
    constraints.gridwidth = GridBagConstraints.REMAINDER;
    gridBag.setConstraints (b, constraints);
    constraints.gridwidth = 1;
    add (b);

    b = new Button ("Seven");
    gridBag.setConstraints (b, constraints);
    add (b);

    b = new Button ("Eight");
    gridBag.setConstraints (b, constraints);
    add (b);
    }

  public void paint (Graphics g)
    {
    g.setColor (Color.green);
    g.fill3DRect (0, 0, size().width, size().height, true);
    }

  }
```

```
class MyButton extends Button
  {
  Dimension dim;

  MyButton (String s, int iWidth, int iHeight)
    {
    super (s);
    dim = new Dimension (iWidth, iHeight);
    }
  public Dimension minimumSize ()
    {
    return (dim);
    }
  }
```

In the picture on the left, Figure 11–8, notice that each row is set to a height that allows room for the tallest component and each column is wide enough to accommodate the widest component.

The picture on the right, Figure 11–9, is the way the applet looks when the two constraint lines are uncommented.

The size of most of the buttons is determined by the text on the face of the button. The size of button *Five* is forced to a larger value by implementing the *minimumSize*() method.

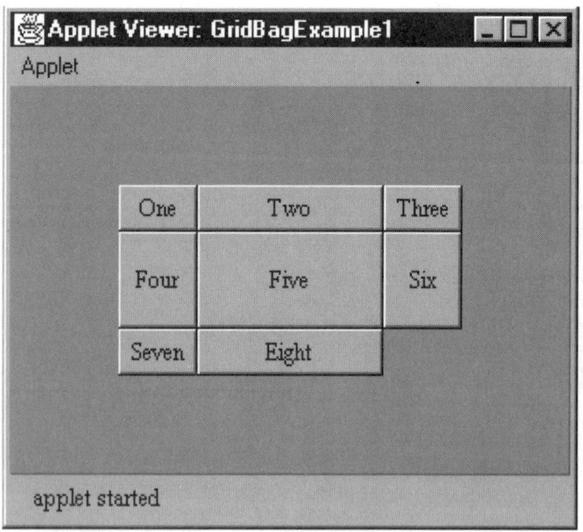

Figure 11–8

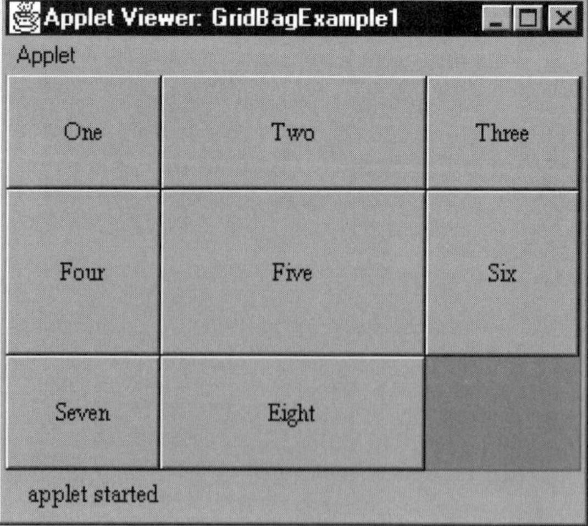

Figure 11–9

To build a variable-sized grid like this, a number of decisions must be made as the new components are added. The feature burden of this task has prompted the Java creaters to factor the parameter behavior into its own class—the *GridBagConstraints* class.

The *GridBagConstraints* object provides a way to set parameters that direct the flow of processing within the GridBagLayout.

To identify a control as the last component on the row, the *gridwidth* variable of the constraints object is set to *GridBagConstraints.REMAINDER*. Then it used the *setConstraints*() method is used to associate the Constraints object with the component. This instructed the Layout Manager to use the remaining space on that row for the component.

Every component that is added to a GridBagLayout should be associated with a *GridBagConstraints* object. The layout behavior is determined by setting fields within the *GridBagConstraints* object. The following are the most important of these fields.

GridBagConstraints.fill.

The *fill* variable determines how to fill the cell with the component if the cell is too large. The value *GridBagConstraints.HORIZONTAL* says to stretch the control's width to fill the cell horizontally. The *GridBagConstraints.VERTICAL* works the same way in the vertical direction. The applet above used the *GridBagConstraints.BOTH,* which caused the control to expand in both directions to fill the cell completely.

GridBagConstraints.weightx and weighty.

When the *weight* fields are set to their default value of "0.0," the layout's overall grid size is built up from the minimum sizes of each of the components in the grid. But when *weight* values are set (to "1.0," for example), the Layout Manager knows how to scale each component so that the overall grid size can fill the display area.

GridBagConstraints.gridwidth and gridheight.

The default value for these fields is "1" and indicates that a component should only take up one cell horizontally or vertically. By setting the *gridwidth* to "3," the Layout Manager is instructed to size the component to a horizontal size that covers three cells in the grid. The *gridheight* variable works the same way vertically.

These fields are also used to indicate end-of-grid conditions. If *gridwidth* is set to *GridBagConstraints.REMAINDER,* then the associated component will occupy the remainder of the cells in that row. Setting the *gridheight* variable to the same value will cause its component to occupy the remainder of the cells in the column down to the bottom of the grid. The special constant *GridBagConstraints.RELATIVE* identifies the component to be the second to last component on the row or column.

GridBagConstraints.gridx and gridy.

These fields provide a way to assign a component to a specific cell in the grid. Cells are numbered beginning at *gridx = 0* and *gridy = 0* for the upper left cell of the grid. To place a component in the third cell of the second row, *gridx* and *gridy* should be set to "2" and "1," respectively.

The example below uses these *grid* variables to place 286 Panel components into a single GridBagLayout to render the American flag (see Figure 11–10). Each panel can fill its display area with a solid color. Each stripe is a panel. Each star is a panel. The blue area is made up of a number of panels to create a grid that places the stars in the proper position.

The first seven stripes have a *gridheight* of three cells to coordinate with the pattern of the stars. The last six stripes have a *gridheight* of one cell, but the cell is made larger by returning a dimension from the panel's *minimumSize*() method that is three times the normal height.

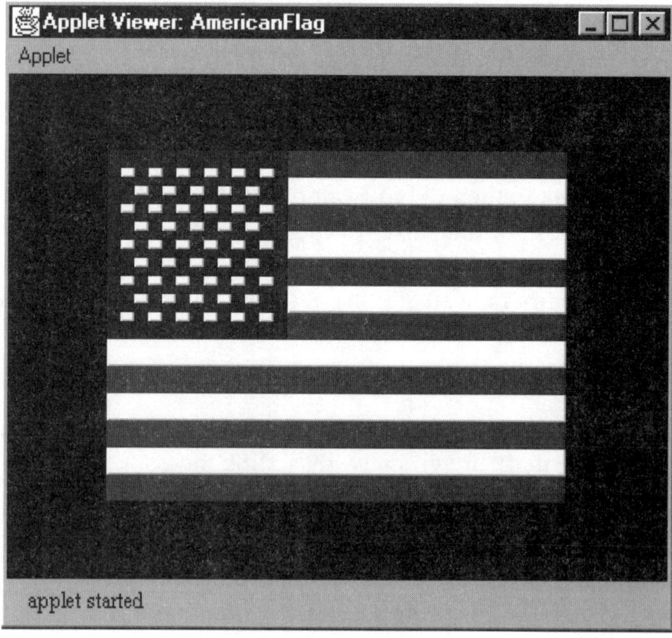

Figure 11–10

This application may tax the performance of some machines and the limits of some Java implementations. After all, most user interfaces will not be creating hundreds of components for a single display area. If anyone experiences difficulty running this example, then they should change line twelve to call for nine star columns. This will reduce the number of components in the layout to 202.

```
import java.applet.Applet;
import java.awt.*;

    public class AmericanFlag extends Applet
/***************************************************************************

    AmericanFlag -- Demonstration of GridBagLayout

***************************************************************************/

    {
    final int iStarColumns = 13;        // If too slow, change to 9


    public String getAppletInfo ()
      {
      return ("Copyright (c) Noel Enete, 1996");
      }


    public void init()
      {
      Panel p;
      GridBagLayout gbl;
      GridBagConstraints c;
      Color cPanelColor;
      int iRow, iColumn;

      gbl = new GridBagLayout ();
      c = new GridBagConstraints ();
      setLayout (gbl);
      c.fill = GridBagConstraints.BOTH;
//    c.weightx = 1.0;                  // Uncomment these to cause the...
//    c.weighty = 1.0;                  // ...grid to fill the window.


/*    Add the stars.
      ==============  */
```

```
      for (iRow = 0; iRow < 21; iRow++)
        {
        for (iColumn = 0; iColumn < iStarColumns; iColumn++)
          {
          c.gridy = iRow;
          c.gridx = iColumn;
          cPanelColor = Color.blue;
          if ((iRow >= 2) && (iRow <= 18)
          && (iColumn >= 1) && (iColumn <= iStarColumns - 2)) //11))
            {
            if (iRow % 2 == 0)                    // Even Rows
              {
              if (((iRow + 2) % 4 == 0)           // Every other Even Row
              && ((iColumn + 1) % 2 == 0))        // Odd Columns
                {
                cPanelColor = Color.white;
                }
              else if ((iRow % 4 == 0)            // Alternating Even Rows
              && (iColumn % 2 == 0))              // Even Columns
                {
                cPanelColor = Color.white;
                }
              }
            }
          addColorPanel (cPanelColor, gbl, c);
          }
        }


/*    Add the first 7 stripes adjacent to the stars.
      ==============================================  */

      c.gridx = 13;
      c.gridheight = 3;

      for (iRow = 0; iRow < 7; iRow++)
        {
        c.gridy = iRow * 3;
        if (iRow % 2 == 0)
          {
          cPanelColor = Color.red;
          }
        else
          {
          cPanelColor = Color.white;
          }
```

```
        addColorPanel (cPanelColor, 20, 1, gbl, c);
        }


/*    Add the last 6 stripes under the stars.
      ========================================  */

      c.gridx = 0;
      c.gridwidth = GridBagConstraints.REMAINDER;
      c.gridheight = 1;

      for (iRow = 7; iRow < 13; iRow++)
        {
        c.gridy = iRow - 7 + 21;
        if (iRow % 2 == 0)
          {
          cPanelColor = Color.red;
          }
        else
          {
          cPanelColor = Color.white;
          }
        addColorPanel (cPanelColor, 13, 3, gbl, c);
        }

      }


    void addColorPanel (Color c, GridBagLayout gbl, GridBagConstraints gbc)
      {
      addColorPanel (c, 1, 1, gbl, gbc);
      }


    void addColorPanel (Color c, int iWidthMultiplier, int iHeightMultiplier,
      GridBagLayout gbl, GridBagConstraints gbc)
      {
      ColorPanel p = new ColorPanel (c, iWidthMultiplier, iHeightMultiplier);
      gbl.setConstraints (p, gbc);
      add (p);
      }


    public void paint (Graphics g)
      {
      g.setColor (Color.black);
```

```
      g.fill3DRect (0, 0, size().width, size().height, true);
      }
    }


    class ColorPanel extends Panel
/*************************************************************************
    ColorPanel -- Fills a Rectangle with Color

*************************************************************************/

    {
    Color cFillColor;
    int iWidthMultiplier;
    int iHeightMultiplier;

    ColorPanel (Color c, int w, int h)
      {
      super ();
      cFillColor = c;
      iWidthMultiplier = w;
      iHeightMultiplier = h;
      }

    public synchronized Dimension minimumSize ()
      {
      return (new Dimension (8 * iWidthMultiplier, 5 * iHeightMultiplier));
      }

    public void paint (Graphics g)
      {
      g.setColor (cFillColor);
      g.fill3DRect (0, 0, size().width, size().height, true);
      }
    }


/*=======================(  End of Source  )===========================*/
```

```
<HTML>
<HEAD>
<TITLE> AmericanFlag </TITLE>
</HEAD>
<BODY>
AmericanFlag
<HR>
<APPLET CODE="AmericanFlag" WIDTH=380 HEIGHT=280>
</APPLET>
<HR>
</BODY>
</HTML>
```

CHAPTER 12

Standalone Windows

Java applications that include a Graphical User Interface are not required to run in a Web browser. They can run independently and create their own windows for graphical rendering.

The independent windows retain many of the familiar services of the applet. They have their own Layout Manager and controls can be added to independent windows in the same way that controls can be added to an applet.

The central class that implements a standalone window in Java is the *Frame* class.

Frame—A Standalone Window

It is helpful to think of a frame as an applet that lives in its own independent window.

Frames have a *paint*() method like an applet does. They have a default Layout Manager (BorderLayout) so components can be added to them. They receive events and handle them in a *handleEvent*() method like an applet.

They just don't need to ride along in a Web browser. They have their own independent window that is framed with a sizing border and a title bar.

When a frame is instantiated, an invisible window is created. This gives one the opportunity to make alterations to the size and composition of the window before it is presented to the users.

The following example instantiates a frame, sizes it, adds a button to it, then asks it to show itself to the users. Since this is a Java application, one runs it by launching the Virtual Machine with the name of the class. Figure 12–1 shows the results of this example.

```
java FrameExample1
```

```
import java.awt.*;

    class FrameExample1
      {
      public static void main (String args[])
        {
        Frame f;

        f = new Frame ();
        f.resize (300, 300);
        f.add ("Center", new Button ("A Frame Window"));
        f.show ();
        }
      }
```

Figure 12–1

This example creates a fully-functioning independent Frame window. There is only one small problem. The window will not close.

Every normal means of closing a window in the native graphical environment sends a WINDOW_DESTROY event to the frame. Unfortunately in the Frame class, the default behavior is to ignore WINDOW_DESTROY events. So the frame persists.

If one's Java environment provides the ability to launch this program from the command line, one can return to the command line and press a control-C to bring the window down. Web browsers can be very ungraceful about this situation and may need to be brought down to cause the Frame window to close.

To get frames to close, one must cause the frame to intercept the WINDOW_DESTROY event and bring itself down. Events are intercepted by coding a *handleEvent*() method and comparing each event *id* field against the constant *Event.WINDOW_DESTROY*.

But where should the *handleEvent*() method be placed?

The WINDOW_DESTROY events are sent to the frame's *handleEvent*() method. The only way to intercept this mechanism is to create a class that extends the Frame class. This extension class should be viewed *as* a Frame class. It can be launched as a Frame window and receive events that are destined for the frame. This extension *becomes* a new kind of frame.

The *handleEvent*() method should be placed in this extension class. When a WINDOW_DESTROY event is sent to this class, it causes the Frame window to close (see Figure 12–2). All other events that are sent to this class are passed up to the Frame class for processing.

```
import java.awt.*;

    class FrameExample2
      {
      public static void main (String args[])
        {
        MyFrame mf;
```

Figure 12–2

```
      mf = new MyFrame ();
      mf.resize (300, 300);
      mf.add ("Center", new Button ("This Frame will Close"));
      mf.show ();
      }
    }


  class MyFrame extends Frame
    {
    public boolean handleEvent (Event evt)
      {
```

```
        if (evt.id == Event.WINDOW_DESTROY)
          {
          System.exit (0);
          }
        return (super.handleEvent (evt));
        }
      }
```

If one wants to draw on the frame's surface directly, one can code a *paint()* method in the extended Frame class. The following code would draw the string *"Hello World"* to the display surface.

```
public void paint (Graphics g)
  {
  g.drawString ("Hello World", 20, 20);
  }
```

The Graphics object that is passed to the *paint()* method is used for any drawing operations. This is exactly the same mechanism that an applet uses to draw on its display surface. Remember that if buttons or other controls are added to the frame, they will overlay any drawing that is performed on the frame's surface by a Graphics object. To see the text above, remove the statement in the main () method that adds the button to the frame.

The Frame class is the home for cursor control in Java. The methods *setCursor()* and *getCursorType()* can be sent to the frame. The cursors that are available are pre-stored and are represented by an integer code. The Frame class provides constants like *Frame.CROSSHAIR_CURSOR* to use when selecting a cursor.

The example below cycles through each of the pre-stored cursors in the Frame class. An interesting quirk about Java's graphical environment is that a new cursor selection does not take effect visually until a mouse move message is received. So click on the button and then move the mouse around to see the new cursor.

```
import java.awt.*;

    class CursorExample
      {
      public static void main (String args[])
        {
        MyFrame mf;
        mf = new MyFrame ();
        }
      }


    class MyFrame extends Frame
      {
      int iCursorIndex = 0;
      Button b;

      final int[] aiCursors =
        {
        Frame.CROSSHAIR_CURSOR,
        Frame.TEXT_CURSOR,
        Frame.WAIT_CURSOR,
        Frame.HAND_CURSOR,
        Frame.MOVE_CURSOR,
        Frame.E_RESIZE_CURSOR,
        Frame.NE_RESIZE_CURSOR,
        Frame.N_RESIZE_CURSOR,
        Frame.NW_RESIZE_CURSOR,
        Frame.W_RESIZE_CURSOR,
        Frame.SW_RESIZE_CURSOR,
        Frame.S_RESIZE_CURSOR,
        Frame.SE_RESIZE_CURSOR,
        Frame.DEFAULT_CURSOR
        };

      final String[] asCursors =
        {
        "Frame.CROSSHAIR_CURSOR",
        "Frame.TEXT_CURSOR",
        "Frame.WAIT_CURSOR",
        "Frame.HAND_CURSOR",
        "Frame.MOVE_CURSOR",
        "Frame.E_RESIZE_CURSOR",
        "Frame.NE_RESIZE_CURSOR",
        "Frame.N_RESIZE_CURSOR",
        "Frame.NW_RESIZE_CURSOR",
```

```
    "Frame.W_RESIZE_CURSOR",
    "Frame.SW_RESIZE_CURSOR",
    "Frame.S_RESIZE_CURSOR",
    "Frame.SE_RESIZE_CURSOR",
    "Frame.DEFAULT_CURSOR"
    };

  MyFrame ()
    {
    super ("Cursor Example");
    resize (300, 200);
    b = new Button ("Click and Move Mouse");
    b.setFont (new Font ("Helvetica", Font.ITALIC, 20));
    add ("Center", b);
    show ();
    }

  public boolean handleEvent (Event evt)
    {
    if (evt.id == Event.WINDOW_DESTROY)
      {
      System.exit (0);
      }

    else if (evt.id == Event.ACTION_EVENT)
      {
      setCursor (aiCursors[iCursorIndex]);
      b.setLabel (asCursors[iCursorIndex]);
      if (iCursorIndex >= aiCursors.length - 1)
        {
        iCursorIndex = 0;
        }
      else
        {
        iCursorIndex++;
        }
      }

    return (super.handleEvent (evt));
    }
  }
```

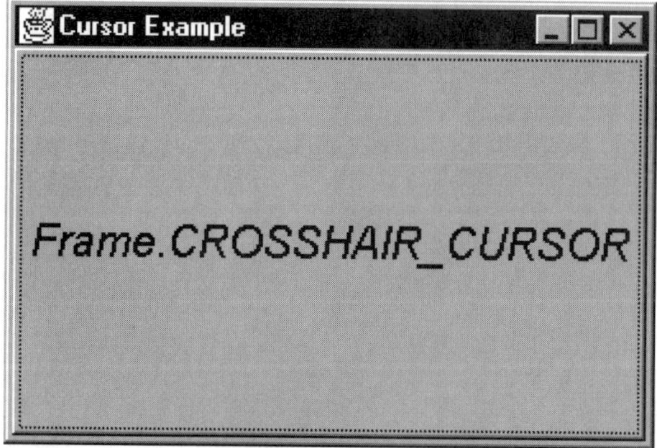

Figure 12–3

Each time the button is pressed in Figure 12–2, the cursor is changed and the cursor description is printed on the button face.

Applet—An Addable Component

There are many similarities between Frame objects and Applet objects. But there is also an interesting interplay between them.

After a close inspection of the Java class hierarchy, one discovers that the Applet class is a subclass of the Component class. This means that an applet *is* a component. Just like a Button, Scrollbar, or other component can be added to a Frame object, an applet can be added to a frame.

At first this seems to have little advantage. What value would an applet that depends upon a Web browser give to a frame that can stand by itself?

The benefit comes when one realizes that an applet can leverage this interplay to allow it to run inside a browser or outside a browser. A applet that is constructed in this way can be placed on a Web page and it will run. It can also be launched from a command line and it will run.

It takes a little careful coding to construct a class that performs in this way; but for the right application, this capability can be a real asset.

To understand the technique, one should begin with a simple applet. Suppose that a *main*() method was added to a simple JAVA applet. What would happen when the applet was launched by a Web browser?

Would the *main*() method be called? No.

All object-oriented systems need a way to begin the processing of an application task. In Java, the *main*() method initiates processing for an application task.

When a Web browser is running, the application task—to browse the Web—has already begun. The applet is loaded by the browser and is sent the *init*() and *start*() methods to signal when it has center stage on the display surface. In the case of the enhanced applet, the *main*() method would be viewed as a superfluous method and would be ignored.

What would happen when the applet was launched from the command line? Would the *main*() method be called? Yes.

When no processing task is active, the class loader must transfer control somewhere after the new class has been loaded. The convention says that when the Virtual Machine is launched with the name of a class, that class must contain a method with the following method signature:

```
public static void main (String args[])
   {
   }
```

After *loading* the new class and before *instantiating* the new class, this *main*() method is called when the class is launched from the command line.

So, placing a *main*() method within an applet allows it to begin processing regardless of whether it was launched from a Web browser or from the command line.

The next step is to place some behavior in the *main*() method that would add the applet to a window. Since frames are independent windows and applets are components that can be added to a frame, the task is to write code in *main*() that launches a frame, instantiates the applet, and adds the applet to the frame.

The following example implements this code and will run from a browser or from the command line.

```
import java.applet.Applet;
import java.awt.*;

  public class StandAloneApplet extends Applet
    {
    boolean bStandAlone = false;

    public void init ()
      {
      Button b;

      setLayout (new BorderLayout ());
      if (bStandAlone) b = new Button ("Stand Alone");
      else             b = new Button ("Applet");
      b.setFont (new Font ("Helvetica", Font.ITALIC | Font.BOLD, 36));
      add ("Center", b);
      }

    public static void main (String args[])
      {
      MyFrame mf;
      StandAloneApplet sa;

      sa = new StandAloneApplet ();
      sa.bStandAlone = true;
      sa.init ();

      mf = new MyFrame ();
      mf.resize (300, 200);
      mf.add ("Center", sa);
      mf.show ();
      }
    }


  class MyFrame extends Frame
    {
    public boolean handleEvent (Event evt)
      {
      if (evt.id == Event.WINDOW_DESTROY)
        {
        System.exit (0);
        }
      return (super.handleEvent (evt));
      }
    }
```

```
<HTML>
<HEAD>
<TITLE> StandAloneApplet </TITLE>
</HEAD>
<BODY>
StandAloneApplet
<HR>
<APPLET CODE="StandAloneApplet" WIDTH=300 HEIGHT=200>
</APPLET>
<HR>
</BODY>
</HTML>
```

The purpose for the code within the applet's *init*() method is to make big buttons that identify how the applet was launched. The picture on the left, Figure 12–4, was launched within the appletviewer (a Web browser substitute); and the picture on the right, Figure 12–5, was launched from the command line.

One will notice the difference in heights between the two buttons. The applet was sized to 300 x 200 and the frame was sized to 300 x 200. But the frame must render a sizing border and a title bar within its space. The remainder of the display area was given to the button.

The following code from the *main*() method created the applet. At this point, the applet is not visible, it is just another object in the Virtual Machine image. It does not become visible until it is added to the frame and the frame is shown.

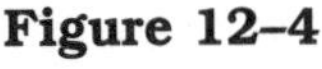
Figure 12–4

Figure 12–5

```
sa = new StandAloneApplet ();
sa.bStandAlone = true;
sa.init ();
```

The second line is not required. It simply registers the fact that the applet was started from the command line. Also, notice the call to the *init*() method. Since this code is taking the place of the Web browser, any methods that the browser would send, like *init*() or *start*(), should be explicitly sent here.

This standalone applet technique works equally well for applets that paint directly to the display surface. If the code in the *init*() method is commented out and the following method is added to the applet, the string *"Hello World"* will be drawn on the display surface.

```
public void paint (Graphics g)
  {
  g.drawString ("Hello World", 20, 20);
  }
```

The Frame window forms the basis of independent window processing in Java. Several other GUI classes depend upon the Frame window and augment its services.

Dialog and (Popup) Window—Dependent Windows

The Dialog class is a window whose primary purpose is to capture user input.

It is very much like a Frame window. It has a default Layout Manager (BorderLayout) and includes a sizing border and a title bar. Unless the programmer traps the WINDOW_DESTROY message and removes the window, the users will have the same problem closing a Dialog as they have closing a Frame window.

A *modal* option can be set when launching a dialog that determines how user input is funneled to the dialog. If the modal parameter is *true*, the thread that launches the dialog is blocked so that other windows in the thread are blocked from receiving input and only the dialog can receive input. If the modal parameter is *false*, the dialog becomes one of many windows that can receive user input.

A dialog looks like an independent Frame window, but it is not completely independent. It must have a Frame window as a parent. Some of the events that are destined to be sent to the Dialog window are sent first to the Frame window's *handleEvent*() method. The Frame window can examine the *target* field of the event to identify the intended destination of the event. Then it can choose to intercept the event or pass it along to its normal destination.

The Frame window is passed as the first parameter to the Dialog constructor.

```
Dialog d = new Dialog (new Frame (), "Cool Dialog", true);

d.resize (200, 200);
d.add ("Center", new Label ("About Box", Label.CENTER));
d.add ("South", new Button ("OK"));
d.show ();
```

This code creates a new Dialog window with the string *"Cool Dialog"* in the title and with the modal option set to *true*. The parent Frame window is created on the fly to demonstrate how to launch a dialog when a Frame window is not readily available. The Frame window remains invisible in this case because its *show*() method was not called.

After the Dialog is created, a Label control is added to the *Center* cell and a button control is added to the *South* cell. Then the dialog is made visible by calling its *show*() method.

Sometimes, one does not require the title bar and sizing border of the Dialog class, but only needs to launch a pop-up window. The Java class that provides pop-up window services is the Window class.

The Window class works like the Dialog class without the modal options. It is a top-level window that must have a Frame window as a parent. It has a BorderLayout and must close itself when it is no longer needed.

```
Window w = new Window (new Frame ());

w.resize (200, 200);
w.add ("Center", new Label ("About Box", Label.CENTER));
w.add ("South", new Button ("OK"));
w.show ();
```

This code fragment creates a new Window object, adds two controls, and makes the window visible. This is another window that will not close by itself.

The following example demonstrates how to launch Dialog and Window objects, handle their Button events, and handle WINDOW_DESTROY events so they close gracefully.

```
import java.awt.*;

    class DialogExample
      {
      public static void main (String args[])
        {
        MyFrame mf;

        mf = new MyFrame ("Dialogs and Windows");
        mf.setLayout (new GridLayout (1, 2, 0, 0));
        mf.reshape (20, 20, 300, 200);
        mf.add (new Button ("Dialog"));
        mf.add (new Button ("Window"));
        mf.show ();
        }
      }


    class MyFrame extends Frame
      {
      MyDialog d;
      MyWindow w;
      Button btnOKDialog;
      Button btnOKWindow;

      public MyFrame (String s)
        {
        super (s);
        }

      public boolean handleEvent (Event evt)
        {
        Label l;

        switch (evt.id)
          {
          case Event.WINDOW_DESTROY:              // Close from System Menu
            System.exit (0);
            break;

          case Event.ACTION_EVENT:
            if ("Dialog".equals (evt.arg))        // Frame's Dialog Button
              {
              d = new MyDialog (this, "Cool Dialog", true);
              d.reshape (40, 40, 200, 200);
```

```
          l = new Label ("Dialog", Label.CENTER);
          l.setFont (new Font ("Helvetica", Font.ITALIC | Font.BOLD, 36));
          d.add ("Center", l);

          btnOKDialog = new Button ("OK");
          d.add ("South", btnOKDialog);
          d.show ();
          }

        else if ("Window".equals (evt.arg))  // Frame's Window Button
          {
          w = new MyWindow (this);
          w.reshape (60, 60, 200, 200);

          l = new Label ("Window", Label.CENTER);
          l.setFont (new Font ("Helvetica", Font.ITALIC | Font.BOLD, 36));
          w.add ("Center", l);

          btnOKWindow = new Button ("OK");
          w.add ("South", btnOKWindow);
          w.show ();
          }
        break;
      }

    return (super.handleEvent (evt));
    }
  }


class MyDialog extends Dialog
  {
  public MyDialog (Frame fr, String s, boolean bModal)
    {
    super (fr, s, bModal);
    }

  public boolean handleEvent (Event evt)
    {
    Label l;

    switch (evt.id)
      {
      case Event.WINDOW_DESTROY:               // Close from System Menu
        this.dispose ();
        break;
```

```
        case Event.ACTION_EVENT:
          if ("OK".equals (evt.arg))             // Dialog's OK Button
            {
            this.dispose ();
            }
          break;
        }
      return (super.handleEvent (evt));
      }
    }


  class MyWindow extends Window
    {
    public MyWindow (Frame fr)
      {
      super (fr);
      }

    public boolean handleEvent (Event evt)
      {
      Label l;

      switch (evt.id)
        {
        case Event.WINDOW_DESTROY:               // Close from System Menu
          this.dispose ();
          break;

        case Event.ACTION_EVENT:
          if ("OK".equals (evt.arg))             // Window's OK Button
            {
            this.dispose ();
            }
          break;
        }
      return (super.handleEvent (evt));
      }
    }
```

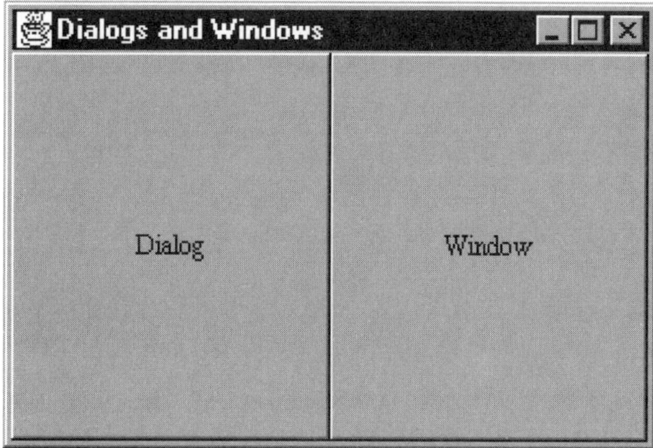

Figure 12–6

Figure 12–7

Figure 12–8

When the example is launched, the user is presented with a window with two large buttons (Figure 12–6). When the "Dialog" button is pressed, a Dialog panel is displayed (Figure 12–7). Pressing the "Window" button launches a Window panel (Figure 12–8). The "OK" button closes either the Dialog or Window panel.

The method *reshape*() in the handle Event method may be new to beginners. This is how a window can be positioned and sized with one method. The first two parameters are the desired *(x, y)* coordinates of the upper left corner of the window. The next two parameters are the desired width and height, respectively.

When a WINDOW_DESTROY event is received, the window is either disposed or the entire application is exited.

```
switch (evt.id)
  {
  case Event.WINDOW_DESTROY:                    // Frame's System Menu Close
    System.exit (0);                           // closes the application.
    break;
  }

          . . .

switch (evt.id)
  {
  case Event.WINDOW_DESTROY:                   // Dialog's System Menu Close
    this.dispose ();                         // disposes the dialog window.
    break;
  }
```

The pressing of an OK Button is identified by the *"OK"* text on the face of the button. When one of these buttons is pressed, an ACTION_EVENT is sent to the parent window and the window is disposed.

```
switch (evt.id)
  {
  case Event.ACTION_EVENT:
    if ("OK".equals (evt.arg))           // Dialog's OK Button.
      {
      this.dispose ();
      }
    break;
  }
```

Menu—A Specialized Dependent Window

Another kind of window that depends on a frame is a pull-down menu.

Pull-down menus are constructed out of three classes: *MenuBar, Menu,* and *MenuItem.* The elemental class in the construction is the MenuItem. The other classes are containers. Menus hold a combination of MenuItems and other Menus. A MenuBar holds a collection of Menus.

The syntax for building a pull-down menu is like the syntax for adding components to a Layout Manager. The method that is called in each case is the *add*() method.

The general procedure is to instantiate a MenuBar,d a Menu object, and a MenuItem. Add the MenuItem to the Menu object, then add the Menu to the MenuBar. After the MenuBar has been constructed, it is passed as a parameter to the Frame window's *setMenuBar*() method.

```
Menu m, m1;
MenuBar mb;

mb = new MenuBar ();
m = new Menu ("File");

m.add (new MenuItem ("Exit"));

mb.add (m);

setMenuBar (mb);
```

The code above was written to execute within a method in a Frame class. If one is moving this code to a class other than a Frame class, the *setMenuBar*() method must be sent to a Frame object.

When the users make a menu selection, an event is sent to the Frame window with the selected MenuItem object in the *target* field. Processing a menu selection is like processing the pressing of a button. The frame's *handleEvent*() method receives an ACTION_EVENT that contain the MenuItem object in the event's *target* field.

To identify the MenuItem that was selected, compare the MenuItem object with the target field in the event. Alternatively, the text of the MenuItem can be compared with the *arg* field in the event.

The following example is a standalone Java application that creates a Frame window that builds its own pull-down menu and processes menu selections. Figure 12–8 displays the pull-down menu.

```
import java.awt.*;

    class MenuExample
      {
      public static void main (String args[])
        {
        MyFrame mf;
        mf = new MyFrame ();
        }
      }


    class MyFrame extends Frame
      {
      Label l;

      MyFrame ()
        {
        super ("Menu Example");

        Menu m, m1;
        MenuBar mb;

        mb = new MenuBar ();

        m = new Menu ("File");
        m.add (new CheckboxMenuItem ("Checkable Item"));
        m.add (new MenuItem ("Exit"));
        mb.add (m);

        m = new Menu ("Numbers");
        m.add (new MenuItem ("0"));
        m.add (new MenuItem ("1"));
        m.add (new MenuItem ("2"));
        m.add (new MenuItem ("3"));
        m.add (new MenuItem ("4"));
        m.add (new MenuItem ("5"));
        m.add (new MenuItem ("6"));
        m.add (new MenuItem ("7"));
        m.add (new MenuItem ("8"));
        m.add (new MenuItem ("9"));
        mb.add (m);

        m = new Menu ("Letters");
        m1 = new Menu ("Vowels");
        m1.add (new MenuItem ("a"));
```

```
        m1.add (new MenuItem ("e"));
        m1.add (new MenuItem ("i"));
        m1.add (new MenuItem ("o"));
        m1.add (new MenuItem ("u"));
        m.add (m1);
        m1 = new Menu ("Consonants");
        m1.add (new MenuItem ("b"));
        m1.add (new MenuItem ("c"));
        m1.add (new MenuItem ("d"));
        m1.add (new MenuItem ("f"));
        m1.add (new MenuItem ("g"));
        m1.add (new MenuItem ("h"));
        m1.add (new MenuItem ("j"));
        m1.add (new MenuItem ("k"));
        m1.add (new MenuItem ("l"));
        m1.add (new MenuItem ("m"));
        m1.add (new MenuItem ("n"));
        m1.add (new MenuItem ("p"));
        m1.add (new MenuItem ("q"));
        m1.add (new MenuItem ("r"));
        m1.add (new MenuItem ("s"));
        m1.add (new MenuItem ("t"));
        m1.add (new MenuItem ("v"));
        m1.add (new MenuItem ("w"));
        m1.add (new MenuItem ("x"));
        m1.add (new MenuItem ("y"));
        m1.add (new MenuItem ("z"));
        m.add (m1);
        mb.add (m);

        m = new Menu ("Musical");
        m.add (new MenuItem ("Do"));
        m.add (new MenuItem ("Ra"));
        m.add (new MenuItem ("Mi"));
        m.addSeparator();
        m.add (new MenuItem ("Fa"));
        m.add (new MenuItem ("Sol"));
        m.addSeparator();
        m.add (new MenuItem ("La"));
        m.add (new MenuItem ("Ti"));
        m.add (new MenuItem (""Do"));
        mb.add (m);

        m = new Menu ("Help");
        m.add (new MenuItem ("Index"));
        m.add (new MenuItem ("Contents"));
```

```
    m.add (new MenuItem ("How Do I..."));
    mb.add (m);
    mb.setHelpMenu (m);

    setMenuBar (mb);

    l = new Label ("Menu", Label.CENTER);
    l.setFont (new Font ("Helvetica", Font.BOLD | Font.ITALIC, 36));
    add ("Center", l);

    resize (300, 200);
    show ();
    }


  public boolean handleEvent (Event evt)
    {
    switch (evt.id)
      {
      case Event.WINDOW_DESTROY:
        if (evt.target == this)
          {
          System.exit (0);
          }
        else
          {
          ((Window) evt.target).dispose ();
          }
        break;

      case Event.ACTION_EVENT:
        if ("Exit".equals (evt.arg))
          {
          System.exit (0);
          }
        else if (evt.target instanceof MenuItem)
          {
          l.setText ((String) evt.arg);
          }
        break;
      }

    return (super.handleEvent (evt));
    }

  }
```

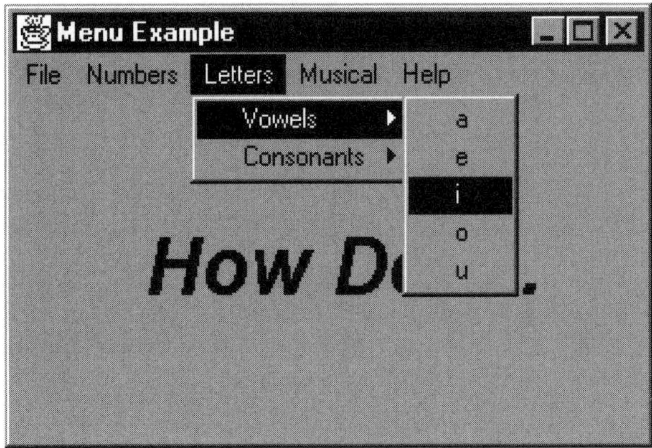

Figure 12–9

Most of the menu items are instances of the MenuItem class. But one of the items in the *File* menu is an instance of the CheckboxMenuItem class. This class works just like MenuItem except it will keep track of a boolean state and render it on the menu surface as a check. The methods *getState*() and *setState*() can be sent to a CheckboxMenuItem to process the state.

The *Letters* menu has multiple levels of menus. Normally MenuItems are added to Menus. But one can also add Menus to Menus. In this case, several MenuItems are added to the *Vowels* Menu and it is added to the *Letters* menu to create the multi-level effect.

To process the menu choices, the *handleEvent*() method examines ACTION_ EVENTs. If MenuItem text equals "Exit," then the application is terminated. If the target object is an instance of the MenuItem class, then the label is set to the text in the MenuItem.

```
case Event.ACTION_EVENT:
  if ("Exit".equals (evt.arg))
    {
    System.exit (0);
    }
  else if (evt.target instanceof MenuItem)
    {
    l.setText ((String) evt.arg);
    }
```

Sometimes it appears to be an unnecessary restriction that pull-down menus must be associated with a Frame window. Why are they not available for Applet windows?

Technically, it may be possible with some browsers to ask the applet for its parent (*getParent*()) and that object for its parent, until one arrives at the browser's Frame window. Then the applet constructed menu might be installed as the frame's MenuBar.

But it seems to go beyond the scope of an applet to take over the browser's menu. An applet is one of many pieces of code that can be collected in a Web page. The browser allows the users to coordinate many Web pages by making selections from the browser's menu.

When menu behavior is required in an applet, it may be more consistent with the browser interface to use Button or Choice controls. If the selection behavior is very complex, one might want to implement a notebook of dialogs. This could be constructed using a CardLayout in the *Center* cell of a BorderLayout and the tabs could be one row of buttons in the *North* cell.

FileDialog—Dependent Window for File Access

Java includes an extension of the Dialog window class for file selection. It is called the FileDialog class. It augments the basic behavior of the Dialog class and requires a Frame window.

It is instantiated with a Frame window, a window title, and a mode constant. The code fragment below identifies the mode as SAVE. This puts the string *"Save"* on the OK button and causes the Dialog to prompt if an existing file is selected to verify that the file can be overlayed.

```
FileDialog fd;

fd = new FileDialog (this, "Save As", FileDialog.SAVE);

fd.setFilenameFilter (this);
fd.setFile ("DebugLog.trc");
fd.show ();

System.out.println ("Filename       = " + fd.getFile ());
System.out.println ("Directory      = " + fd.getDirectory ());
System.out.println ("FilenameFilter = " + fd.getFilenameFilter ());
System.out.println ("Mode           = " + fd.getMode ());
```

After it is instantiated, several attributes can be set in the FileDialog. When the dialog is fully tailored, the *show*() method is sent to make the window visible. The dialog is modal, so no more code in the launching method is executed until the dialog is closed.

When the users close the FileDialog, control is passed to the line right after the *show*() call. This is the place to extract the users' selection from the FileDialog object. One can request the filename with *getFile*() and the directory path with *getDirectory*(). The *getMode*() method returns either the *FileDialog.SAVE* constant or the *FileDialog.LOAD* constant.

An interface has been designed to give programmers control over what files are displayed by the FileDialog. The interface is called a FilenameFilter and has only one method—*accept*(). When the FileDialog is enumerating a directory's contents, it will pass the directory and filename of each file to the *accept*() method. The *accept*() method returns *true* if the filename should be displayed and *false* if it should be ignored.

To make use of this service, one must implement the *FilenameFilter* interface by coding an *accept*() method in one of the classes. In the following example, the *accept*() method always returns *true*, so all the files in a directory are displayed. The handle to this object is passed as a parameter to the FileDialog's *setFilenameFilter*() method before the dialog is made visible.

The following example illustrates how to use a FileDialog to save program data to a file. Figure 12–10 displays the screen as viewed by the users.

```
import java.awt.*;
import java.io.*;

    class FileDialogExample
      {
      public static void main (String args[])
        {
        DebugLog log;

        log = new DebugLog ();
        for (int i = 0; i < 50; i++)
          {
          log.println ("Debug Line #" + i);
          }
        }
      }
```

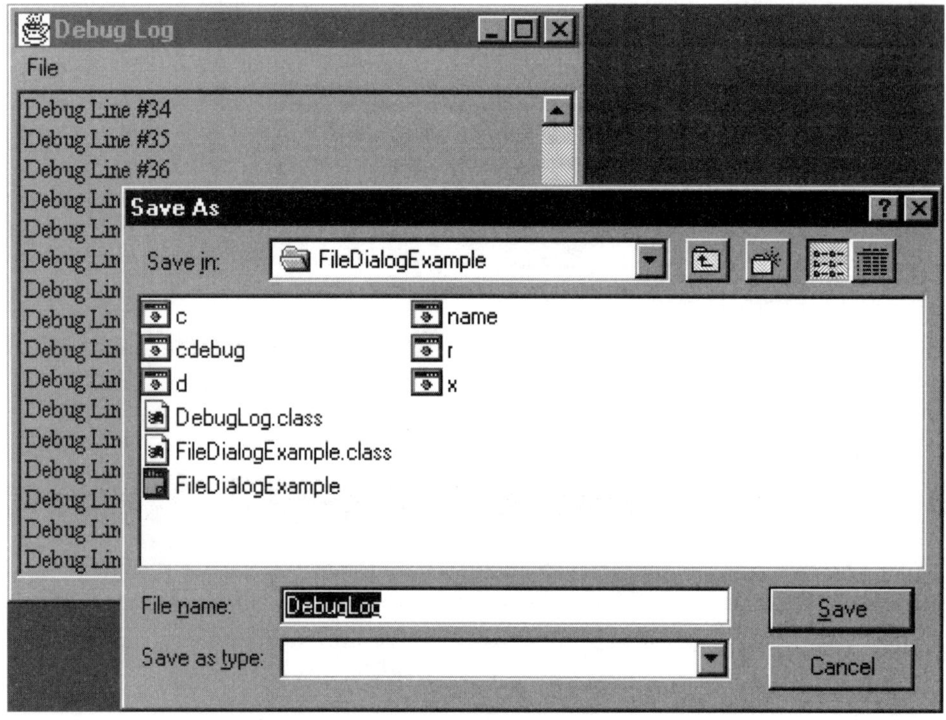

Figure 12–10

```
class DebugLog extends Frame implements FilenameFilter
  {
  final int iMaxCount = 1000;
  List l;

  public DebugLog ()
    {
    super ("Debug Log");

    Menu a,b,c,m;
    MenuBar mb;

    mb = new MenuBar ();
    m = new Menu ("File");
    m.add (new MenuItem ("Clear"));
    m.add (new MenuItem ("Save"));
    m.add (new MenuItem ("Exit"));
    mb.add (m);
    setMenuBar (mb);
```

```
        l = new List ();
        add ("Center", l);

        resize (300, 300);
        show ();
        }


    public void println (String s)
        {
        if (l.countItems () >= iMaxCount)
            {
            l.delItem (0);
            }
        l.addItem (s);
        l.makeVisible (l.countItems () - 1);
        }


    public boolean accept (File f, String s)
        {
        return (true);
        }


    public boolean handleEvent (Event evt)
        {
        int i;
        String sFilename;
        FileDialog fd;
        FilenameFilter ff;
        File fOut;
        FileOutputStream fos;
        DataOutputStream dos;

        switch (evt.id)
            {
            case Event.WINDOW_DESTROY:
                if (evt.target == this)
                    {
                    System.exit (0);
                    }
                else
                    {
                    ((Window) evt.target).dispose ();
                    }
                break;
```

```
    case Event.ACTION_EVENT:
      if ("Clear".equals (evt.arg))
        {
        l.delItems (0, l.countItems () - 1);
        }
      else if ("Save".equals (evt.arg))
        {
        fd = new FileDialog (this, "Save As", FileDialog.SAVE);
        fd.setFilenameFilter (this);
        fd.setFile ("DebugLog.trc");
        fd.show ();

        System.out.println ("*-------------------------------*");
        System.out.println ("Directory      = " + fd.getDirectory ());
        System.out.println ("FilenameFilter = "
          + fd.getFilenameFilter ());
        System.out.println ("Mode           = " + fd.getMode ()
          + "    (0=load, 1=save)");
        System.out.println ("Filename       = " + fd.getFile ());
        sFilename = fixFilename (fd.getFile ());
        System.out.println ("Fixed Filename = " + sFilename);

        try
          {
          fOut = new File (fd.getDirectory (), sFilename);
          fos = new FileOutputStream (fOut);
          dos = new DataOutputStream (fos);
          for (i = 0; i < l.countItems (); i++)
            {
            dos.writeBytes (l.getItem (i) + "\r\n");
            }
          dos.close ();
          }
        catch (Exception e)
          {
          System.out.println ("Exception writing the file: " + e);
          }
        }

      else if ("Exit".equals (evt.arg))
        {
        System.exit (0);
        }
      break;
    }

  return (super.handleEvent (evt));
  }
```

```
        String fixFilename (String s)     // Removes ".*.*" bug from filename.
          {
          int i;

          i = s.indexOf (".*.*");
          if (i > -1)
            {
            return (s.substring (0, i));
            }
          return (s);
          }

        }
```

The *DebugLog* class in the example is a frame that accepts calls to its *println*() method and displays the strings in a large List control. To use this class to help debug an applet, copy the *DebugLog.class* file into the applet's directory, instantiate it, and send *println*() messages to it.

This syntax is all that is needed.

```
DebugLog log;

log = new DebugLog ();

log.println ("Debug String");
```

Each call to *println*() adds an item to *DebugLog's* List component. When the maximum allowable number of items (*iMaxCount*) is reached, the oldest items are deleted. The *File* menu gives the user the option to *Clear* the list of all items or to *Save* the string items in a text file.

The *DebugLog* class was selected to *implement* the *FilenameFilter* interface. This interface has only one method, the accept() method. One will notice the accept() method instructs the caller that every file is acceptable for displaying in the FileDialog.

```
public boolean accept (File f, String s)
{
return (true);
}
```

Frame windows and their dependents windows provide a way to construct standalone graphical programs in the Java environment or programs that can also serve as applets. Their judicious use can greatly extend the range of application possibilities in the Java environment.

CHAPTER 13

Sound

Just as images are pixel samples of the actual picture, sound files are also digital samples of the actual sound.

PCM—How to Represent Sound as Data

It is quite a trick to translate the pulsating waves of air that we call *sound* into a lifeless stream of data. Several approaches have been attempted, but one approach has gained widespread acceptance—the *Pulse Code Modulated* technique.

In this technique, the continuous air waves are broken up into many tiny pieces of sound. Each piece represents the state of a sound in a single segment of time. Then each slice of sound is reduced to a code and stored in a file.

A sound file is a stream of codes that represent slices of sound.

The real trick is how the slice of sound, also known as a *sample* of sound, is reduced to a code. To understand this, it may be helpful to picture a stereo speaker for a moment. Picture a speaker that is outside of its enclosure and the large magnet and paper cone are exposed (see Figure 13–1). When that speaker is hooked up to a stereo system and it starts generating pulsating sound waves, one can quickly see how the waves are generated. The entire paper cone is moving back and forth—almost vibrating—in response to the speaker's electronic magnet. As the paper cone pushes on the air next to it, pulses of air eminate in all directions from the speaker.

While that speaker is playing, if time suddenly stood still, the cone would be deflected a certain distance from its starting position. Let's say at this moment it was deflected 5 mm. The number "5" could be stored as a number in a file.

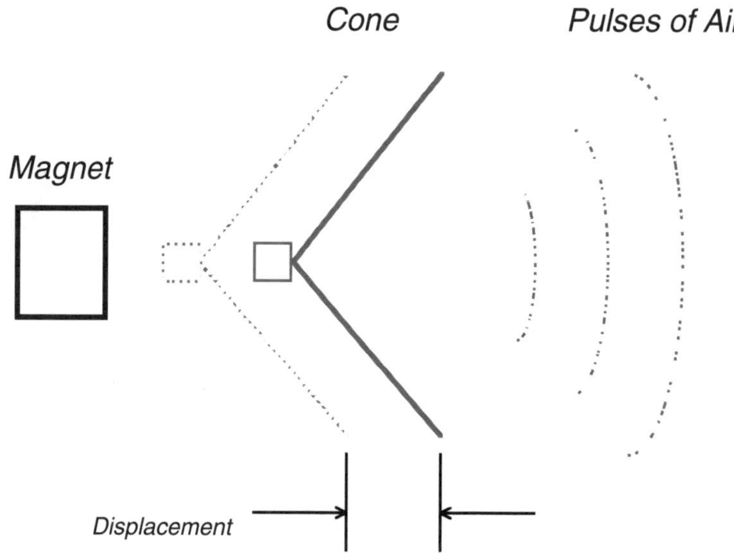

At any Moment, the Cone of a Speaker is Displaced from its Original Position

Figure 13–1

Let's say the speaker was allowed to play a little more, then stopped, and that its new deflection at this time slice was 13 mm from its starting position. That number can be stored right after the "5" in the file. Each time the speaker is stopped, a *sample* of its position is measured and stored in the file. After a number of *samples* have been taken and saved, the resulting file is known as a sound file that is full of Pulse Code Modulated (PCM) codes.

The *pulse* is how often the *sample* is taken. The more often it is taken, the more accurate the sound pattern. To record good quality sound, several thousand *samples* must be taken each second.

To play back the sound, each pulse code is read from the file and the speaker's cone is forcefully deflected by that amount from its original position. So the cone would be deflected 5 mm at the moment of the first *sample* and 13 mm at the moment of the second *sample*. If the playback is timed to occur at the same rate as the original *samples*, the speaker will generate approximately the same sound waves.

The actual codes that are stored in PCM data are not in millimeters. For 8-bit sound, the PCM codes vary from "0" to "255". The "0" code represents no deflection from the cone's original position. The "255" code represents the maximum deflection from the cone's original position.

AU—How to Format a Sound File for Java

Almost *all* sampled sound is stored as PCM data. But almost *all* sound files have a header on the front of the PCM data to explain how to interpret the data. The entire sound file is known by its header type. All WAV files have a WAV header. All AU files have an AU header, and so on.

The header is needed to identify how many samples of sound were taken each second and how many bits wide each sample is. In the absence of a standard format for the header, each vendor created their own: WAV (Microsoft), AU (Sun and NeXT), AIF (Apple), and VOX (Dialogic).

Until a clear standard emerges for sound files, Java has chosen to initially support only one sound file format—the AU format. There is much discussion about expanding Java's sound support and one would expect a number of enhancements over the course of time.

Until the enhancements are made, there is a simple way to convert *almost* any sound file to the AU format. Remember, that the actual data is PCM data and that the only difference in the files is the header of the data. One can use a simple sound editing utility to read in a WAV file, for example, and to save it back to disk as an AU file.

An especially capable shareware utility for doing this is called *Cool* and is available from:

Syntrillium Software Corporation
P.O. Box 60274
Phoenix, AZ 85082-0274
USA

Play()—How to Render a Sound File

Once the sound files have been converted to the AU format, Java provides some Applet methods to load and render the sound on machines that have a sound card. In Java version 1.0, there is no support in the *image* for capturing sound.

A sound file is represented in the Java image as an AudioClip. AudioClip is an interface in the *java.applet* package. Since it is not a class, one can not instantiate it directly. To instantiate it, call the Applet method *getAudioClip()*, passing an URL location and a string *resource* identification.

```
AudioClip audioDo1;

audioDo1 = getAudioClip (getCodeBase (), "audio/do1.au");
```

This example asks the applet to supply the current default URL and then identifies the *do1.au* sound file in the subdirectory *audio*. The object that is returned to the *audioDo1* variable is an AudioClip and represents the sound file within the *image*.

One can ask an AudioClip to *play*(), *loop*(), or *stop*(). The *loop*() method causes the sound to play over and over again.

In the example below, eight sound files are loaded in the applet's *init*() method. As the users press one of the buttons on the panel (see Figure 13–2), a corresponding sound is asked to *play*().

Each sound file is the naturally occurring chord for each tone of a major scale. The chord is played as an arpeggio on a classical guitar.

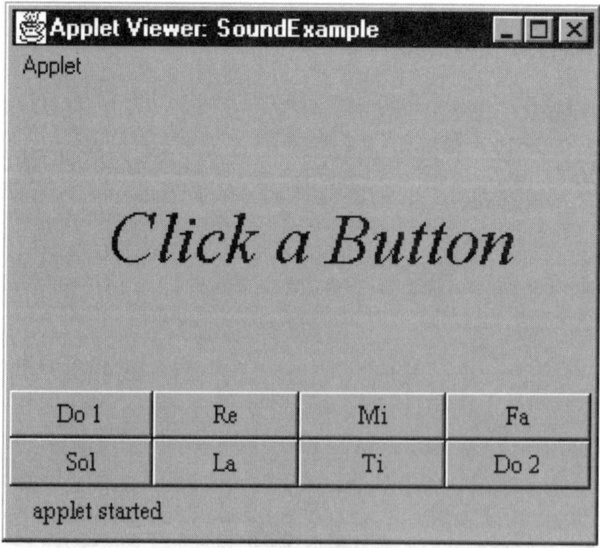

Figure 13–2

```
import java.applet.*;
import java.awt.*;

  public class SoundExample extends Applet
    {
    Label lCenterLabel;
    AudioClip
      audioDo1,
      audioRe,
      audioMi,
      audioFa,
      audioSol,
      audioLa,
      audioTi,
      audioDo2;

    public void init()
      {
      Panel p;

      setLayout (new BorderLayout (0, 0));

      lCenterLabel = new Label ("Click a Button", Label.CENTER);
      lCenterLabel.setFont (new Font ("TimesRoman", Font.ITALIC, 36));
      add ("Center", lCenterLabel);

      p = new Panel ();
      p.setLayout (new GridLayout (2, 4, 0, 0));
      p.add (new Button ("Do 1"));
      p.add (new Button ("Re"));
      p.add (new Button ("Mi"));
      p.add (new Button ("Fa"));
      p.add (new Button ("Sol"));
      p.add (new Button ("La"));
      p.add (new Button ("Ti"));
      p.add (new Button ("Do 2"));
      add ("South", p);

      showStatus ("Fetching Sounds");
      audioDo1 = getAudioClip (getCodeBase (), "audio/do1.au");
      audioRe  = getAudioClip (getCodeBase (), "audio/re.au");
      audioMi  = getAudioClip (getCodeBase (), "audio/mi.au");
      audioFa  = getAudioClip (getCodeBase (), "audio/fa.au");
      audioSol = getAudioClip (getCodeBase (), "audio/sol.au");
      audioLa  = getAudioClip (getCodeBase (), "audio/la.au");
```

```
   audioTi  = getAudioClip (getCodeBase (), "audio/ti.au");
   audioDo2 = getAudioClip (getCodeBase (), "audio/do2.au");
   }


public boolean handleEvent (Event evt)
   {
   String s;

   if (evt.id == Event.ACTION_EVENT)
     {
     s = (String) evt.arg.toString ();

     lCenterLabel.setText (s);

     if      ("Do 1".equals (s)) audioDo1.play ();
     else if (  "Re".equals (s)) audioRe.play ();
     else if (  "Mi".equals (s)) audioMi.play ();
     else if (  "Fa".equals (s)) audioFa.play ();
     else if ( "Sol".equals (s)) audioSol.play ();
     else if (  "La".equals (s)) audioLa.play ();
     else if (  "Ti".equals (s)) audioTi.play ();
     else if ("Do 2".equals (s)) audioDo2.play ();
     }

   return (super.handleEvent (evt));
   }
}
```

```
<HTML>
<HEAD>
<TITLE> SoundExample </TITLE>
</HEAD>
<BODY>
SoundExample
<HR>
<APPLET CODE="SoundExample" WIDTH=300 HEIGHT=200>
</APPLET>
<HR>
</BODY>
</HTML>
```

CHAPTER 14

File I/O

Java provides two approaches for accessing data in files. The first uses classes that are specific to a file system. The second uses classes that are generalized to provide access to data from a number of sequential sources.

The approach that is the most familiar is to use the File and RandomAccessFile classes to provide access to data in a file system.

File—Name and Location

The File class represents the name of a file. It does not provide any access to the data of a file. Rather, it identifies a node in a directory and provides services to maintain the directory.

From the command line, when a person asks for the names of all the files in a directory, each line of the resulting report would be considered a Java File—a read-only file, a subdirectory, a superdirectory, the current directory, or an executable file.

To instantiate a File object, one needs to identify a node in a directory. The constructor can accept a single path string, a directory with a filename, or a File object with a filename. In the latter case, the File object must represent the directory in which the file is located.

```
File f;

f = new File ("dirpath");

f = new File ("dirpath", "filename");

f = new File (FileObject, "filename");
```

The File class is the class to use when searching a file system directory tree.

In the example below, the *walkTree()* method instantiates a File object with the path to a directory. Then it calls the *processNode()* method to process that directory.

The *processNode()* method calls the file's *isDirectory()* method to see if the File object represents a directory. If it does not represent a directory, the *length()* method is sent to accumulate the total file sizes and the name of the file is written to the standard output device.

If it does represent a directory, the file's *list()* method is called to get a list of all the filenames in the directory. Then a File object is created for each filename from the File object that represents the current directory and the name of the file. This File object is sent recursively to the *processNode()* method for processing.

```
import java.io.*;

    class FileExample
      {
      String sBasePath;
      long lBasePathSize;


      FileExample (String s)
        {
        sBasePath = s;
        lBasePathSize = 0;
        }


      void walkTree ()
        {
        File f;

        f = new File (sBasePath);
        processNode (f);
```

```
    System.out.println ("\n    Dir Node " + sBasePath + " represents "
      + lBasePathSize + " bytes\n");
    }


  void processNode (File fIn)
    {
    File f;
    String[] as;
    int i;

    if (fIn.isDirectory ())                      // If it is a directory..
      {
      as = fIn.list ();                          // ..Get its file names

      for (i = 0; i < as.length; i++)
        {                                        // ....For every file name
        f = new File (fIn, as[i]);               // ......Create a file object
        processNode (f)                          // ........and process it.
        }

      System.out.println ("    Finished Dir: " + fIn.getPath ());
      return;
      }

    lBasePathSize += fIn.length ();
    System.out.println (fIn.getPath ());
    }


  public static void main (String[] args)
    {
    FileExample x;

    if (args.length < 1)
      {
      System.out.println ("Format: java FileExample BasePath");
      System.exit (1);
      }

    x = new FileExample (args[0]);
    x.walkTree ();
    }
  }
```

```
1.0 C:\JumpStrt\examples\FileExample>java FileExample \JumpStrt\examples
        .
        .
        .
\JumpStrt\examples\put.bat
\JumpStrt\examples\InstanceOf\InstanceOf.java
\JumpStrt\examples\InstanceOf\name.bat
\JumpStrt\examples\InstanceOf\x.bat
\JumpStrt\examples\InstanceOf\c.bat
\JumpStrt\examples\InstanceOf\cdebug.bat
\JumpStrt\examples\InstanceOf\r.bat
\JumpStrt\examples\InstanceOf\d.bat
\JumpStrt\examples\InstanceOf\InstanceOf.class
    Finished Dir: \JumpStrt\examples\InstanceOf
\JumpStrt\examples\FileExample\FileExample.java
\JumpStrt\examples\FileExample\name.bat
\JumpStrt\examples\FileExample\x.bat
\JumpStrt\examples\FileExample\c.bat
\JumpStrt\examples\FileExample\cdebug.bat
\JumpStrt\examples\FileExample\r.bat
\JumpStrt\examples\FileExample\d.bat
\JumpStrt\examples\FileExample\FileExample.class
    Finished Dir: \JumpStrt\examples\FileExample
    Finished Dir: \JumpStrt\examples

    Dir Node \JumpStrt\examples represents 997675 bytes
```

The File class also provides *delete()* to erase the file, *mkDir()* to create a subdirectory, *getParent()* to get a path to the parent directory, and *lastModified()* to get the date the file was last updated.

Whenever data from the File system is accessed, the most precise method of identifying the target file is to instantiate a File object.

RandomAccessFile—Direct File System Access

The *RandomAccessFile* class provides methods that directly access the data in a particular file. This is not a generalized I/O class. It can only be used with file system data.

A File object is used to instantiate a RandomAccessFile. The second parameter is a string that indicates whether the file should be open for reading *"r"*, writing *"w"*, or for both *"rw"*.

Methods are sent to the *RandomAccessFile* object to retrieve or store data in the file.

```
File f;
RandomAccessFile raf;
String s;

f = new File ("RandomAccessFileExample.java");
raf = new RandomAccessFile (f, "r");
s = raf.readLine ();
```

When the object is created, the file pointer is at offset 0 in the file. The pointer can be positioned using the *skipBytes()* or *seek()* methods. There are read and write methods for each simple data type: *readBoolean(), readByte(), readChar(), readDouble(), readFloat(), readInt(),* and *read()* for byte arrays. There is also a method to read character data until encountering an end of line character, *readLine().*

The *source* file for the example below is opened for reading and the first three lines are read and printed on the standard output device. Then the *class* file is opened for reading and selected codes are read and printed. The *skipBytes()* and *seek()* methods are used to position the file pointer to the correct spot before calling the read method. Note: the constant pool count in the class file is one more that the number of items in the constant pool.

```
import java.io.*;

    class RandomAccessFileExample
      {
      public static void main (String args[])
        {
        File f;
        RandomAccessFile raf;
        int iMagicNumber;
        short sVersion;
        short sPoolItemCount;
        String s;

        try
          {
          f = new File ("RandomAccessFileExample.java");
          raf = new RandomAccessFile (f, "r");
```

```
      s = raf.readLine ();
      System.out.println ("\nSource Line 1 -->" + s);
      s = raf.readLine ();
      System.out.println ("Source Line 2 -->" + s);
      s = raf.readLine ();
      System.out.println ("Source Line 3 -->" + s);

      raf.close ();


      f = new File ("RandomAccessFileExample.class");
      raf = new RandomAccessFile (f, "r");

      iMagicNumber = raf.readInt ();
      System.out.println ("\nThe Java class magic number is "
        + iMagicNumber);

      raf.skipBytes (2);
      sVersion = raf.readShort ();
      System.out.println ("\nThe Java class version number is "
        + sVersion);

      raf.seek (8);
      sPoolItemCount = raf.readShort ();
      System.out.println ("\nThe Java class constant pool contains "
        + (sPoolItemCount - 1) + " items\n");

      raf.close ();
      }

    catch (Exception e)
      {
      System.out.println ("Exception: " + e);
      }
    }
  }
```

```
1.0 C:\JumpStrt\examples\RandomAccessFileExample>java RandomAccessFile
  Example

Source Line 1 --->import java.io.*;
Source Line 2 --->
Source Line 3 --->    class RandomAccessFileExample

The Java class magic number is -889275714

The Java class version number is 45

The Java class constant pool contains 102 items
```

Stream—Sequential Access

Although the *RandomAccessFile* class gives access to file data, the power of Java I/O is not tapped until one comes to terms with the Java Stream classes. These are generalized classes that give sequential access to data from a wide variety of sources.

When one figures out how to use a stream, they know how to access files and how to interact with TCP/IP sockets and how to parse through memory buffers. Stream syntax is simple and universal. Streams are used throughout the Java system and can provide a familiar technique for accessing data sequentially.

From an object-oriented perspective, a *stream* is an object that contains a buffer and a position. The buffer could be entirely present in the Stream object in the form of an array of bytes, or the stream might be fetching the bytes one by one in response to a read request. In either case, the stream represents the entire block of data.

A stream provides access to its data sequentially. Whenever a read method is called, the data at the current position is returned to the caller and the current position is incremented to point to the next piece of data. Most streams maintain a long variable that holds the offset of the current position in the stream.

ByteArrayInputStream, ByteArrayOutputStream and StringBufferInputStream

These classes implement the purest form of a stream. They hold their entire buffer in a memory variable and provide access to it sequentially. In this case, the stream *represents* the buffer and the Stream *contains* the buffer.

One might wonder why a string or an array of bytes should be placed into one of these classes. Why not create loops that directly access each element of the array?

Sometimes loops are the best way to process an array. But most of the time, a stream is the preferred approach because it provides a simple interface that invokes high performance routines.

To append one array onto the end of another array, one would have to create a third array that was big enough to hold both arrays. Then it would loop through and copy the data from the first array, then copy the data from the second array to the third array.

Using the ByteArrayOutputStream, one simply writes each array to the stream. Then when all the data has been added, the stream is converted back to an array by sending the *toByteArray()* method to it. This method does not copy data. It just returns the internal array buffer to the caller.

Sometimes the need arises to convert a string to an array so it can be used in a block I/O operation. The *StringBufferInputStream* class provides a *read()* method that will copy a certain number of bytes from the stream's internal buffer to an identified array variable.

These two techniques are illustrated in the example below. A StringBufferInputStream is the input object and a ByteArrayOutputStream is the output object. The input stream is instantiated with a string for its data buffer. In the processing loop, sections of the string are converted to arrays of bytes and each array is written to a ByteArrayOutputStream which appends the data to its internal buffer. After each write operation, the output stream is converted to an array by sending the *toByteArray()* method and the array is printed on the standard output device. This displays the current state of the buffer in the output stream.

One will notice the parameters that are also passed to the read and write methods. The first number identifies the offset within the array at which to begin processing. The second number identifies the number of bytes to process.

```
import java.io.*;

    class InMemoryStreamExample
      {
      public static void main (String args[])
        {
        StringBufferInputStream sbis;
        ByteArrayOutputStream baos;
        byte[] abOutput;
        byte[] ab;
        int iReadLength;
        String s;
```

```
        try
          {
          ab = new byte[3];
          s = "abcdefghijklmnopqrstuvwxyz";
          sbis = new StringBufferInputStream (s);
          baos = new ByteArrayOutputStream ();

          while ((iReadLength = sbis.read (ab, 0, 3)) != -1)
            {
            baos.write (ab, 0, iReadLength);

            abOutput = baos.toByteArray ();
            s = new String (abOutput, 0);
            System.out.println ("The output array is -->" + s + "<--");
            }
          }

        catch (Exception e)
          {
          System.out.println ("Exception: " + e);
          }
        }
      }
```

```
1.0 C:\JumpStrt\examples\InMemoryStreamExample>java InMemoryStreamExample
The output array is -->abc<--
The output array is -->abcdef<--
The output array is -->abcdefghi<--
The output array is -->abcdefghijkl<--
The output array is -->abcdefghijklmno<--
The output array is -->abcdefghijklmnopqr<--
The output array is -->abcdefghijklmnopqrstu<--
The output array is -->abcdefghijklmnopqrstuvwx<--
The output array is -->abcdefghijklmnopqrstuvwxyz<--
```

FileInputStream and FileOutputStream

These classes do not hold their entire data buffer in memory. They hold a File object that points to their data and they provide the same kind of sequential access to file data that the ByteArrayStreams provide to array data.

Because this kind of stream is buffering the data, it is hard to tell when data written to a FileOutputStream is actually written to the file system. The *flush()*

method can be sent to any output stream and it makes sure to flush any data from its internal buffers.

To instantiate a FileStream, one passes a File object rather than a complete data buffer to the constructor. The File object represents the name and location of a block of data that has been stored in the file system.

The FileInputStream uses that information to provide sequential read access to this block of data. The FileOutputStream provides sequential write or append access to the file. As the Stream methods *read()* and *write()* are called, the FileStreams update their position variables to point to the next available position in the stream.

The example below reads an array of bytes from the FileInputStream and writes it to the FileOutputStream until the read length indicates that the end of input has been reached (-1).

```
import java.io.*;

    class FileInputStreamExample
      {
      public static void main (String args[])
        {
        File fIn;
        File fOut;
        FileInputStream fis;
        FileOutputStream fos;
        int iNumBytesRead;
        byte[] ab;

        try
          {
          fIn = new File ("FileInputStreamExample.java");
          fis = new FileInputStream (fIn);
          fOut = new File ("FileInputStreamExample.java.copy");
          fos = new FileOutputStream (fOut);

          ab = new byte[2048];

          while ((iNumBytesRead = fis.read (ab)) != -1)
            {
            fos.write (ab, 0, iNumBytesRead);
            }
```

```
            fis.close ();
            fos.close ();
            }

          catch (Exception e)
            {
            System.out.println ("Exception: " + e);
            }

          System.out.println ("FileInputStreamExample.java has been copied to "
            + "FileInputStreamExample.java.copy");
          }
        }
```

```
1.0 C:\JumpStrt\examples\FileInputStreamExample>java FileInputStreamExample
FileInputStreamExample.java has been copied to
FileInputStreamExample.java.copy
```

SequenceInputStream

This class provides a clever way to concatenate input streams so that they appear to be one large stream of data. The class is not restricted to FileStreams. It can be used with any kind of stream.

To construct a SequenceInputStream, one passes an enumeration of streams to the constructor. The easiest way to create an enumeration is to create a Vector object, add streams to the vector, then ask for the vector's elements. The *elements()* method returns an enumeration.

```
Vector v;
SequenceInputStream sis;

sis = new SequenceInputStream (v.elements ());
```

When a *read()* method is sent to the SequenceInputStream, the data from the first stream in the enumeration is returned to the caller. As the data in the first stream is exhausted, the SequenceInputStream transparently selects the next stream and continues to service *read()* calls. To the calling programs, the many input streams appear to be one large concatenated stream.

The example below creates three FileInputStreams; each point to the example's own source code file. Each of the streams are added to a vector. Then a SequenceInputStream is created with an enumeration from the vector. The arrays are read from the SequenceInputStream and written to the standard output device.

When this program runs, the source below is written to the standard output device three consecutive times.

```
import java.io.*;
import java.util.*;

    class SequenceInputStreamExample
      {
      public static void main (String args[])
        {
        File fIn;
        Vector v;
        FileInputStream fis;
        SequenceInputStream sis;
        int iNumBytesRead;
        byte[] ab;

        ab = new byte[2048];
        v = new Vector ();

        try
          {
          fIn = new File ("SequenceInputStreamExample.java");
          fis = new FileInputStream (fIn);
          v.addElement (fis);

          fIn = new File ("SequenceInputStreamExample.java");
          fis = new FileInputStream (fIn);
          v.addElement (fis);

          fIn = new File ("SequenceInputStreamExample.java");
          fis = new FileInputStream (fIn);
          v.addElement (fis);

          sis = new SequenceInputStream (v.elements ());

          while ((iNumBytesRead = sis.read (ab)) != -1)
            {
            System.out.write (ab, 0, iNumBytesRead);
            }
```

```
            sis.close ();
            }

         catch (Exception e)
            {
            System.out.println ("Exception: " + e);
            }
         }
      }
```

FilterStream—Smart Sequential Access

When reading data sequentially, it is often handy to access data in intelligent units that can be placed directly into memory variables. The FilterStreams implement a number of methods that allow data to be read or written as units of formatted data.

DataInputStream and DataOutputStream

These streams allow the program to read or write formatted data variables directly from the stream. They include read and write methods for *readBoolean()*, *readByte()*, *readChar()*, *readDouble()*, *readFloat()*, *readInt()*, *read()* for byte arrays, and *readLine()* for lines of text.

This parsing service is particularly useful when performing high performance buffered I/O. The data from these services is normally returned to the program as an array of bytes. It can be difficult to identify how to process multiple byte data variables that are returned to the program as an array of single byte variables.

The following example illustrates three different ways to use the DataStreams. First, some primitive data is written to a DataOutputStream. The stream was created by first instantiating a file, then using the file to instantiate a FileOutputStream, then using the stream to instantiate the DataOutputStream. When data is written to this stream, it ends up being added to the associated file.

Then a similar process is used to open a DataInputStream and read the data back into the primitive data variables.

The next section of the example reads the data as an array of bytes. This array is placed in a ByteArrayInputStream and the stream is placed in a DataInputStream. Notice that when read methods are sent to the DataInputStream, the data is actually being read from the array of bytes. This is the way formatted data can be extracted from a byte array.

The last section of the example shows how to read lines of textual data from a stream. The stream could have been connected to a socket or to a byte array. In this case, it is connected to a FileInputStream that is pointing to the source file. Each *readLine()* method that is sent to the DataInputStream returns a string that holds one text line from the file. The string includes the end-of-line delimiter.

```
import java.io.*;

    class DataInputStreamExample
      {
      public static void main (String args[])
        {
        File fIn;
        File fOut;
        FileInputStream fis;
        DataInputStream dis;
        ByteArrayInputStream bais;
        FileOutputStream fos;
        DataOutputStream dos;
        int iNumBytesRead;
        byte[] ab;
        int i;
        boolean b;
        double d;
        String s;

        ab = new byte[2048];
        try
          {


/*        Create a file that contains primitive data types.
          ================================================   */

          fOut = new File ("DataInoutStreamExample.data");
          fos = new FileOutputStream (fOut);
          dos = new DataOutputStream (fos);

          i = 24;
          dos.writeInt (i);
          b = true;
          dos.writeBoolean (b);
          d = 3.1416;
          dos.writeDouble (d);

          dos.close ();
```

```
/*          Read the file using a DataInputStream.
            ======================================  */

            fIn = new File ("DataInoutStreamExample.data");
            fis = new FileInputStream (fIn);
            dis = new DataInputStream (fis);

            i = dis.readInt ();
            b = dis.readBoolean ();
            d = dis.readDouble ();

            System.out.println ("Data from file:  i = " + i
              + ",  b = " + b + ",  d = " + d);
            dis.close ();


/*          Read the file as an array of bytes and use a DataInputStream
            to step through the array.
            ============================================================  */

            fIn = new File ("DataInoutStreamExample.data");
            fis = new FileInputStream (fIn);
            iNumBytesRead = fis.read (ab);

            bais = new ByteArrayInputStream (ab, 0, iNumBytesRead);
            dis = new DataInputStream (bais);

            i = dis.readInt ();
            b = dis.readBoolean ();
            d = dis.readDouble ();

            System.out.println ("Data from array: i = " + i
              + ",  b = " + b + ",  d = " + d);
            dis.close ();


/*          Read this source file using a DataInputStream.
            ==============================================  */

            fIn = new File ("DataInputStreamExample.java");
            fis = new FileInputStream (fIn);
            dis = new DataInputStream (fis);

            while ((s = dis.readLine ()) != null)
              {
              System.out.println (s);
              }
```

```
         dis.close ();
         }

      catch (Exception e)
         {
         System.out.println ("Exception: " + e);
         }
      }
   }
```

```
1.0 C:\JumpStrt\examples\DataInputStreamExample>java DataInputStreamExample
Data from file:  i = 24,  b = true,  d = 3.1416
Data from array: i = 24,  b = true,  d = 3.1416
import java.io.*;

    class DataInputStreamExample
      {
      public static void main (String args[])
         {
         File fIn;
           .
           .
           .
```

PrintStream

This class provides intelligent formatting for the writing of textual data. The *System.out* object is an instance of this class and the *print()* and *println()* methods are implemented in this class. Any output stream can be turned into a PrintStream by passing it to the *PrintStream* constructor.

In the following code fragment, the string *"A Text Line"* is written to the file.

```
File fOut;
FileOutputStream fos;
PrintStream ps;

fOut = new File ("DataInoutStreamExample.data");
fos = new FileOutputStream (fOut);
ps = new PrintStream (fos);
ps.println ("A Text Line");
ps.close ();
```

LineNumberInputStream

This is a very small class that works much like a FileInputStream. The only difference is that it counts end-of-line delimiters as they are encountered. Then at any point during processing, the *getLineNumber()* method can be sent to the LineNumberInputStream to get the count of the current line.

There is no behavior for reading by lines in this class. To read by lines and keep track of the line number, one would need to chain input streams in the following manner:

```
File fIn;
FileInputStream fis;
LineNumberInputStream lnis;
DataInputStream dis;
String s;

fIn = new File ("DataInputStreamExample.java");
fis = new FileInputStream (fIn);
lnis = new LineNumberInputStream (fis);
dis = new DataInputStream (lnis);

while ((s = dis.readLine ()) != null)
   {
   System.out.println (lnis.getLineNumber () + ": " + s);
   }

dis.close ();
```

This kind of chaining of streams is what makes the Java streams so flexible and so powerful. Although there are four objects involved, there is only one data source. Each stream simply attaches to the data source and makes its unique services available while accessing the data.

The *readLine()* method is sent to the *DataInputStream* object to read the data one line at a time. The *getLineNumber()* method is sent to the *LineNumberInputStream* object to identify how many lines have been read.

BufferedInputStream and BufferedOutputStream

These are high performance streams that have the same interface as the FileStreams. They move data to and from their destination in blocks. The size of the block can be passed to the constructor.

With so much data present in buffers, it is important to send the *flush()* method whenever the application requires the data to reach its destination. With careful use, this stream can improve the performance of many kinds of algorithms.

```
File fIn;
FileInputStream fis;
BufferedInputStream bis;

fIn = new File ("DataInputStreamExample.java");
fis = new FileInputStream (fIn);
bis = new BufferedInputStream (fis, 16384);
```

PushbackInputStream

This is a very small class that gives the caller the ability to *unread()* a single byte. The *unread()* method does more than decrement the stream location by one position. It stages the parameter that is passed to *unread()* as the next byte that the stream will read.

It only allows the stream to be pushed back one byte. But with its ability to replace the byte that was read with another byte, this stream works like a very shallow stack.

PipedInputStream and PipedOutputStream

These classes implement piped I/O between Java threads. One thread writes data to a PipedOutputStream and another thread reads data from a PipedInputStream.

When creating the stream objects, the output stream must be connected to the input stream. This can be done by passing one of the streams to the constructor of the other as is illustrated in the following example. One can also connect the streams by sending the *connect()* method to one of the streams and passing the other stream as a parameter to the method.

In the example below, a PipedInputStream is accessed through a DataInputStream from the main thread. A PipedOutputStream is created and connected to the PipedInputStream. When a new thread is created, the PipedOuputStream is passed as a parameter.

So the launched thread has the *output* stream and the main thread has the *input* stream. When the launched thread writes to the output stream, the main thread receives the data from its input stream and writes it to the standard output device.

```
import java.io.*;

    class PipedInputStreamExample
      {
      public static void main (String args[])
        {
        PipedInputStream pis;
        PipedOutputStream pos;
        DataInputStream dis;
        MyThread th;
        String s;

        try
          {
          pis = new PipedInputStream ();          // Stays in this thread
          dis = new DataInputStream (pis);        // Allows line access
          pos = new PipedOutputStream (pis);      // Goes to launched thread

          th = new MyThread (pos);
          th.start ();

          try
            {
            while ((s = dis.readLine ()) != null)
              {
              System.out.println ("Main Thread Received: " + s);
              }
            }

          catch (Exception e)
            {
            System.out.println ("The launched thread just stopped. . .");
            }
          }
```

```
      catch (Exception e)
        {
        System.out.println ("Error occured: " + e);
        }
      }
    }


  class MyThread extends Thread
    {
    PipedOutputStream pos;

    MyThread (PipedOutputStream posIn)
      {
      pos = posIn;
      }

    public void run ()
      {
      int i;
      PrintStream ps;

      ps = new PrintStream (pos);

      for (i = 0; i < 100; i++)
        {
        ps.println ("The count is " + i);
        }
      }
    }
```

```
1.0 C:\JumpStrt\examples\PipedInputStreamExample>java PipedInputStream
  Example
Main Thread Received: The count is 0
Main Thread Received: The count is 1
      .
      .
      .

Main Thread Received: The count is 95
Main Thread Received: The count is 96
Main Thread Received: The count is 97
Main Thread Received: The count is 98
Main Thread Received: The count is 99
The launched thread just stopped. . .
```

When performing File I/O, one should use the Stream classes as much as possible. The stream concept may seem awkward at first. But the skill that one gains in using streams is multiplied by the many places in which Java makes streams available.

CHAPTER 15

Sockets and a Simple Server

Client/Server applications rely on the ability of programs to communicate naturally and easily.

The rise of the Internet has brought a flexible new mechanism for communicating between client and server programs. This technique has been employed by a wide range of global applications and has been stress-tested by millions of users. In the history of computing, no other communication technique has received as much field testing.

This technique centers around the use of a *socket* in the TCP/IP protocol suite. Since many people are unfamiliar with the TCP/IP protocol suite, it is described in the appendix chapter *Introduction to the World Wide Web.*

Many programmers have no experience with communications. Java is a great place to gain that experience. The Java designers have crafted classes that make it remarkably easy to use a socket.

Probably the biggest problem with *sockets* is the name. It puts people off. The name does not suggest very much about what it is or what it does.

What is a Socket?

From an application program's point of view, a *socket* is like a file handle. It represents the source and destination of data. It provides services to read and write data. It knows how to store data and how to fetch data.

But instead of the destination of the data being a local file system, the destination is a program on another computer. Instead of the data being converted to magnetic spots on a disk, the data is processed. Instead of the data being reconstructed from stored bit patterns, it is generated on-the-fly by the other program.

A socket is a file handle to another program's data.

The analogy with the file handle continues. A file handle can be opened and closed. A socket can be opened and closed. When a file handle is opened, it is given the path of the file to open. When a socket is opened, it is given the machine and program identification so a connection can be made. Read and write services are available for files and for sockets.

So, a socket is the local interface to a remote program which is serving as the source and destination for data.

This is the perspective from one side of the conversation. A program opens a local socket to represent a remote program and to exchange data with it.

From the other side of the conversation, the remote program opens up its own socket to represent the local program and to exchange data with *it*. All conversations involve two programs and two sockets (see Figure 15–1). Each socket represents the other program and moves data to it and from it.

Each socket gives its program the illusion that it is interacting directly with the remote program. To get the data to the other program, the socket passes it to the TCP/IP stack and it flows across the network to the other computer according the rules of Internet routing. When it reaches the other computer, it passes up through the TCP/IP stack and becomes the return value for a pending *read*() request.

The sockets, which connect two programs, provide the same set of services and functions for each program. There is a slightly different task that a socket must perform to begin a conversation.

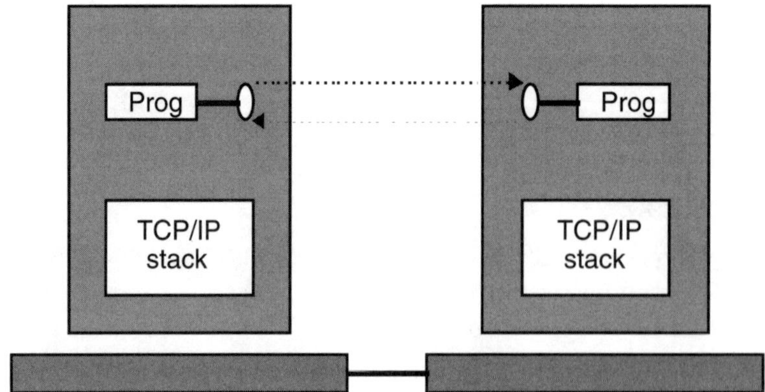

Figure 15–1 A conversation involves two programs and two sockets.

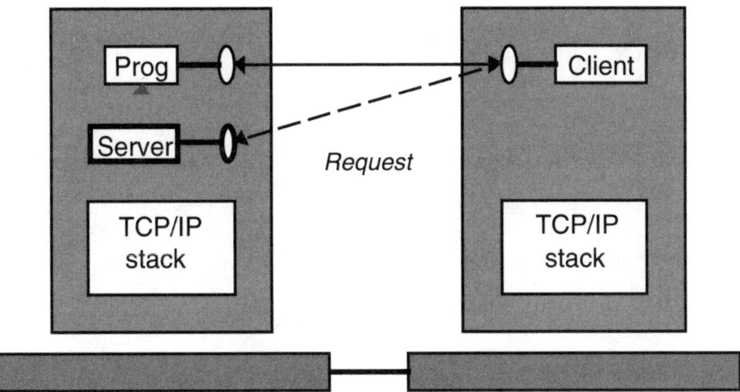

Figure 15–2 The ServerSocket waits for a new request, then launches a new thread with a new socket to carry on the conversation.

To begin a conversation, one program must be running and must have opened a socket to *listen* for incoming requests for a conversation. This program is known as the *server*, because it is waiting to serve a request.

When an incoming request arrives, it is conceivable that the program could immediately engage in a conversation with the requester. But if it did that, it would not be available to service additional requests that may arrive while it is conversing with the first request.

So, the architecture says that a server socket should create a new socket and a new thread to process the incoming request (see Figure 15–2). This delegation scheme keeps the server free to process new requests, even though the old requests have not been fully satisfied.

In Java, the class that waits for new requests is called the *ServerSocket* class and the class that is used on both sides of an existing conversation is called the Socket class. Both classes are in the *java.net* package.

ServerSocket—The Starting Point of a Conversation

Sometimes the operation of a server program can seem mysterious. It is really quite straightforward.

There are three programs involved in a conversation—one that waits for new connections (the *server* program), one that requests a connection (the *client* program), and one that is launched to service the new connection (the *server extension* program).

When the server program begins, it should create a *ServerSocket* object and ask it to wait for incoming connection requests.

```
Socket sock;
ServerSocket ssock;

ssock = new ServerSocket (8080);

sock = ssock.accept ();
```

The number that is passed to the *ServerSocket*() constructor is called the *port* number. This is a way to connect an incoming request with a server. Both the client and the server agree (ahead of time) to use a particular number. Then when the client uses the *port* number to make a connection request, it will reach the desired ServerSocket and server program.

There are certain "well understood" *port* numbers that identify popular Internet applications like ftp (port 21), telnet (port 23), mail (port 25), and Web (port 80). When picking a number for a new application, choose a number well above 1000. Most of the numbers from 1 to 1000 have been associated with "well understood" applications.

When a program creates a *ServerSocket* object, Java opens it. To begin listening for incoming requests, one calls the ServerSocket's *accept*() method.

This method *blocks* or halts any further processing in the thread until a connection is received. When a request is received, the ServerSocket returns a new regular socket to the server program. This regular socket can be used to read and write data to the client program.

The server program delegates the actual conversation to another thread. It launches the new thread with the new socket and allows that thread to converse with the client. Since the server thread has been freed up, it goes back to listening for new connection requests. When the new thread has concluded the conversation, it normally stops and deallocates itself.

In the example below, the new thread that the server launches is called a ServerExtension.

```
import java.net.*;
import java.io.*;

    class SimpleServer
      {
      public static void main (String argv[])
        {
        Socket sock;
        ServerSocket ssock;
        Thread thServx;
        ServerExtension servx;

        System.out.println ("Serv: Initializing to port 8080");

        try
          {
          ssock = new ServerSocket (8080);

          while (true)
            {
            System.out.println ("Serv: Waiting for a connection...");
            sock = ssock.accept ();
            System.out.println ("Serv: Received a connection");

            servx = new ServerExtension (sock);
            thServx = new Thread (servx);
            thServx.start ();
            }
          }
        catch (Exception e)
          {
          System.err.println ("Serv: Exception in main loop: " + e);
          }
        }
      }


    class ServerExtension implements Runnable
      {
      private Socket sock;
      private InputStream isIn;
      private PrintStream psOut;
```

```
    public ServerExtension (Socket s)
      {
      sock = s;
      }

    public void run ()
      {
      System.out.println ("*-----------------------------------*");
      System.out.println ("SrvX: Connected to: "
        + sock.getInetAddress () + ":" + sock.getPort ());

      try
        {
        isIn = sock.getInputStream ();
        psOut = new PrintStream (sock.getOutputStream ());
        psOut.print ("This is a msg from the server's connection");
        sock.close ();
        }
      catch (Exception e)
        {
        System.err.println ("SrvX: Exception sending a string to the "
          + "client: " + e);
        }

      System.out.println ("SrvX: Disconnecting: "
        + sock.getInetAddress () + ":" + sock.getPort ());
      System.out.println ("*-----------------------------------*");
      }
    }
```

Notice the *while*() loop that waits for new connections and dispatches *ServerExtension* threads to handle them. The new socket is passed to the new program when the *ServerExtension* object is created.

```
while (true)
  {
  sock = ssock.accept ();                  // Wait for new connection

  servx = new ServerExtension (sock);    // Dispatch thread to handle it
  thServx = new Thread (servx);
  thServx.start ();
  }
```

When the thread is created, it is passed to the *ServerExtension* object as a parameter. This establishes internal linkage between the two objects.

The thread's *start*() method is written so that it behaves differently if this internal linkage exists. When this linkage exists, the default behavior is for the *start*() method to call the ServerExtension's *run*() method to carry out the run behavior. This causes the *run*() method in the *ServerExtension* object to be the code that is executed in the new thread.

Once the *run*() method begins execution, the conversation has begun. The special role of the ServerSocket is out of the picture. There are only two programs involved now—the client and the server extension. Each of them has normal *sockets* that represent the other as a dynamic network resource. Data can be written to or read from either socket.

Now it is time to look at how a normal conversation proceeds.

Sockets—The End Points of a Conversation

A Java socket represents a remote network resource and provides services to read or write data to that resource.

A socket can be instantiated in two ways. A ServerSocket can instantiate a socket when it receives a new connection request or the socket can be created directly. When a socket is created directly, the desired remote resource is identified by machine name and port number.

```
Socket sock;

sock = new Socket ("localhost", 8080);
```

This creates a new socket and dispatches a request for connection to the machine known as *"localhost"*. The machine name is a string that could either be a domain name like *"java.sun.com"*, a dotted decimal string like *"199.23.185.119"*, or the string *"localhost"*.

The latter option indicates that the destination machine is the same as the originating machine. This gives a way of testing the client and the server programs on the same machine.

When Java sends the connection request, it includes the port number in the request. This number identifies the server program from which service is requested, because it corresponds to the port number that the server program used to instantiate its ServerSocket.

The process of creating a socket directly sends a connection request to the server. When the server responds, the new Socket object is constructed and returned to the caller.

Once the socket is created, Java provides services to read and write to the socket. Since a socket is like a file handle, Java's socket services follow an analogy with its File I/O services. The services are all based on stream classes.

To get the Stream objects that allow data to be moved to and from the remote program, one sends *getInputStream*() and *getOutputStream*() to the Socket object. The following code fragment instantiates a new socket, then fetches its InputStream and OutputStream.

```
Socket sock;
InputStream isIn;
OutputStream osOut;
PrintStream psOut;

sock = new Socket ("localhost", 8080);

isIn = sock.getInputStream ();
osOut = sock.getOutputStream ();

psOut = new PrintStream (osOut);
```

If the methods that are available in the *OutputStream* class do not suit one's needs, the OutputStream can be used to instantiate a PrintStream that provides several more services to facilitate textual processing.

To read data from a socket, one sends the *read*() method to the socket's input stream. In the code fragment below, the array of bytes *abIn* is passed as a parameter to the *read*() method, along with the position in the array to begin placing the incoming data and the maximum size of the array.

```
byte abIn[] = new byte[1024];
int iNumRead;

isIn = sock.getInputStream ();

while (true)
  {
  iNumRead = isIn.read (abIn, 0, 1024);
  if (iNumRead < 0)
    {
    break;
    }
  }
```

The reason the *read*() call is inside a loop is that socket protocol does not guarantee how much data will be returned for each call to *read*(). The only guarantee is that it will not overflow the specified array size. When there is no more data to be received, Java returns a "−1" number of bytes read.

Another unusual thing to remember about the *read*() method is that it will block or stop the thread until data is ready to be retrieved from the socket.

For this reason, the client and server programs must be clear on whose turn it is to write data and whose turn it is to read data. If they get out of sync, both programs can end up waiting to receive data from the other one.

The Web protocol that is described in the next chapter is a set of rules that the client and server follow, so they both realize whose turn it is to read data and whose turn it is to write data.

The easiest way to write data to a socket is to select a *PrintStream* object as the output object and send a *print*() method to it. The only parameter needed is the string to send.

```
OutputStream osOut;
PrintStream psOut;

sock = new Socket ("localhost", 8080);

osOut = sock.getOutputStream ();
psOut = new PrintStream (osOut);

psOut.print ("This is a msg from the server's connection");
```

The *print*() method does not need to be sent several times to send the string. A single call will send the entire string.

Internally, the string may be broken up into several pieces to be sent efficiently across the network. This will only become visible as the other socket is examining the data that it gets back from each call to its *read*() method.

The SimpleServer application illustrates this process. The output from the application is displayed below.

The application consists of the two files. The *SimpleServer.java* file, which has already been displayed above, contains the classes *SimpleServer* and *ServerExtension*. The *SimpleClient.java* file is displayed below.

```
import java.net.*;
import java.io.*;

    class SimpleClient
      {
      public static void main (String args[])
        {
        Socket sock;
        InputStream isIn;
        PrintStream psOut;
        byte abIn[] = new byte[1024];
        int iNumRead;

        try
          {
          sock = new Socket ("localhost", 8080);
          isIn = sock.getInputStream ();
          psOut = new PrintStream (sock.getOutputStream ());

          while (true)
            {
            iNumRead = isIn.read (abIn, 0, 1024);
            if (iNumRead < 0)
              {
              break;
              }

            String str = new String (abIn, 0, 0, iNumRead);

            System.out.println
              (
              "Clnt: Received from server: "
```

```
                + str + "  (" + iNumRead + " bytes)"
                );
              }
            }

        catch (Exception exception)
            {
            System.out.println ("Clnt: Exception reading server data: "
              + exception);
            }
        }
    }
```

When this application is run, the client and server portions of the application are run on the same machine in two separate windows.

To run it, one must open two command line windows. Start the SimpleServer in one of the windows. Then run the SimpleClient one or more times in the other window. The display from the two windows will look something like the following.

Server	**Client**
1.0 C:\SimpleServer>java SimpleServer	
Serv: Initializing to port 8080	
Serv: Waiting for a connection...	
	1.0 C:\SimpleServer>java SimpleClient
Serv: Received a connection	
Serv: Waiting for a connection...	

SrvX: Connected to: 127.0.0.1:1037	
	Clnt: Received from server: T (1 bytes)
	Clnt: Received from server: his is a msg from the server's connection (41 bytes)
SrvX: Disconnecting: 127.0.0.1:1037	

	1.0 C:\SimpleServer>java SimpleClient
Serv: Received a connection	
Serv: Waiting for a connection...	

`*-----------------------------------*` `SrvX: Connected to: 127.0.0.1:1038`	
	`Clnt: Received from server: T  (1 bytes)` `Clnt: Received from server: his is a msg from the server's connection  (41 bytes)`
`SrvX: Disconnecting: 127.0.0.1:1038` `*-----------------------------------*`	
	`1.0 C:\SimpleServer>java SimpleClient`

`Serv: Received a connection`
`Serv: Waiting for a connection...`
`*-----------------------------------*`
`SrvX: Connected to: 127.0.0.1:1039`	

	`Clnt: Received from server: T  (1 bytes)` `Clnt: Received from server: his is a msg from the server's connection  (41 bytes)`
`SrvX: Disconnecting: 127.0.0.1:1039` `*-----------------------------------*`	

Notice that the server receives the connection, launches the server extension, then waits for the next connection. As the server extension comes to life, it notifies the log of its presence; then it sends the string to the client. The client receives the string in two chunks: one that is 1 byte long and one that is 41 bytes long. The size of the transfer units varies widely and depends on the current system load.

When the server extension (SrvX) has completed, it disconnects and exits. At that point, the client program exits to the command line and the server program continues to wait for the next request.

To take the server program down, type a *control-C* into its window and the command line will reappear.

If the user experiences unusually slow performance, there are several possible causes and resolutions. Be aware that some installations have implemented Web servers to achieve performance gains over traditional servers. Installations that launch a high number of CGI (Common Gateway Interface) programs can install classes to a running Java image much more efficiently than launching CGI programs. They also achieve overall performance gains.

Here are some things to examine if one's performance is substandard. Marginal memory conditions and slow processor speed is sometimes the cause for slow performance of this kind of application. Some versions of Windows95 and WindowsNT have significantly slower performance for "localhost" destinations than for truly remote destinations.

Communication is Java's greatest strength. Whether a Java program is an applet acting as a client or an application acting as a server, distributed processing is unusually straightforward to implement in Java.

CHAPTER 16

A Simple Web Server

When a person types in the location of a Web site and the browser fetches the Web page, a short Client/Server conversation has occurred.

The steps in the conversation are exactly like those described in the previous chapter.

The server program, called a Web Server, was already running at the Web site and had opened a ServerSocket on port 80. The client program, called a Web Browser, opened a regular socket and specified the location of the Web site. The socket requested a conversation with the program on port 80 of the Web site. The server accepted the request and launched a new server extension thread with a regular socket to carry on the conversation.

Now the conversation between the client program and the server extension program can begin.

HTTP—The Format of Web Requests and Web Responses

Web *requests* and *responses* follow a set of rules known as the *Hyper Text Transfer Protocol(HTTP).* This is a series of rules (a *protocol*) that govern the movement (*transfer*) of requests and responses of Web data (consisting of text with *hyper* links to other resources).

Conversations between Web clients and Web servers are always the same. The client makes one request, the server makes one response, and the conversation is terminated. When a Web page is fetched, the Web client requests a particular Web page and the Web server responds by sending that page back.

The server extension reads the request from its socket. The data in the request is in the form of ASCII text lines. The lines are delimited by a carriage return and a line feed character (on all platforms).

The first line of the request looks like this:

```
GET /echo.html HTTP/1.0
```

The second field is the name of the Web page to retrieve. Some optional lines may follow the request to give further information about the request or about the requester. A blank line marks the end of the request.

The response looks like this:

```
HTTP/1.0 200 Document follows
Content-type: text/html

< - -  Web Page Data  - - >
```

The response consists of a few lines of administrative information, a blank line, then the Web page data.

After the server extension sends its response, it closes the socket and deallocates itself. The client knows to read the response lines until there is a socket error marking the end of the response data.

WebServer—Responds to a Web Browser Request

To illustrate the basic flow of a Web request and response, a SimpleWebServer is constructed below to simply receive a request from a Web browser and respond back with a Web page.

This SimpleWebServer will compile and service a Web request. Note: Since Unix platforms will only allow the root user to open a socket on a well-known point like 80, the Unix version of these examples was port 8000 to conduct Web interactions.

```
import java.net.*;
import java.io.*;

    class SimpleWebServer
      {
      public static void main (String argv[])
        {
        Socket sock;
        ServerSocket ssock;
        Thread thServx;
        WebServerExtension servx;

        System.out.println ("Serv: Initializing WebServer to port 80");

        try
          {
          ssock = new ServerSocket (80);

          while (true)
            {
            System.out.println ("Serv: Waiting for a connection...");
            sock = ssock.accept ();
            System.out.println ("Serv: Received a connection");

            servx = new WebServerExtension (sock);
            thServx = new Thread (servx);
            thServx.start ();
            }
          }
        catch (Exception e)
          {
          System.err.println ("Serv: Exception in main loop: " + e);
          }
        }
      }


    class WebServerExtension implements Runnable
      {
      private Socket sock;
      private PrintStream psOut;
      private DataInputStream disIn;
```

```
public WebServerExtension (Socket s)
  {
  sock = s;
  }


public void run ()
  {
  System.out.println ("*--------------------------------------*");
  System.out.println ("SrvX: Connected to: "
    + sock.getInetAddress () +":"+ sock.getPort ());

  try
    {
    disIn = new DataInputStream (sock.getInputStream ());
    psOut = new PrintStream (sock.getOutputStream ());

    getRequest ();
    sendReply ("This is from SimpleWebServer");

    sock.close ();
    }
  catch (Exception e)
    {
    System.err.println ("SrvX: Exception processing request: " + e);
    }

  System.out.println ("SrvX: Disconnecting: "
    + sock.getInetAddress () +":"+ sock.getPort ());
  System.out.println ("*--------------------------------------*");
  }


void getRequest ()
  {
  String sLineIn;

  try
    {
    while (((sLineIn = disIn.readLine ()) != null)
    && (!sLineIn.equals ("")))
      {
      processLineIn (sLineIn);
      }
    }
```

```
    catch (Exception e)
      {
      System.out.println ("SrvX: Exception getting request: " + e);
      }
    }


  void processLineIn (String s)
    {
    System.out.println ("SrvX: Received: " + s);
    }


  void sendReply (String s)
    {
    StringBufferInputStream sbis;
    String sHtmlText;
    byte[] ab;
    int iLength;

    System.out.println ("SrvX: Sending the MIME...");

    sHtmlText = "HTTP/1.0 200 Document follows\n"
      + "Server: Java/" + getClass().getName() + "\n"
      + "Content-type: text/html\n\n";

    sbis = new StringBufferInputStream (sHtmlText);
    iLength = sbis.available ();                        // String to array
    ab = new byte[iLength];
    sbis.read (ab, 0, iLength);
    psOut.write (ab, 0, iLength);                       // Write array

    System.out.println ("SrvX: Sending the Web Page...");

    sHtmlText = "<html><head><title>SimpleWebServer"
      + "</title></head>\n<body><h1>"
      + s + "</h1>\n";

    sbis = new StringBufferInputStream (sHtmlText);
    iLength = sbis.available ();                        // String to array
    ab = new byte[iLength];
    sbis.read (ab, 0, iLength);
    psOut.write (ab, 0, iLength);                       // Write array

    System.out.println ("SrvX: Finished sending.");
    }
  }
```

Notice the similarity between this code and the SimpleServer of the previous chapter.

The server opens a ServerSocket, then waits for a client to make a request. When a Web client makes a request, a regular socket is returned from the *accept()* method and the server launches a server extension thread that processes the request.

All the server extension code descends from the *run*() method, which reads the request from the socket with a call to *getRequest*() and writes the response back to the socket with a call to *sendReply*(). These two methods are in the WebServerExtension class.

The code in the *getRequest*() method reads and displays each line in the request until it encounters a blank line. In this example, the actual contents of the lines are ignored. The next chapter will demonstrate how to examine these lines.

The code in the *sendReply*() method sends the administrative lines in the Web response, followed by a blank line and the actual Web page data. In a more normal Web server, the code at this point would probably fetch the Web page data from a file. The next chapter will illustrate how to perform that processing.

The instructions for running this server are the same as the previous chapter, except the client must be a Web client program. Anyone who does not have a Web browser can use the SimpleWebClient that is constructed in the next section.

Anyone who does have a Web browser can use it in this way. Start the *SimpleWebServer* application from the command line. Then open the Web browser and enter the following URL:

```
http://localhost/echo.html
```

Unix users should specify the port number following the machine name:

```
http://localhost:8000/echo.html
```

Using the Netscape *Navigator*, the conversation ends up looking like Figure 16–1.

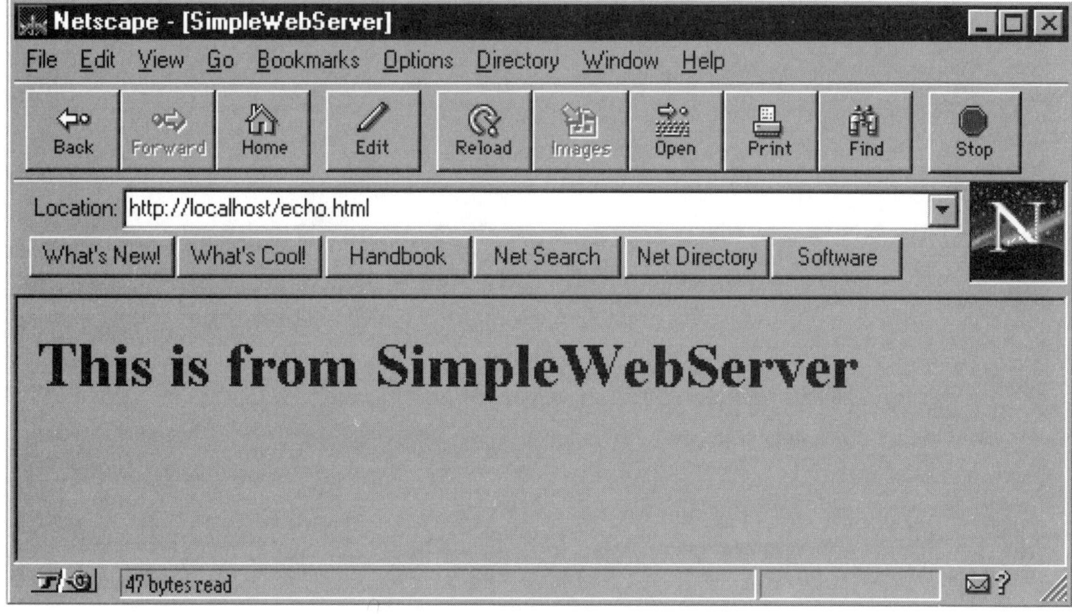

Figure 16–1

In the example, the SimpleWebServer's server extension thread has displayed each line that the Netscape client sent in the Web request. Notice the first line sent was the *request line* that begins with GET. The lines that follow each start with a keyword, followed by ":", then a value. These are called *header fields* and each field gives some more information about the request. All of these fields are optional.

```
1.0 C:\JumpStrt\examples\SimpleWebServer>java SimpleWebServer
Serv: Initializing WebServer to port 80
Serv: Waiting for a connection...
Serv: Received a connection
Serv: Waiting for a connection...
*-------------------------------------------*
SrvX: Connected to: 127.0.0.1:1032
SrvX: Received: GET /echo.html HTTP/1.0
SrvX: Received: Connection: Keep-Alive
SrvX: Received: User-Agent: Mozilla/2.0GoldB1 (Win95; I)
SrvX: Received: Pragma: no-cache
SrvX: Received: Host: localhost
SrvX: Received: Accept: image/gif, image/x-xbitmap, image/jpeg,
      image/pjpeg, */*
```

```
SrvX: Sending the MIME...
SrvX: Sending the Web Page...
SrvX: Finished sending.
SrvX: Disconnecting: 127.0.0.1:1032
*-----------------------------------------*
```

WebClient—Generates a Web Browser Request

The following example builds upon the SimpleClient of the previous chapter and enhances it to send the exact request that the Netscape browser sent previously.

The socket is pointed to a Web server (*port 80*) on the local machine (*"localhost"*).

```
import java.net.*;
import java.io.*;

    public class SimpleWebClient
      {
      public static void main (String[] args)
        {
        Socket sock;
        InputStream isIn;
        PrintStream psOut;
        byte abDataIn[] = new byte[1024];
        int iNumBytes;

        try
          {
          sock = new Socket ("localhost", 80);
          isIn = sock.getInputStream ();
          psOut = new PrintStream (sock.getOutputStream ());

          System.out.println ("Clnt: Sending a GET request...");
          psOut.println ("GET /echo.html HTTP/1.0");
          psOut.println ("Connection: Keep-Alive");
          psOut.println ("User-Agent: Mozilla/2.0GoldB1 (Win95; I)");
          psOut.println ("Pragma: no-cache");
          psOut.println ("Host: localhost");
          psOut.println ("Accept: image/gif, image/x-xbitmap, "
            + "image/jpeg, image/pjpeg, */*");
          psOut.println ("");
          System.out.println ("Clnt: Sent a GET request...\n");
```

```
            while (true)
              {
              iNumBytes = isIn.read (abDataIn, 0, 1024);
              if (iNumBytes < 0)
                {
                break;
                }

              String str = new String (abDataIn, 0, 0, iNumBytes);
              System.out.println "--------------Received-------------- "
                + iNumBytes + " bytes");
              System.out.println (str);
              System.out.println ("----------------------------------\n");
              }
            }

          catch (Exception exception)
            {
            System.out.println ("Clnt: Exception interacting with socket: "
              + exception);
            }
          }
        }
```

After the socket is instantiated and the PrintStream is established, there are a series of calls to the PrintStream's *println*() method.

```
psOut.println ("GET /echo.html HTTP/1.0");
psOut.println ("Connection: Keep-Alive");
psOut.println ("User-Agent: Mozilla/2.0b3 (WinNT; I)");
psOut.println ("Pragma: no-cache");
psOut.println ("Host: localhost");
psOut.println ("Accept: image/gif, image/x-xbitmap, "
  + "image/jpeg, image/pjpeg, */*");
psOut.println ("");
```

These calls send the Web *request* through the socket to the Web server. Each of these calls sends one line. These lines correspond to the lines received from the Netscape browser.

When the Web server sends a response back, the SimpleWebClient displays the data that is returned. Instead of holding all of the data and displaying the whole response at once, this client displays the data that is returned from each *read*()

method. This helps to underscore how the *read*() method must be continually called until it returns a byte count of "-1".

When the SimpleWebClient is executed, it should exit back to the command line by itself.

Here is the output from this program:

```
1.0 C:\JumpStrt\examples\SimpleWebClient>java SimpleWebClient
Clnt: Sending a GET request...
Clnt: Sent a GET request...

-------------Received------------- 1 bytes
H
---------------------------------

-------------Received------------- 86 bytes
TTP/1.0 200 Document follows
Server: Java/WebServerExtension
Content-type: text/html


---------------------------------

-------------Received------------- 94 bytes
<html><head><title>SimpleWebServer</title></head>
<body><h1>This is from SimpleWebServer</h1>

---------------------------------
```

```
1.0 C:\JumpStrt\examples\SimpleWebServer>java SimpleWebServer
Serv: Initializing WebServer to port 80
Serv: Waiting for a connection...
Serv: Received a connection
Serv: Waiting for a connection...
*-------------------------------------------*
SrvX: Connected to: 127.0.0.1:1035
SrvX: Received: GET /echo.html HTTP/1.0
SrvX: Received: Connection: Keep-Alive
SrvX: Received: User-Agent: Mozilla/2.0GoldB1 (Win95; I)
SrvX: Received: Pragma: no-cache
SrvX: Received: Host: localhost
SrvX: Received: Accept: image/gif, image/x-xbitmap, image/jpeg,
    image/pjpeg, */*
SrvX: Sending the MIME...
SrvX: Sending the Web Page...
SrvX: Finished sending.
SrvX: Disconnecting: 127.0.0.1:1035
*-------------------------------------------*
```

This simplified Web client could be used to go out and pull a Web page from a computer on the Internet by changing two things. First, the *"localhost"* parameter in the *Socket*() call should be changed to the domain name of the target site (*i.e., "java.sun.com"*).

Second, the parameter right after the "GET" on the first line of the request should be changed to the actual Web page file name. One could request the home page by using the following statement:

```
psOut.println ("GET / HTTP/1.0");
```

URL—A Convenient WebClient Class

When one needs to fetch a Web resource and does not want to go to the trouble of specifying a Web request or parsing through a Web response, Java has provided a class that issues basic *"GET"* requests.

The class's name is URL and represents one Web resource. The URL class is located in the *java.net* package and is an acronym for a *Uniform Resource Locator*. It is pronounced *eerl*.

URL is a common term in Web browsing. Any time anyone types a location into a Web browser that looks generally like the following, they have entered an URL:

```
http://java.sun.com/index.html
```

The following example accepts command line parameters and uses a Java URL to copy a Web resource from its location on the Internet to a local file.

The first parameter, *args[0]*, is the URL that identifies the desired Web resource. The second and third parameters, *args*[1] and *args*[2], are the directory and filename where the data should be stored.

Here is an example of how to launch this program.

```
1.0 C:\GoGetUrl>java GoGetUrl http://java.sun.com/ /GoGetUrl
JavaHomePage.html
```

The *java GoGetUrl* launches the Java Virtual Machine and loads the *GoGetUrl* class. The next parameter is an URL that specifies the default home page of the *java.sun.com* site. The next two parameters give the directory and filename in which to place the home page data.

```
import java.net.*;
import java.io.*;

    class GoGetUrl
      {
      public static void main (String[] args)
        {
        URL url;
        InputStream isIn;
        File fOut;
        FileOutputStream fosOut;
        int iChar;
        int iCount = 0;
        int iTotCount = 0;

        if (args.length < 3)
          {
          System.out.println
            (
            "\nFormat:  " +
            "java GoGetUrl FullyQualifiedUrl LocalDirectory LocalFileName\n"
            );
          System.exit (1);
          }
```

```
        try
          {
          url = new URL (args[0]);
          isIn = url.openStream ();
          fOut = new File (args[1], args[2]);
          fosOut = new FileOutputStream (fOut);

          while ((iChar = isIn.read ()) != -1)
            {
            iCount++;
            if (iCount >= 1000)
              {
              iTotCount += iCount;
              System.out.println ("Received " + iTotCount + " bytes...");
              iCount = 0;
              }
            fosOut.write (iChar);
            }
          }
        catch (Exception e)
          {
          System.out.println ("Exception receiving the data: " + e);
          }

        iTotCount += iCount;

        System.out.println
          (
          "Received " + iTotCount + " bytes and stored them in"
          + args[1] + "/" + args[2]
          );
        }
      }
```

An URL is a little like a socket. When one instantiates an URL object, they can ask it to open an InputStream.

```
URL url;
InputStream isIn;

url = new URL (args[0]);
isIn = url.openStream ();
```

This InputStream is used to read the data from its Internet location into local variables in this program.

When the URL is instantiated, it opens a socket and makes the request for the specified resource. When the program calls the URL InputStream's *read*() method, it is actually calling a filtered version of the Socket InputStream's *read*() method. The administrative lines are removed from the Web response and only the targeted data is allowed through.

The main processing loop simply reads a character from the Internet and writes it to the FileOutputStream.

```
int iChar;
InputStream isIn;
FileOutputStream fosOut;

while ((iChar = isIn.read ()) != -1)
  {
  fosOut.write (iChar);
  }
```

There is some additional logic to print out a progress message for every 1000 bytes that are copied.

This URL class is an excellent way to make short requests for Web resources. Its limitation is that it can only issue *"GET"* requests. When the Java application needs to access more sophisticated CGI (Common Gateway Interface) programs, a *"POST"* request is the preferred method. POST requests must be issued through a socket.

The Web request and Web response architecture provide a convenient mechanism for conducting Client/Server conversations across the World Wide Web.

CHAPTER 17

A Web Server for Client/Server Programming

There is no reason why the Web request and response protocol needs to be restricted to Hypertext applications.

All Client/Server applications make requests and receive responses. The format of the Web conversations includes enough flexibility to meet the needs of a wide range of applications. The more a programmer understands about how a Web server works, the more feasible it seems to adapt the Web server to address the needs of other applications that require servers.

This chapter explains how to enhance the SimpleWebServer of the previous chapter so that it serves as a platform for many kinds of application services.

With the combination of Java extensions on the browser and Java extensions on the server, it is possible to build custom Client/Server applications on top of the existing infrastructure of the World Wide Web.

How to Open Up the Web

Client/Server applications are made up of two programs—a client and a server. Usually they are custom programs that work together to accomplish a specific task. The client makes a request and the server fulfills the request (see Figure 17–1).

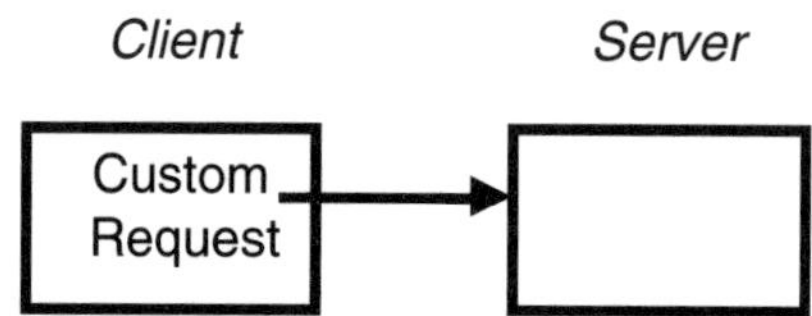

Figure 17–1 A Client/Server application.

The World Wide Web is a Client/Server application. The two programs work together to make files on the serving computer available to anyone with a Web client program. In this application, the client requests and displays files. The server program supplies files to any client that asks for them (see Figure 17–2).

In order for a Client/Server application to be useful, the client and server programs must be easily available to a large number of people. If the client program is difficult to acquire, fewer people will be able to access the services. If the server program is difficult to acquire or set up, there will be fewer services available.

The Web has enjoyed a staggering growth rate. The number of services that are available and the number of people that can access the services have become so great that the Web has become woven into the fabric of the computer industry.

Wouldn't it be nice if a custom-written Client/Server application could hitchhike on the existing Web infrastructure? In this scenario, the server program would be an extension of the Web server, and the client program would be an extension of the Web browser program.

It is not normally possible to extend the services of a client or server program in this way. Most Client/Server applications are written as closed systems that do their job and nothing else.

But any program that supports Java gains the ability to extend itself.

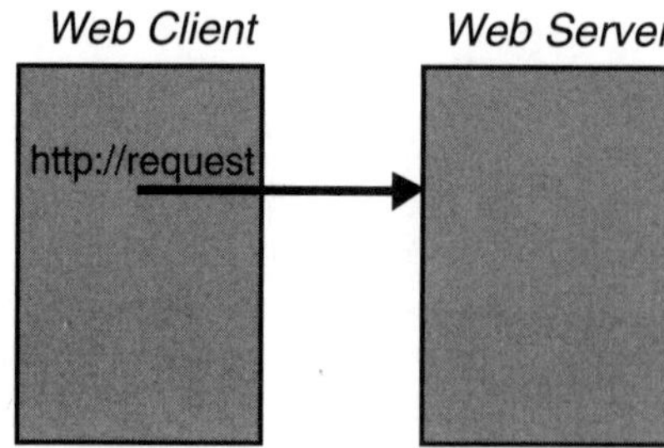

Figure 17–2 The Web is a Client/Server application for fetching files.

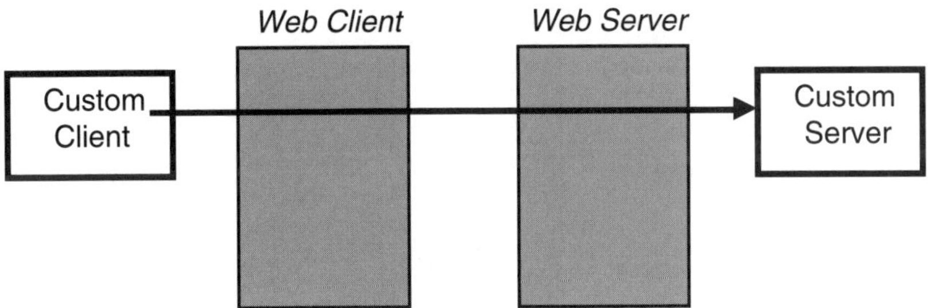

Figure 17–3 A custom Client/Server application over the existing web infrastructure.

Java applets *already* extend the services of the Web browser. In this role, the applet is functioning as a custom client program that is dynamically added to the Web browser.

If the Web server program was written so that it could add Java classes on demand, the loadable classes would be extending the services of the Web server.

By coordinating these server-extending classes with browser-extending applets, a custom Client/Server application can be constructed to run across the Web's infrastructure (see Figure 17–3).

Attaching a Client to the Web Browser

Web browsers that support Java inherit the unusual ability to add functionality on demand.

Java programs run in a memory area called an *image,* which is managed by the Virtual Machine. The memory area contains a number of class objects and instance objects. Each object in the image operates as a peer and has the potential to ask for services from another image.

If one class in a Java image would like to add a new class to the image, it can dynamically load that class, create an object from the class, and then request service from it.

Objects from the newly-loaded class operate as peers with the rest of the objects in the image. Once the new class is in place, it is as if the class was part of the original program—a seamless extension of the original program.

If a custom client was written as a Java applet, it could easily be added to a Web browser on-the-fly and it would not require the users to install any software (see Figure 17–4). It would be a seamless client extension to the Web browser program.

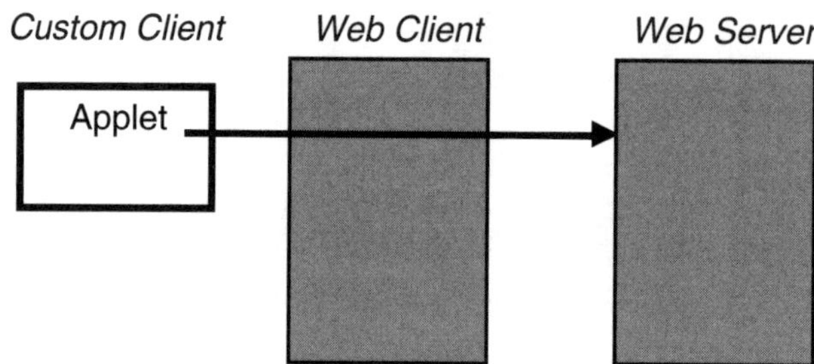

Figure 17–4 A custom client can be written as a Java applet.

Once loaded, the custom client could communicate with the server in the same way that the Web browser communicates with its server—it could issue Web *requests* and receive Web *responses.*

Most Web browsers place security restrictions on an applet to protect the client-side system from malicious programs. This includes some communications restrictions. But most browsers allow an applet to "phone home" and carry on a conversation with the Web site from which it was loaded.

In the following example, the applet *GetUrlClient* illustrates how to code the client-side of a Client/Server application. It is an applet that issues a Web request when one of its buttons is pressed, and it sets the text of a TextArea control to the contents that it receives from the Web server.

In the *urlRequest()* method, the applet illustrates how to use the URL class to issue a Web request. In the method *socketRequest()*, the applet illustrates how to issue a Web request using a socket.

To run this example, one needs to use a Java Enabled Web browser and the Web server that is described in the next section of this chapter. This example will not work with the appletviewer.

Open a command line and go to *c:\JumpStrt\examples\ExtendableWebServer*. Start the *ExtendableWebServer* from the command line with the command:

```
java ExtendableWebServer
```

After it is ready for incoming requests, point the Web browser to the following URL:

```
http://localhost/GetUrlClient.html
```

The browser fetches the Web page from the local Web server, fetches the *GetUrlClient* class from the local Web server, then presents the applet to the user. If the browser window and the server window are arranged so that both are visible, one will see both sides of the conversation as they occur.

When the applet has arrived and is rendered (Figure 17–5), press the *urlRequest* button to see the applet issue a Web request using the URL class. The request is directed to the server from which it was launched. Press the *socketRequest* button to see the same request issued through a Socket class.

```
import java.applet.Applet;
import java.awt.*;
import java.net.*;
import java.io.*;

    public class GetUrlClient extends Applet
      {
      TextArea ta;
      final String sInitText = "After Server is running, Press the Button";


      public void init()
        {
        Panel p;

        setLayout (new BorderLayout (0, 0));

        ta = new TextArea (sInitText);
        add ("Center", ta);

        p = new Panel ();
        p.setLayout (new GridLayout (1, 2, 0, 0));
        p.add (new Button ("Clear"));
        p.add (new Button ("urlRequest"));
        p.add (new Button ("socketRequest"));
        add ("South", p);
        }


      public boolean action (Event evt, Object obj)
        {
        if ("Clear".equals (obj))
          {
          ta.setText (sInitText);
          return (true);
```

```
      }
    else if ("urlRequest".equals (obj))
      {
      urlRequest ();
      return (true);
      }
    else if ("socketRequest".equals (obj))
      {
      socketRequest ();
      return (true);
      }
    return (false);
    }


  void urlRequest ()
    {
    URL url;
    InputStream isIn;
    byte[] ab = new byte[1024];
    StringBuffer sb;
    int iNumBytes;

    sb = new StringBuffer ();

    try
      {
      url = new URL ("http://localhost/GetUrlClient.html");
      isIn = url.openStream ();

      while ((iNumBytes = isIn.read (ab, 0, 1024)) >= 0)
        {
        sb.append (new String (ab, 0, 0, iNumBytes));
        }
      }
    catch (Exception e)
      {
      System.out.println ("Exception receiving the data: " + e);
      }

    ta.setText (sb.toString ());
    }
```

```
void socketRequest ()
  {
  Socket sock;
  InputStream isIn;
  PrintStream psOut;
  byte[] ab = new byte[1024];
  StringBuffer sb;
  int iNumBytes;

  sb = new StringBuffer ();

  try
    {
    sock = new Socket ("localhost", 80);
    isIn = sock.getInputStream ();
    psOut = new PrintStream (sock.getOutputStream ());

    psOut.println ("GET /GetUrlClient.html HTTP/1.0");
    psOut.println ("Connection: Keep-Alive");
    psOut.println ("User-Agent: Mozilla/2.0GoldB1 (Win95; I)");
    psOut.println ("Pragma: no-cache");
    psOut.println ("Host: localhost");
    psOut.println ("Accept: image/gif, image/x-xbitmap, "
      + "image/jpeg, image/pjpeg, */*");
    psOut.println ("");

    while ((iNumBytes = isIn.read (ab, 0, 1024)) >= 0)
      {
      sb.append (new String (ab, 0, 0, iNumBytes));
      }
    }

  catch (Exception exception)
    {
    System.out.println ("Clnt: Exception interacting with socket: "
      + exception);
    }

  ta.setText (sb.toString ());
  }
}
```

```
<HTML>
<HEAD>
<TITLE> GetUrlClient </TITLE>
</HEAD>
<BODY>
GetUrlClient
<HR>
<APPLET CODE="GetUrlClient" WIDTH=300 HEIGHT=200>
</APPLET>
<HR>
</BODY>
</HTML>
```

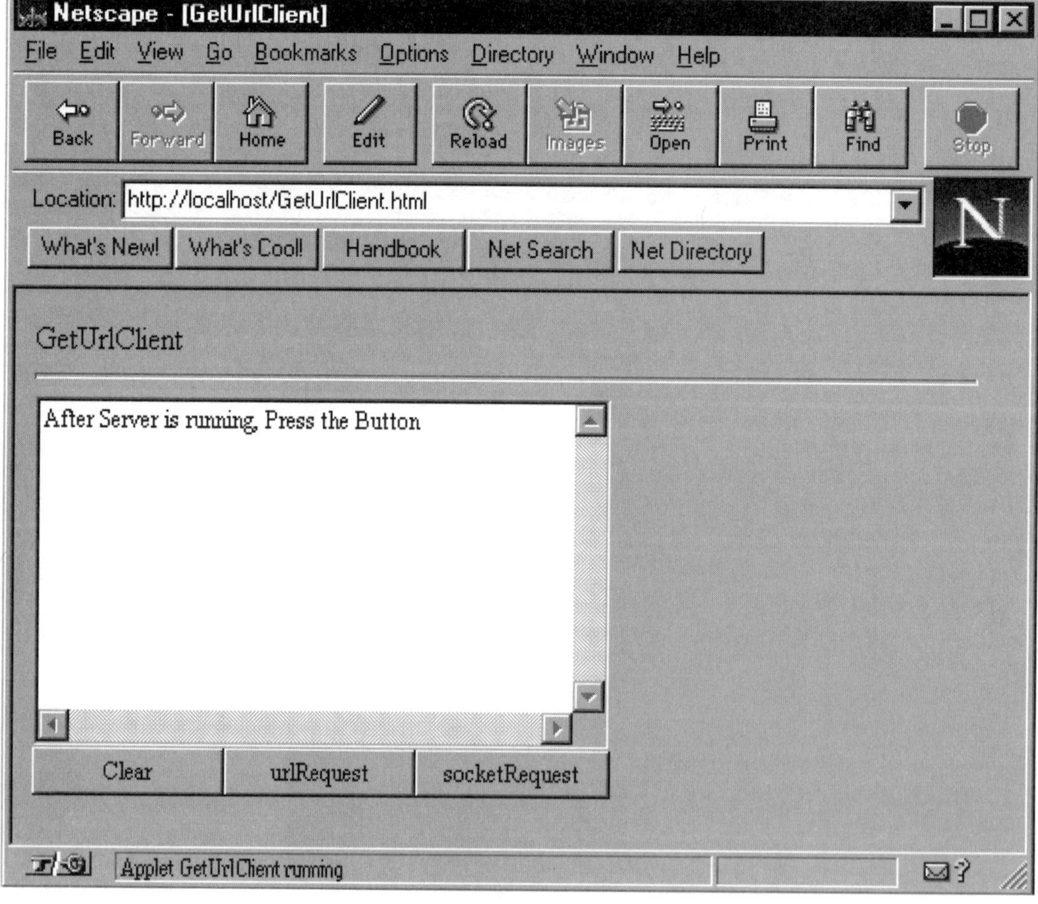

Figure 17–5

When the Web page data arrives, the applet places the data in the TextArea as one long string. The tags are not interpreted. Notice the difference between the data that is received over a socket and the data that is received using the URL class. The socket has direct visibility of the entire Web response. The URL class provides methods to access the administrative lines of the Web response.

The applet convention provides a natural way for custom clients to participate in the widely available Web architecture. But a custom client must be able to converse with a custom server that is extending the services of a Web server to have a complete Client/Server application.

What does it take to make a Web server *extendable*?

Attaching a Server to the Web Server

The Web designers have recognized the need to extend the services of a Web server beyond the simple fetching of files. To address this need, they have implemented the CGI architecture in most Web servers. Every HTML form that is filled out and sent to a server is processed by a CGI program.

CGI—Extending traditional web servers

When a traditional Web server receives a request that points to the name of a program rather than to the name of a file, it launches the program and passes the Web request to it. The technique for passing the request and for receiving the reply from the launched program is known as the *Common Gateway Interface* (CGI).

CGI specifies that a launched program should receive the Web request in one of two ways. If the Web request is using the GET method, the request is available through environment variables. If the request is using the POST method, the request is read from the standard input device. In either case, the program writes the response back to the standard output device (*stdout*).

The CGI technique for extending a Web server has been available for a number of years and can be used when designing Client/Server applications. To use it, one would write the client as a Java applet and write the server as a CGI program. This approach will work, but it has some disadvantages.

Although CGI programs could be written in Java, they would load very slowly. CGI programs are loaded in the same way a program is loaded from a command line. When a Java program is loaded from the command line, the Virtual Machine must first be loaded (which loads a number of classes to condition a fully-functional image before the identified Java class is made ready to run). This can be a relatively slow process.

Writing the CGI program in C adds to the logistics complexity of a Client/Server application. There are usually many modules in a productional Client/Server application. Performing bug fixes, establishing test systems, and tracking maintenance releases becomes much more difficult when the modules are in multiple languages.

There are also performance issues with CGI programs. If a Web site processes a large number of HTML forms in a day, then they launch a large number of CGI programs each day. The performance hit for this activity can become the bottleneck of the entire Web site.

Several Web sites have achieved performance gains by writing Web server programs in Java and preloading Java classes to do the job of the CGI programs. Although the Java code executes slower, the seamless integration has resulted in greater throughput.

ExtendableWebServer—A Web server that launches Java classes

As an alternative to CGI programming, the ExtendableWebServer provides a way to extend a Web server with Java classes.

When a Web request specifies the name of a Java class rather than the name of a file, the ExtendableWebServer creates a new instance of that class. This allows it to process the Web request and send the Web response back. If the class is not present in the running image, then it is dynamically added to the image.

The ExtendableWebServer is written so that only certain classes can qualify to be requested. Only classes that are subclasses of the *ServerExtension* class can be loaded to extend this Web server.

Just like a custom Java client must be an extension of the Applet class, a custom Java server must be an extension of the *ServerExtension* class. This class and several extensions to it are included in the code below.

All requests are processed by a *ServerExtension* class. The FileServerExtension processes Web requests for file data. The FormServerExtension processes an HTML form.

To run the ExtendableWebServer, all the files in the *ExtendableWebServer* directory are required. Open a command line window, change to the directory *c:\JumpStrt\examples\ExtendableWebServer*, and launch the server like a Java application:

```
java ExtendableWebServer
```

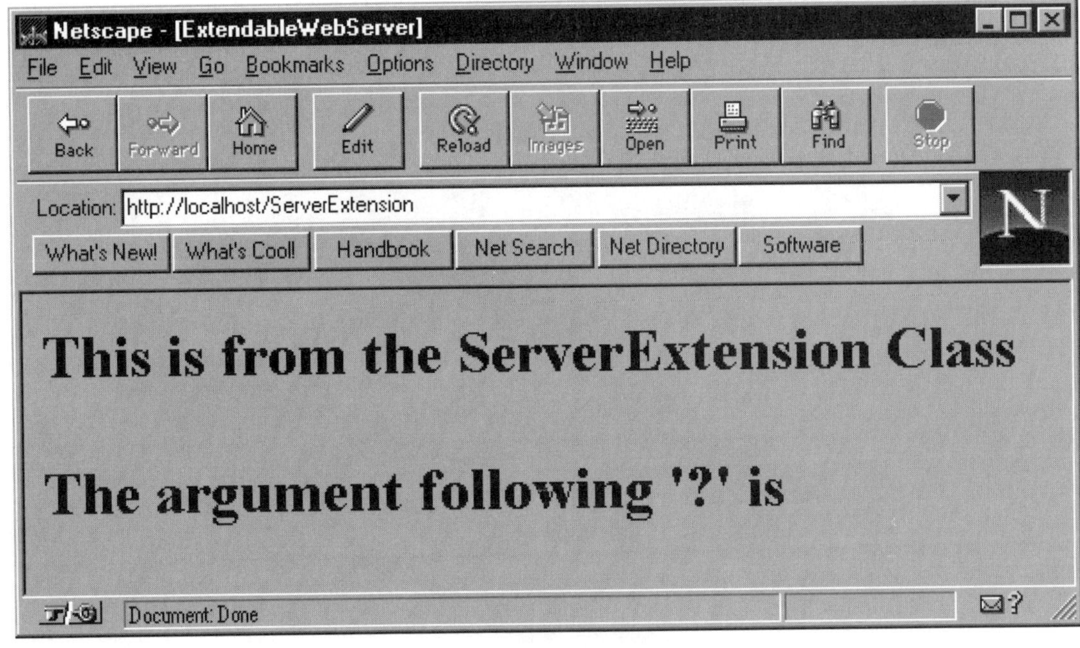

Figure 17–6

After a moment, it will signal that it is waiting for a connection request. At this point, start a Web browser and point to the following URL:

```
http://localhost/ServerExtension
```

The ExtendableWebServer will load the *ServerExtension* class and that class will send a default response to the Web browser (Figure 17–6). Here are some other URLs to try:

```
http://localhost/ServerExtension?k1=one&k2=two

http://localhost/file1
http://localhost/file2
http://localhost/file3

http://localhost/form.html
```

In the latter request, the server retrieves the *form.html* file and the browser displays an HTML form. When a button on the form is pressed, a Web request is sent to *http://localhost/FormServerExtension* and the server loads the FormServerExtension class to process the request.

Here is the complete code to the ExtendableWebServer.

```
import java.net.*;
import java.io.*;
import java.util.*;

    class ExtendableWebServer
      {
      final String sTag = "Copyright (c) 1996 Noel Enete";

      public static void main (String argv[])
        {
        Socket sock;
        ServerSocket ssock;
        Thread thConn;
        SConnection conn;

        System.out.println ("Serv: Initializing WebServer to port 80");

        try
          {
          ssock = new ServerSocket (80);

          while (true)
            {
            System.out.println ("Serv: Waiting for a connection...");
            sock = ssock.accept ();
            System.out.println ("Serv: Received a connection");

            conn = new SConnection (sock);
            thConn = new Thread (conn);
            thConn.start ();
            }
          }
        catch (Exception e)
          {
          System.err.println ("Serv: Exception in main loop: " + e);
          }
        }
      }


    class SConnection implements Runnable
      {
      final String sTag = "Copyright (c) 1996 Noel Enete";
      private Socket sock;
      private DataInputStream disIn;
```

```
    private PrintStream psOut;
    String sResource = null;
    String sResourceParms = null;


    public SConnection (Socket s)
      {
      sock = s;
      }


    public void run ()
      {
      ServerExtension serverX;

      System.out.println ("*------------------------------------*");
      System.out.println ("Conn: Connected to: "
        + sock.getInetAddress () +":"+ sock.getPort ());

      try
        {
        disIn = new DataInputStream (sock.getInputStream ());
        psOut = new PrintStream (sock.getOutputStream());

        getRequest ();


/*      The requested resource is first interpreted as a class name,
        the class is dynamically loaded, and an instance is created.
        ==============================================================  */

        serverX = ServerExtension.getClassInstance (sResource);


/*      If the class is not found, the resource is interpreted as a
        filename and a file loading ServerExtension is created.
        ==============================================================  */

        if (serverX == null)
          {
          serverX = new FileServerExtension ();
          sResourceParms = sResource;
          }
```

```
/*      The get() method is sent to the ServerExtension, which sends
        back an appropriate response to the client.
        ==============================================================  */

        serverX.get (this, sResourceParms);
        sock.close ();
        }

      catch (Exception e)
        {
        System.err.println ("Conn: Exception processing request: " + e);
        }

      System.out.println ("Conn: Disconnecting: "
        + sock.getInetAddress () +":"+ sock.getPort ());
      System.out.println ("*--------------------------------------*");
      }

    void getRequest ()
      {
      String sLineIn;

      try
        {
        while (((sLineIn = disIn.readLine ()) != null)
        && (!sLineIn.equals ("")))
          {
          processLineIn (sLineIn);
          }
        }
      catch (Exception e)
        {
        System.out.println ("Conn: Exception getting request: " + e);
        }
      }


    void processLineIn (String s)
      {
      StringTokenizer st;
      String sRequestParms;

      System.out.println ("Conn: Received: " + s);

      if (sResource == null)          // Only process the request line.
        {
```

```
    st = new StringTokenizer (s);
    st.nextToken ();
    sRequestParms = st.nextToken().substring(1);

    st = new StringTokenizer (sRequestParms, "? ", false);
    sResource = st.nextToken ();
    if (st.hasMoreTokens ())
      {
      sResourceParms = st.nextToken ();
      }
    else
      {
      sResourceParms = "";
      }
    }
  }

void sendReply (String s)
  {
  sendMime ();

  System.out.println ("Conn: Sending the Resource...");
  psOut.print
    (
    "<html>"
    + "<head><title>ExtendableWebServer</title></head>\n"
    + "<body><h1>"
    + s
    + "</h1>\n"
    );
  System.out.println ("Conn: Finished sending.");
  }


void putReply (byte[] ab, int iStartPosition, int iEndPosition)
  {
  sendMime ();

  System.out.println ("Conn: Putting the Resource...");
  psOut.write (ab, iStartPosition, iEndPosition);
  System.out.println ("Conn: Finished putting.");
  }


void sendMime ()
  {
```

```
        System.out.println ("Conn: Sending the MIME...");
        psOut.print
          (
          "HTTP/1.0 200 Document follows\n" +
          "Server: Java/" + getClass().getName() + "\n" +
          "Content-type: text/html\n\n"
          );
        }
      }



/*************************************************************************

    ServerExtension Classes

*************************************************************************/

    interface ServerExtendable
      {
      final String sTag = "Copyright (c) 1996 Noel Enete";

      public abstract void get (SConnection conn, String sArg);
      }



    class ServerExtension implements ServerExtendable
      {
      final String sTag = "Copyright (c) 1996 Noel Enete";
      SConnection conn;

      public ServerExtension ()
        {
        }

      static ServerExtension getClassInstance (String s)
        {
        Class clsNew;
        ServerExtension servx = null;
        int i;

        try
          {
          clsNew = Class.forName (s);
```

```
      try
        {
        servx = (ServerExtension) clsNew.newInstance();
        }
      catch (java.lang.IllegalAccessException ex)
        {
        System.out.println ("SrvX: IllegalAccessException, class = "
           + s);
        }
      catch (java.lang.InstantiationException ex)
        {
        System.out.println ("SrvX: InstantiationException, class = "
           + s);
        }
      }

    catch (java.lang.ClassNotFoundException ex )
      {
      System.out.println ("SrvX: Class " + s + " not found" );
      }

    if (servx != null)
      {
      System.out.println ("SrvX: Class " + s + " found" );
      }

    return (servx);
    }


  public void get (SConnection conn, String sArg)
    {
    conn.sendReply
      (
      "This is from the ServerExtension Class"
      + "<p>The argument following '?' is "
      + sArg
      );
    }
  }



class MyServerExtension extends ServerExtension
  {
  public void get (SConnection conn, String sArg)
```

```
    {
    conn.sendReply ("Hello World");
    }
  }


class TimeServer extends ServerExtension
  {
  final String sTag = "Copyright (c) 1996 Noel Enete";

  public void get (SConnection conn, String sArg)
    {
    Date d;
    String s;
    StringTokenizer st;
    byte[] ab = new byte[100];
    long lTime;
    int iReqTimezoneOffset;

    if ("West".equals (sArg))
      {
      iReqTimezoneOffset = 420;
      }
    else if ("Central".equals (sArg))
      {
      iReqTimezoneOffset = 300;
      }
    else
      {
      iReqTimezoneOffset = 240;
      }

    d = new Date ();
    lTime = d.getTime ();
    lTime += (d.getTimezoneOffset () - iReqTimezoneOffset) * 60 * 1000;
    d.setTime (lTime);

    st = new StringTokenizer (d.toLocaleString ());
    s = st.nextToken ();
    s = sArg + ": " + st.nextToken ();
    s.getBytes (0, s.length (), ab, 0);
    conn.putReply (ab, 0, s.length());
    }
  }
```

```
class FileServerExtension extends ServerExtension
  {
  final String sTag = "Copyright (c) 1996 Noel Enete";

  public void get (SConnection conn, String sArg)
    {
    FileInputStream fisIn = null;
    byte[] abBuffer = new byte[20000];
    int iBytesRead;

    try
      {
      fisIn = new FileInputStream (sArg);
      }
    catch (Exception e)
      {
      System.out.println ("FilX: Can't find " + sArg);
      e.printStackTrace ();
      conn.sendReply ("Can not find the file " + sArg);
      return;
      }
    System.out.println( "FilX: File " + sArg + " found" );

    try
      {
      iBytesRead = fisIn.read (abBuffer);
      conn.putReply (abBuffer, 0, iBytesRead);
      fisIn.close ();
      }
    catch (Exception eReadWrite)
      {
      System.out.println ("FilX: Can't read the file " + sArg);
      eReadWrite.printStackTrace ();
      conn.sendReply ("Cannot read the file " + sArg);
      return;
      }
    }
  }


class FormServerExtension extends ServerExtension
  {
  final String sTag = "Copyright (c) 1996 Noel Enete";
```

```
public void get (SConnection conn, String sArg)
  {
  StringBuffer sb;
  StringTokenizer st;

  sb = new StringBuffer ();
  st = new StringTokenizer (sArg, "&", false);

  while (st.hasMoreTokens ())
    {
    sb.append (st.nextToken ());
    sb.append ("\n");
    }

  conn.sendReply ("A Form was received by "
    + "the FormServerExtension Class. "
    + "<p>The Arguments were as follows:"
    + "<pre>"
    + sb.toString ()
    + "</pre>");
  }
}
```

```
C:\JumpStrt\examples\ExtendableWebServer>java ExtendableWebServer
Serv: Initializing WebServer to port 80
Serv: Waiting for a connection...
Serv: Received a connection
Serv: Waiting for a connection...
*--------------------------------*
Conn: Connected to: 127.0.0.1:1130
Conn: Received: GET /ServerExtension HTTP/1.0
Conn: Received: Connection: Keep-Alive
Conn: Received: User-Agent: Mozilla/2.0GoldB1 (Win95; I)
Conn: Received: Host: localhost
Conn: Received: Accept: image/gif, image/x-xbitmap, image/jpeg,
image/pjpeg, */*
SrvX: Class ServerExtension found
Conn: Sending the MIME...
Conn: Sending the Resource...
Conn: Finished sending.
Conn: Disconnecting: 127.0.0.1:1130
*--------------------------------*
```

Notice, in the source above, the ServerExtension classes occupy the last half of the source file. The classes *MyServerExtension*, *FileServerExtension*, *FormServerExtension*, and *TimeServer* are all subclasses of ServerExtension and are included in this section, so they are easy to locate.

As the server log shows above, a request for the *ServerExtension* class was made and the *ServerExtension* class was found. The ServerExtension used the *SConnection* object to send the MIME administrative lines and Web page back to the client.

This program works very much like the SimpleWebServer, but there are a few differences. When a connection request is received by the ExtendableWebServer, a connection object, rather than an extension object, is instantiated to process the request.

```
Socket sock;
ServerSocket ssock;
Thread thConn;
SConnection conn;

ssock = new ServerSocket (80);

while (true)
  {
  sock = ssock.accept ();

  conn = new SConnection (sock);
  thConn = new Thread (conn);
  thConn.start ();
  }
```

A *Server Connection (SConnection)* object stands between the client and the *ServerExtension* object. It handles all of the HTTP interaction with the client and also instantiates the appropriate *ServerExtension* class to process the request.

When an SConnection starts running, it calls the *getRequest*() method to read the Web request from the socket. During that process, it surfaces the requested resource (a filename or a class name) and places it in the *sResource* variable.

```
Socket sock;
DataInputStream disIn;
PrintStream psOut;
String sResource = null;
String sResourceParms = null;
ServerExtension serverX;

getRequest ();

serverX = ServerExtension.getClassInstance (sResource);

if (serverX == null)
  {
  serverX = new FileServerExtension ();
  sResourceParms = sResource;
  }

serverX.get (this, sResourceParms);
sock.close ();
```

To find the resource, it first assumes that a class is being requested and tries to instantiate it. The static method *getClassInstance*() will load the class if it is not found in the running image and will return an object to the *serverX* variable. If the name cannot be instantiated, then the resource is assumed to be a file. To processes this file request, a *FileServerExtension* object is instantiated and placed in the *serverX* variable.

Once the ServerExtension is instantiated, its *get*() method is called. Any parameters that are sent in the Web request are stored in the variable *sResourceParms* and passed as a parameter to the *get*() method. When the call to the *get*() method returns, the Web request has been processed and a response has been sent back to the client.

Dynamic class loading occurs in the *forName*() method (which is called by *getClassInstance*()). Class loading occurs in two steps. A Class object is obtained, then an instance is created from the Class object.

```
Class clsNew;
ServerExtension servx;

clsNew = Class.forName ("MyServerExtensionClassName");
servx = (ServerExtension) clsNew.newInstance();
```

One normally does not think about Class objects. Each Class object represents a class in the image. They hold the code of a class and they know how to create a new instance of a class.

When a class is being dynamically loaded, the name of the class is not known in advance. So a Class object must be dynamically created out of a string that holds the name of a class.

This is accomplished in the *Class.forName*() method. The search for the class begins in the current memory image to see if it has already been loaded. If it is not found, then the *classpath* is searched for a class that matches the requested class name. If the class is found, it is loaded into the image as a Class object. If it is not found, then *null* is returned.

The second step is to create an instance of the class by sending the *newInstance*() method to the Class object. Once the ServerExtension is created, the *get*() method is called and the Web request is processed.

ServerExtension—A class that extends the Web server

The class that is loaded on demand by the Web server is called the *ServerExtension* class. It provides a simple way to extend the functionality of the Web server. It does for the Web server what a Java applet does for the Web client, as shown in Figure 17–7.

When a Web request arrives at the *ServerExtension* object, the request has already been received from the socket and parsed. The task of the *ServerExtension* class is to send back an appropriate response.

Here are the essential parts to include when coding a *ServerExtension* class:

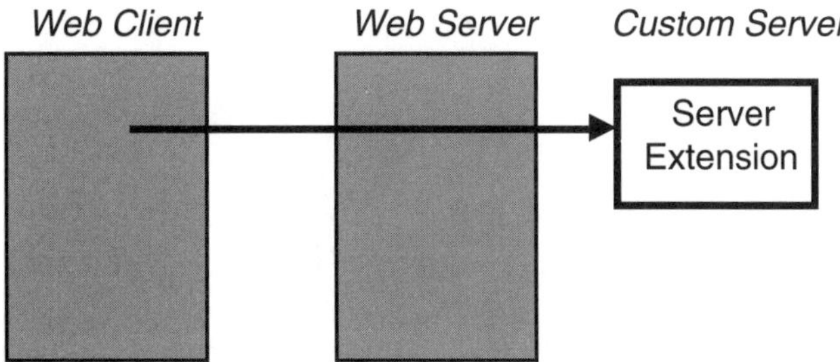

Figure 17–7 A ServerExtension is a Java class that extends the function of the Web server.

```
class MyServerExtension extends ServerExtension
  {
  public void get (SConnection conn, String sArg)
    {
    conn.sendReply ("Hello World");
    }
  }
```

The entire Web request is processed within the *get*() method.

The *SConnection* object, which is passed to the *get*() method, includes the behavior that sends responses back to the Web client. The method *sendReply*() is the simplest method for sending Web pages. It sends an administrative MIME, then it sends a Web page title and main body back to the client. The Web page is constructed from the string that is passed to the method.

The *sArg* variable contains parameters that are passed with the Web GET request. In the ExtendableWebServer, multiple parameters are passed as a single parameter string and must be parsed. In the next chapter, the CaffeineCafe parses the parameters and places them in an array of strings that it sends to the *get*() method.

FormServerExtension—A class to process an HTML form

One of the most popular ways to extend a Web server is to create a program that processes an HTML form. When the Web user clicks on an HTML form, a request is sent to the server with the contents of the fields in the form. The request is normally directed to a CGI program to process the fields.

In the ExtendableWebServer, CGI requests are processed by ServerExtensions. The following example demonstrates how to construct a ServerExtension that processes an HTML form. The FormServerExtension processes the form in the file *form.html*. This file is stored in the same directory as the ExtendableWebServer.

To execute this example, launch the ExtendableWebServer in one window; then start a Web browser and point it to the following URL:

```
http://localhost/form.html
```

This will fetch the file *form.html* and present an HTML form to the user (Figure 17–8). When a button on the form is clicked, the browser makes a CGI request to the server and passes the contents of the fields. The FormServerExtension receives the fields in the *sArg* parameter of the *get*() method and formats a reply back to the client.

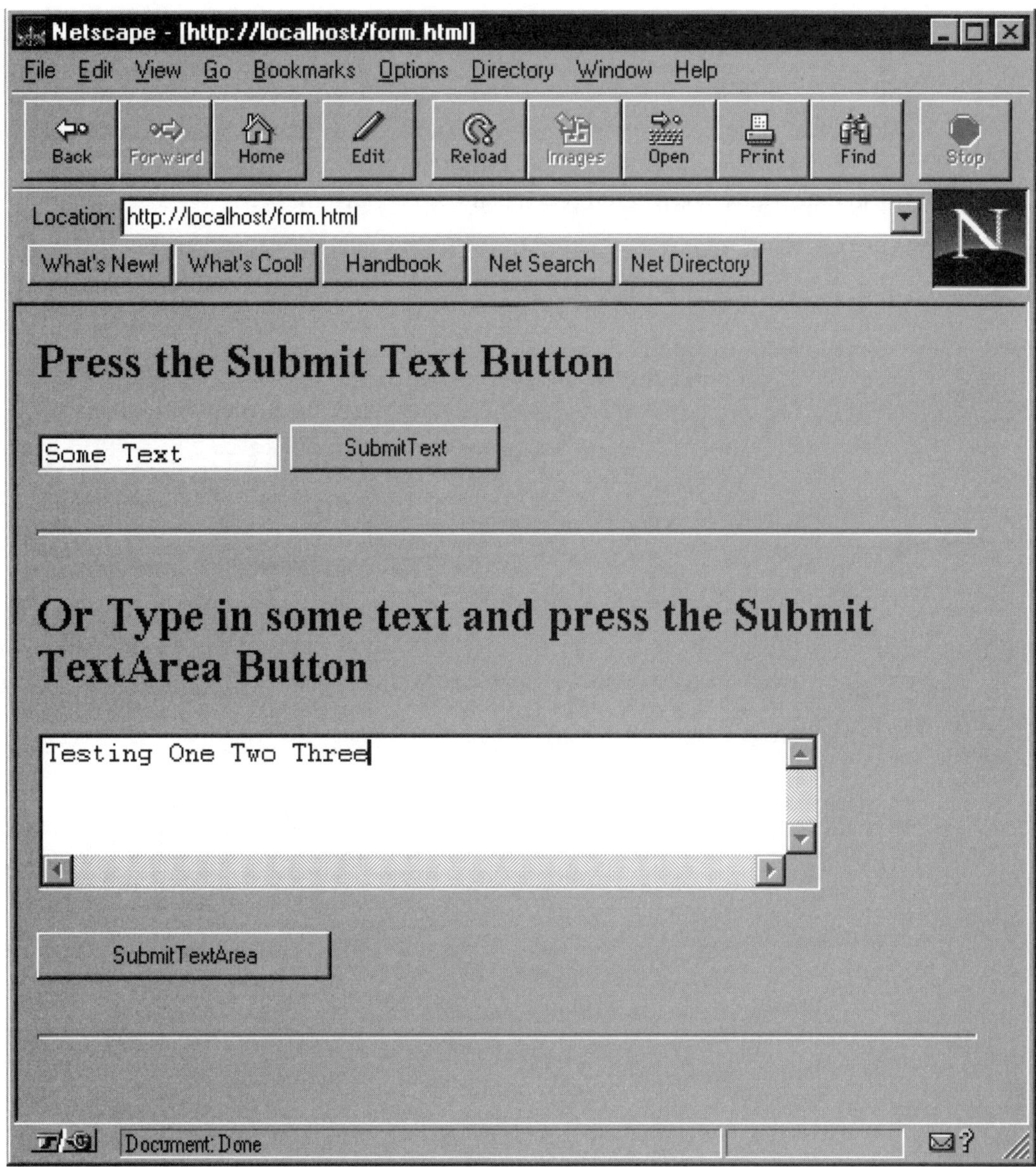
Netscape - [http://localhost/form.html]
File Edit View Go Bookmarks Options Directory Window Help
Back Forward Home Edit Reload Images Open Print Find Stop
Location: http://localhost/form.html
What's New! What's Cool! Handbook Net Search Net Directory
Press the Submit Text Button
Some Text
SubmitText
Or Type in some text and press the Submit TextArea Button
Testing One Two Three
SubmitTextArea
Document: Done

Figure 17–8

The data from the form is passed to the *get*() method in the *sArg* variable. According to the Web convention, each field parameter is separated by an ampersand (&) character.

The FormServerExtension parses through these "&" characters and sends each parameter back on a separate line. This can help the programmer *see* what HTML form data looks like when it reaches the server program.

The following source is included in the *ExtendableWebServer*.java file.

```
class FormServerExtension extends ServerExtension
    {
    final String sTag = "Copyright (c) 1996 Noel Enete";

    public void get (SConnection conn, String sArg)
      {
      StringBuffer sb;
      StringTokenizer st;

      sb = new StringBuffer ();
      st = new StringTokenizer (sArg, "&", false);

      while (st.hasMoreTokens ())
        {
        sb.append (st.nextToken ());
        sb.append ("\n");
        }

      conn.sendReply ("A Form was received by "
        + "the FormServerExtension Class. "
        + "<p>The Arguments were as follows:"
        + "<pre>"
        + sb.toString ()
        + "</pre>");
      }
    }
```

```
1.0 C:\JumpStrt\examples\ExtendableWebServer>java ExtendableWebServer
Serv: Initializing WebServer to port 80
Serv: Waiting for a connection...
Serv: Received a connection
Serv: Waiting for a connection...
*----------------------------------------*
Conn: Connected to: 127.0.0.1:1128
Conn: Received: GET /form.html HTTP/1.0
Conn: Received: Connection: Keep-Alive
Conn: Received: User-Agent: Mozilla/2.0GoldB1 (Win95; I)
Conn: Received: Host: localhost
Conn: Received: Accept: image/gif, image/x-xbitmap, image/jpeg,
  image/pjpeg, */*
SrvX: Class form.html not found
FilX: File form.html found
Conn: Sending the MIME...
Conn: Putting the Resource...
Conn: Finished putting.
Conn: Disconnecting: 127.0.0.1:1128
*----------------------------------------*
Serv: Received a connection
Serv: Waiting for a connection...
*----------------------------------------*
Conn: Connected to: 127.0.0.1:1129
Conn: Received: GET /FormServerExtension?suggestions=Testing+One+Two+Three
&SubmitTextAreaButton=SubmitTextArea HTTP/1.0
Conn: Received: Referer: http://localhost/form.html
Conn: Received: Connection: Keep-Alive
Conn: Received: User-Agent: Mozilla/2.0GoldB1 (Win95; I)
Conn: Received: Host: localhost
Conn: Received: Accept: image/gif, image/x-xbitmap, image/jpeg,
  image/pjpeg, */*
SrvX: Class FormServerExtension found
Conn: Sending the MIME...
Conn: Sending the Resource...
Conn: Finished sending.
Conn: Disconnecting: 127.0.0.1:1129
*----------------------------------------*
```

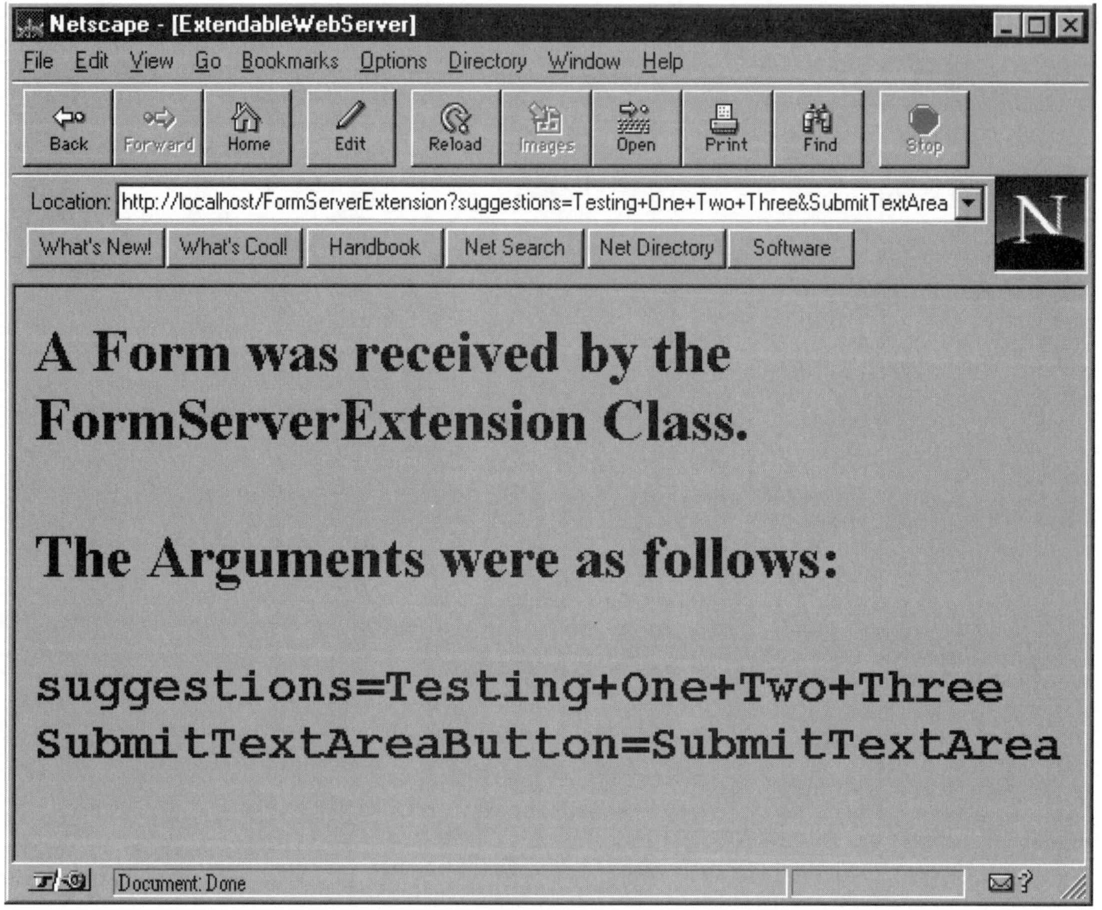

Figure 17–9

Implementing a Client/Server Application

Now that the Web client can be extended and the Web server can be extended, a true Client/Server application can be constructed over the Web. The client can be constructed in the form of an applet. The server can be constructed in the form of a ServerExtension. This is described in Figure 17–10.

Both client and server classes can be loaded from the Web server on demand.

New users are not required to go through software installation. The new client classes are added to the users' browsers when they visit the application's Web site. The new client class makes requests for service back to a ServerExtension on the application Web site. The ServerExtension is dynamically loaded and responds with the requested updates and information.

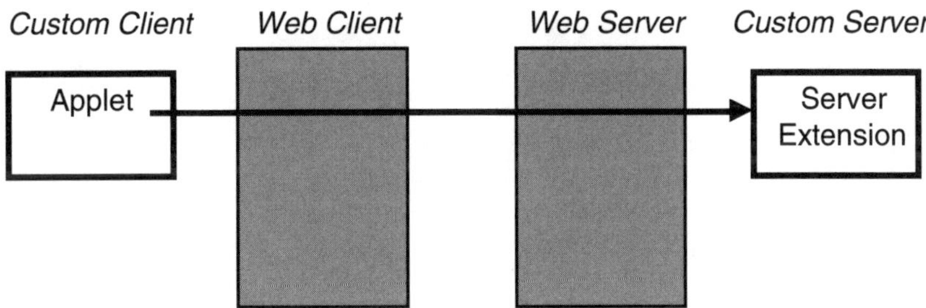

Figure 17–10 A Custom Client/Server application over the existing web infrastructure.

This architecture allows Client/Server applications to be constructed from dynamic distributable Java classes.

SqlQuery—A look at JDBC syntax

This kind of design lends itself to back end database services. With the introduction of Java's DataBase Connectivity (JDBC) classes, a *ServerExtension* class could function as a database server.

JDBC provides an interface to execute SQL queries into third-party database management systems like Oracle and Sybase. The databases do not need to reside on the local machine. The JDBC syntax includes an URL-like address to locate the target database table. Any Java application class (like a ServerExtension) can issue SQL requests to machines anywhere on the Internet. Browser restrictions limit database access for applets to the local machine for security reasons.

JDBC is not restricted to one vendor's database. As the name might suggest, it was based on Microsoft's ODBC, but not built on top of it. Each vendor provides database access to their system by coding native JDBC methods in a Dynamic Link Library (.DLL). The users add these .DLLs to the Java BIN directory and can access them through the methods of the *java.sql.** package.

Although an explanation of JDBC is beyond the scope of this current edition, the source below will give a demomstration of database access in Java. For more information on JDBC, contact Sun Computers at http://java.sun.com.

```
import java.net.URL;
import java.sql.*;

    class SqlQuery
/*****************************************************************************

    SqlQuery - An Example of an SQL Query using JDBC

    This code fragment will not compile and is intended merely for reading.

 *****************************************************************************/

    {
    public static void main (String[] args)
      {
      String sDBUrl;
      Connection conn;
      Statement stmt;
      ResultSet rs;
      int i;

      int iField;
      Numeric nField;
      boolean bField;
      String sKey;

      try
        {

/*      Create an URL specifying a database accessable through ODBC and
        connect to it.
        ===============================================================  */

        sDataBaseUrl = "jdbc:odbc:MyDataBase";
        conn = Environment.getConnection (sDataBaseUrl, "username", "passwrd");


/*      Create a statement and execute an SQL query. The result set is
        placed in rs.
        ===============================================================  */

        stmt = conn.createStatement ();
        rs = stmt.executeQuery
          (
          "SELECT iField, nField, sKey, acField, bField FROM MyTable"
          );
```

```
/*      Each cycle of this loop processes one row of the result set. Get
        each field value in a row using data-type specific methods and
        using the position of the field in the query. Then print the row.
        =================================================================
*/

        while (rs.next ())
          {
          iField = rs.getInteger (1);
          nField = rs.getNumeric (2);
          sKey = rs.getVarChar (3);
          char[] acField = rs.getVarChar(4).tocharArray();
          bField = rs.getBit (5);

          System.out.println ("sKey >>" + sKey + "<<");
          System.out.println ("  iField  >>" + iField + "<<");
          System.out.println ("  nField  >>" + nField + "<<");
          System.out.print   ("  acField >>");
          for (i = 0; i < acField.length; i++)
            {
            System.out.print (acField[i]);
            }
          System.out.println ("<<");
          System.out.println ("  bField >>" + bField + "<<");
          }
        stmt.close ();
        conn.close ();
        }

      catch (Exception e)
        {
        System.out.println ("Exception processing query: " + e);
        }
      }
    }
```

TimeClient/TimeServer—A client/server application to fetch the current time

The following example creates a complete Client/Server application. The client is an applet called TimeClient. The server is a ServerExtension called TimeServer.

The applet presents three buttons for requesting the current time. When a button is pressed, a request is sent to the *TimeServer* extension, which returns the current time as a string. The applet presents the string in a Label control. The applet also sends the parameter *west*, *central*, or *east* with the request to identify the desired time zone.

This application begins by fetching the Web page *TimeClient.html*. This is a file in the ExtendableWebServer directory. The page contains an <APPLET> tag that launches the *TimeClient* applet. Once the applet has arrived and a button is pressed, the applet issues a CGI request to the server which invokes the *time-server* class and fetches the time.

To run the application, start the ExtendableWebServer from a command line:

```
java ExtendableWebServer
```

Then point a Web browser to the following URL to load the client Web page and the Applet class:

```
http://localhost/TimeClient.html
```

When the applet is visible (Figure 17–11), press one of the buttons and watch the server process the request and return the result (Figure 17–12).

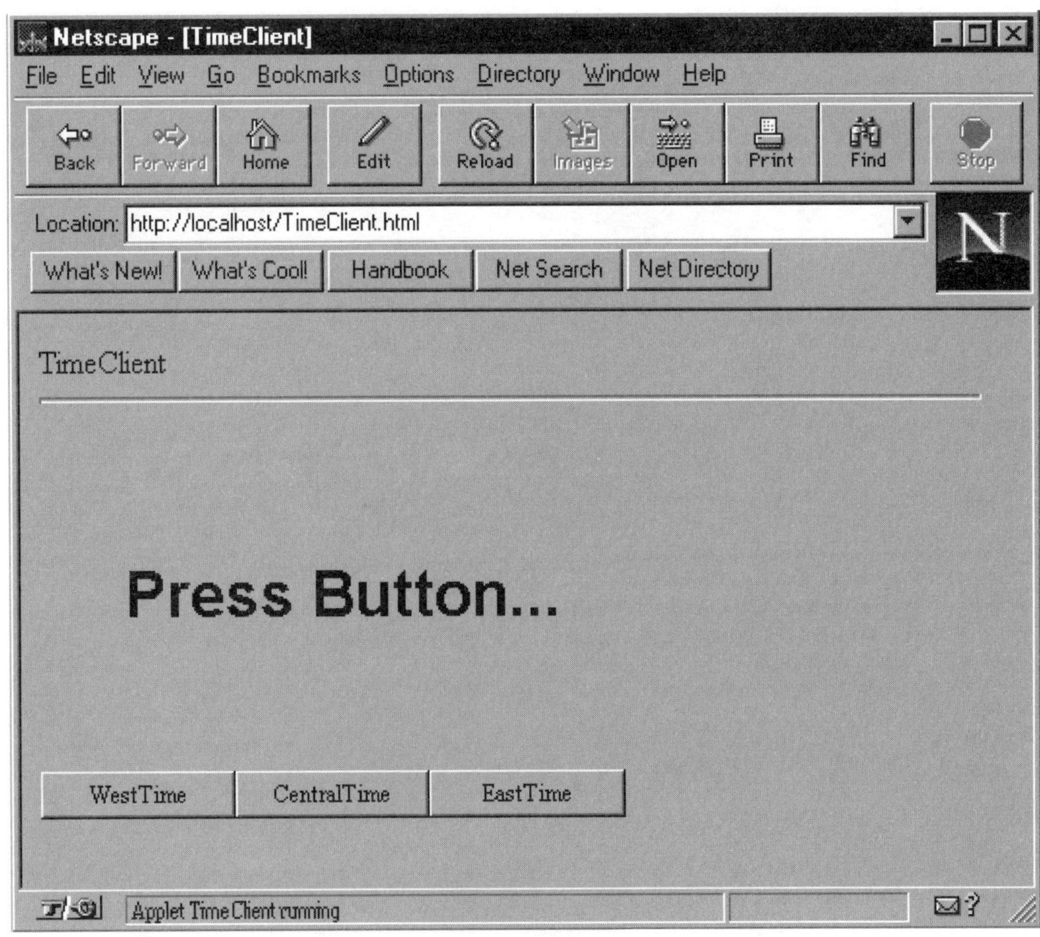
Netscape - [TimeClient]
File Edit View Go Bookmarks Options Directory Window Help
Back Forward Home Edit Reload Images Open Print Find Stop
Location: http://localhost/TimeClient.html
What's New! What's Cool! Handbook Net Search Net Directory
TimeClient
Press Button...
WestTime CentralTime EastTime
Applet TimeClient running

Figure 17–11

```
import java.applet.Applet;
import java.awt.*;
import java.net.*;
import java.io.*;

    public class TimeClient extends Applet
      {
      Label l;

      public void init()
        {
        Panel p;

        setLayout (new BorderLayout (0, 0));

        l = new Label ("Press Button...", Label.CENTER);
        l.setFont (new Font ("Helvetica", Font.BOLD, 32));
        add ("Center", l);

        p = new Panel ();
        p.setLayout (new GridLayout (1, 3, 0, 0));
        p.add (new Button ("WestTime"));
        p.add (new Button ("CentralTime"));
        p.add (new Button ("EastTime"));
        add ("South", p);
        }


      public boolean action (Event evt, Object obj)
        {
        if ("WestTime".equals (obj))
          {
          urlRequest ("West");
          l.setFont (new Font ("Helvetica", Font.BOLD, 32));
          return (true);
          }
        else if ("CentralTime".equals (obj))
          {
          urlRequest ("Central");
          l.setFont (new Font ("Courier", Font.BOLD, 24));
          return (true);
          }
        else if ("EastTime".equals (obj))
          {
          urlRequest ("East");
```

```
      l.setFont (new Font ("TimesRoman", Font.BOLD | Font.ITALIC, 32));
      return (true);
      }
    return (false);
    }


  void urlRequest (String s)
    {
    URL url;
    InputStream isIn;
    byte[] ab = new byte[1024];
    StringBuffer sb;
    int iNumBytes;

    sb = new StringBuffer ();

    try
      {
      url = new URL ("http://localhost/TimeServer?" + s);
      isIn = url.openStream ();

      while ((iNumBytes = isIn.read (ab, 0, 1024)) >= 0)
        {
        sb.append (new String (ab, 0, 0, iNumBytes));
        }
      }
    catch (Exception e)
      {
      System.out.println ("Exception receiving the data: " + e);
      }

    l.setText (sb.toString ());
    }
  }
```

```
<HTML>
<HEAD>
<TITLE> TimeClient </TITLE>
</HEAD>
<BODY>
TimeClient
<HR>
<APPLET CODE="TimeClient" WIDTH=300 HEIGHT=200>
</APPLET>
<HR>
</BODY>
</HTML>
```

The *ServerExtension* class below is actually included in the source for the ExtendableWebServer, but is included here for easy reference.

```
class TimeServer extends ServerExtension
  {
  final String sTag = "Copyright (c) 1996 Noel Enete";

  public void get (SConnection conn, String sArg)
    {
    Date d;
    String s;
    StringTokenizer st;
    byte[] ab = new byte[100];
    long lTime;
    int iReqTimezoneOffset;

    if ("West".equals (sArg))
      {
      iReqTimezoneOffset = 420;
      }
    else if ("Central".equals (sArg))
      {
      iReqTimezoneOffset = 300;
      }
    else
      {
      iReqTimezoneOffset = 240;
      }
```

```
    d = new Date ();
    lTime = d.getTime ();
    lTime += (d.getTimezoneOffset () - iReqTimezoneOffset) * 60 * 1000;
    d.setTime (lTime);

    st = new StringTokenizer (d.toLocaleString ());
    s = st.nextToken ();
    s = sArg + ": " + st.nextToken ();
    s.getBytes (0, s.length (), ab, 0);
    conn.putReply (ab, 0, s.length());
    }
  }
```

```
1.0 C:\JumpStrt\examples\ExtendableWebServer>java ExtendableWebServer
Serv: Initializing WebServer to port 80
Serv: Waiting for a connection...
Serv: Received a connection
Serv: Waiting for a connection...
*-------------------------------------------*
Conn: Connected to: 127.0.0.1:1043
Conn: Received: GET /TimeServer?East HTTP/1.0
Conn: Received: Connection: Keep-Alive
Conn: Received: User-Agent: Mozilla/2.0GoldB1 (Win95; I)
Conn: Received: Pragma: no-cache
Conn: Received: Host: localhost
Conn: Received: Accept: image/gif, image/x-xbitmap, image/jpeg,
image/pjpeg, */*
SrvX: Class TimeServer found
Conn: Sending the MIME...
Conn: Putting the Resource...
Conn: Finished putting.
Conn: Disconnecting: 127.0.0.1:1043
*-------------------------------------------*
```

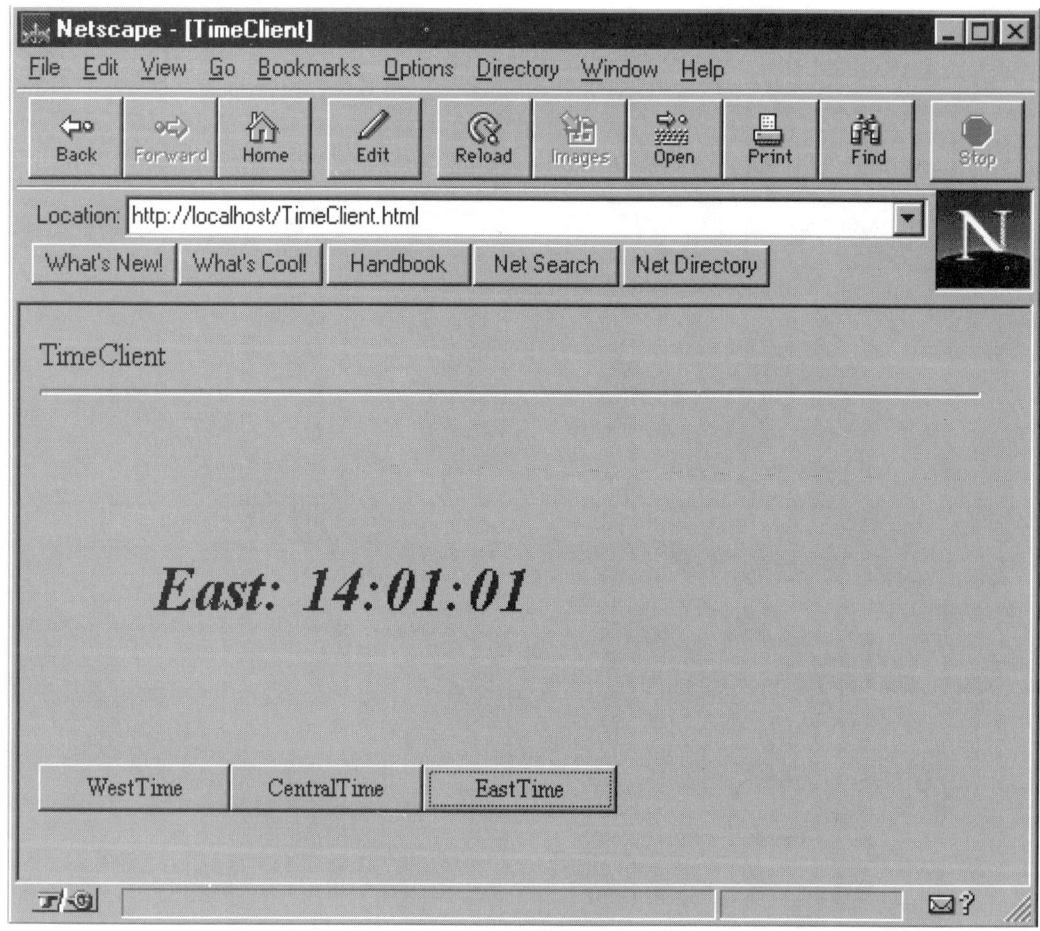
Netscape - [TimeClient]
File Edit View Go Bookmarks Options Directory Window Help
Back Forward Home Edit Reload Images Open Print Find Stop
Location: http://localhost/TimeClient.html
What's New! What's Cool! Handbook Net Search Net Directory
TimeClient
East: 14:01:01
WestTime CentralTime EastTime

Figure 17–12

The server log above shows the activity that follows pressing one of the applet's buttons. In the figure, the *EastTime* button was pressed. In response, the applet sent a request to the server that began with the line:

```
GET /TimeServer?East HTTP/1.0
```

When the *get*() method of the *TimeServer* class received the request, the *sArg* variable carried the string "*East*". The code inside the *get*() method calculated the current time, then displaced it for the Eastern time zone and called *putReply*() to return the time string.

By coding clients in applets and servers in ServerExtensions, a distributed application can ride the infrastructure of the Web. The application can be deployed on demand to users as they visit the application's Web site.

The only requirement is that the Web server supports the dynamic launching of Java classes. The ExtendableWebServer was designed to be as simple as possible to help new Java programmers understand how server extensions are implemented.

The final chapter leverages the design of the ExtendableWebServer to construct a Web server that is more complete and better structured for enhancements. If one wants to start a Web site with one of the Web servers in this book, consider using the CaffeineCafe.

CHAPTER 18

The CaffeineCafe

At some point in the development process, the time comes to convert a prototype into a real maintainable application. As the size of a program grows, the need to segment it grows.

The ExtendableWebServer of the previous chapter has reached that point. This chapter enhances the server to make it more of a complete application program. Along the way several of the Java facilities for managing larger system development will be illustrated. The final result is a Web server that would be suitable for creating a Web site for the Internet *or* the Intranet.

Although it is not a requirement for productional programs to have "catchy" names, the name *ExtendableWebServer* leaves something to be desired. What could a server be called that delivers many small portions of Java service? How about a *CaffeineCafe*? The new name may be a little corny, but it usually brings a smile to the face of those who hear it.

There is a similar problem with the name of the *ServerExtension* class. The name may be descriptive, but it lacks personality. So what should a class be called that doles out small portions of service from a *CaffeineCafe*? How about a *Dripper*? . . . Give it a minute, you might like it. . . . If not, you have the source and can give it a better name.

Beyond the name issues, the services in the CaffeineCafe are more upgraded and generalized than those available in the ExtendableWebServer. The source code is organized as several separate files to facilitate a controlled growth of features. The source is commented and the comments are automatically formatted into HTML documentation using Java's documentation generator. The documentation is easily viewed from the *\JumpStart\index.html* Web page.

The server now supports both GET and POST requests and can construct a more intelligent MIME when responding to Web requests. It can also preload a list of Drippers to speed up the processing of CGI requests.

There is an object that maintains a non-volatile list of system-wide defaults. The services in this class allow the users to specify a list of aliases that translate certain incoming requests into different requests. It also allows the Webmaster to specify the base directory for file fetches and a list of packages to search for loading Dripper classes.

To introduce the CaffeineCafe, it would be helpful to take it out for a spin.

Several examples, which follow, provide a sense for how the CaffeineCafe operates. To get the most benefit from the examples, try to position the browser window and the command line window so both are visible at one time. As one clicks on Web pages and watches the requests and responses flow through the Web server, they develop an irreplaceable instinct for how the Web works.

Try It Out—How to Run CaffeineCafe

If the CD example programs have been installed and the code was placed in the *JumpStrt* directory, the CaffeineCafe is ready to run. If there is any doubt, one should verify that the contents of the CaffeineCafe directory are placed in the directory:

```
\JumpStrt\examples\CaffeineCafe
```

Open a command line window and change directories to the home directory, which is *\JumpStrt\examples\CaffeineCafe*. Launch the CaffeineCafe with the following syntax:

```
java com.enete.CaffeineCafe.CaffeineCafe
```

This application has been compiled into a *package,* which must be specified as part of the class name. There is more information on packages later in this chapter. When the server starts, it loads a number of system-wide defaults and several Dripper classes. The startup log should look like this:

```
Beta1 C:\JumpStrt\examples\CaffeineCafe>java com.enete.CaffeineCafe.
  CaffeineCafe
*-----------Default Directories------------*
-- listing properties --
BaseDocDir=/JumpStrt/examples/CaffeineCafe
BaseClassDir=/JumpStrt/examples/CaffeineCafe
*--------------Default Packages------------*
-- listing properties --
com.enete.CaffeineCafe=com.enete.CaffeineCafe
*------------Default Aliases--------------*
– listing properties –
stats=EchoDripper
echo.html=EchoDripper
echo=EchoDripper
*-----------Default Preloades-------------*
-- listing properties --
PackageMaint=PackageMaint
FileDripper=FileDripper
EchoDripper=EchoDripper
AliasMaint=AliasMaint
PreloadMaint=PreloadMaint
*-----------------------------------------*
Drip: Class com.enete.CaffeineCafe.PackageMaint found
Drip: Class com.enete.CaffeineCafe.FileDripper found
Drip: Class com.enete.CaffeineCafe.EchoDripper found
Drip: Class com.enete.CaffeineCafe.AliasMaint found
Drip: Class com.enete.CaffeineCafe.PreloadMaint found
Cafe: Initializing to port 80 on aptiva/199.5.187.134
Cafe: Waiting for a connection...
```

At this point, the server is waiting for a connection request from a Web browser. Startup a browser and enter one of the following URLs:

```
http://localhost/EchoDripper
http://localhost/file1
http://localhost/file2
http://localhost/file3
http://localhost/SimpleDripper
http://localhost/FormDripper
http://localhost/FileMaintClient.html
```

To stop the CaffeineCafe, press a *control-C* in the window from which the server was launched.

The first request causes the server to load the *EchoDripper* class, which sends back a dynamically generated Web page. When the server receives a file request, it launches the FileDripper to find and return the file to the Web browser. The *SimpleDripper* class is the smallest example of a class that extends the CaffeineCafe.

The FormDripper is a hollow version of a system maintenance Dripper program. It demonstrates how data from an HTML form is received by a Dripper object. There are three classes based on this example that come with the CaffeineCafe that allow the users to maintain the system-wide defaults. They are constructed so that maintenance can be performed from a Web browser.

The maintenance classes are the *AliasMaint*, *PreloadMaint*, and *PackageMaint* classes. Be careful with them. They alter the system defaults and affect how the server runs.

To run them, use one of their names in place of EchoDripper on the URL above. The maintenance class responds by sending an HTML form to the browser. Make changes to the multi-line text area. Make sure there are no blank lines. Then press the *Update* button and the dripper will update the system defaults. The *AliasMaint* Dripper sends the page, which is shown in Figure 18–1, back to the browser: *http://localhost/AliasMaint.*

The alias defaults give the Web administrator the opportunity to translate Web requests before the server processes the request. According to the list in Figure 18–1, users could make a request for the *echo.html* file and the *EchoDripper* class would actually be invoked.

When the *Update* button is pressed, the field data is sent to the *AliasMaint* Dripper. It pulls the data from the multi-line text area field and updates the alias Properties object. Then it creates a new form that displays the new aliases and sends it back to the browser for more changes. Each time the *Update* button is pressed, the change is saved to disk.

The maintenance drippers illustrate how to construct server-side applications that use dynamic HTML forms and Web pages for the entire visual presentation of the program.

The last URL mentioned above launches the FileMaint application. This is a custom Client/Server application whose client is an applet and whose server is a Dripper. The client manages the presentation and the server manages the data storage and retrieval. The application is not written to be fast. It is written to be easy to read. As a result, it loads all of its data each time it processes a request. There is much room for optimization.

The data that is presented by the *FileMaint* application is genuine *surf speak*. The terms that are included identify common situations that occur while ocean surfing. A second copy of the data is stored in the file *SurfSpeak* in the *CaffeineCafe* directory.

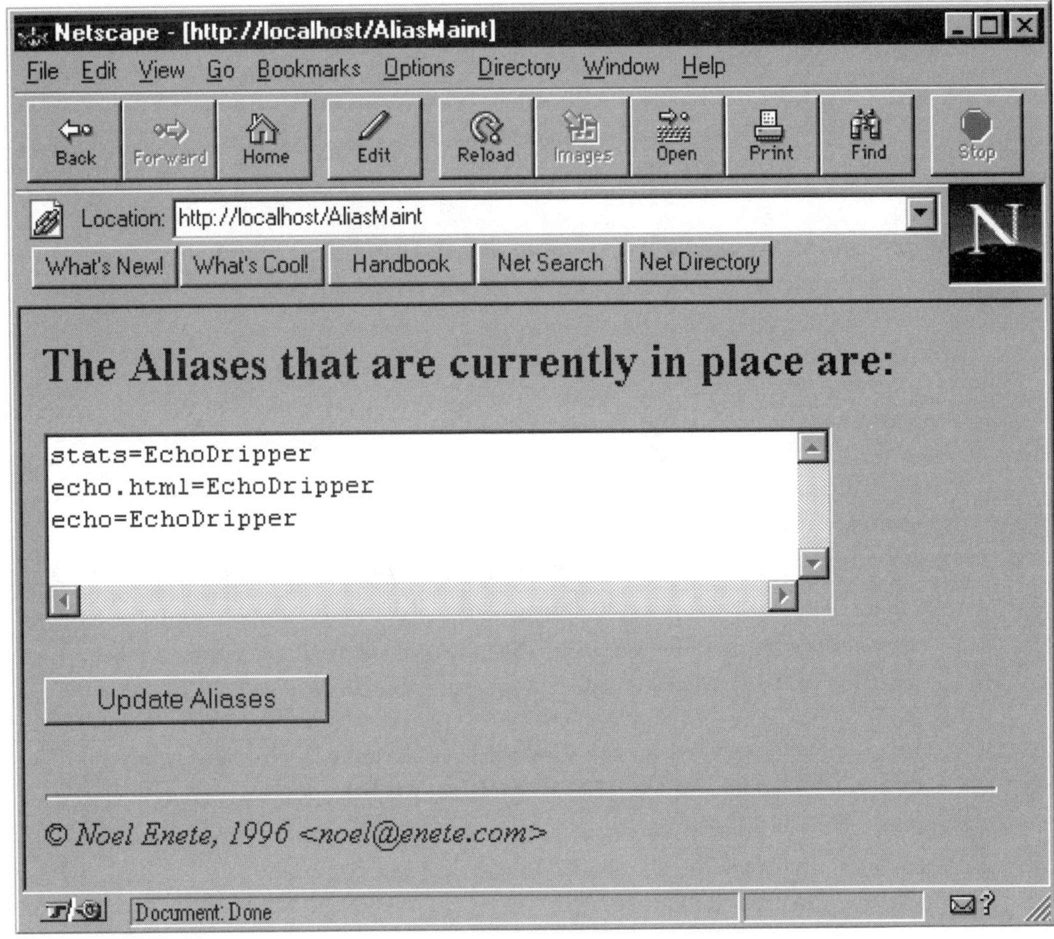

Figure 18–1

Extend It—How to Code Drippers

How to code a simple dripper

The services of the CaffeineCafe can be extended by coding Dripper classes. This is the Java equivalent to a CGI program. The job of a Dripper is to return an appropriate Web page to the requester.

The following Dripper class returns a Web page that contains the string *"Hello World"*. The source for this class is in the *SimpleDripper.java* file and is located in the CaffeineCafe home directory.

```
import com.enete.CaffeineCafe.*;

    public class SimpleDripper extends Dripper
      {

      public void get (SConnection conn, String[] args)
        {
        conn.reply ("Hello World");
        }

      }
```

Drippers make use of the Dripper and *SConnection* classes and so they need to import the *com.enete.CaffeineCafe* package. Each class that extends the services of the CaffeineCafe must be an extension of the *Dripper* class. This follows the analogy that browser extension classes must extend the Applet class.

The *get*() method receives control when a Web request arrives and asks the *SConnection* object to send an appropriate response to the browser.

To create a new dripper, copy this file and replace the name *SimpleDripper* with the name of the new service extension—for example, *MyDripper*. Replace the *"Hello World"* string with the HTML text string that should be sent back to the browser. After the class is compiled into the CaffeineCafe directory, invoke the service by entering the following URL at the browser:

`http://localhost/MyDripper`

Remember to have the CaffeineCafe running in a command line window before pointing the browser to this URL.

How to code a forms processing dripper

The normal role that a dripper plays is to be a dynamic Web page generator. But it can also be a complete application.

If the dripper delivered a Web page that contained an HTML form, the dripper could code the form so that it pointed back to the Dripper class. Then, when the users press the button, the data would be sent back to the Dripper class for processing. If the dripper maintained this cycle of interaction, it would become a complete application whose entire user interface consisted of dynamic Web pages.

The following dripper demonstrates how to generate this kind of dripper. The class is stored in the *FormDripper.java* file and is located in the CaffeineCafe home directory. To run it, point a browser to:

`http://localhost/FormDripper`

```
import com.enete.CaffeineCafe.*;
import java.io.*;
import java.util.*;

    public class FormDripper extends Dripper
      {

      final String sForm =
        "<form method=\"post\" action=\"http://localhost/FormDripper\">" +
        "<h2>A Dripper Generated HTML Form</h2><p>"                      +
        "The FormDripper generated and sent this form to the Web "       +
        "browser. When you send this form back, it will go back to "     +
        "the FormDripper for processing. Type in this "                  +
        "text area</i> and press the button to see how the form "        +
        "data is delivered to the Dripper.<p>"                           +
        "<textarea name=\"TextAreaControl\" cols=48 rows=4>"             +
        "</textarea><p>"                                                 +
        "<input type=submit name=SendButton value=\"Send\">"             +
        "</form>"                                                        +
        "<hr>";


      public void get (SConnection conn, String[] args)
        {
        conn.putHtmlMime ();
        conn.put (sForm);
        }


      public void post (SConnection conn, Hashtable ht)
        {
        conn.putHtmlMime ();
        conn.put ("<h3><i>The Dripper's post() method received the follow-
        ing "
          + "parameters as a hashtable:</i></h3><p>" + ht);
        }
      }
```

The data for the Web page is stored in string variable *sForm*. When the users key in the URL that points to this dripper, the *get*() method sends the Web page back to the browser.

When the users press the button on the form, the Web request is relayed to the *post*() method in the dripper. This receives the data variables from the form and sends a diagnostic message back to the users. To make this a complete application, the full Web page would be sent back to the users at this point.

This dripper illustrates the two principle methods that receive a Web request: *get*() and *post*().

```
public void get (SConnection conn, String[] args)
   {
   }

public void post (SConnection conn, Hashtable ht)
   {
   }
```

These two methods correspond with the two kinds of Web requests–the GET and POST requests. If the browser makes a GET request, control is passed to the *get*() method and any parameters are placed in the *args* string array (one parameter per string). If the browser makes a POST request, control is passed to the *post*() method and any parameters are placed in the *ht* Hashtable variable as a collection of key/value pairs.

The dripper uses the *SConnection* methods *putHtmlMime*() and *put*() to send the data to the client rather than using the single *reply*() method above. This provides a way to send one MIME header followed by several data strings. The *reply*() method sends a MIME header with each data string that it sends to the client.

```
conn.putHtmlMime ();
conn.put (sForm1);
conn.put (sForm2);
conn.put (sForm3);
```

The HTML form includes the statement *method=post*, which instructs the browser to make a POST request when sending the form back to the server.

```
final String sForm1 =
  "<form method=\"post\" action=\"http://localhost/FormDripper\">" +
```

So, when the users press the *Send* button, the browser sends this form to the server by way of a POST and control is passed to the dripper's *post*() method. In the *post*() method above, a diagnostic Web page is returned and it displays the data that it received.

To create a full application from this dripper, the *post*() method should process the HTML field data and send back a new Web page with the new data.

The following example is one of the drippers that maintains system-wide defaults for the CaffeineCafe. It is a complete application. Use it carefully because it makes changes to CaffeineCafe's properties files. To run it, point a browser at the URL:

`http://localhost/AliasMaint`

```
package com.enete.CaffeineCafe;
import java.io.*;
import java.util.*;
import com.enete.CaffeineCafe.*;

/*************************************************************************

    AliasMaint -- Maintains the System-Wide Default Alias List.

    To the this application's HTML form, point a browser to
    http://localhost/AliasMaint, then interact with the form.

    * @author    Noel Enete
    * @version   1.0 alpha1, 04/09/96

*************************************************************************/

    public class AliasMaint extends Dripper
    {
    final String sTag = "Copyright (c) 1996 Noel Enete";

    final String sForm1 =
      "<form method=\"post\" action=\"http://localhost/AliasMaint\">" +
      "<h2>The Aliases that are currently in place are:</h2><p>"      +
      "<textarea name=\"updates\" cols=48 rows=4>";
```

```
    final String sFormn9 =
      "</textarea><p>"                                                +
      "<input type=submit name=update value=\"Update Aliases\">"      +
      "</form>"                                                       +
      "<hr>"                                                          +
      "<address>"                                                     +
      "&copy; Noel Enete, 1996 &lt;noel@enete.com&gt;"                +
      "</address>";


/*************************************************************************/


/** The get() method is called when someone requests this class in an
    URL without any parameters (http://localhost/AliasMaint). The
    method returns a form that displays the system-wide aliases for
    the CaffeineCafe system and allows the user to update it. When
    the Update button is pressed, this class is called again, only
    it is called with the POST method followed by the values from
    the form fields.*//*
    ==================================================================  */

    public void get (SConnection conn, String[] args)
      {
      Enumeration enum;
      Properties pr;
      String sKey;


/*    Output the MIME and the first part of the HTML form.
      ======================================================  */

      conn.putHtmlMime ();
      conn.put (sForm1);


/*    Output each of the current system-wide aliases.
      ==================================================  */

      pr = CaffeineCafe.getDefaults().getAliases();
      enum = pr.propertyNames ();
      while (enum.hasMoreElements ())
        {
        sKey = (String) enum.nextElement ();
        conn.put
```

```
        (
        sKey + "=" + pr.getProperty (sKey)
        + "\r\n"
        );
      }


/*   Output the remainder of the form.
     ==================================  */

     conn.put (sForm9);
     }


/** This method is called from the self contained HTML form in this
    class. It pulls the contents of the form fields and updates the
    system-wide aliases with the contents of the fields.*//*
    =================================================================  */

    public void post (SConnection conn, Hashtable ht)
      {
      Enumeration enum;
      Properties pr;
      String sKey;
      String sArgument;
      String sUpdates;
      Hashtable htNewAliases;
      CaffeineCafeDefaults defs;


/*    Output the MIME and the first part of the form back to the client.
      ==================================================================== */

      defs = CaffeineCafe.getDefaults ();
      conn.putHtmlMime ();
      conn.put (sForm1);


/*    If the update button was pressed, update the default aliases
      with the contents of the 'updates' field.
      =============================================================  */

      if (ht.get ("update") != null)
        {
        System.out.println ("FrmD: Updating Aliases");
```

```
        sUpdates = (String) ht.get ("updates");
        htNewAliases = getNewAliases (sUpdates);


/*      Reload the system-wide aliases from the contents of the form
        field.
        ===========================================================  */

        defs.clearAliases ();
        enum = htNewAliases.keys ();
        while (enum.hasMoreElements ())
          {
          sKey = (String) enum.nextElement ();
          sArgument = (String) htNewAliases.get (sKey);
          defs.putAlias (sKey, sArgument);
          }
        defs.saveDefaults ();
        }


/*    Output the current aliases to the client.
      ========================================  */

      pr = defs.getAliases();
      enum = pr.propertyNames ();
      while (enum.hasMoreElements ())
        {
        sKey = (String) enum.nextElement ();
        conn.put
          (
          sKey + "=" + pr.getProperty (sKey)
          + "\r\n"
          );
        }

      conn.put (sForm9);
      }


    Hashtable getNewAliases (String s)
      {
      String sKey;
      String sArgument;
      StringTokenizer st;
      Hashtable ht;
```

```
        ht = new Hashtable ();
        st = new StringTokenizer (s, "\n= ", false);
        while (st.hasMoreTokens ())
          {
          sKey = st.nextToken ();
          sKey.trim ();
          sArgument = st.nextToken ();
          sArgument = sArgument.replace ('\r', ' ');
          sArgument = sArgument.trim ();
          ht.put (sKey, sArgument);
          }
        return (ht);
        }

    }

/*========================(  End of Source  )===========================*/
```

More examples of drippers that implement server-side applications are AliasMaint.java, PreloadMaint.java, and PackageMaint.java and can be found in the following directory:

`\JumpStrt\examples\CaffeineCafe\com\enete\CaffeineCafe`

This kind of dripper is a complete application that lives on the Web server. Since it does not require any Java class on the client side, it could be called a server-side application and will work with all browsers, even if they do not support Java.

How to code a Client/Server application

The previously mentioned drippers have always returned Web pages to the requester. But they do not need to return a Web page. If the requester is an applet rather than a browser, the dripper could return any kind of data and the applet would decide how to render the data.

To implement a Client/Server application within the infrastructure of the Web, one would design applet and dripper pairs so that the applet/dripper exchange would accomplish the work of an application program.

The example below implements a Client/Server application that performs maintenance on a file on the server. It is composed of four files: *FileMaintClient.html*, *FileMaintClient.java*, *FileMaintServer.java*, and *FileMaintServerProperties*. Each file can be located in:

`\JumpStrt\examples\CaffeineCafe`

To run the application, point a browser to:

```
http://localhost/FileMaintClient.html
```

After the Web page and applet are featured, the user is given the opportunity to perform file maintenance on a simple key word/definition file (Figure 18–2).

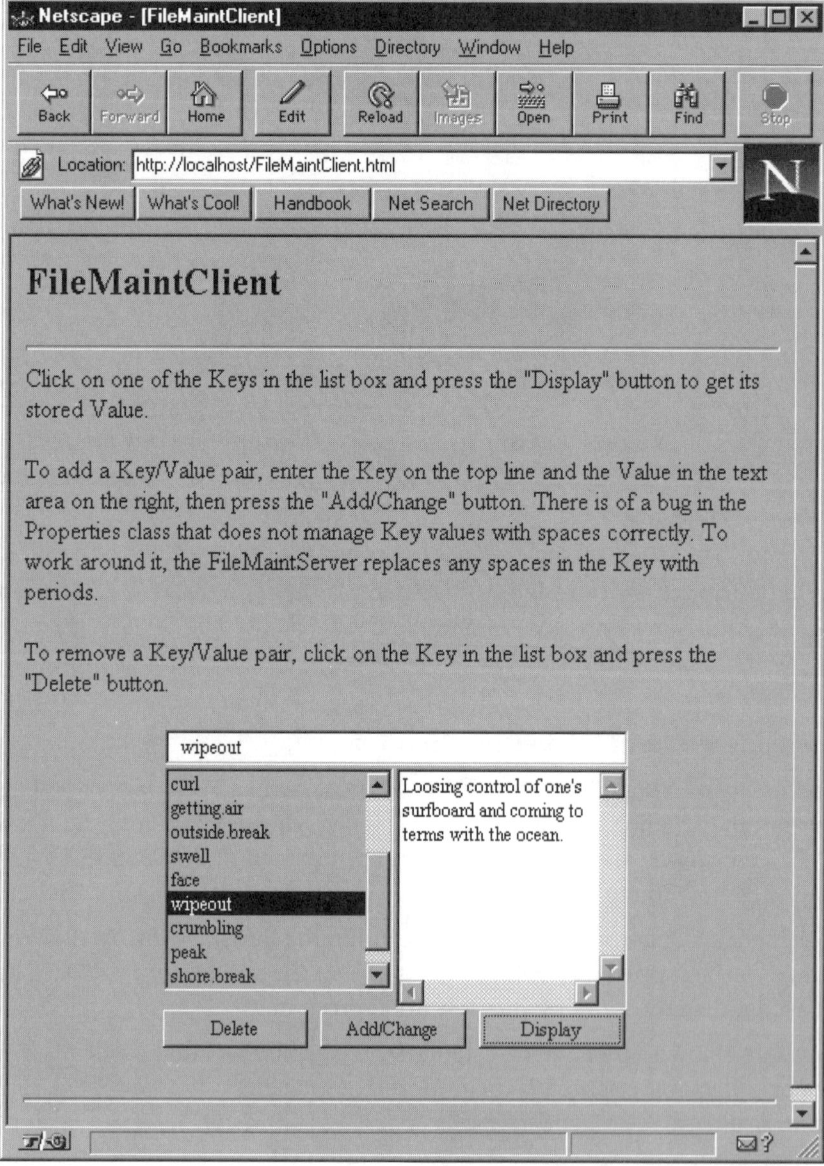

Figure 18–2

The client program is an applet called the *FileMaintClient*. It presents a list of keys in a List control. These keys represent key/value records that are managed by the server. Click on a key, then click the *Display* button and the key's value will be fetched from the server.

To enter a new key/value pair, enter the key through the TextField on the top and enter the value in the TextArea control in the middle. After entering the data, click the *Add* button and the values are sent to the FileMaintServer to add to the file. The FileMaintServer returns a new list of keys which the FileMaintClient places in the list control.

The text in the key/value fields must be specially encoded to flow as parameters to a GET request. The spaces must be replaced with "+"s and non-printable characters must be turned into escape sequences that take the form of a percent sign followed by two hexadecimal characters (e.g., "%12").

Java provides the static method *encode*() in the URLEncode class to accomplish this transformation.

```
TextField tf;
TextArea ta;
String s;
String sResponse;

s = "&" + URLEncoder.encode (tf.getText ())
  + "&" + URLEncoder.encode (ta.getText ());
urlRequest ("Put", s);
updateList (sResponse);
```

When the request is encoded, it looks like this:

`FileMaintServer?REQUEST&PARM1&PARM2`

The "?" separates the resource name from its parameters. The parameters are separated by an "&" character.

The REQUEST parameter is defined by the FileMaintServer to be one of the following strings: *"Put"*, *"Get"*, *"Remove"*, or *"List"*. The PARM1 and PARM2 parameters have different meanings for each REQUEST. The rules for each request are described in the source to the FileMaintServer.

Here is the FileMaintClient:

```
import java.applet.Applet;
import java.awt.*;
import java.net.*;
import java.io.*;
import java.util.*;

    public class FileMaintClient extends Applet
      {
      TextField tf;
      TextArea ta;
      List l;
      String sResponse = "";

      public void init()
        {
        Panel p;

        setLayout (new BorderLayout (0, 0));

        tf = new TextField ();
        add ("North", tf);

        p = new Panel ();
        p.setLayout (new GridLayout (1, 2, 0, 0));
        l = new List ();
        p.add (l);
        ta = new TextArea ();
        p.add (ta);
        urlRequest ("List", "");
        updateList (sResponse);
        tf.setText (l.getSelectedItem ());
        add ("Center", p);

        p = new Panel ();
        p.setLayout (new GridLayout (1, 3, 8, 0));
        p.add (new Button ("Delete"));
        p.add (new Button ("Add/Change"));
        p.add (new Button ("Display"));
        add ("South", p);

        l.select (0);
        l.makeVisible (0);
        }
```

```
public boolean action (Event evt, Object obj)
  {
  String s;

  if ("Delete".equals (obj))
    {
    s = "&" + URLEncoder.encode (l.getSelectedItem ());
    urlRequest ("Remove", s);
    updateList (sResponse);
    return (true);
    }

  else if ("Add/Change".equals (obj))
    {
    if (("".equals (tf.getText ())) || ("".equals (ta.getText ())))
      {
      showStatus ("Data must be entered in the Key and Value fields");
      return (true);
      }
    s = "&" + URLEncoder.encode (tf.getText ())
      + "&" + URLEncoder.encode (ta.getText ());
    urlRequest ("Put", s);
    updateList (sResponse);
    return (true);
    }

  else if ("Display".equals (obj))
    {
    s = "&" + URLEncoder.encode (l.getSelectedItem ());
    urlRequest ("Get", s);
    ta.setText (sResponse);
    return (true);
    }

  return (false);
  }


public boolean handleEvent (Event evt)
  {
  if (evt.id == Event.LIST_SELECT)
    {
    tf.setText (l.getSelectedItem ());
    ta.setText ("");
    }
```

```
    return (super.handleEvent (evt));
    }


  void urlRequest (String sResource, String sParm)
    {
    URL url;
    InputStream isIn;
    byte[] ab = new byte[1024];
    StringBuffer sb;
    int iNumBytes;

    sb = new StringBuffer ();

    try
      {
      url = new URL ("http://localhost/FileMaintServer?"
        + sResource + sParm);
      isIn = url.openStream ();

      while ((iNumBytes = isIn.read (ab, 0, 1024)) >= 0)
        {
        sb.append (new String (ab, 0, 0, iNumBytes));
        }
      }
    catch (Exception e)
      {
      System.out.println ("Exception receiving the data: " + e);
      }

    sResponse = sb.toString ();
    }


  void updateList (String s)
    {
    StringTokenizer st;
    String sSelected = "";
    String sItem;
    int i = 0;

    if (l.countItems () > 0)
      {
      sSelected = l.getSelectedItem ();
      l.delItems (0, l.countItems () - 1);
      }
```

```
        st = new StringTokenizer (s, "\r\n", false);

        while (st.hasMoreElements ())
          {
          sItem = st.nextToken ();
          l.addItem (sItem);
          if (sItem.equals (sSelected))
            {
            i = l.countItems () - 1;
            }
          }

        l.select (i);
        l.makeVisible (i);
        tf.setText (l.getSelectedItem ());
        ta.setText ("");
        }
      }
```

```
<HTML>
<HEAD>
<TITLE> FileMaintClient </TITLE>
</HEAD>
<BODY>
<H2>FileMaintClient</H2>
<HR>
Click on one of the Keys in the list box and press the "Display" button
to get its stored Value.<p>

To add a Key/Value pair, enter the Key on the top line and the Value
in the text area on the right, then press the "Add/Change" button. There
is a bug in the Properties class that does not manage Key values
with spaces correctly. To work around it, the FileMaintServer
replaces any spaces in the Key with periods.<p>

To remove a Key/Value pair, click on the Key in the list box and
press the "Delete" button.<p>

<CENTER>
<APPLET CODE="FileMaintClient" WIDTH=300 HEIGHT=200>
</APPLET>
</CENTER>
</BODY>
</HTML>
<p>
<HR>
```

On the server side of the application is the *FileMaintServer* class. This Dripper is invoked each time the FileMaintClient makes a Web request. The client issues one of four requests—*"Get"*, *"Put"*, *"Remove"*, or *"List"*. The FileMaintServer performs the request and sends back a response.

The FileMaintServer performs all of its processing in the *get*() method. The request parameters arrive in the *args* variable. The *args*[*0*] string holds the REQUEST verb. The next two strings in the *args* array hold the PARM1 and PARM2 parameters.

The data file that the FileMaintServer is maintaining is a Properties file. At the beginning of every request, the FileMaintServer calls its local method *openProperties*() to open the properties file.

```
void openProperties ()
        {
        p = new Properties ();

        try
          {
          fis = new FileInputStream ("FileMaintServerProperties");
          p.load (fis);
          fis.close ();
          }
        catch (Exception e)
          {
          System.out.println ("Mant: Can not open FileMaintServer"
            "Properties");
            }
        }
```

This method instantiates a Properties object from the contents of the saved file *FileMaintServerProperties*. Once instantiated, the Properties object works like a Hashtable to store and maintain the key/value pairs. Every time a change is made to the Properties object, the new contents of the object are saved to disk. The local method, *saveProperties*(), is called to write the file.

The Properties file is a text file. Each line is delimited by a single line feed character (regardless of the platform). One should avoid editing it directly unless the editor correctly processes line feed delimited lines. If the *FileMaintServerProperties* file becomes damaged, there is an extra copy of the data in the *SurfSpeak* file.

Each REQUEST issues a response to the client. The *"Put"*, *"Remove"*, and *"List"* REQUESTs, return a CRLF delimited list that identify the current keys in the

Properties object. The *"Get"* REQUEST returns the value of the key that was specified in PARM1.

When parameter data arrives at the *get*() method, it is still in its encoded form for travel across the Web. To decode it, the method *httpToString*() in the *SConnection* class is called.

This code fragment implements the *"Remove"* REQUEST.

```
        else if ((args.length > 1) && "Remove".equals (args[0]))
          {
          p.remove (SConnection.httpToString (args[1]));
          saveProperties ();
          returnKeys (conn);
          return;
          }
```

Here is the FileMaintServer:

```
import com.enete.CaffeineCafe.*;
import java.io.*;
import java.util.*;

    public class FileMaintServer extends Dripper
      {
      Properties p;
      FileInputStream fis;
      FileOutputStream fos;


      public void get (SConnection conn, String[] args)
        {
        openProperties ();
        String s;


/*      Get:  args[1] = key, reply = value.
        ===================================  */

        if ((args.length > 1) && "Get".equals (args[0]))
          {
          returnString
            (
            conn,
```

```
            (String) p.get (SConnection.httpToString (args[1]))
            );
          return;
          }


/*      Put:  args[1] = key, args[2] = value, reply = CRLF delimited keys.
        To work around a bug in the Properties class, spaces in the key
        are replaced with periods.
        ===================================================================
*/

        else if ((args.length > 2) && "Put".equals (args[0]))
          {
          s = SConnection.httpToString (args[1]);
          s = s.replace (' ', '.');
          p.put
            (
            s,
            SConnection.httpToString (args[2])
            );
          saveProperties ();
          returnKeys (conn);
          return;
          }


/*      Remove:  args[1] = key, reply = CRLF delimited keys.
        ==================================================  */

        else if ((args.length > 1) && "Remove".equals (args[0]))
          {
          p.remove (SConnection.httpToString (args[1]));
          saveProperties ();
          returnKeys (conn);
          return;
          }


/*      List:  reply = CRLF delimited keys.
        ===================================  */

        else if ("List".equals (args[0]))
          {
          returnKeys (conn);
```

```
        return;
        }
      }


    void returnString (SConnection conn, String s)
      {
      conn.putMime (200, "text/plain");
      conn.put (s);
      }


    void returnKeys (SConnection conn)
      {
      Enumeration enum;

      conn.putMime (200, "text/plain");
      enum = p.propertyNames ();

      while (enum.hasMoreElements ())
        {
        conn.put ((String) enum.nextElement () + "\r\n");
        }
      }


    void openProperties ()
      {
      p = new Properties ();

      try
        {
        fis = new FileInputStream ("FileMaintServerProperties");
        p.load (fis);
        fis.close ();
        }
      catch (Exception e)
        {
        System.out.println ("Mant: Cannot open FileMaintServerProperties");
        }
      }
```

```
void saveProperties ()
  {
  try
    {
    fos = new FileOutputStream ("FileMaintServerProperties");
    p.save (fos, "FileMaintServer Data File");
    fos.close ();
    }
  catch (Exception e)
    {
    System.out.println ("Mant: Cannot save FileMaintServerProperties");
    }
  }
}
```

The following server log traces the execution of the FileMaintServer as it processes the *"Get"* REQUEST for the key *"wipeout"*.

```
*-------------------------------------------*
Cafe: Received a connection
Cafe: Waiting for a connection...
*-------------------------------------------*
Conn: Connected to: 127.0.0.1:1237
Conn: Received: GET /FileMaintServer?Get&wipeout HTTP/1.0
Conn: Received: Connection: Keep-Alive
Conn: Received: User-Agent: Mozilla/2.01Gold (Win95; I)
Conn: Received: Pragma: no-cache
Conn: Received: Host: localhost
Conn: Received: Accept: image/gif, image/x-xbitmap, image/jpeg,
  image/pjpeg, */*
Drip: Class FileMaintServer found
Conn: Sending Text Data...
Conn: Sending Text Data...
Conn: Disconnecting: 127.0.0.1:1237
*-------------------------------------------*
```

Notice that the client made a GET Web request and that the application REQUEST was *"Get"* and PARM1 was *"wipeout"*.

The applet/Dripper structure of the *FileMaint* application provides an example for constructing Client/Server applications over the Web infrastructure.

All the files for the application can be stored on the application Web server and delivered to the client on demand. When new users browse the application's Web page, a tag in the page also delivers the applet client to the users. As the users interact with the applet, the applet makes requests to the dripper.

This can be a very convenient mechanism for delivering applications to users on an Intranet or to users on the Internet.

Packages—How CaffeineCafe is Organized

The examples that have been presented in the book so far have consisted of one or two source files in a single directory. As the complexity of an application grows, it is often helpful to collect Java classes into groups of related responsibilities.

The Java mechanism for grouping related class files is the *package*.

This book has already presented several Java packages. The classes in the Abstract Window Toolkit are stored in the package *java.awt*. The utility classes are stored in the package *java.util*. The socket and URL classes are stored in the package *java.net*.

A package name corresponds to the name in which the class file is stored. All the AWT classes are in the directory *java\awt* and the network classes are in the directory *java\net*.

Package names are *relative* directory paths. They do not specify the complete path from the root of the directory tree. The base of the path is specified by the environment variable CLASSPATH. Why go outside the Java system to specify the base path to Java classes? This is to allow each computer installation to identify the directory where it has placed the Java classes.

```
CLASSPATH=C:\JAVA\JAVA.102\CLASSES
```

If the CLASSPATH variable was set to the value above (as it often was in the early versions of Java), the classes for the *java.awt* package would be found in the directory:

```
C:\JAVA\JAVA.102\CLASSES\JAVA\AWT
```

Current versions of Java include a CLASSPATH that looks like this:

```
CLASSPATH=C:\JAVA\JAVA.102\LIB\CLASSES.ZIP
```

Although it is possible that *classes.zip* was the name of a directory, it is usually the name of a file in the LIB directory. If this path provides the base of the path for locating Java classes, how does one use this to construct the fully qualified path to the class files?

When the CLASSPATH specifies the name of a .ZIP file, rather than a directory, the system assumes that the .ZIP file was constructed with the recursive subdirectory option and that it contains a number of subdirectories and files within it. Java version 1.0 also assumes that the .ZIP file was saved with the option that saves the files in an *uncompressed* format.

To find the AWT classes, one would have to use a .ZIP utility and expand the *classes.zip* file. Then they would notice a *java\awt* subdirectory and all the class files for the Abstract Window Toolkit would be found in that directory.

Why would Java choose such a complicated technique as a .ZIP file for storing the classes in its packages? Because it yields a significant performance improvement. When the Java Virtual Machine starts, it must load a large number of classes to create a useful image. By putting all of the classes in one file, the VM can replace 50–100 file open calls (expensive operations) with a single file open. Even though the VM must parse through the .ZIP file to find the class files, this is much quicker than numerous directory searches and file opens.

The CLASSPATH gives the root of the directory path and the *package name* gives the remainder of the path to each Java class.

During development, it is helpful to create several different directory trees to manage new projects, projects in testing, or projects that are in production. For this reason, one can code many root directory paths in the CLASSPATH variable. The paths must be separated by a ";" and Java searches them in order from left to right. The following is a typical CLASSPATH setting. It is displayed on two lines because it will not fit on one.

```
CLASSPATH=.;C:\JAVA\JAVA.100\classes;
            C:\JAVA\JAVA.100\lib\classes.zip
```

The examples in this book work because the default CLASSPATH includes the current directory (identified in the path as "."). In Java 1.0 and above, all the system classes are fetched from the *classes.zip* file and the CLASSPATH must include an entry for that file. To get the default CLASSPATH in one's Java system, execute the ArrayApplication example that is in the */JumpStart/examples/Array Application* directory.

To specify a package for one's own class, place a package statement as the first line of a Java source file.

```
package MyPackage;

    class PackageExample
      {
      public static void main (String args[])
        {
        System.out.println ("Greetings from the PackageExample!");
        }
      }
```

This says that the *PackageExample.class* is a member of the package *MyPackage.*

If no package name is specified in a source file, a default package (that has no name) is assigned to the class. The complete name of a class prefixes the package name on the front of the class name. In the case of classes that do not specify a package, their formal name and their class name are the same. The class in the previous example is formally known as the *MyPackage.PackageExample* class.

This program is part of the examples on the CD. When the examples are installed on one's disk, the *PackageExample.java* file should be in the following directory:

```
c:\JumpStrt\examples\PackageExample\MyPackage
```

Although many Java programmers recommend adding a directory to the CLASSPATH for each new base of development, there is a way to never need to modify the CLASSPATH.

The programmer can leverage the fact that the default CLASSPATH includes the default directory. In the previous example, if the default directory is *c:\JumpStrt\examples\PackageExample*, then one can compile and launch this class with the statements:

```
javac MyPackage\PackageExample.java
java MyPackage.PackageExample
```

In the launching of the class, the complete path will be constructed from the current directory, plus the package name, plus the class name and class file extension:

```
c:\JumpStrt\examples\PackageExample\MyPackage\PackageExample.class
```

Periods in the package name indicate levels in a directory tree. If the package in the previous example was assigned the name *My.Great.Package* rather than *MyPackage*, then the Java source file and the Java class file should be in the *My\Great\Package* subdirectory rather than in the *MyPackage* subdirectory. Then the class would be compiled and launched with the following statements:

```
javac My\Great\Package\PackageExample.java
java My.Great.Package.PackageExample
```

It is often assumed that the *"class not found"* message is due to a problem with the CLASSPATH variable, but that is rarely the problem. The most frequent cause is a capital letter where a lowercase letter should be. Class names and package names are both case-sensitive in Java.

The classes in the CaffeineCafe are organized into the package *com.enete.CaffeineCafe*. This conforms to the naming scheme that Java recommends. The scheme attempts to provide package names that are unique over the entire Internet. The scheme suggests that a package name should be constructed from an Internet domain name.

This author's domain name is *enete.com*. The scheme says to reverse the domain name, then add the application name. This scheme results in very long package names and it is too early to see if the scheme will receive widespread acceptance.

Whatever scheme is chosen, package names provide a helpful technique for organizing compiled Java classes.

JavaDoc—How CaffeineCafe is Documented

As a program grows in size and complexity, it becomes necessary to generate documentation so that the program and its services can be understood and used effectively.

Java's Lisa Friendly and Arthur van Hoff created a tool that generates documentation for the programmer automatically. It is included with each version of Java and is based on Donald Knuth's CWEB system of structured documentation. Java uses this tool to document its API.

The *javadoc* utility reads the source file for each class in a package and constructs Web pages that describe the classes and methods of the package. Information is gathered from public class definitions, public or protected method definitions, and public or protected instance variable definitions.

Any comments that proceed class, method, or variable definitions and that begin with "/**" are used as text to describe the definition in the generated Web page.

The text within these comment blocks is allowed to contain certain HTML tags for limited text formatting. Although other tags are allowed and are passed through to the final Web page, one should avoid tags that alter how the tool formats the overall page. The following tags are recommended:

<b> … </b>	*Bold text*
<i> … </i>	*Italic text*
<tt> … </tt>	*Constant Pitch Typewriter text*

Within the comments, one can also place a code field called a *doc tag*. This includes codes for specifying:

@see class	*Links to other classes*
@version text	*Version information*
@author text	*Author's name or link to a Web site*
@param variable description	*Method parameter description*
@return description	*Description of method return object*
@throws class description	*Exceptions that a method throws*

The following example suggests a source code format that conforms to the requirements of *javadoc* and also suggests a highly readable source style. By studying the source file and the resulting Web page, one can quickly adapt their coding style to make use of the services of *javadoc*. The Web page can be accessed quickly from the *index.html* file that is in the *\JumpStrt* directory.

Keep in mind that *javadoc* was designed to work with source files that were members of a package. Although the program will run on other source files, it does not generate anything worthwhile unless the source file is a member of a package.

To run *javadoc* on the following example program, change directory to the *c:\JumpStrt\examples\JavaDocExample* directory and issue the command:

```
javadoc MyPackage
```

A portion of one of the resulting Web pages is displayed in Figure 18–3.

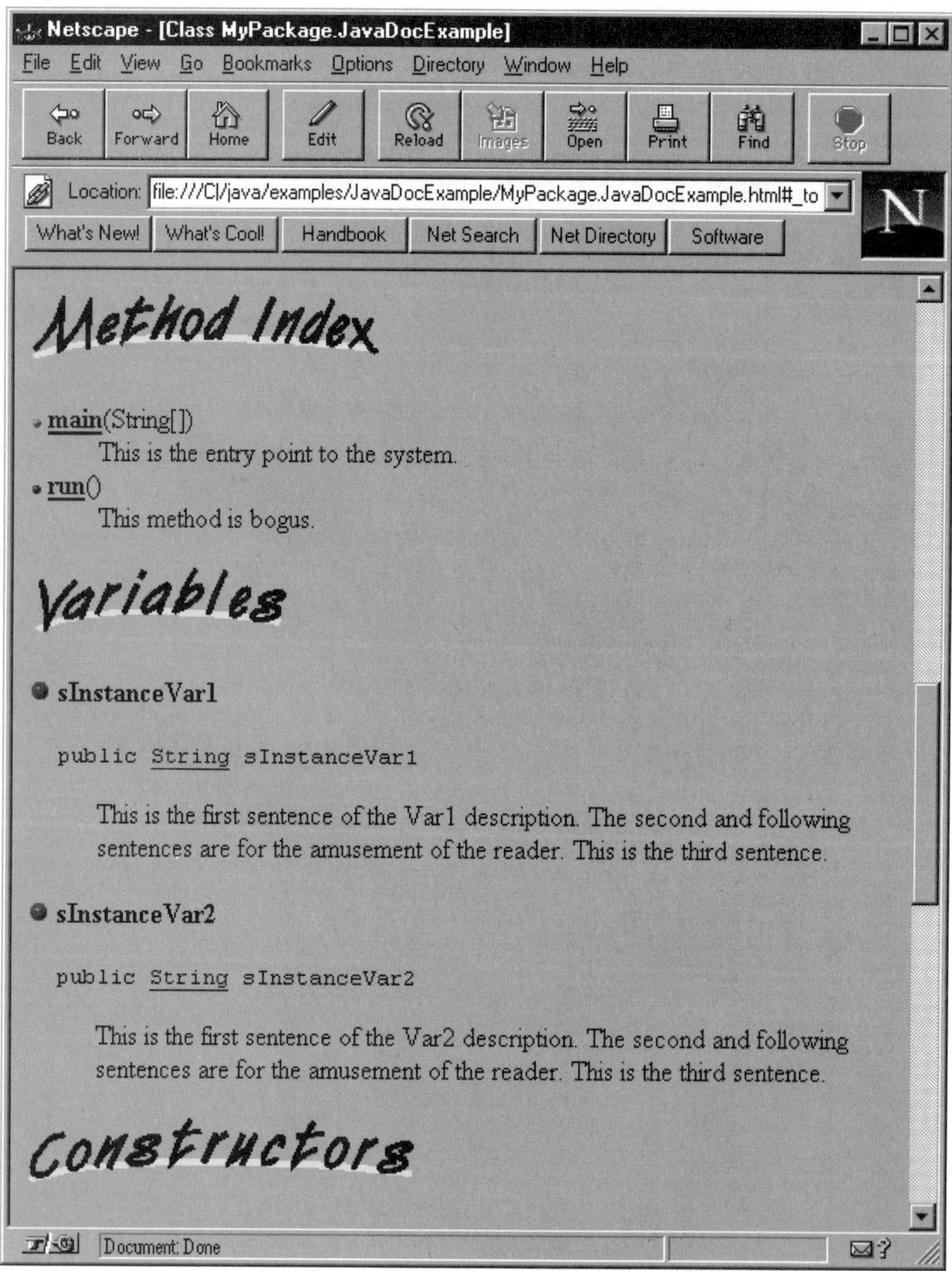
Netscape - [Class MyPackage.JavaDocExample]
File Edit View Go Bookmarks Options Directory Window Help
Back Forward Home Edit Reload Images Open Print Find Stop
Location: file:///C|/java/examples/JavaDocExample/MyPackage.JavaDocExample.html#_to
What's New! What's Cool! Handbook Net Search Net Directory Software
Method Index
main(String[])
This is the entry point to the system.
run()
This method is bogus.
Variables
sInstanceVar1
public String sInstanceVar1
This is the first sentence of the Var1 description. The second and following sentences are for the amusement of the reader. This is the third sentence.
sInstanceVar2
public String sInstanceVar2
This is the first sentence of the Var2 description. The second and following sentences are for the amusement of the reader. This is the third sentence.
Constructors
Document: Done

Figure 18–3

```
package MyPackage;

/***************************************************************************

    JavaDocExample -- How to Automatically Generate Documentation.

    This example demonstrates the various source codes that allow the
    JavaDoc program to generate HTML documentation from Java source
    files.<p>

    From the JavaDocExample directory, one invokes the javadoc utility
    with the following syntax:

    * <pre>
    *     javadoc MyPackage
    * </pre>

    One can insert some HTML tags to enhance the look of the text. For
    example one can call for <i>Italics</i>, <tt>Constant width Typewriter
    like font</tt>, or a <b>Bold Font</b>.<p>

    * @author     Noel Enete
    * @version    1.0 alpha1, 04/18/96
    * @see        java.lang.Object


***************************************************************************/

    public class JavaDocExample implements Runnable
    {

    String sInstanceVar0;              /* Only public vars get documented. */


 /** This is the first sentence of the Var1 description. The second
    and following sentences are for the amusement of the reader. This
    is the third sentence.*//*
    =================================================================   */

    public String sInstanceVar1;

 /** This is the first sentence of the Var2 description. The second
    and following sentences are for the amusement of the reader. This
    is the third sentence.*//*
    =================================================================   */
```

```
    public String sInstanceVar2;

/*************************************************************************/

/** This is the normal constructor. It is the constructor that is most
    often used to construct this class.*//*
    ======================================================================= */

    public JavaDocExample ()
      {
      System.out.println ("Greetings from the JavaDocExample!");
      }

/** This constructs the class from a string object. The string is used as
    an example of the class that needs to be constructed.
    * @param sModel the String to use as the model.
    * @return The object instantiated from sModel.
    * @throws InstantiationException if a problem was encountered.*//*
    ======================================================================= */

    public JavaDocExample (String sModel)
      {
      System.out.println ("Greetings from the JavaDocExample(String)!");
      }

/** This method is bogus. It was just included here to illustrate
    how the <i>implements</i> phrase on the class definition looks
    when it is documented.*//*
    ================================================================= */

    public void run ()
      {
      }

/** This is the entry point to the system. It simply instantiates
    a new JavaDocExample object.*//*
    ================================================================= */
```

```
    public static void main (String args[])
      {
      new JavaDocExample ();
      }
    }

/*==========================(  End of Source  )==========================*/
```

The web pages that are generated make use of image files that come with the Java system. The tool assumes that the image files will be in a subdirectory called <i>*images.* One will find all of these files in the directory c:*JumpStrt\\examples\\JavaDocExample\\images.*

Source—How CaffeineCafe Works

Design—Enhances the ExtendableWebServer

The entry point for the *CaffeineCafe* system is the *CaffeineCafe* class. It includes a *main*() method and it opens a ServerSocket on port 80 (port 8000 for Unix systems). It runs a dispatching loop that waits for new connections.

The CaffeineCafe spawns a new thread to process each new Web request. It starts an *SConnection* object inside the thread to receive the Web request from the client and to determine how to process it. After the thread has been launched, the CaffeineCafe goes back to listening for new connection requests.

When the *SConnection* object has received the Web request, an appropriate Dripper object is instantiated to process the request (see Figure 18–4). When a response has been prepared, the *Dripper* object asks the *SConnection* object to send the response back to the client.

After the response has been sent, the request processing thread exits and dies.

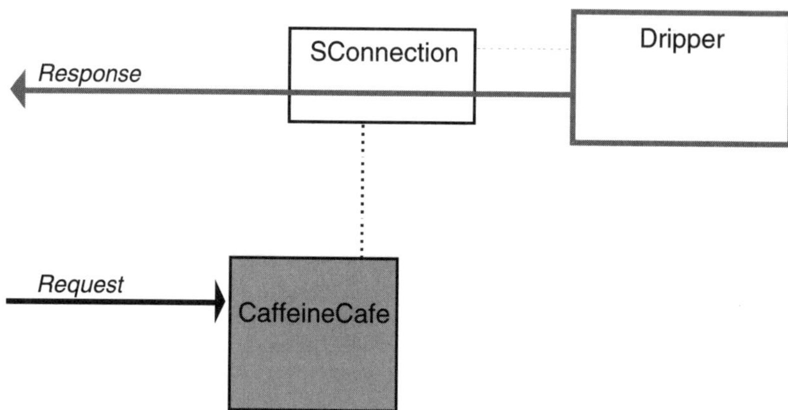

Figure 18–4 A new connection and Dripper are launched to process each request.

The overall thread design is common to most server programs. The dynamic launching of a Dripper class to process each server request is the special feature of this server. It provides a way for Java classes to extend the services of the Web server. With the facility for preloading selected Dripper classes, performance of the CaffeineCafe can be optimized.

CaffeineCafe—Listens for new connections

This is the entry point for the system.

It begins the application by instantiating a *CaffeineCafeDefaults* object and asking the object to preload each Dripper class that should be preloaded.

Then it opens a ServerSocket and begins a long running loop. Each cycle of the loop processes one Web request. At the top of the loop, the thread waits to *accept* incoming connection requests. Until a request is received, this thread is blocked. When a request is received, the object creates a new thread and passes an *SConnection* object to it. This new thread is started and processes the entire Web request.

After the thread is launched, the *CaffeineCafe* object cycles back to the top of the loop and waits for another connection request. This loop is terminated manually when the users press a *control-C* on the keyboard.

```
package com.enete.CaffeineCafe;
import java.net.*;
import java.io.*;
import com.enete.CaffeineCafe.*;

/***************************************************************************

    CaffeineCafe -- The Entry Point for the CaffeineCafe Web Server.

    It listens to a ServerSocket for connections. When it receives a
    connection, it launches a connection object in a new thread. The
    connection object receives the service requests from the Web client
    and launches the appropriate server extension ('Dripper') object to
    service the request.<p>

    Use the following syntax to invoke this server from the command line:

    * <pre>
    *    java com.enete.CaffeineCafe.CaffeineCafe
    * </pre>

    To exit the program, press control-C.<p>

    * @author    Noel Enete
    * @version   1.0 alpha1, 04/09/96


***************************************************************************/

    public class CaffeineCafe
    {
    final String sTag = "Copyright (c) 1996 Noel Enete";

    static CaffeineCafeDefaults defs; /* System wide default properties. */

/***************************************************************************/


    public CaffeineCafe (int iPort)
      {
      Socket sock;
      ServerSocket ssock;
      Thread thConn;
      SConnection conn;
      InetAddress ia = null;
```

```
    defs = new CaffeineCafeDefaults ();
    defs.fetchPreloads ();

    try
      {
      ia = InetAddress.getLocalHost ();
      System.out.println ("Cafe: Initializing to port " + iPort
        + " on " + ia);
      ssock = new ServerSocket (iPort);

      while (true)
        {
        System.out.println ("Cafe: Waiting for a connection...");
        sock = ssock.accept ();
        System.out.println ("Cafe: Received a connection");

        conn = new SConnection (sock);
        thConn = new Thread (conn);
        thConn.start ();
        }
      }
    catch (Exception e)
      {
      System.err.println ("Cafe: Exception in main loop: " + e);
      }
    }


  public static CaffeineCafeDefaults getDefaults ()
    {
    return (defs);
    }


  public static void main (String argv[])
    {
    new CaffeineCafe (80);
    }

  }


/*========================(  End of Source  )==========================*/
```

SConnection—Handles communications between client and dripper

There is one *SConnection* object for each Web request that is being processed. Its job is to stand in between the client and the Dripper and manage all of the details of HTTP communication. It uses a socket to conduct a conversation with the client.

Its first job is to receive the Web request. The first line of the request carries the most important information and is processed in the method *processFirstLine*().

This line arrives as three fields separated by blanks. The fields are called the *method*, the *resource*, and the *protocol version* respectively.

```
GET /echo.html HTTP/1.0
```

The first field is called the *method* because when a client sends a request for service, it is much like a program calling a method. The method field identifies which service is being requested. The two main services are GET and POST. The GET method appends its parameters on the end of the second field of this line. The POST method sends its parameters after the last line of the normal Web request.

The other two fields act like parameters for the method.

The request above is asking the server to find and return a particular Web page. The *resource* that is being requested is the Web page */echo.html*. If there were any parameters with this request, a "?" would be added to the end of the resource and the parameters would be added onto that.

When the Web began in 1990, the *Hyper Text Transfer Protocol* (HTTP) did not carry a version number. But when the Web became popular and the protocol was expanded to allow more services, the first version was assigned the version number of *0.9* and the newer version number was set to *1.0*.

In the request above, the protocol version is HTTP/1.0. In the 0.9 version of the rules, the protocol version field is not present. If a Web server encounters a request that includes only a method field and a resource field, they can assume that the client is operating under 0.9 rules.

In 1996, a new version of HTTP came out and was assigned the version number *1.1*. It expanded the number of methods from 3 to 13 and architected rules to help optimize the performance of the Web's request/response conversations.

The complete HTTP rules are written in the form of an Internet Engineering Task Force *Draft*. To get a copy, one can ask their local Internet expert to go to their favorite ftp site that keeps IETF drafts and print *draft-ietf-http-v10-spec-04.txt* (for versions 0.9 and 1.0) and *draft-ietf-http-v11-spec-01.txt* (for version 1.1).

An easier way to get a copy of the rules it to visit Roy Fielding's Web page at *http://www.ics.uci.edu/~fielding/*. Roy is one of the three authors of this document and contains links from his home page to the documents themselves.

Each line after the first line of the request is processed by the *processNextLine*() method. Each line holds a key/value pair that is known as a *header field*. The key is separated from the value by a ":" character. SConnection places each key/value pair in the *htParms* Hashtable and provides accessing methods so that other classes can fetch the details about the request.

The formal request is terminated by an empty line. The following code in *receiveRequest*() receives lines until a blank line is received.

```
while ((sLineIn = disIn.readLine ()) != null && !sLineIn.equals (""))
  {
  processLineIn (sLineIn);
  }
```

If the request is a POST request, parameter data follows the blank line. In this case, the method *receivePostParms*() receives the remainder of the request from the socket.

After the Web request has been received, the *run*() method of this class asks the dripper's *fromConnection*() method to instantiate an appropriate Dripper object to process the Web request. After the dripper has been created, the *run*() method calls the *get*() or *post*() method in the dripper to process the request.

When the dripper is ready to send data back to the client, the *SConnection* object provides several services to do the sending. The simplest service is the *reply*() method. This accepts an HTML text string and does all the work to get the text back to the client as a Web page. For more precise control over the sending mechanism, the methods *putHtmlMime*(), *putMime*(), and *put*() are provided.

To translate parameter data to and from the Web's URL encoding scheme, the methods *httpToString*() and *stringToHttp*() are provided.

```
package com.enete.CaffeineCafe;
import java.net.*;
import java.io.*;
import java.util.*;
import com.enete.CaffeineCafe.*;

/**********************************************************************

    SConnection -- The Server Side Connection.

    This manages all HTTP interaction with the client. It has a socket
    and keeps track of the HTTP details. This object determines the
    appropriate Dripper to launch and rides along with it.<p>

    The Dripper is sent a method that corresponds to the method in the
    HTTP request. The Dripper uses routines in this class to ship
    appropriate responses back to the client. <p>

    The htParms instance variable stores the HTTP request as a collection
    of key/value pairs. The first line of the request is cracked into
    the key=value pairs: VERB=[GET or POST], REQUEST=/path/filename, and
    PROTOCOL=HTTP/1.0. Objects can access this information through the
    getMethod(), getResource(), and getProtocol() methods in this class.<p>

    * @author    Noel Enete
    * @version   1.0 alpha1, 04/09/96

**********************************************************************/

    public class SConnection implements Runnable
    {
    final String sTag = "Copyright (c) 1996 Noel Enete";

    static final String METHOD        = "METHOD";
    static final String RESOURCE      = "RESOURCE";
    static final String RESOBJECT     = "RESOBJECT";
    static final String RESPATH       = "RESPATH";
    static final String RESNAME       = "RESNAME";
    static final String RESPARMS      = "RESPARMS";
    static final String POSTPARMS     = "POSTPARMS";
    static final String PROTOCOL      = "PROTOCOL";
    static final String CONTENTLENGTH = "Content-length";

    private Socket sock;
    private DataInputStream disIn;
    private PrintStream psOut;
```

```
    Dripper drip;                        /* Dripper that uses this class.   */
    Hashtable htParms;                   /* Holds the HTTP request.         */

/***********************************************************************/


    public SConnection (Socket s)
      {
      htParms = new Hashtable ();
      sock = s;
      }


    public void run ()
      {
      System.out.println ("*---------------------------------------*");
      System.out.println ("Conn: Connected to: "
        + sock.getInetAddress () + ":" + sock.getPort ());

      try
        {
        disIn = new DataInputStream (sock.getInputStream ());
        psOut = new PrintStream (sock.getOutputStream ());

        receiveRequest ();                      // Get the main request.
        drip = Dripper.fromConnection (this);  // Instantiate a server extn.

        if (getMethod().equals("GET"))          // If it is a GET req...
          {
          drip.get (this, getResParms ());      // ...pass it on to extn,
          }
        else if (getMethod().equals("POST")    // If it is a POST req...
          {
          receivePostParms ();                  // ...Get rest of req. data
          drip.post (this, getPostParms ());    // ......& pass it on to extn.
          }

        sock.close ();
        }

      catch (Exception e)
        {
        System.err.println ("Conn: Exception processing request: " + e);
        }
```

```
    System.out.println ("Conn: Disconnecting: "
      + sock.getInetAddress () + ":" + sock.getPort ());
    System.out.println ("*---------------------------------------*");
    }


  public void reply (String s)
    {
    putHtmlMime ();                       // Send the MIME

    put                                   // Send the Web Page
      (
      "<html><head><title>" + s + "</title></head>\n"
      + "<body><h1>" + s + "</h1>\n"
      );
    }


  public void putHtmlMime ()
    {
    putMime (200, "text/html");
    }


  public void putMime (int iReturnCode, String sContentType)
    {
    if (expectsMime ())
      {
      put
        (
        "HTTP/1.0 " + iReturnCode + " Document follows\n"    // Status-line
        + "Content-type: " + sContentType + "\n"             // Mime
        + "\n"                                               // Empty Line
        );
      }
    }


  public void put (String s)
    {
    System.out.println ("Conn: Sending Text Data...");
    psOut.print (s);
    }
```

```
public void put (byte[] ab, int iStartPosition, int iEndPosition)
  {
  System.out.println ("Conn: Sending Binary Data...");
  psOut.write (ab, iStartPosition, iEndPosition);
  }


void receiveRequest ()
  {
  String sLineIn;

  try
    {
    while ((sLineIn = disIn.readLine ()) != null && !sLineIn.equals (""))
      {
      processLineIn (sLineIn);
      }
    }
  catch (Exception e)
    {
    System.out.println ("Conn: Error receiving request: " + e);
    }
  }


void receivePostParms ()
  {
  String sLineIn;
  StringTokenizer st;
  String sKey;
  String sValue;
  Hashtable htPostParms;

  htPostParms = new Hashtable ();

  try
    {
    sLineIn = disIn.readLine ();
    st = new StringTokenizer (sLineIn, "&=", false);

    while (st.hasMoreElements ())
      {
      sKey = SConnection.httpToString (st.nextToken ());
      sValue = SConnection.httpToString (st.nextToken ());
      htPostParms.put (sKey, sValue);
```

```
        }
      htParms.put (POSTPARMS, htPostParms);
      }

    catch (Exception e)
      {
      System.out.println ("Conn: Error receiving post parms: " + e);
      }
    }


  void processLineIn (String s)
    {
    System.out.println ("Conn: Received: " + s);

    if (htParms.elements().hasMoreElements())
      {
      processNextLine (s);
      }
    else
      {
      processFirstLine (s);
      }
    }


/*  This parses the first request line. All functional units are
    identified and placed into the Hashtable with descriptive keys.
    It handles resources specified like this:
    "/cgi-bin/gmtconvert.cgi?year=96&month=01&day=19&time=22:00:00"*//*
    ==================================================================  */

    void processFirstLine (String s)
      {
      StringTokenizer st;
      String sToken;
      String sResource;
      String sResObject;
      StringBuffer sbResPath;
      Vector vResParms;
      String[] as;

      st = new StringTokenizer (s, " \n\r", false);
```

```
try
  {
  htParms.put (METHOD, st.nextToken ());              // Pull the method

  sResource = st.nextToken ();
  htParms.put (PROTOCOL, st.nextToken ());            // Protocol

  htParms.put (RESOURCE, sResource);                  // Resource

  st = new StringTokenizer (sResource, "?", false);  // Res w/o Parms
  sResObject = st.nextToken ();
  htParms.put (RESOBJECT, sResObject);

  vResParms = new Vector ();                          // Res Parms
  while (st.hasMoreElements ())
    {
    vResParms.addElement (st.nextToken ("&"));
    }
  as = new String[vResParms.size ()];
  vResParms.copyInto (as);
  htParms.put (RESPARMS, as);

  st = new StringTokenizer (sResObject, "/\\", true); // Res Path
  sbResPath = new StringBuffer ();
  sToken = st.nextToken ();
  while (st.hasMoreElements ())
    {
    sbResPath.append (sToken);
    sToken = st.nextToken ();
    }
  htParms.put (RESPATH, sbResPath.toString ());

  htParms.put (RESNAME, sToken);                      // Res Name
  }

catch (Exception e)
  {
  System.out.println
    (
    "Conn: Error processing request line "
    + s + "  " + e
    );
  }
}
```

```
void processNextLine (String s)
  {
  StringTokenizer st;
  String sKey;
  String sValue;

  st = new StringTokenizer (s, ":\n\r", false);

  try
    {
    sKey = st.nextToken ();
    sValue = st.nextToken().trim();
    htParms.put (sKey, sValue);
    }
  catch (Exception e)
    {
    System.out.println ("Conn: Unable to parse request line -->" + s
      + "<--");
    }
  }


public static String stringToHttp (String s)
  {
  StringBuffer sbReturn;
  StringBuffer sbHexChar;
  StringBufferInputStream sbis;
  int iIn;
  String sByte;

  sbReturn = new StringBuffer ();
  sbis = new StringBufferInputStream (s);

  while ((iIn = sbis.read ()) != -1)
    {
    switch (iIn)
      {
      case '%':
        sbReturn.append ('%');
        sbReturn.append ('%');
        break;

      case ' ':
        sbReturn.append ('+');
        break;
```

```
        default:
          if (iIn < 20)
            {
            sbReturn.append ('%');
            sByte = Integer.toString (iIn, 16);
            if (sByte.length () == 1) sByte = "0" + sByte;
            sbReturn.append (sByte);
            }
          else
            {
            sbReturn.append ((char) iIn);
            }
          break;
        }
      }

    return (sbReturn.toString ());
    }


  public static String httpToString (String s)
    {
    StringBuffer sbReturn;
    StringBuffer sbHexChar;
    StringBufferInputStream sbis;
    char cIn;

    sbReturn = new StringBuffer ();
    sbis = new StringBufferInputStream (s);

    while ((cIn = (char) sbis.read ()) != (char) -1)
      {
      switch (cIn)
        {
        case '%':
          sbHexChar = new StringBuffer ();
          sbHexChar.append ((char) sbis.read ());
          sbHexChar.append ((char) sbis.read ());
          cIn = (char) Integer.parseInt (sbHexChar.toString (), 16);
          break;

        case '+':
          cIn = ' ';
          break;
        }
```

```
        sbReturn.append (cIn);
        }

      return (sbReturn.toString ());
      }



    public String getMethod ()
      {
      return ((String) htParms.get (METHOD));
      }


    public String getResource ()
      {
      return ((String) htParms.get (RESOURCE));
      }


    public String getResObject ()
      {
      return ((String) htParms.get (RESOBJECT));
      }


    public String getResPath ()
      {
      return ((String) htParms.get (RESPATH));
      }


    public String getResName ()
      {
      return ((String) htParms.get (RESNAME));
      }


    public String[] getResParms ()
      {
      return ((String[]) htParms.get (RESPARMS));
      }
```

```
    public Hashtable getPostParms ()
      {
      return ((Hashtable) htParms.get (POSTPARMS));
      }


    public String getProtocol ()
      {
      return ((String) htParms.get (PROTOCOL));
      }


    boolean expectsMime ()
      {
      return (htParms.containsKey (PROTOCOL));
      }


    int getContentLength ()
      {
      return (Integer.valueOf
        (
        (String) htParms.get(CONTENTLENGTH)).intValue()
        );
      }

    }

/*========================(  End of Source  )===========================*/
```

Dripper—Implements default dripper behavior

The primary service of the Dripper class is to provide default behavior for the *get*() and *post*() methods.

It also stores the *SConnection* object so that any Dripper method can get back to the client.

The unusual service that is provided in the Dripper class is the ability to examine a Web request and instantiate a dripper that would be appropriate to process the request. This service is implemented in the *fromConnection*() method.

To determine the correct dripper, this method first assumes that the resource field of the *request line* is a reference to a class name and sends the string to the *newDripper*() method to instantiate an object of that class. If that attempt fails, the resource field is assumed to be a filename and a *FileDripper* object is instantiated. In either case, a Dripper object is returned to the calling object.

As the *newDripper*() method is searching for a class to match the resource name, it uses the *package path* from the *CaffeineCafeDefaults* object to construct the fully qualified class name. The class name is constructed from each of the packages in the *package path* plus the resource name. This design allows drippers that do not have a package and drippers from different packages to extend the services of the CaffeineCafe. The *package path* can be edited by pointing a browser at the *PackageMaint* class and editing the lines that are returned.

The ability to instantiate a Dripper object is located in this class so that the Dripper class can control which dripper is appropriate to process particular Web requests.

```
package com.enete.CaffeineCafe;
import java.net.*;
import java.io.*;
import java.util.*;
import com.enete.CaffeineCafe.*;

/***********************************************************************

    Dripper -- This Server Extension Processes one HTTP Request.

    This class is dynamically loaded and serves to extend the WebServer
    in a way that is analogous to a CGI program. It uses its Connection
    instance variable for all interaction with the client. This class
    is normally subclassed.<p>

    * @author    Noel Enete
    * @version   1.0 alpha1, 04/09/96

***********************************************************************/

    public class Dripper
    {
    final String sTag = "Copyright (c) 1996 Noel Enete";

    SConnection conn;

/**********************************************************************/
```

```
    public Dripper ()
      {
      }


/** This reads a Web request and instantiates the appropriate Dripper.
    It uses the connection to read the request up to the blank line.
    It determines the appropriate Dripper to instantiate from the
    resource field of request. It instantiates the Dripper, attaches
    the connection, and returns it to the sender.*//*
    ====================================================================  */

    public static Dripper fromConnection (SConnection conn)
      {
      Dripper drip;
      String sResName;
      String sAliasName;

      sResName = conn.getResName ();

      sAliasName = CaffeineCafe.getDefaults().getAlias(sResName);
      if (sAliasName != null)
        {
        System.out.println ("Drip: Request aliased from " + sResName
          + " to " + sAliasName);
        sResName = sAliasName;
        }

      drip = newDripper (sResName);     // First, assume resource is a
                                        classname.

      if (drip == null)                 // If not, assume it is a filename.
        {
        drip = new FileDripper ();
        }

      drip.conn = conn;
      return (drip);
      }


/** Accepts a string and tries to instantiate an object from a class by
    that name. Each of the packages in the package search path is used
```

```
    to look for the class. If successful, the Dripper instance is
    returned. If not, null is returned.*//*
    ===================================================================    */

    public static Dripper newDripper (String s)
      {
      Class clsNew;                        /* Class desc for desired class.    */
      Dripper drip = null;                 /* The new object.                  */
      String[] asPackages;                 /* Each package name to try.        */
      String sFullClassName = null;        /* Package + class name.            */
      int i;

      asPackages = CaffeineCafe.getDefaults().getPackagePath();

      for (i = 0; i <= asPackages.length; i++)
        {
        if (i == asPackages.length)
          {
          sFullClassName = s;
          }
        else
          {
          sFullClassName = asPackages[i] + "." + s;
          }

        try
          {
          clsNew = Class.forName (sFullClassName);

          try
            {
            drip = (Dripper) clsNew.newInstance ();
            }
          catch (java.lang.IllegalAccessException e)
            {
            System.out.println ("Drip: IllegalAccessException, class = " + s);
            }
          catch (java.lang.InstantiationException e)
            {
            System.out.println ("Drip: InstantiationException, class = " + s);
            }
          }

        catch (java.lang.ClassNotFoundException e)
          {
          }
```

```
        if (drip != null)
          {
          break;
          }
        }

      if (drip != null)
        {
        System.out.println ("Drip: Class " + sFullClassName + " found");
        }
      else
        {
        System.out.println ("Drip: Class " + sFullClassName + " not found");
        }

      return (drip);
      }



    public void get (SConnection conn, String[] args)
      {
      int i;

      conn.putHtmlMime ();

      conn.put ("This is from the Dripper>>get() method. Arguments = ");
      for (i = 0; i < args.length; i++)
        {
        conn.put ("<p>" + i + ": " + args[i]);
        }
      }



    public void post (SConnection conn, Hashtable ht)
      {
      conn.reply ("This is from the Dripper>>post() method. Parameters = "
        + ht);
      }

    }


/*========================(  End of Source  )============================*/
```

EchoDripper—Presents an "About Box" for the server

This is an example of a Dripper class that returns the current data and time to the requester. This kind of class allows the client to get a simple description of the Web site. This class could be customized by each Web site to give details that would be interesting to a first time visitor.

The only caution is to avoid telling the client exactly what Web server is being run or exactly what operating system is executing the server. Sometimes hackers make use of that information to target a Web site for break-in.

In the alias property of the *CaffeineCafeDefaults* object, there is an entry that translates all requests that do not specify a resource like *http://localhost/* to request this EchoDripper. This can be changed by executing the *AliasMaint* class from a browser and editing the line that says */=EchoDripper*.

```
package com.enete.CaffeineCafe;
import java.io.*;
import java.util.*;
import com.enete.CaffeineCafe.*;

/***********************************************************************

    EchoDripper -- Returns some information about the Web Site.

    This is the Web equivalent to an "About Box" in a GUI environment.
    There is an important difference between standalone GUI information
    and information about a remote server -- the more information that
    is given out about a Web site, the more information a hacker can use
    to compromise the site.<p>

    * @author    Noel Enete
    * @version   1.0 alpha1, 04/09/96

***********************************************************************/

    public class EchoDripper extends Dripper
    {
    final String sTag = "Copyright (c) 1996 Noel Enete";

/**********************************************************************/


    public void get (SConnection conn, String[] args)
      {
      Date d;
```

```
        d = new Date ();
        conn.reply
          (
          "Welcome to this Web site.<p>  The current date and time is "
          + d.toLocaleString ()
          );
        }

      }

/*========================(  End of Source  )============================*/
```

FileDripper—Fetches files for the server

This class processes all file requests for the CaffeineCafe.

Since most sites want to keep their Web page data separate from their server program files, a *default document directory* in the *CaffeineCafeDefaults* object is used to construct the fully qualified path to the requested file.

To change the default directory, one must go to the fifth line of the constructor for the *CaffeineCafeDefaults* class and enter a new path for the *BASEDOCDIR* key and recompile. This must be done by hand so that hackers can not get access to this path. If hackers could change the path, then they could point the base directory to the root directory and take over the computer.

Once the file is located, the *content-type* header information for the MIME is determined from the extension of the filename and the file is written back to the client.

```
package com.enete.CaffeineCafe;
import java.io.*;
import com.enete.CaffeineCafe.*;

/***************************************************************************

    FileDripper -- This processes one Web File Request

    This service uses the system wide defaults to attach a document base
    path to the beginning of the requested document.<p>

    * @author    Noel Enete
    * @version   1.0 alpha1, 04/09/96
```

```
*************************************************************************/

    public class FileDripper extends Dripper
    {
    final String sTag = "Copyright (c) 1996 Noel Enete";

/*************************************************************************/


    public void get (SConnection conn, String[] args)
      {
      FileInputStream fisIn = null;
      byte[] abBuffer = new byte[20000];
      int iBytesRead;
      String sFileName;
      String sResourceName;
      String sContentType;


/*    Find the file resource.
      ======================  */

      sFileName = conn.getResObject ();
      sResourceName = CaffeineCafe.getDefaults().getBaseDocDir() + sFileName;

      try
        {
        fisIn = new FileInputStream (sResourceName);
        }
      catch (Exception e)
        {
        System.out.println ("Drip: Can't find " + sResourceName);
        e.printStackTrace ();
        conn.putMime (404, "text/html");
        conn.put ("Can't find " + sFileName);
        System.out.println ("Drip: Exception handled");
        return;
        }
      System.out.println( "Drip: File " + sResourceName + " found" );


/*    From the filename determine the type of data in the file.
      =========================================================  */

      if (sResourceName.endsWith (".html"))
        {
        sContentType = "text/html";
```

```
        }
      else if (sResourceName.endsWith (".gif"))
        {
        sContentType = "image/gif";
        }
      else if ((sResourceName.endsWith (".txt"))
      || (sResourceName.endsWith (".bat"))
      || (sResourceName.endsWith (".java"))
      || (sFileName.indexOf (".") == -1))
        {
        sContentType = "text/plain";
        }
      else
        {
        sContentType = "application/octet-stream";
        }


/*    Send the file data back to the client.
      ======================================  */

      try
        {
        conn.putMime (200, sContentType);

        while ((iBytesRead = fisIn.read (abBuffer)) >= 0)
          {
          conn.put (abBuffer, 0, iBytesRead);
          }

        fisIn.close ();
        }

      catch (Exception eReadWrite)
        {
        System.out.println ("Drip: Can't read " + sResourceName);
        eReadWrite.printStackTrace ();
        conn.put ("Can't read " + sFileName);
        System.out.println ("Drip: Can't read exception handled");
        return;
        }
      }

    }


/*========================(  End of Source  )===========================*/
```

CaffeineCafeDefaults—Maintains system-wide defaults

There is one *CaffeineCafeDefaults* object in the system and it keeps track of system-wide defaults.

The object is stored as an instance variable for the *CaffeineCafe* object and the static method *getDefaults*() in the *CaffeineCafe* class gives any object access to the system defaults.

All of the defaults are stored in Properties objects and are saved to disk files.

Methods are included for setting and getting each of the default values. The following methods retrieve various defaults.

getPackagePath()	*An array of package names*
getAliases()	*A Properties object of aliases*
getAlias(String)	*An alias value for the passed key*
getPreloadClasses()	*An array of class names*
getBaseDocDir()	*A directory path base for file fetches*

Whenever a Dripper has done maintenance to the system defaults and would like to force an update to the Properties files, it can call the *saveDefaults*() method. This method updates all the Properties files with the current values.

Notice the initialization of the *BASEDOCDIR*. This key identifies the directory from which Web pages are fetched. It is hard coded as ".", which is the current directory. Replace this value with a path to the Web page files. The path should use forward slash "/" characters and should *not* end with a slash. Then recompile the class. From the *\JumpStrt\examples\CaffeineCafe* directory, the compile syntax is:

```
javac com\enete\CaffeineCafe\CaffeineCafeDefaults.java
```

```
package com.enete.CaffeineCafe;
import java.io.*;
import java.util.*;
import com.enete.CaffeineCafe.*;

/************************************************************************

    CaffeineCafeDefaults -- This Maintains System-Wide Properties.

    This class manages system-wide defaults like the default document
    directory, the default base class directory, and a package search
    path. By calling the saveDefaults() method, the defaults can
    be saved in text files and will be reloaded from these files each
    time the server is started.<p>
```

```
    * @author    Noel Enete
    * @version   1.0 alpha1, 04/09/96

***************************************************************************/

    public class CaffeineCafeDefaults
    {
    final String sTag = "Copyright (c) 1996 Noel Enete";

    static final String PKGFILENAME    = "CaffeineCafePackages";
    static final String ALIASFILENAME  = "CaffeineCafeAliases";
    static final String PRELOADFILENAME= "CaffeineCafePreloades";
    static final String DIRFILENAME    = "CaffeineCafeDirectories";
    static final String BASEDOCDIR     = "BaseDocDir";
    static final String BASECLASSDIR   = "BaseClassDir";

    Properties prPackages;              /* Holds package names to search.   */
    Properties prAliases;               /* Holds alias file and class names.*/
    Properties prPreloadClasses;        /* Holds class names to preload.    */
    Properties prDirectories;           /* Holds directory defaults.        */

/***************************************************************************/


    public CaffeineCafeDefaults ()
      {
      Properties prDefaults;
      FileInputStream fis;

      prDefaults = new Properties ();
      prDefaults.put (BASEDOCDIR, ".");
      prDefaults.put (BASECLASSDIR, ".");
      prDirectories = new Properties (prDefaults);

      prDefaults = new Properties ();
      prDefaults.put ("com.enete.CaffeineCafe", "com.enete.CaffeineCafe");
      prPackages = new Properties (prDefaults);

      prDefaults = new Properties ();
      prDefaults.put ("echo.html", "EchoDripper");
      prDefaults.put ("/", "EchoDripper");
      prAliases = new Properties (prDefaults);

      prDefaults = new Properties ();
      prDefaults.put ("EchoDripper", "EchoDripper");
      prPreloadClasses = new Properties (prDefaults);
```

```
System.out.println ("*---------Default Directories--------*");
try
  {
  fis = new FileInputStream (DIRFILENAME);
  prDirectories.load (fis);
  fis.close ();
  }
catch (Exception e)
  {
  System.out.println ("Defs: No directory overrides found in "
    + DIRFILENAME);
  }
prDirectories.list (System.out);

System.out.println ("*----------Default Packages----------*");
try
  {
  fis = new FileInputStream (PKGFILENAME);
  prPackages.load (fis);
  fis.close ();
  }
catch (Exception e)
  {
  System.out.println ("Defs: No package overrides found in "
    + PKGFILENAME);
  }
prPackages.list (System.out);

System.out.println ("*-----------Default Aliases----------*");
try
  {
  fis = new FileInputStream (ALIASFILENAME);
  prAliases.load (fis);
  fis.close ();
  }
catch (Exception e)
  {
  System.out.println ("Defs: No alias overrides found in "
    + ALIASFILENAME);
  }
prAliases.list (System.out);

System.out.println ("*---------Default Preloades----------*");
try
  {
  fis = new FileInputStream (PRELOADFILENAME);
```

```
      prPreloadClasses.load (fis);
      fis.close ();
      }
    catch (Exception e)
      {
      System.out.println ("Defs: No preload overrides found in "
        + PRELOADFILENAME);
      }
    prPreloadClasses.list (System.out);
    System.out.println ("*-----------------------------------*");
    }


  public void fetchPreloads ()
    {
    String[] as;
    int i;

    as = getPreloadClasses ();

    for (i = 0; i < as.length; i++)
      {
      if (Dripper.newDripper (as[i]) == null)
        {
        System.out.println ("Defs: Unable to preload " + as[i] + " class!");
        }
      }
    }


  public void saveDefaults ()
    {
    FileOutputStream fos;
    String sFileName = "";

    try
      {
      sFileName = DIRFILENAME;
      fos = new FileOutputStream (sFileName);
      prDirectories.save (fos, "Directories for CaffeineCafe");
      fos.close ();

      sFileName = PKGFILENAME;
      fos = new FileOutputStream (sFileName);
      prPackages.save (fos, "Package Path for CaffeineCafe");
      fos.close ();
```

```
      sFileName = ALIASFILENAME;
      fos = new FileOutputStream (sFileName);
      prAliases.save (fos, "Aliases for CaffeineCafe");
      fos.close ();

      sFileName = PRELOADFILENAME;
      fos = new FileOutputStream (sFileName);
      prPreloadClasses.save (fos, "Preloaded Classes for CaffeineCafe");
      fos.close ();
      }
    catch (Exception e)
      {
      System.out.println ("Defs: Unable to save properties " + sFileName);
      }
    }


  public void setBaseDocDir (String s)
    {
    prDirectories.put (BASEDOCDIR, s);
    saveDefaults ();
    }


  public String getBaseDocDir ()
    {
    return (prDirectories.getProperty (BASEDOCDIR, "/"));
    }


  public void setBaseClassDir (String s)
    {
    prDirectories.put (BASECLASSDIR, s);
    saveDefaults ();
    }


  public String getBaseClassDir ()
    {
    return (prDirectories.getProperty (BASECLASSDIR, "/"));
    }


  public String[] getPackagePath ()
    {
    Vector v;
```

```
      Enumeration enum;
      String[] as;

      v = new Vector ();
      enum = prPackages.propertyNames ();
      while (enum.hasMoreElements ())
        {
        v.addElement (enum.nextElement ());
        }
      as = new String[v.size ()];
      v.copyInto (as);
      return (as);
      }


   public void putPackagePath (String s)
      {
      prPackages.put (s, s);
      }


   public void clearPackagePath ()
      {
      prPackages.clear ();
      }


   public Properties getAliases ()
      {
      return (prAliases);
      }


   public String getAlias (String sKey)
      {
      return (prAliases.getProperty (sKey));
      }


   public void putAlias (String sKey, String sValue)
      {
      prAliases.put (sKey, sValue);
      }
```

```
    public void clearAliases ()
      {
      prAliases.clear ();
      }


    public String[] getPreloadClasses ()
      {
      Vector v;
      Enumeration enum;
      String[] as;

      v = new Vector ();
      enum = prPreloadClasses.propertyNames ();
      while (enum.hasMoreElements ())
        {
        v.addElement (enum.nextElement ());
        }
      as = new String[v.size ()];
      v.copyInto (as);
      return (as);
      }


    public void putPreloadClass (String s)
      {
      prPreloadClasses.put (s, s);
      }


    public void clearPreloadClasses ()
      {
      prPreloadClasses.clear ();
      }

    }

/*========================(  End of Source  )===========================*/
```

APPENDIX A

How Do I . . .

This chapter provides short answers to commonly asked Java questions.

String and Array

How do I concatenate strings?

Strings are concatenated by using the "+" operator. The string "z" below contains the characters "abcdef".

```
class ConcatStrings
  {
  public static void main (String args[])
    {
    String x = "abc";
    String y = "def";
    String z = x + y;

    System.out.println ("x + y = " + z);
    }
  }
```

How do I parse through a string?

Use the *StringTokenizer* class. This is found in the *java.util* package and is very handy. When the *StringTokenizer* is instantiated below, the second parameter (", ") identifies two characters as token delimiters: a comma and a space character. Each time the *nextToken*() method is called, it returns the next token as a string. The example below filters out all of the spaces and commas in the input string.

```
import java.util.*;

    class ParseString
      {
      public static void main (String args[])
        {
        String s = "first,second, third fourth,  fifth";
        StringTokenizer st;

        st = new StringTokenizer (s, ", ");

        while (st.hasMoreTokens ())
          {
          System.out.println ("--->" + st.nextToken () + "<---");
          }
        }
      }
```

How do I dimension and load an array at the same time?

Java allows an array to be initialized and dimensioned at one time. But this is only legal when it occurs in the same statement that declares the variable. In the example below, an Integer array and a String array are initialized and dimensioned in single statements.

```
class LoadArray
  {
  public static void main (String args[])
    {
    int i;
    int[] ai =
      {
      2, 4, 6, 8, 10, 12
      };
    String[] as =
      {
      "String line one",
      "String line two",
      "String line three"
      };

    for (i = 0; i < ai.length; i++)
      {
      System.out.println ("array of integer " + i + " = " + ai[i]);
      }
    System.out.println ();

    for (i = 0; i < as.length; i++)
      {
      System.out.println ("array of string  " + i + " = " + as[i]);
      }
    }
  }
```

How do I append one array with another array?

The first array should be put in a ByteArrayOutputStream. Then the second array should be passed as a parameter in the *write*() method to this stream. Then the stream's *toByteArray*() method should be called to get the final large array.

In the example below, the first array is created by loading a string into a String-BufferInputStream and reading arrays from it. Each array that is read from the StringBufferInputStream is written to the ByteArrayOutputStream. When all arrays have been written to the output stream, the *toByteArray*() method is sent and the final array is printed.

```
import java.io.*;

    class AppendArray
      {
      public static void main (String args[])
        {
        StringBufferInputStream sbis;
        ByteArrayOutputStream baos;
        byte[] abOutput;
        byte[] ab;
        int iReadLength;
        String s;

        try
          {
          ab = new byte[3];
          s = "abcdefghijklmnopqrstuvwxyz";
          sbis = new StringBufferInputStream (s);
          baos = new ByteArrayOutputStream ();

          while ((iReadLength = sbis.read (ab, 0, 3)) != -1)
            {
            baos.write (ab, 0, iReadLength);
            }

          abOutput = baos.toByteArray ();
          s = new String (abOutput, 0);
          System.out.println ("The final array is ->" + s + "<-");
          }

        catch (Exception e)
          {
          System.out.println ("Exception: " + e);
          }
        }
      }
```

Loop

How do I code a for() loop?

This loop is used to iterate for a specific number of times and is coded exactly as a *for()* loop in C.

```
class ForLoop
  {
  public static void main (String args[])
    {
    int i;

    for (i = 0; i < 4; i++)
      {
      System.out.println ("Iteration = " + i);
      }
    }
  }
```

How do I code a while() loop?

This loop is used to iterate through a block of code an unspecified number of times. It is coded like the *while()* loop in C. The expression within the parentheses must resolve to a *boolean*. Each of Java's comparison operations, like (2 < 3) and (9 == 6), resolve to *boolean* values.

```
class WhileLoop
  {
  public static void main (String args[])
    {
    boolean bMore;
    int iCount;

    bMore = true;
    iCount = 0;

    while (bMore)
      {
      System.out.println ("Iteration = " + iCount);
      if (iCount >= 5)
        {
        bMore = false;
        }
      iCount++;
      }
    }
  }
```

How do I code a do/while() loop?

This is equivalent to a *while()* loop, except the block of code is executed at least one time before any exit condition is checked.

```
class DoLoop
  {
  public static void main (String args[])
    {
    boolean bMore;
    int iCount;

    bMore = true;
    iCount = 0;

    do
      {
      System.out.println ("Iteration = " + iCount);
      if (iCount >= 5)
        {
        bMore = false;
        }
      iCount++;
      } while (bMore);
    }
  }
```

How do I abruptly exit a loop (break)?

The statement to use is *break*. This will exit the current loop. Java has added a refinement to normal *break* processing in C. One can specify a label just before the loop statement. If that label is specified after the break command, control is passed to the next statement after the labeled loop.

The example below shows simple *break* processing and then *labeled break* processing.

```
class BreakLoop
  {
  public static void main (String args[])
    {
    int i;
    int j;
    int k;

    for (i = 0; i < 4; i++)
      {
      if (i == 2)
        {
        break;
        }
      System.out.println ("Iteration A = " + i);
      }

    loopI:
    for (i = 0; i < 2; i++)
      {
      loopJ:
      for (j = 0; j < 3; j++)
        {
        loopK:
        for (k = 0; k < 4; k++)
          {
          System.out.println
            (
            "Iteration B  i = " + i
            + " j = " + j
            + " k = " + k
            );
          if ((i >= 1) && (j >= 2) && (k >= 3))
            {
            break loopI;
            }
          }
        }
      }
    }
  }
```

How do I skip some statements and return to the top of the loop (continue)?

The *continue* statement is the command that aborts the execution of the remaining statements in a loop and jumps back to the top of the loop to begin the next iteration. It works with each kind of Java loop.

There is also a *labeled* form of the *continue* statement. It transfers control to the label in the same way that the *labeled break* statement does.

```
class ContinueLoop
  {
  public static void main (String args[])
    {
    int i;

    for (i = 0; i < 4; i++)
      {
      System.out.println ("Iteration A = " + i);
      if (i >= 2)
        {
        continue;
        }
      System.out.println ("Iteration B = " + i);
      }
    }
  }
```

How do I process an Enumeration?

An *enumeration* represents a linked list of objects. One retrieves the elements in the list by repeatedly calling the enumeration's *nextElement*() method. When the enumeration's *hasMoreElements*() method returns *false*, the end of the list has been reached.

```
import java.util.*;

    class ProcessEnumeration
      {
      public static void main (String args[])
        {
        String s;
        Enumeration enum;
        Properties prSystemProperties;

        prSystemProperties = System.getProperties ();

        enum = prSystemProperties.propertyNames ();

        while (enum.hasMoreElements ())
          {
          s = (String) enum.nextElement ();
          System.out.println ("Property Name = " + s);
          }
        }
      }
```

How do I create an Enumeration?

The Vector object will return an Enumeration object by calling its *elements*() method. To create an enumeration that links a series of objects, create a vector and add the objects to the vector. Then call the vector's *elements*() method.

```
import java.util.*;

    class CreateEnumeration
      {
      public static void main (String args[])
        {
        Enumeration enum;
        Vector v;
        Integer i;
        Double d;
        String s;

        i = new Integer (12);
        d = new Double (3.1416);
        s = "A New World";

        v = new Vector ();
        v.addElement (i);
        v.addElement (d);
        v.addElement (s);
        enum = v.elements ();

        while (enum.hasMoreElements ())
          {
          System.out.println ("Element: " + enum.nextElement ());
          }
        }
      }
```

Flow of Control

How do I code if/then/else logic?

If/Then/Else logic is coded in Java like it is coded in C. The only difference is the nature of a comparison. In C, comparisons resolve to a number and the false state is defined as the number *0*. In Java, comparisons resolve to a *boolean* data type (which is not a number). To write a loop that repeats forever, one should use the boolean *true* literal inside the *while*() parenthesis rather than following the C convention of the number "1".

```
class IfThenElse
  {
  public static void main (String args[])
    {
    if (1 == 2)
      {
      System.out.println ("1 == 2");
      }
    else
      {
      System.out.println ("1 does not = 2");
      }
    if (1 != 2)
      {
      System.out.println ("1 != 2");
     }
    if (true)
      {
      System.out.println ("To force a 'true' state, use true");
      }
    }
  }
```

How do I perform case logic (switch)?

Case logic is performed with a *switch*() statement. The value within the *switch*() parentheses is an integer. Without the *break* statements, the code would continue executing through the next case. If no case is trapped, control is passed to the (optional) *default* statement. The *break* in the default is not required.

```
class SwitchLogic
  {
  public static void main (String args[])
    {
    int i = 3;

    switch (i)
      {
      case 1:
        System.out.println ("i = 1  (i=" + i + ")");
        break;
      case 2:
        System.out.println ("i = 2  (i=" + i + ")");
        break;
      case 3:
        System.out.println ("i = 3  (i=" + i + ")");
        break;
      default:
        System.out.println ("There is no case for i  (i=" + i + ")");
        break;
      }
    }
  }
```

How do I force a program exit with a return code (exit)?

The System class provides an abstract method called *exit*(), which will terminate a program immediately. The integer that is passed to the method is returned to the operating system as the program return code.

```
class Exit
  {
  public static void main (String args[])
    {
    System.exit (0);
    }
  }
```

How do I code bitwise AND/OR logic?

Bitwise AND ("&") or OR (" | ") operators can be used with integer data. One should keep in mind that they produce integer results, not *boolean* results. Logical constructions require a *boolean* data type.

So, if bitwise operators are used in logical constructions, they must be used in conjunction with a comparison operator like ("!="). Comparison operators resolve to *boolean* data types.

```
class BitwiseAnd
      {
      public static void main (String args[])
        {
        int i;

        i = 0x0104;

        if ((i & 0x0004) != 0)
          {
          System.out.println ("Bit 3 is turned on");
          }
        if ((i & 0x0100) != 0)
          {
          System.out.println ("Bit 9 is turned on");
          }

        System.out.println ("This forces " + i + " to the odd number: "
          + (i | 1));
        }
      }
```

Conversion

How do I convert a String into an int, float, or double?

The conversion must be performed by a class. But the target data types are not classes. One must create a new wrapper object (like *Integer* or *Float*) using the String to be converted. Then use a wrapper method like *intValue*() to return the number as a non-class data variable.

```
class StringToNumber
  {
  public static void main (String args[])
    {
    int iWk;
    float fWk;
    double dWk;

    iWk = (new Integer("123")).intValue();
    fWk = (new Float("123.45")).floatValue();
    dWk = (new Double("123.45")).doubleValue();

    System.out.println ("iWk = " + iWk);
    System.out.println ("fWk = " + fWk);
    System.out.println ("dWk = " + dWk);
    }
  }
```

How do I convert an int, float, or double to a String?

The String class provides a method called *valueOf()* for converting other data types into Strings. The method is a static method, so the class name is used (e.g., String.valueof()), rather than an instance variable name. The numeric data variable is passed as a parameter and a String object is returned.

```
class NumberToString
  {
  public static void main (String args[])
    {
    int iWk = 123;
    float fWk = (float) 123.45;
    double dWk = 123.45;
    String sWk;

    sWk = String.valueOf (iWk);
    System.out.println ("iWk = " + iWk);
    sWk = String.valueOf (fWk);
    System.out.println ("fWk = " + fWk);
    sWk = String.valueOf (dWk);
    System.out.println ("dWk = " + dWk);
    }
  }
```

How do I convert a String to an array and back?

Use the String to instantiate a StringBufferInputStream. Then read an array from it. The example performs this operation, then also converts the array back to a string so it can be printed on the standard output device.

```
import java.io.*;

    class StringToArray
      {
      public static void main (String args[])
        {
        StringBufferInputStream sbis;
        byte[] ab;
        int iLength;
        String s;

        s = "abcdefghijklmnopqrstuvwxyz";               // String to stream
        sbis = new StringBufferInputStream (s);

        iLength = sbis.available ();                    // Stream to array
        ab = new byte[iLength];
        sbis.read (ab, 0, iLength);

        s = new String (ab, 0);                         // Print array
        System.out.println ("The final array is -->"
          + s + "<--");
        }
      }
```

How do I convert a Boolean/Integer/Double to a boolean/int/double?

For each *simple type* like int, double, and boolean, there is a corresponding *composite type* that is a full class with services that can be called. The *composite types,* also called *wrappers,* have names that are usually capitalized versions of the *simple types*: Integer, Double, and Boolean.

This example shows how to convert from the *simple type* to the *composite type* and back:

```
class ValueHolderConversions
  {
  public static void main (String args[])
    {
    int i;
    double d;
    boolean b;
    Integer ii;
    Double dd;
    Boolean bb;

    i = 7;
    d = 3.1416;
    b = true;
    System.out.println
      (
      "Initial values:                    i=" + i
      + "  d=" + d
      + "  b=" + b
      );

    ii = new Integer (i);
    dd = new Double (d);
    bb = new Boolean (b);
    System.out.println
      (
      "Converted to value holder objects:    ii=" + ii
      + "  dd=" + dd
      + "  bb=" + bb
      );

    i = 0;
    d = 0.0;
    b = false;
    System.out.println
      (
```

```
      "Reinitialized to bogus values:        i=" + i
      + "  d=" + d
      + "  b=" + b
      )

    i = ii.intValue ();
    d = dd.doubleValue ();
    b = bb.booleanValue ();
    System.out.println
      (
      "Converted from value holders vars:    i=" + i
      + "  d=" + d
      + "  b=" + b
      );
    }
  }
```

File

How do I code basic file I/O?

To work with files, one usually works with two classes for each file. The File class stores the file's path and name. The behavior for accessing the data of a file is in a Stream class.

The example below uses the FileInputStream to read data from the *BasicFileIOInData* file in the default (".") directory and the FileOutputStream to write it to the *BasicFileIOOutData* file in the default (".") directory. The input file is in the *examples\how_do_i\BasicFileIO* directory.

```
import java.io.*;

    class BasicFileIO
      {
      public static void main (String args[])
        {
        File fIn;
        FileInputStream fisIn;
        File fOut;
        FileOutputStream fosOut;
        int iChar;

        try
          {
          fIn = new File (".", "BasicFileIOInData");
          fisIn = new FileInputStream (fIn);
          fOut = new File (".", "BasicFileIOOutData");
          fosOut = new FileOutputStream (fOut);

          while ((iChar = fisIn.read ()) != -1)
            {
            fosOut.write (iChar);
            }

          fisIn.close ();
          fosOut.close ();
          }

        catch (Exception e)
          {
          System.out.println ("Error processing files: " + e);
          }
        }
      }
```

How do I read from stdin and write to stdout and stderr?

In Java, the standard I/O streams are instantiated when the image is started. They are available as instance variables of the System class. The following streams are used:

System.in	*An InputStream object*
System.out	*A PrintStream object*
System.err	*A PrintStream object*

Since the streams are already open, they can be immediately read and written. To run the following program, one can use a piped file for input as follows:

```
java StdFileIO < StdFileIOInData
```

The input file is included in the directory *examples\How_Do_I\StdFileIO*.

```
import java.io.*;

    class StdFileIO
      {
      public static void main (String args[])
        {
        int iChar;

        try
          {
          while ((iChar = System.in.read ()) != -1)
            {
            System.out.write (iChar);
            }
          System.err.println ("A Stupendously Successful Run");
          }

        catch (Exception e)
          {
          System.out.println ("Error processing files: " + e);
          }
        }
      }
```

Math

How do I code arithmetic?

The standard symbols for arithmetic are used in Java.

```
class Arithmetic
  {
  public static void main (String args[])
    {
    int i;
    double d;

    i = 3 + 4;
    i = 9 - 2;
    i = 3 * 5;
    i = 8 / 4;                      // Integer division truncates.
    d = 8.5 / 3.7;                  // Real number division.

  System.out.println ("i = " + i + "  d = " + d);
  }
}
```

How do I round a number or get its ceiling or floor?

The Math class provides static methods to *round*(), *ceil*(), or *floor*().

```
class Round
  {
  public static void main (String args[])
    {
    long l;
    double d;

    d = 3.67;

    l = Math.round (d);
    System.out.println (d + " rounded is " + l);

    l = (long) Math.floor (d);
    System.out.println ("The floor of " + d + " is " + l);

    l = (long) Math.ceil (d);
    System.out.println ("The ceiling of " + d + " is " + l);
    }
  }
```

How do I truncate a number?

The Math class provides the *floor*() method to return the largest whole number less than the number passed to it.

```
class Truncate
  {
  public static void main (String args[])
    {
    int i;
    double d;

    d = 7.82;

    i = (int) Math.floor (d);       // Truncates and converts to an int.
    d = Math.floor (d);             // Truncates to a double.

    System.out.println ("i = " + i + "  d = " + d);
    }
  }
```

How do I calculate a division remainder?

The remainder for the division of two integers is available by using the modulus operator "%". To get the remainder for the division of real numbers, use the static Math method *IEEEremainder*().

```
class Remainder
  {
  public static void main (String args[])
    {
    int i;
    double d;

    i = 10 % 4;
    System.out.println ("The mod or remainder of 10 / 4 = " + i);

    d = Math.IEEEremainder (10.0, 4.0);
    System.out.println ("The mod or remainder of 10.0 / 4.0 = " + d);
    }
  }
```

How do I raise a number to a power?

The static Math method *pow*() accepts two doubles. It raises the first to the power specified by the second. It returns a double.

The exponential constant *e* has a dedicated method to raise it to a power. The *exp*() method is passed the power and it returns *e* raised to that power.

```
class RaiseToPower
  {
  public static void main (String args[])
    {
    int i;
    double d;

    i = (int) Math.pow (2.0, 16.0);
    System.out.println ("2 raised to the 16th power = " + i);

    d = Math.pow (5.3, -3.2);
    System.out.println ("5.3 raised to the -3.2 power = " + d);

    d = Math.exp (5.0);
    System.out.println ("e raised to the 5.0 power = " + d);
    }
  }
```

How do I specify the constant "Pi" or the constant "e"?

These two constants are stored in variables in the Math class.

```
class Pi
  {
  public static void main (String args[])
    {
    double d;

    d = Math.PI;
    System.out.println ("Pi = " + d);

    d = Math.E;
    System.out.println ("e = " + d);
    }
  }
```

How do I invoke sin, cos, and tan functions?

The trigonometry functions are available as static methods in the Math class.

```
class Trig
  {
  public static void main (String args[])
    {
    double d;

    d = Math.sin (45.0);
    System.out.println ("The sine of 45 degrees = " + d);

    d = Math.cos (60.0);
    d = Math.tan (60.0);

    d = Math.asin (60.0);
    d = Math.acos (60.0);
    d = Math.atan (60.0);
    }
  }
```

Language

How do I code literals?

Here are a number of examples of literals.

```
class SomeLiterals
  {
  public static void main (String args[])
    {
    int iWk;
    long lWk;
    float fWk;
    double dWk;
    String sWk;
    boolean bWk;

                                    // Literal Integers:
    iWk = 25;                       // Decimal integer
    iWk = 025;                      // Assumed to be octal 25 = 21 decimal
    iWk = 0x25;                     // Assumed to be hex 25 = 37 decimal
    lWk = 25L;                      // Forced to be a long integer.

                                    // Literal floating points:
    dWk = 2.0d;                     // Double precision
    fWk = 2.0f;                     // Float
    dWk = 2.0;                      // Default is double

                                    // Literal String:
    sWk = "Hello World";            // A string

                                    // Literal Booleans:
    bWk = true;                     // true
    bWk = false;                    // false
    }
  }
```

How do I create a variable?

Simple type variables like *int, double,* and *boolean,* are created when the variable is declared. Composite type variables that are objects of real classes need to be declared and then created with the *new* operator.

```
class Variable
      {
      public static void main (String args[])
         {
         int i;                           // Simple Type var created here.
         StringBuffer sb;                 // Composite Type var defined here.

         i = 3;                           // Assign a value to the var.
         sb = new StringBuffer ("abc");   // Create the var object with a
                                          // value.
         }
      }
```

How do I create a single variable that all instances of a class can access?

Add the *static* attribute to the definition of the variable. Each time the class below is instantiated, the static variable *iInstanceCount* is incremented. At the end of the example, the value of *iInstanceCount* is printed out as "3". If it was not a static variable, it would have a value of *0.*

```
class StaticVariableExample
  {
  static int iInstanceCount = 0;

  StaticVariableExample ()
    {
    iInstanceCount++;
    }

  public static void main (String args[])
    {
    StaticVariableExample x, y, z;

    x = new StaticVariableExample ();
    y = new StaticVariableExample ();
    z = new StaticVariableExample ();
    System.out.println ("There are "
      + StaticVariableExample.iInstanceCount
      + " StaticVariableExample instances");
    }
  }
```

How do I call a method?

The method *printAMessage*() below is called by creating an object of the *CallMethod* class, then appending the method name to the object name: *cm.printAMessage*().

```
class CallMethod
  {
  void printAMessage ()
    {
    System.out.println ("Hello World");
    }

  public static void main (String args[])
    {
    CallMethod cm;

    cm = new CallMethod ();

    cm.printAMessage ();
    }
  }
```

How do I call a method that throws an Exception?

The general format is to enclose the call that throws the exception within a *try*{} block and follow it with a *catch*(){} block. The catch statement takes an exception as a parameter.

Since all exceptions are derived from the class *Exception*, one can always specify the Exception class as the catch parameter, regardless of which exception is thrown. To get more control over exception handling, one would specify the exact Exception class that could be thrown as the parameter to the catch block.

```
class CallWithException
   {
  public static void main (String args[])
    {
    int i;

    for (i = 0; i < 3; i++)
      {
      try
        {
        System.out.println ("Iteration = " + i);
        Thread.sleep (1000);
        }
      catch (Exception e)
        {
        System.out.println ("An exception occurred: " + e);
        }
      }
    System.out.println ("Done!");
    }
  }
```

How do I explicitly call a method in a super class?

Use the variable called *super*. In line 7 below, the object *super* is sent the method *myMethod*(). When that happens, the *myMethod*() of HigherClass is executed rather than the local version of *myMethod*().

```
class CallSuper extends HigherClass
  {
  void myMethod (String sParam)
    {
    System.out.println ("CallSuper>>myMethod() was called with "
      + sParam);
    super.myMethod (sParam);
    }

  public static void main (String args[])
    {
    CallSuper x = new CallSuper ();
    x.myMethod ("** Param List **");
    }
  }


class HigherClass
  {
  void myMethod (String sParam)
    {
    System.out.println ("HigherClass>>myMethod() was called with "
      + sParam);
    }
  }
```

How do I use an Interface?

An interface is a structure that looks like a class. But the methods do not have any code in them. They are simply defined. When a class *implements* an interface, it supplies the code for each method that is included in the interface structure. This allows many different classes to contain the behavior that is specified in a single interface.

In the example below, the interface *Displayer* has specified one method, *display*(). Both classes have implemented this interface and provided behavior for the *display()* method. Notice how the *main()* method is able to instantiate both classes into a variable that is defined to be of type *Displayer*. The interface stands in the place of a class and can be used like a class.

```
class InterfaceExample implements Displayer
  {
  public void display ()
    {
    System.out.println ("An instance of InterfaceExample");
    }

  public static void main (String args[])
    {
    Displayer d;

    d = new InterfaceExample ();
    d.display ();
    d = new MyClass ();
    d.display ();
    }
  }

class MyClass implements Displayer
  {
  public void display ()
    {
    System.out.println ("An instance of MyClass");
    }
  }

interface Displayer
  {
  public void display ();
  }
```

How do I see if an object is an instance of a particular class?

One can use the *instanceof* operator (notice that it is all lowercase). Since this is an operator, it is placed between an instance variable and a class name. The statement resolves to a boolean that can be used in comparisons.

```
class InstanceOfExample
  {
  public static void main (String args[])
    {
    Object obj;

    obj = "Distributed Applications";

    if (obj instanceof Integer)
      {
      System.out.println ("obj is an instance of Integer");
      }
    else if (obj instanceof String)
      {
      System.out.println ("obj is an instance of String");
      }
    else if (obj instanceof Double)
      {
      System.out.println ("obj is an instance of Double");
      }
    }
  }
```

User Interface

How do I cut, copy, and paste inside a TextField or TextArea?

In the Windows95 platform, when the TextField or TextArea is visible, click the right mouse button in the control and a menu pops up with the options to *Cut, Copy, Paste, Delete, Select All,* or *Undo*. These services are provided without any work on the programmer's part.

How do I receive keyboard input?

For Java applications, keyboard input must be read from the standard input stream (*System.in*). This is described in the first part of the chapter on *User Input*. For Java applets, keyboard input arrives in the form of events. The applet should implement a *handleEvent*() method to detect the *key down* and *key up* events. This is described in the latter part of the chapter on *User Input*.

How do I pass parameters to a command line Java application?

Parameters are passed on the command line in the same manner as other programs. The Java system passes them to an application as an array of String objects. The first parameter is indexed as the [*0*] position of the array.

```
class ParmsToApplication
  {
  public static void main (String args[])
    {
    if (args.length == 0)
      {
      System.out.println ("No parameters were specified on command line");
      }
    if (args.length >= 1)
      {
      System.out.println ("The 1st command line parameter: " + args[0]);
      }
    if (args.length >= 2)
      {
      System.out.println ("The 2nd command line parameter: " + args[1]);
      }
    if (args.length >= 3)
      {
      System.out.println ("The 3rd command line parameter: " + args[2]);
      }
    }
  }
```

How do I pass parameters to an applet?

To pass a parameter to an applet, the parameter must be coded in the Web page that launches the applet. In the Web page, the parameter is coded as a <PARAM . . . > tag within the <APPLET> . . . </APPLET> area. The name of the parameter and the value of the parameter are both strings.

The applet receives the parameter by calling the *getParameter*() method with the name of the desired parameter. In Figure A–1 the parameter is written to the screen.

```
import java.applet.Applet;
import java.awt.*;

    public class PassParmsToApplet extends Applet
      {
      String s;

      public void init ()
        {
        s = getParameter ("MyParameter");
        }

      public void paint (Graphics g)
        {
        g.drawString (s, 20, 20);
        }
      }
```

Figure A–1

```
<HTML>
<HEAD>
<TITLE> PassParmsToApplet </TITLE>
</HEAD>
<BODY>
PassParmsToApplet
<APPLET CODE="PassParmsToApplet" WIDTH=300 HEIGHT=200>
<PARAM NAME=MyParameter VALUE="Network Centered Computing">;
<HR>
</APPLET>
</BODY>
</HTML>
```

How do I write text on an Applet window?

Text is normally written when the applet is processing the *paint*() method. Each *paint*() method is handed a Graphics object as a parameter. The Graphics object contains the drawing functions needed for writing text.

The Graphics *drawString*() method accepts the string to be drawn and the *x* and *y* pixel location where the string should be drawn on the window. The left end of the baseline is positioned to the location specified and the characters of the string are positioned to the right of this position.

```
import java.applet.Applet;
import java.awt.*;

    public class TextApplet extends Applet
      {
      public void paint (Graphics g)
        {
        g.drawString ("Hello Distributed World", 20, 20);
        }
      }
```

```
<HTML>
<HEAD>
<TITLE> TextApplet </TITLE>
</HEAD>
<BODY>
TextApplet
<APPLET CODE="TextApplet" WIDTH=300 HEIGHT=200>
<HR>
</APPLET>
</BODY>
</HTML>
```

How do I get FontMetrics for a Font?

Fonts never take on physical dimensions until they are scaled to a physical display device and point size. For that reason, the *FontMetrics* object is only available from the Graphics object that manages the display surface.

In the example below, a new font is created and is made the default font in the current Graphics object. Then the *FontMetrics* object is acquired by calling the Graphics object's *getFontMetrics*() method. All the dimensions for the current Font in the current display device is stored in the *FontMetrics* object. Using the height of the selected font as the beginning y coordinate, the large string is written to the screen (Figure A–2).

Figure A–2

```
import java.applet.Applet;
import java.awt.*;

    public class FontMetricsExample extends Applet
      {
      public void paint (Graphics g)
        {
        Font fFont;
        FontMetrics fm;
        int x, y;

        fFont = new Font ("Helvetica", Font.ITALIC | Font.BOLD, 120);
        g.setFont (fFont);

        fm = g.getFontMetrics ();

        x = 10;
        y = fm.getHeight ();
        g.drawString ("Java", x, y);
        }
      }
```

```
<HTML>
<HEAD>
<TITLE> FontMetricsExample </TITLE>
</HEAD>
<BODY>
FontMetricsExample
<APPLET CODE="FontMetricsExample" WIDTH=300 HEIGHT=200>
<HR>
</APPLET>
</BODY>
</HTML>
```

How do I place a button at a particular (x, y) spot?

First, remove the applet's default Layout Manager. Then call the button's *reshape*() method to set two things: the *(x, y)* position of the upper left corner of the button and the width and height of the button.

```
import java.applet.Applet;
import java.awt.*;

    public class ButtonAtSpot extends Applet
      {
      public void init ()
        {
        Button b;

        setLayout (null);
        b = new Button ("Button 1");
        b.reshape (100, 30, 150, 100);
        add (b);
        }
      }
```

```
<HTML>
<HEAD>
<TITLE> ButtonAtSpot </TITLE>
</HEAD>
<BODY>
ButtonAtSpot
<APPLET CODE="ButtonAtSpot" WIDTH=300 HEIGHT=200>
</APPLET>
</BODY>
</HTML>
```

How do I draw lines, circles, and rectangles on the face of an applet?

All of the drawing and filling methods are in the Graphic object in the *java.awt* package. Lines are drawn from an *x*, *y* coordinate ((0, 0) is upper left) to an *x*, *y* coordinate. Circles or ovals are drawn within the rectangle that is specified by an upper left coordinate (*x*, *y*) and the width and height of the rectangle. Rectangles are specified in the same way.

```
import java.applet.Applet;
import java.awt.*;

    public class CircleApplet extends Applet
      {
      public void paint (Graphics g)
        {
        int x, y;

        x = size().width - 1;           // Width of the applet.
        y = size().height - 1;          // Height of the applet.

        g.drawLine (0, 0, x, y);

        g.drawOval (0, 0, x, y);

        g.drawRect (0, 0, x, y);
        }
      }
```

```
<HTML>
<HEAD>
<TITLE> CircleApplet </TITLE>
</HEAD>
<BODY>
CircleApplet
<APPLET CODE="CircleApplet" WIDTH=300 HEIGHT=200>
<HR>
</APPLET>
</BODY>
</HTML>
```

How do I copy pixels from one spot in the window to another?

The Graphics object has a *copyArea*() method that will copy all the pixels within a specified rectangle to another spot in the window. The first four parameters to this function identify the *x* and *y* offset of the upper left corner and the width and height of the rectangle. The last two parameters identify how far to displace the new rectangle from the first rectangle. If these two parameters were both "0," then the pixels would be copied on top of the old pixels. If they were "5" and "7," then the pixels would all be copied 5 pixels to the right and 7 pixels down.

The example below writes the string "*Java*" on the display surface, identifies the rectangle that encompasses it, and copies that rectangle to positions that tile the window's surface. The results are shown in Figure A–3.

```
import java.applet.Applet;
import java.awt.*;

    public class CopyImageExample extends Applet
      {
      public void paint (Graphics g)
        {
        Font fFont;
        FontMetrics fm;
        String s;
```

Figure A–3

```
        int x, y;
        int w, h;
        int i, j;

        fFont = new Font ("Helvetica", Font.ITALIC | Font.BOLD, 36);
        g.setFont (fFont);
        fm = g.getFontMetrics ();

        s = "Java";
        x = 0;
        y = fm.getLeading () + fm.getAscent ();
        w = fm.stringWidth (s);
        h = fm.getHeight () - fm.getLeading ();

        g.drawString (s, x, y);

        for (i = 0; i < 4; i++)
          {
          for (j = 0; j < 5; j++)
            {
            g.copyArea (0, 0, w, h, w * i, h * j);
            }
          }
        }
      }
```

```
<HTML>
<HEAD>
<TITLE> CopyImageExample </TITLE>
</HEAD>
<BODY>
CopyImageExample
<APPLET CODE="CopyImageExample" WIDTH=300 HEIGHT=200>
<HR>
</APPLET>
</BODY>
</HTML>
```

How do I draw in one cell of a Layout Manager?

Create a class that is a subclass of Canvas or Panel and implement its *paint()* method. Then put an instance of the new class in one of the cells of the Layout-Manager.

The example below extends the Panel class and places the new *MyPanel* class in each of the cells of the BorderLayout (Figure A–4). MyPanel draws an oval each time it renders itself. All further drawing can be handled in MyPanel's *paint()* method.

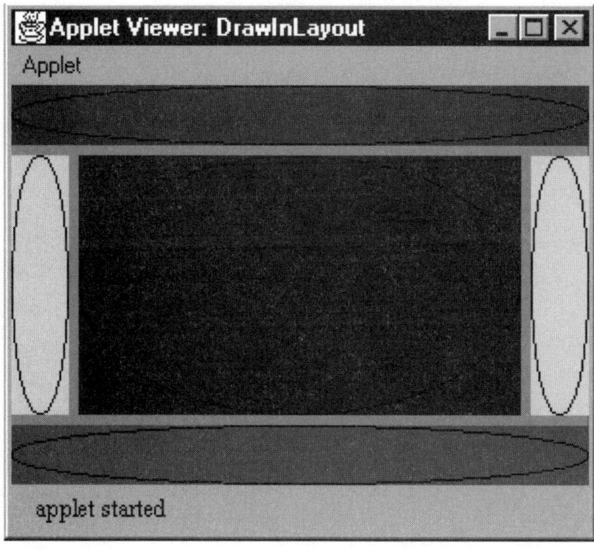

Figure A–4

```
import java.applet.Applet;
import java.awt.*;

    public class DrawInLayout extends Applet
      {
      public void init()
        {
        MyPanel p;

        setLayout (new BorderLayout (5, 5));

        p = new MyPanel ();
        p.setBackground (Color.red);
        add ("North", p);

        p = new MyPanel ();
        p.setBackground (Color.blue);
        add ("Center", p);

        p = new MyPanel ();
        p.setBackground (Color.magenta);
        add ("South", p);

        p = new MyPanel ();
        p.setBackground (Color.yellow);
        add ("West", p);

        p = new MyPanel ();
        p.setBackground (Color.yellow);
        add ("East", p);
        }

      public void paint (Graphics g)
        {
        g.setColor (Color.green);
        g.fill3DRect (0, 0, size().width, size().height, true);
        }
      }
```

```
class MyPanel extends Panel
  {
  public Dimension preferredSize ()
    {
    return (new Dimension (30, 30));
    }

  public void paint (Graphics g)
    {
    g.drawOval (0, 0, size().width - 1, size().height - 1);
    }
  }
```

```
<HTML>
<HEAD>
<TITLE> DrawInLayout </TITLE>
</HEAD>
<BODY>
DrawInLayout
<APPLET CODE="DrawInLayout" WIDTH=300 HEIGHT=200>
<HR>
</APPLET>
</BODY>
</HTML>
```

How do I place an independent window at a particular (x, y) spot?

The first two parameters of the *reshape*() method specify the coordinate of the upper left corner of the Frame window. The other two parameters specify the width and height of the window.

```
import java.awt.*;

    class LocationWindow
      {
      public static void main (String args[])
        {
        MyFrame mf;

        mf = new MyFrame ();

        mf.reshape (75, 75, 300, 300);

        mf.add ("Center", new Button ("Upper Left Corner is at (75,75)"));
        mf.show ();
        }
      }


    class MyFrame extends Frame
      {
      public boolean handleEvent (Event evt)
        {
        if (evt.id == Event.WINDOW_DESTROY)
          {
          System.exit (0);
          }
        return (super.handleEvent (evt));
        }
      }
```

How do I get an independent window to close?

The WINDOW_DESTROY event must be trapped and the application must be closed in the trap. In an independent window, this event is sent to the Frame window. To trap the event, one must extend frame with a new class and implement the *handleEvent*() method in the new class. When the event *id* field equals *Event.WINDOW_DESTROY,* then exit the application.

```
import java.awt.*;

    class CloseWindow
      {
      public static void main (String args[])
        {
        MyFrame mf;

        mf = new MyFrame ();
        mf.resize (300, 300);
        mf.add ("Center", new Button ("This Window will Close"));
        mf.show ();
        }
      }


    class MyFrame extends Frame
      {
      public boolean handleEvent (Event evt)
        {
        if (evt.id == Event.WINDOW_DESTROY)
          {
          System.exit (0);
          }
        return (super.handleEvent (evt));
        }
      }
```

Client/Server

How do I get Netscape to reload the applet?

During development, sometimes an applet needs to be recompiled and redisplayed in the Netscape browser. If the applet is already loaded in the browser, one would guess that pressing the *Reload* button would reload the HTML page and the applet. But the Java class is not reloaded when the HTML page is reloaded.

If one is developing both sides of the application on the local machine, they can try placing the HTML page in an editor and re-save the page to disk. Then press *Reload* in Netscape. In most environments, Netscape will identify the new HTML page and fetch a new copy of the applet.

System

How do I get the IP number of this machine?

The *InetAddress* object provides *Internet Address* services. The static method, *getLocalHost*(), returns an *InetAddress* object that contains the address information for the local host.

To extract the IP number from the InetAddress object, one can call its *toString*() method and parse the dotted decimal number from the string that is returned. Another method is to call the *getAddress*() method and format the byte array that is returned. The array consists of the four bytes of the IP address in network byte order.

```
import java.net.*;

    class GetIPNumber
      {
      public static void main (String[] args)
        {
        InetAddress ia = null;

        try
          {
          ia = InetAddress.getLocalHost ();
          }
        catch (Exception e)
          {
          System.out.println ("Error fetching local host name: " + e);
          }

        System.out.println ("Host Name/Address = " + ia);
        }
      }
```

How do I find the font face names that are available?

The Toolkit object has a service that returns the font face names that are available in a particular Java environment. They are returned as an array of strings.

```
import java.awt.Toolkit;

    class FontFacenames
      {
      public static void main (String args[])
        {
        int i;
        String[] asFaceName;

        asFaceName = Toolkit.getDefaultToolkit().getFontList();

        for (i = 0; i < asFaceName.length; i++)
          {
          System.out.println (asFaceName[i]);
          }
        System.exit (0);
        }
      }
```

How do I find out how much memory is available?

The Runtime object keeps track of image statistics while a program is running.

```
class MemoryAvailable
  {
  public static void main (String args[])
    {
    Runtime rt;

    rt = Runtime.getRuntime ();
    System.out.println ("Total Memory = " + rt.totalMemory ());
    System.out.println ("Free Memory = " + rt.freeMemory ());
    }
  }
```

How do I launch a thread?

One way to launch a thread is to make a new class that extends the Thread class. The only method that needs to be implemented is the *run*() method.

To actually launch the thread, instantiate the new Thread object and send it the *start*() method. Control in the new thread will pass to the new class's *run*() method. The original thread will continue to execute the next instruction.

In the example below, the *join*() method is sent to the thread to cause the launching thread to wait with no time out (0) until the launched thread has completed processing. When execution is complete in the *run*() method of the launched thread and the method exits, the thread is automatically stopped and deallocated.

```
class LaunchThread
  {
  public static void main (String args[])
    {
    MyThread th;

    try
      {
      th = new MyThread ();
      th.start ();
      th.join (0);
      }
    catch (Exception e)
      {
      System.out.println ("Error occured: " + e);
      }
    }
  }


class MyThread extends Thread
  {
  public void run ()
    {
    int i;

    for (i = 0; i < 300; i++)
      {
      System.out.print ("\rThe count is " + i);
      }
    System.out.println ("");
    }
  }
```

How do I dynamically load a class?

If one is starting with a string that contains a class name, one must call the class's static *forName*() method to obtain a Class object for the new class. This method searches the CLASSPATH, locates the Class file, and loads it into the *image* if it is not already present.

Then the new Class object must be sent the *newInstance*() method to get a new instance of the new class. The object that is returned from this call can be used as an instance of the desired class. In the example below, the target class is MyClass. After it is loaded and instantiated, the *printAString*() method is sent to it.

```
class LoadClass
  {
  public static void main (String args[])
    {
    Class cls;
    MyClass x = null;

    try
      {
      cls = Class.forName ("MyClass");

      try
        {
        x = (MyClass) cls.newInstance ();
        }
      catch (java.lang.IllegalAccessException e)
        {
        System.out.println ("IllegalAccessException");
        }
      catch (java.lang.InstantiationException e)
        {
        System.out.println ("InstantiationException");
        }
      }
```

```
    catch (java.lang.ClassNotFoundException e)
      {
      System.out.println ("ClassNotFoundException");
      }

    x.printAString ();
    }
  }

class MyClass
  {
  void printAString ()
    {
    System.out.println ("This is from MyClass");
    }
  }
```

Special Services

How do I create a bit coded variable?

The *BitSet* object provides services to store and retrieve bit coded information. The variable width is specified when the object is created. The internal variable width is selected in increments of 64 bits.

The *set()* method turns a bit on. The *clear()* method turns a bit off. The methods *and()*, *or()*, and *xor()* return a BitSet that is the result of a logical bitwise operation between two specified BitSets.

```
import java.util.*;

    class BitSetExample
      {
      public static void main (String args[])
        {
        BitSet bits1;
        BitSet bits2;
        BitSet bits3;

        bits1 = new BitSet (64);           // 1-64 == 64, 65-128 == 128
        bits2 = new BitSet (64);           // 1-64 == 64, 65-128 == 128
        System.out.println
          (
          "\nbits1.size() == " + bits1.size ()
          + " possible bit positions."
          );
        System.out.println ();

        bits1.set(0);                      // Set bit number 0 in bits1
        bits1.set(2);                      // Set bit number 2 in bits1
        bits2.set(1);                      // Set bit number 1 in bits2
        bits2.set(2);                      // Set bit number 2 in bits2
        bits3 = (BitSet) bits1.clone ();   // Create bits3 as a copy of bits1

        System.out.println ("The bits that are on in bits1 are " + bits1);
        System.out.println ("The bits that are on in bits2 are " + bits2);
        System.out.println ();
```

```
    bits1.and (bits2);
    System.out.println ("After: bits1 AND bits2...");
    System.out.println ("bits1: bit 0 is set?  " + bits1.get (0));
    System.out.println ("bits1: bit 1 is set?  " + bits1.get (1));
    System.out.println ("bits1: bit 2 is set?  " + bits1.get (2));
    System.out.println ("bits1 = " + bits1);
    System.out.println ();

    bits1 = (BitSet) bits3.clone ();
    bits1.or (bits2);
    System.out.println ("After: bits1 OR bits2...");
    System.out.println ("bits1: bit 0 is set?  " + bits1.get (0));
    System.out.println ("bits1: bit 1 is set?  " + bits1.get (1));
    System.out.println ("bits1: bit 2 is set?  " + bits1.get (2));
    System.out.println ("bits1 = " + bits1);
    System.out.println ();

    bits1 = (BitSet) bits3.clone ();
    bits1.xor (bits2);
    System.out.println ("After: bits1 XOR bits2...");
    System.out.println ("bits1: bit 0 is set?  " + bits1.get (0));
    System.out.println ("bits1: bit 1 is set?  " + bits1.get (1));
    System.out.println ("bits1: bit 2 is set?  " + bits1.get (2));
    System.out.println ("bits1 = " + bits1);
    System.out.println ();

    bits1 = (BitSet) bits3.clone ();
    System.out.println ("Before any bits are cleared, bits1 = " + bits1);
    bits1.clear (0);
    System.out.println ("After clearing bit 0,        bits1 = " + bits1);
    System.out.println ();
    }
}
```

Utilities

How do I generate documentation?

Take a look at the *JavaDoc* section of the CaffeineCafe chapter for instructions about running Java's automatic documentation generator.

How do I list the Class Hierarchy of Java classes?

The API documentation that is in the form of HTML pages has several links at the top of most of the pages. One of those links says *Class Hierarchy*. This selection will fetch an HTML page that has each class listed under its parent class.

APPENDIX B

Introduction to the World Wide Web

How Did the Internet Start?

In the late 1960s, scientists working for the US Department of Defense created a new technique for communicating information between computers. This technique was designed to be flexible enough to continue functioning in the event of a nuclear attack.

The new technique came to be known by the acronym TCP/IP (*Transmission Control Protocol/Internet Protocol*), because it was a set of rules (*PROTOCOL*) that *CONTROLLED* the *TRANSMISSION* of information between computers on INTERconnected NETworks.

TCP/IP was adaptable to a wide variety of computing platforms and it was free to license. It enabled computers that were manufactured by different vendors to communicate over incompatible networks. A Macintosh computer on an Ethernet network could communicate with an IBM PC on a Token Ring without concern for the incompatibilities between their environments.

TCP/IP extended this adaptability by providing a way to connect one network with another network. Computers on any of the connected networks were able to access any of the other computers without concern for geographical location or local incompatibilities.

The ease and benefits of TCP/IP caused it to spread quickly. As Local Area Networks (LAN) grew in popularity, they began connecting with each other using TCP/IP. As they did, a movement to interconnect networks began.

The breadth of the movement spread quickly across the nation and then around the world. This unending chain, which consisted of networks connected to networks connected to networks, became known collectively as the Global *Internet*.

This Internet has succeeded in making connections across hardware vendor boundaries, across operating system boundaries, across national boundaries, and across continental boundaries. This is all possible because of the TCP/IP communication technique. But TCP/IP was not the first technique for connecting computers together.

Why did it succeed? Because it was so simple and flexible.

How Does the Internet Work?

In many ways, the Internet was patterned after a LAN. In a physical LAN, each computer is assigned a unique address. In the Internet, each computer is assigned a unique address.

The address is a four byte number. The number is sometimes represented in *dotted decimal* form (199.5.187.27), where the numbers between the dots represent the value of each of the bytes. The address can also be represented by a name (www.netscape.com). In this format, the dots simply make the name easier to read and categorize. Before any communication takes place, names are changed back into numerical addresses.

The four byte addresses have two parts.

One portion of the address stores a number that uniquely identifies the local network to which the computer is connected. The other portion of the address stores a number that uniquely identifies the computer on the local network. The first part of the address is called the *network* number and the second part is called the *host* number (Figure B–1). The Internet refers to all computers that run their own operating system as *hosts*. The opposite of a *host* is a *terminal*.

The *network number* is unique. No two networks are assigned the same number. The *host number* is only unique within a local network. The combination of the two numbers forms a unique address for identifying each single computer on the Global Internet.

The Internet sends data to these addresses in much the same way that Local Area Networks send data to their addresses.

The unit of data that a LAN sends is called a *frame* and consists of a header portion and a data portion. The header portion includes the address of the destina-

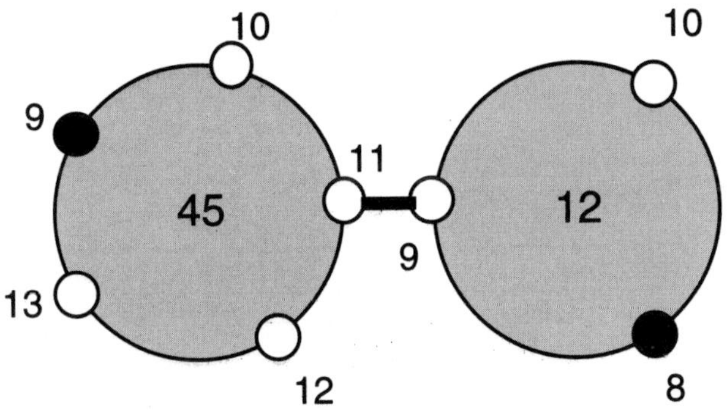

Two Networks

IP Address for Host on Left 45 | 9

IP Address for Host on Right 12 | 8

Network Number *Host Number*

Figure B–1

tion and the address of the originator of the transmission. The data portion holds the actual data that the program is sending.

The unit of transmission for the Internet is a *datagram*.

Like a LAN *frame,* an Internet *datagram* has two parts: a header and a data portion. The header includes Internet addresses for the source and destination of the message.

Why have two headers with two destination addresses? It is a matter of scope. The Internet header gives the ultimate destination. The local header gives the local destination.

Remember that the Internet connects networks together. One machine on each network is selected to manage data that is flowing between the networks. This computer is called a *gateway* or a *router*.

Datagrams

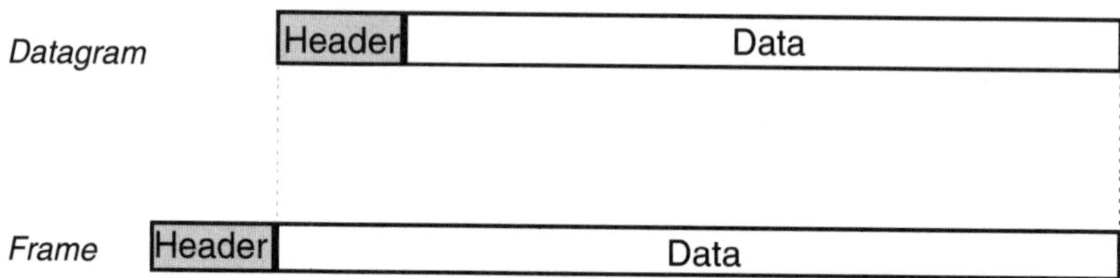

Figure B–2 Internet datagrams ride within local network frames.

The local destination field gives the address of the gateway machine on the local network. The Internet destination field gives the network number and host number of the final destination of the Internet *datagram.*

One of the flexibilities of TCP/IP comes from the way datagrams make their way across networks to their destination. Each datagram is independently routed to its destination.

In a network with multiple gateways (Figure B–3), the first two datagrams may be sent through *gateway 12,* but by the time the third datagram needs to be sent, *gateway 13* may have a lighter load. Thus, the third datagram would be routed through *gateway 13.* This helps to balance the load between gateways. All three datagrams arrive at their destination. They just might travel different routes to get there.

If a nuclear attack destroyed networks in one or two regions of the country, *datagrams* would select *gateways* that were still working and the network would continue to function.

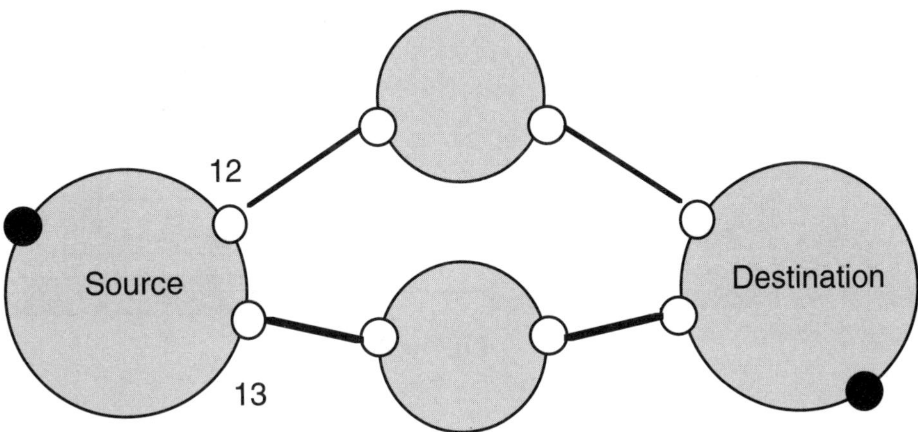

Figure B–3 This shows the process of independent routing.

How is Internet Software Structured?

The software that builds datagrams and routes them to Internet addresses is organized into several pieces that build one upon the other. To show this relationship, they are often represented as blocks stacked one upon the other. Collectively, they are known as the *TCP/IP stack*.

Each layer has a precise responsibility. The *Link* layer contains drivers for managing the physical issues, like a LAN card. The *Internet Protocol (IP)* layer manages addressing, routing, and constructs the datagrams. The *Transmission Control Protocol (TCP)* layer makes sure the datagrams are presented to the program in order, even if they arrive out of order. TCP also calls for the retransmission of datagrams that were lost along the way.

Any application program that wants to communicate with another machine accesses the other machine by opening a TCP *socket*. Opening a socket is much like opening a file. When the socket is opened, the program receives a number that represents the socket; and it is passed as a parameter for any further read or write operations. This socket handle is similar to a file handle.

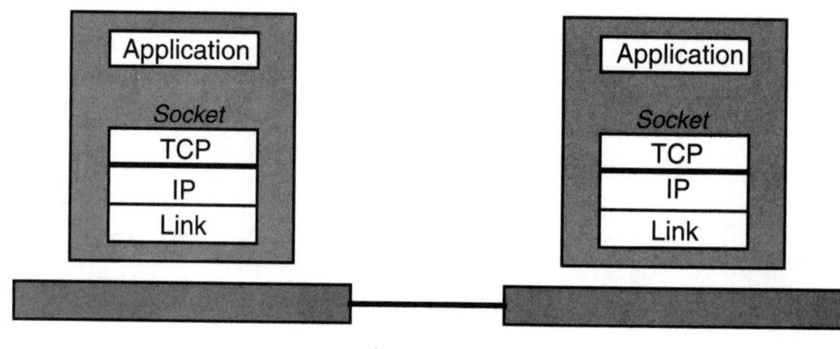

Figure B–4

As shown in Figure B–4, the data that is read from a socket comes from an application program that has opened a corresponding socket on another computer. As the two programs read and write data to their corresponding sockets, the protocol stack constructs datagrams and routes the data between the computers.

How Does a Program Use the Internet?

Application programs that open sockets and make use of the TCP/IP Protocol Stack are usually written in two parts—a client and a server. The client program opens a socket on one machine and the server program opens a socket on another machine. The two read and write to their sockets.

Over the years, several TCP/IP application programs have become so common that they are considered necessary components of a TCP/IP implementation.

The *ftp (File Transfer Protocol)* program is one of these standard services. It provides a way to transfer files from one computer to another. It provides a command line interface by which the users can display another computer's directory and copy specific files. There is no provision for displaying the files.

The *Gopher* (as in "go for" something) program adds a scrolling window interface to file transfer service. Text files can also be viewed. But there is no provision for formatting the files after they arrive. What is displayed is the straight text.

The *mail* (E-mail or electronic mail) program allows users to send small text files between computers. This has become very popular. Users can send a letter to Paris using *mail* and it arrives at its destination within seconds and costs nothing.

The *Usenet* news group program organizes E-mail messages into discussion forums dedicated to one of a number of special interest topics. There are over 2,500 news group categories. Many groups have over a million participants. Some have tens of millions of participants.

But, by far, the most popular application program designed to run on the Internet is the *World Wide Web.*

How Does a Web Browser Use the Internet?

The Web application program displays a friendly scrolling window through which users can view data files and fetch other data files.

The Web client program (also known as a Web browser) fetches a data file and displays it in the graphical window. The file that is being displayed is a text file. It could be opened by a normal text editor; and it could be edited.

One of the special things about the text file is that it includes formatting codes, called *tags*, that tell the browser how to format the text for viewing.

```
<h1>HotJava(tm) Documentation </h1>

Welcome to the HotJava Documentation Home Page. This page contains links to
the on-line documentation available with this release. You can also
<a href="http://java.sun.com/misc/JavaSearchHelp.html">search the documen-
  tation</a>. If you need help using HotJava, see the
<a href="http://java.sun.com/misc/using.html"><em>User's Guide</em></a>.
```

One can locate the *tags* in the text file above because they are surrounded by angular brackets.

For example, *<h1>* indicates that the text that follows should be formatted as a first level header, which usually places it in a large font. The *</h1>* indicates the end of the first level header formatting. On the last line, the *<em>* indicates that the text should be rendered in an *emphasized* font.

This collection of tags that specify how text should be formatted for viewing is collectively known as the Hyper Text Markup Language (HTML). A file that uses these tags is known as a Web page. The primary job of a Web browser is to fetch, format, and display Web pages.

How are Web Pages Connected to One Other?

Once the browser has fetched one Web page, there is a mechanism within the page for specifying other Web pages to fetch.

Embedded within the Hypertext Markup Language is a special tag for making reference to other Web pages. It is called an *anchor* tag and can be seen on the last line of the example above.

The full location of the new page is specified right after the *href=* (hypertext reference) parameter. The location is coded in three sections: the protocol (http: hypertext transfer protocol), the machine (java.sun.com), and the file path (/misc/using.html).

The format for the location of other Web documents has become an Internet standard and is known as a Uniform Resource Locator or URL.

When users click on the text between an *<a href=...>* tag and an *</a>* tag, the Web browser makes a request for the Web resource and displays it upon arrival.

The progressive chain of references from one text document to another by means of *anchor* tags is the Internet's implementation of *hypertext.* The collection of links between Web pages is collectively known as the World Wide Web.

How Do Web Pages Support Multimedia?

Anchor tags can point to any kind of Web resource. This includes Web pages, picture files, sound files, movie files, and programs.

When a Web resource arrives, the browser determines what kind of data is in the file and passes that data to routines that know how to render the data for the users.

Since the Web browser can coordinate so many different kinds of media files, it has assumed the position as the multimedia window into the Internet.

How are Java Programs Shared Across the Internet?

With HotJava and the other Java enabled Web browsers, a new kind of Web resource can be fetched by a Web browser—a program. Now Web browsers can fetch and render more than lifeless data files. They can fetch and run programs.

To specify a program resource within a Web page, the HotJava team added a new tag to the markup language—the <APPLET> tag. It works like the anchor tag. Instead of specifying the location of a data file, it specifies the location of a compiled Java program.

When a Java Enabled browser fetches this program file, it loads it into memory and runs the Java program. A rectangular portion of the current Web page is set aside as the window for the program. All program output is written to this region and user input into this area is relayed to the program.

Java Enabled Web browsers make program sharing and program cooperation as simple as linking together Web pages.

APPENDIX C

Introduction to Java's Virtual Machine

The primary reason that Java is well-suited for applications that are spread across the Internet is that Java programs run on a Virtual Machine.

The Virtual Machine concept has been around for a number of years. It is the design upon which UCSD's p-system compilers were built. It is also the way most of the Smalltalk environments are designed.

Virtual Machine technology is unfamiliar to most people. To understand why this technology makes program sharing easier, one needs to gain an awareness of how Java's Virtual Machine works and about how programming tasks can be spread between machines on the Internet.

How does the Virtual Machine Work?

What is a Virtual Machine?

A Virtual Machine is a program.

In Java, the Virtual Machine is a collection of C functions that are invoked when the JAVA command is typed on the command line.

How do you use the Virtual Machine?

The real computer runs Java's Virtual Machine the same way it would run any other program. If the user typed *java* on the command line, Java's VM would be loaded into memory and then its instructions would be executed (see Figure C–1). As far as the real computer knows, the only part of the Java system that is running is the Java Virtual Machine.

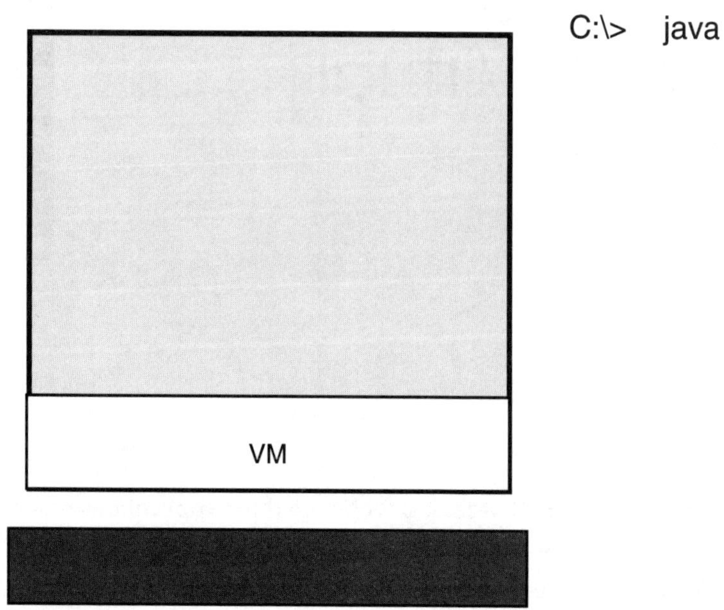

Figure C–1 The Virtual Machine is a program.

Once the VM program is running, it takes over the task of loading and running Java programs for the real computer. If the user typed *java Hello* on the command line, Java's VM would be loaded into memory. Then it would load the Java program *Hello.class* (Java uses *.class* instead of *.exe* for a file extension) into memory and run it (see Figure C–2).

If one has installed CD into the *c:\JumpStrt* directory and has included Java's BIN directory in their system's search path, they can try this out. From a command line, switch to the *\JumpStrt\examples\Hello* directory and type the following command:

```
C:\JumpStrt\examples\Hello>java Hello
Hello world!
```

This loads the VM and runs the *Hello.class* program.

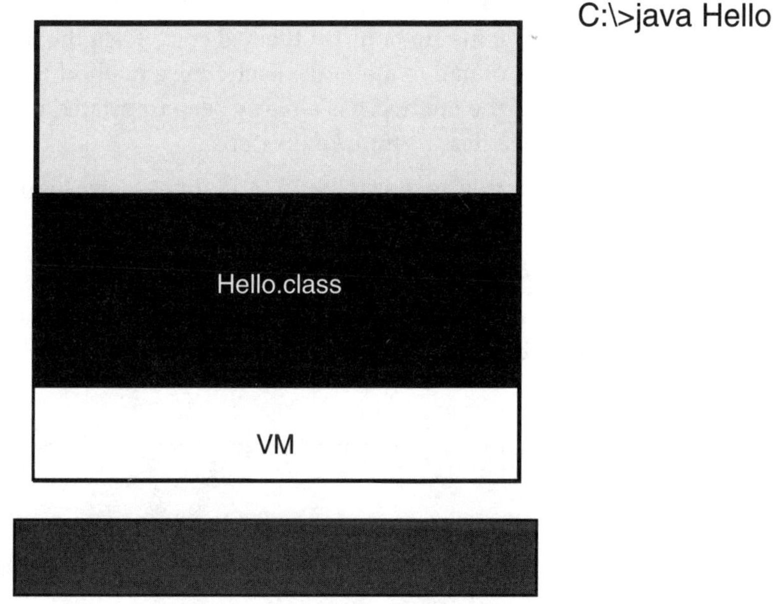

Figure C–2

What does the VM do when it runs?

After the real computer has loaded the VM into memory, and after the VM has loaded a Java program into memory, processing can begin.

The Virtual Machine that is distributed from Sun fetches each Java instruction in the *Hello.class,* and it translates it into an instruction that is understandable to the real processor. Then it passes it to the real processor to be carried out. This is sometimes called a Virtual Machine *interpreter,* because it processes instructions one by one.

Other vendors have created Virtual Machines called *Just-In-Time* compilers (JIT for short). They are not really compilers. They do not read Java source. They are Virtual Machines and read Java instructions.

Instead of reading each Java instruction one by one, they translate all the instructions in a method into a block of instructions for the real chip. Then the native instructions are cached in a pool of native methods. Each time a method is called, this cache is consulted to see if the method has already been translated into native instructions. This saves needless re-translation steps.

This technique can cause execution speeds to be 10 to 15 times faster than the interpreted translation approach.

What instructions does the VM interpret?

The source of the *Hello.java* program is listed below. The *main*() method is turned into three VM instructions when it is compiled.

```
class Hello
  {
  public static void main (String argv[])
    {
    System.out.println ("Hello world!");
    }
  }
```

```
The three instructions for the main method in VM Assembly Language:

    getstatic #7 <Field java/lang/System.out Ljava/io/PrintStream;>
    idc1 #1 <String "Hello world!">
    invokevirtual #8 <Method java/io/PrintStream.println(Ljava/lang/String;)V>

The three instructions as they appear in the Byte Code Stream (in hex):

    B2 00 07
    12 01
    B6 00 08
```

Although this looks like a lot of data, the byte stream is highly abbreviated. The VM only has to look at eight bytes to process the three instructions above.

When the Java Virtual Machine is "running" this part of the program, it processes the *getstatic* command first. To process this instruction, it stores the location of field #7 (the *System.out* object) in the current object register.

Unfortunately, the abbreviations of these instructions are not very helpful in remembering what they do. There are reasons for the abbreviation of each command, but they only make sense when one takes into account the architecture of the Virtual Machine.

The *idc1* command remembers the address of a data item from the constant pool. In this case, it is remembering the first item in the constant pool, which is the string *"Hello World!"*

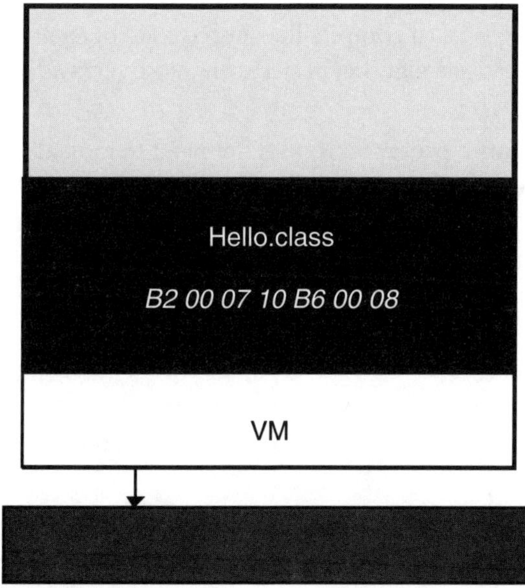

Figure C–3 The Virtual Machine translates the VM instructions and fulfills them by invoking service from the real processor.

The third instruction invokes virtual function #8—the *println*() function. This is a general service function in the object *System.out*. To process this instruction, the VM finds the instructions for the *println*() function and interprets them just as it interpreted these instructions. This is shown in Figure C–3.

Exactly which services of the real computer the VM uses when processing the instructions is a matter of VM design. Some designs use the real processors' storage areas, like its registers and stacks. Other designs create their own storage areas and treat them like registers and stacks. Almost all designs make use of the processor's services to send data to output devices like the screen.

But one thing is clear. The Java program is not concerned with the instruction set or operating system of the real computer upon which it is running. It is only aware that it is running on a virtual computer. It is running on the Java Virtual Machine.

Is the Virtual Machine an interpreter?

Since the VM interprets the instructions in the Java class, sometimes Java is called an *interpreted* language, like interpreted BASIC, or a script language, like the PC BAT language or REXX.

Interpreted languages must compile the source code of each line of the program at run-time. This carries a significant performance overhead, especially in loop processing.

When Java's VM runs a program, it does not need to look at a Java source file. The source has been already compiled. All the VM needs to do is look at Java instructions and translate them into native instructions that a particular chip can understand.

The VM is an interpreter in the sense that it translates between two different instruction sets. However, Java programs are not source files. They are compiled programs.

Java's VM Opens Up Distributed Processing

By adding the Virtual Machine to Java's environment, it is now possible to pass a compiled Java program between computers and have it run properly on either platform. All of the incompatibilities that exist between computer systems and operating systems are managed in the Virtual Machine.

The Java Virtual machine makes program sharing as easy as text sharing is on the World Wide Web.

APPENDIX D

How to Parse a Java Class File

Everything that is known about a Java class is stored in the class file. As Java code is moved around the network, it is the class file that is being communicated to each machine.

The larger the class file is, the slower the program is fetched and is loaded. Many parts of the original source program are removed in the compilation process (like comments and many variable names). But a surprising amount of the source program is retained in the class file.

As one learns what is stored in the class file and what is not stored there, one can select coding techniques that decrease the size of the executable and increase the speed of startup.

A Class File Is a Collection of Fields

Surprisingly, the class file has a fairly simple format. It is a collection of fields.

Some fields live at a fixed location and are unique in the file. Others are stored as elements of an array.

The first field in the file is four bytes wide and is known as the Java *Magic Number*. It is a fixed location field at the very beginning of the file and identifies the file as a Java class file.

The value in this field is the same for each class file and its choice was completely arbitrary. The lively tone of the Java team is reflected in their selection of the value of the *Magic Number*. They selected the number *Café Babe*! The four byte number is 3,405,691,582 in decimal. But in hex, the number is CAFEBABE.

In addition to the fixed location fields, there are fields that serve as elements in an array. The Constant Pool is an array of every field, class, and method in the class file. When the Java instructions reference a field, they reference it by its index in the Constant Pool.

There are many different kinds of fields in the Constant Pool. Each field has a one byte numeric code that indicates the type of the field. For example, the first byte of a String field has the value of "1," which identifies it as an AscII string. The next two bytes identify the length of the string, and the string data follows the length.

```
0000:  CAFE BABE 0003 002D  0020 0800 1A07 001D     *Ê_º_...-. ......*
0010:  0700 1C07 000E 0700  160A 0005 0009 0900    *................*
0020:  0300 0B0A 0004 000A  0C00 1900 1E0C 000C    *................*
0030:  0015 0C00 1400 1B01  0007 7072 696E 746C    *..........printl*
0040:  6E01 000D 436F 6E73  7461 6E74 5661 6C75    *n...ConstantValu*
0050:  6501 0013 6A61 7661  2F69 6F2F 5072 696E    *e...java/io/Prin*
0060:  7453 7472 6561 6D01  000A 4578 6365 7074    *tStream...Except*
0070:  696F 6E73 0100 0F4C  696E 654E 756D 6265    *ions...LineNumbe*

0080:  7254 6162 6C65 0100  0A53 6F75 7263 6546    *rTable...SourceF*
0090:  696C 6501 000E 4C6F  6361 6C56 6172 6961    *ile...LocalVaria*
00A0:  626C 6573 0100 0443  6F64 6501 0003 6F75    *bles...Code...ou*
00B0:  7401 0015 284C 6A61  7661 2F6C 616E 672F    *t...(Ljava/lang/*
00C0:  5374 7269 6E67 3B29  5601 0010 6A61 7661    *String;)V...java*
00D0:  2F6C 616E 672F 4F62  6A65 6374 0100 046D    */lang/Object...m*
00E0:  6169 6E01 0016 285B  4C6A 6176 612F 6C61    *ain...([Ljava/la*
00F0:  6E67 2F53 7472 696E  673B 2956 0100 063C    *ng/String;)V...<*

0100:  696E 6974 3E01 000C  4865 6C6C 6F20 776F    *init>...Hello wo*
0110:  726C 6421 0100 154C  6A61 7661 2F69 6F2F    *rld!...Ljava/io/*
0120:  5072 696E 7453 7472  6561 6D3B 0100 106A    *PrintStream;...j*
0130:  6176 612F 6C61 6E67  2F53 7973 7465 6D01    *ava/lang/System.*
0140:  0005 4865 6C6C 6F01  0003 2829 5601 000A    *..Hello...()V...*
0150:  4865 6C6C 6F2E 6A61  7661 0000 0002 0005    *Hello.java......*
0160:  0000 0000 0002 0009  0017 0018 0001 0013    *................*
0170:  0000 0025 0002 0001  0000 0009 B200 0712    *...%........2...*

0180:  01B6 0008 B100 0000  0100 1000 0000 0A00    *.¶..±...........*
0190:  0200 0000 0500 0800  0300 0000 1900 1E00    *................*
01A0:  0100 1300 0000 1D00  0100 0100 0000 052A    *...............**
01B0:  B700 06B1 0000 0001  0010 0000 0006 0001    *·..±............*
01C0:  0000 0001 0001 0011  0000 0002 001F 0000    *................*
01D0:  0000 0000 0000 0000  0000 0000 0000 0000    *................*
01E0:  0000 0000 0000 0000  0000 0000 0000 0000    *................*
01F0:  0000 0000 0000 0000  0000 0000 0000 0000    *................*
```

At offset 0x0037 above, a String field begins. The single byte value "1" indicates that the field is an AscII string. The next two bytes, 0x0007, indicate that the string is seven characters long. The string data, *println*, follows. The next byte, at offset 0x0041, indicates the start of another String field.

Since the Java environment provides for Unicode Strings made up of two byte characters, it is interesting to notice that the class file stores an AscII string, which is using one byte characters. Java is following the Unicode processing convention of only storing characters as one byte values when the most significant byte of each character is a zero. All of the methods that use strings in the image assume that strings consist of two byte characters.

The Fields Are Organized into Groups

The Constant Pool array starts at offset 0x0008 and continues through offset 0x0159. The Constant Pool is one of the five arrays of fields in the class file. Their positions in the class file are indicated in Figure D–1. Notice that each array of fields is preceded by two bytes that indicate the number of fields in the array.

At offset 0x0008 is the four byte Constant Pool Count variable. This gives the number of items in the Constant Pool array. There are actually *Count - 1* items in the Constant Pool and the first item is considered index position "1".

To parse through the Constant Pool section of the class file, this book includes a utility called *dumpclass*. The utility is automatically installed from the CD into the *\JumpStrt\java\classes* directory. Since this directory is included in the default CLASSPATH, one can use the utility from any directory.

To parse through the *Hello.class* file above, use the following syntax:

```
c:\JumpStrt\examples\Hello>java dumpclass Hello.class

                  .
                  .
                  .

0x0001 String Item
          Item Tag
            000A:  0x08
```

```
         String Index
           000B:  0x001A
              .
              .
              .

0x001A Ascii String Item
         Item Tag
           0105:  0x01

         Length and Bytes
           0106:  0x000C        Hello world!

0x001B Ascii String Item
         Item Tag
           0114:  0x01

         Length and Bytes
           0115:  0x0015        Ljava/io/PrintStream;

              .
              .
              .
```

The number on the far left is the one-based index of the field in the Constant Pool. The other numbers are either offsets within the class file or data at that spot.

These Constant Pool fields make reference to one another. The first field in the array (index 1) points to a String field by using its index in the Constant Pool (index 0x001A). The field at index 0x001A carries the data for the string *"Hello world!"*

These fields sometimes carry some odd-looking additional symbols in the string data. The *L* on the beginning of the *java/io/PrintStream* data indicates that this string is more than a string of data. It is actually an object that is an instance of the *class java/io/PrintStream*. Other data type signatures are indicated by other codes including *I* for integer, *B* for byte, and *S* for short.

One can find the complete list of signature codes in the Java Virtual Machine documentation under the *Class File Format—Signatures* section. The quickest way to this documentation is to point a browser at the *BookTour.html* file that is installed into the *\JumpStrt* directory and follow the last link on the page.

Single Field Area 1	
Magic Number	4 bytes
Version Number	4 bytes
Constant Pool	
Number of Constant Pool Fields	2 bytes
Array of Constant Pool Fields	CPField[]
Single Field Area 2	
Access Flags	2 bytes
This Class	2 bytes
Super Class	2 bytes
Interfaces	
Number of Interface Indexes	2 bytes
Array of CP Indexes to Interfaces	short[]
Fields	
Number of Field Reference Fields	2 bytes
Array of Field Reference Fields	FRefField[]
Methods	
Number of Method Reference Fields	2 bytes
Array of Method Reference Fields	MRefField[]
Attributes	
Number of Attribute Reference Fields	2 bytes
Array of Attribute Reference Fields	ARefField[]

Figure D–1

The compiler loads these Constant Pool fields with the information for each class, field, and method that it encounters. The field is referenced by citing its index position in Constant Pool array. This way the field data is stored in one location, and each reference to the field points to the spot where its data is stored.

Inspecting the Class File Can Suggest Optimizations

Although much of the source program is stripped out during compilation, it is still surprising how many of the identifiers are retained in the class file.

It is helpful to pipe the output of *dumpclass* to a file and search the file to see which identifiers are being removed by the compiler and which ones are not being removed. To optimize a Java program for space and loading speed, one should choose relatively short names for those identifiers that are retained in the class file.

```
0280:  6A61 7661 2F6C 616E  672F 5374 7269 6E67    *java/lang/String*
0290:  0100 204D 792F 5665  7279 2F42 6967 2F50    *.. My/Very/Big/P*
02A0:  6163 6B61 6765 2F50  4173 6369 6953 7472    *ackage/PAsciiStr*
02B0:  696E 6701 0020 506F  6F6C 3E3E 6D61 696E    *ing.. Pool>>main*
02C0:  3A20 496E 7075 7420  6669 6C65 206E 6F74    *: Input file not*
02D0:  2066 6F75 6E64 0100  4328 4C6A 6176 612F    * found..C(Ljava/*
02E0:  6C61 6E67 2F53 7472  696E 673B 4C4D 792F    *lang/String;LMy/*
02F0:  5665 7279 2F42 6967  2F50 6163 6B61 6765    *Very/Big/Package*

0300:  2F50 4669 656C 643B  4C6A 6176 612F 6C61    */PField;Ljava/la*
0310:  6E67 2F53 7472 696E  673B 2956 0100 0328    *ng/String;)V...(*
0320:  2949 0100 1828 4C6A  6176 612F 696F 2F49    *)I...(Ljava/io/I*
0330:  6E70 7574 5374 7265  616D 3B29 5601 0018    *nputStream;)V...*
0340:  4D79 2F56 6572 792F  4269 672F 5061 636B    *My/Very/Big/Pack*
0350:  6167 652F 506F 6F6C  0100 2943 6F6E 7374    *age/Pool..)Const*
0360:  616E 7420 506F 6F6C  2043 6F75 6E74 2028    *ant Pool Count (*
0370:  6974 7320 7265 616C  6C79 2074 6869 7320    *its really this *
```

All of the class names are retained in the file. In addition, the class name is prefixed by the class's package name. The selection of a long package name can quickly consume precious space in the class file. In the previous dump of a portion of a class file, notice how much space is taken by the package name My.Very.Big.Package.

In addition to the class identifiers, all of the class's method names are saved in the Constant Pool. This is true even if the method name is declared to be a private method.

Fortunately not all identifiers are retained in the class file. Identifiers that are declared within the body of a method are not retained in the class file. Method parameter names are also discarded.

The wise use of space in the class file can improve how quickly the class is loaded into the image. The class file is the component that must squeeze through the network and the longer it takes to arrive at a client's workstation, the more sluggish the application appears.

Inspecting the Class File Can Locate Errors

An examination of the class file can also help when debugging the elusive "class not found" error message.

It is often difficult to understand how Java cannot find a class when it is in the same directory from which Java is being launched. The default CLASSPATH includes the "." directory. How could Java not find the class?

Java is not just looking for a class file. It is also looking within a class file for a particular class signature. Inside the class file, class names are prefixed by their package name. If no package name was used, nothing is prefixed to the name.

When debugging "class not found" messages, it can be helpful to dump the class file and identify the class's complete signature. If a package name is prefixed to the class name, both must be used or the class will not be found.

When debugging, it can be very helpful to examine the contents of a Java class file. With the utility mentioned above and a grasp of the general structure, the class file can shed light on a number of programming issues in Java.

APPENDIX E

Enete Utilities

Included in the CD is an early alpha copy of some Java utility programs that may be useful. At the time of this writing, most of these utilities are only available for the Windows platform. Check the Web site *http://www.enete.com* for the most current enhancements and platforms supported.

The utility classes are installed into the *\JumpStrt\java\classes* directory because this directory is on the default CLASSPATH. In the Windows CD, batch files are also included to simplify the invocation of the services. The batch files are installed into the *\JumpStrt\java\bin* directory because this is in the system path. The utilities can be invoked from any command line prompt.

Image Scanning Utilities

These utilities scan the classes in the current CLASSPATH and return a report of all the methods that *implement* the indicated method name or all the methods that *pass* or *return* the indicated class name. Wildcard characters are supported and the parameter names are *not* case sensitive.

Implementers—All the methods that implement the requested method

Sometimes when programming in an object-oriented environment, one knows the method name that one wants to call, but one can't remember which class implements the method. One can find all the classes that implement a certain method name by running this utility.

This utility accepts a method name parameter. The method name is *not* case sensitive and can include the leading or trailing wildcard character "*". The "*" character indicates the return value type. The optional second parameter narrows the search to classes that match a particular class filename mask.

`implementers` *`MethodMask [ClassesToSearchMask]`*

— or —

`java EU implementers` *`MethodMask [ClassesToSearchMask]`*

The name *EU* is the actual name of the class that implements these image scanning utilities. To invoke the class directly, the class name needs to be followed by the requested service and parameters. The first line demonstrates the syntax for using the batch file. Help is available for either syntax by executing the command without parameters.

```
c:\> implementers elements *

      - or -

c:\> java EU implementers elements *


*---------------------------------------------*
      .
      .
      .
*---------------------------------------------*
EUSpider-->EUSpider::elements ()    ^Enumeration
Hashtable-->Hashtable::elements ()    ^Enumeration
Dictionary-->Dictionary::elements ()    ^Enumeration
Vector-->Vector::elements ()    ^Enumeration
Cache-->Cache::elements ()    ^Enumeration
*---------------------------------------------*
```

Passers—All the methods that pass the requested class

As one studies the Java Class Hierarchy, one may come across a class that seems useful but it is hard to figure out how to use it. The *passers* utility scans the class hierarchy and returns each method that passes the class in its parameter list.

The *ClassNameMask* can be a class name, an interface name, or a simple data type name like *int* or *float*. The parameters are not case sensitive, and leading or trailing wildcard characters may be used.

`passers` *`ClassNameMask [ClassesToSearchMask]`*

— or —

`java EU passers` *`ClassNameMask [ClassesToSearchMask]`*

```
c:\> passers Vector *

      - or -

c:\> java EU passers Vector *


*----------------------------------------------*
      .
      .
      .
*----------------------------------------------*
EUClass--->EUClass::references (Vector)   ^void
EUVector--->EUVector::addVector (Vector)   ^void
VectorEnumerator-->VectorEnumerator::<init> (Vector)   ^void
DocumentationGenerator--->DocumentationGenerator::getComment (Vector)   ^String
DocumentationGenerator--->DocumentationGenerator::getReturn (Vector)   ^String
DocumentationGenerator--->DocumentationGenerator::getVersion (Vector)   ^String
DocumentationGenerator--->DocumentationGenerator::getSees (Vector,
ClassDeclaration)   ^Vector
DocumentationGenerator--->DocumentationGenerator::getAuthors (Vector)   ^String
DocumentationGenerator--->DocumentationGenerator::getParameters (Vector)
^Vector
DocumentationGenerator--->DocumentationGenerator::getThrows (Vector,
FieldDefinition)   ^Vector
DocumentationGenerator--->DocumentationGenerator::genPackagesDocumentation
(Vector)   ^void
AppletSecurity--->AppletSecurity::parseACL (Vector, String, String)   ^void
*----------------------------------------------*
```

Returners—All the methods that return the requested class

If one is new to a class like the Enumeration class, it would be nice to know which methods return objects of this class. The *returners* utility searches the Java class library and finds each method that returns a certain class name.

The *ClassNameMask* can be a class name, an interface name, or a simple data type name like *int* or *float*. The parameters are not case sensitive, and leading or trailing wildcard characters may be used.

`returners` *`ClassNameMask [ClassesToSearchMask]`*

— or —

`java EU returners` *`ClassNameMask [ClassesToSearchMask]`*

```
c:\> returners Enumeration *

       - or -

c:\> java EU returners Enumeration *


*---------------------------------------------*
      .
      .
      .
*---------------------------------------------*
EUSpider--->EUSpider::elements ()   ^Enumeration
Hashtable--->Hashtable::keys ()   ^Enumeration
Hashtable--->Hashtable::elements ()   ^Enumeration
Properties--->Properties::propertyNames ()   ^Enumeration
Dictionary--->Dictionary::keys ()   ^Enumeration
Dictionary--->Dictionary::elements ()   ^Enumeration
Vector--->Vector::elements ()   ^Enumeration
AppletContext--->AppletContext::getApplets ()   ^Enumeration
ClassPath--->ClassPath::getFiles (String, String)   ^Enumeration
ClassDefinition--->ClassDefinition::getAbstractFields (Environment)
^Enumeration
Package--->Package::getSourceFiles ()   ^Enumeration
Package--->Package::getBinaryFiles ()   ^Enumeration
BinaryClass-->BinaryClass::getDependencies ()   ^Enumeration
BatchEnvironment--->BatchEnvironment::getClasses ()   ^Enumeration
ZipFile--->ZipFile::entries ()   ^Enumeration
SwitchData--->SwitchData::sortedKeys ()   ^Enumeration
Cache--->Cache::keys ()   ^Enumeration
Cache--->Cache::elements ()   ^Enumeration
AppletViewer--->AppletViewer::getApplets ()   ^Enumeration
*---------------------------------------------*
```

General Utilities

GenApplet—Generate a skeleton Java applet

This utility creates a skeleton applet. It uses the *AppletClassName* to create a subdirectory, an .html file, and a .java source file. The source is a simple "Hello World" skeleton that compiles and runs. The utility also creates several batch files for common operations like compiling *(c.bat)*, editing *(x.bat)*, and running *(r.bat)* the applet.

`applet` *`AppletClassName`*

— *or* —

`java GenApplet` *`AppletClassName`*

```
c:\JumpStrt\exercises>applet MyApplet

      - or -

c:\JumpStrt\exercises>java GenApplet MyApplet

c:\JumpStrt\exercises\MyApplet>dir

X        BAT            40  10-06-96  1:49p x.bat
C        BAT            65  10-06-96  1:49p c.bat
R        BAT            41  10-06-96  1:49p r.bat
D        BAT            68  10-06-96  1:49p d.bat
P        BAT           317  10-06-96  1:49p p.bat
CDEBUG   BAT            87  10-06-96  1:49p cdebug.bat
MYAPPL~1 HTM           164  10-06-96  1:49p MyApplet.html
MYAPPL~1 JAV           213  10-06-96  1:49p MyApplet.java
```

GenApplication—Generate a skeleton Java application

This utility creates a skeleton Java application. It uses the *ApplicationClassName* to create a subdirectory and a .java source file. The source is a simple "Hello World" skeleton that compiles and runs. The utility also creates several batch files for common operations like compiling *(c.bat)*, editing *(x.bat)*, and running *(r.bat)* the application.

`application` *`ApplicationClassName`*

— *or* —

`java GenApplication` *`ApplicationClassName`*

```
c:\JumpStrt\exercises>application MyApplication

      - or -

c:\JumpStrt\exercises>java GenApplication MyApplication

c:\JumpStrt\exercises\MyApplication>dir

X         BAT          45  10-06-96  1:58p x.bat
C         BAT          75  10-06-96  1:58p c.bat
R         BAT          33  10-06-96  1:58p r.bat
D         BAT          78  10-06-96  1:58p d.bat
P         BAT         221  10-06-96  1:58p p.bat
CDEBUG    BAT          97  10-06-96  1:58p cdebug.bat
MYAPPL~1 JAV          158  10-06-96  1:58p MyApplication.java
```

MakeNugget—Create a self-extracting archive of files

This class will collect all the files in the current directory and in subdirectories and create a Java class from them. When the Java class is executed, the files and subdirectory structure is recreated.

This utility will faithfully recreate the subdirectory structure that it archives. Empty subdirectories are carried in the archive and recreated when expanded. It also detects text files and will supply the proper line delimiting character(s) for the platform at runtime. If the self-extracting class file becomes larger than 1.44 MB, additional class files are created. The first filename ends with a "1" *(Nugget1.class)*, the second filename ends with a "2" *(Nugget2.class)*, etc.

Command line options allow the users to specify the base name of the class. The "-s" (small) option was used to create smaller class files to facilitate moving archive files to a Macintosh. The *BeginPath* option specifies a different base directory (relative or absolute) from which to gather the files.

To extract the files, place all the self-extracting class files (nuggets) into the target directory and execute the first Java class. It will extract the files that it contains, then invoke the next class file. Each class file extracts itself until all of the files and subdirectories are recreated.

The purchase of this book entitles the reader to a shareware license of this utility.

```
java MakeNugget        (to create the archive)
java Nugget1           (to restore the archive)
```

```
c:\JumpStrt\exercises\MyApplication>java MakeNugget

MakeNugget v1.0.1 by Noel Enete (options: 'java MakeNugget -?')  Shareware
  $15

Building Nugget1 from '.' ...
appending ./* 0 binary...
appending ./x.bat 45 ascii...
appending ./c.bat 75 ascii...
appending ./r.bat 33 ascii...
appending ./d.bat 78 ascii...
appending ./p.bat 221 ascii...
appending ./cdebug.bat 97 ascii...
appending ./MyApplication.java 158 ascii...


c:\JumpStrt\exercises\MyApplication>dir

X        BAT              45  10-06-96  1:58p x.bat
C        BAT              75  10-06-96  1:58p c.bat
R        BAT              33  10-06-96  1:58p r.bat
D        BAT              78  10-06-96  1:58p d.bat
P        BAT             221  10-06-96  1:58p p.bat
CDEBUG   BAT              97  10-06-96  1:58p cdebug.bat
MYAPPL~1 JAV             158  10-06-96  1:58p MyApplication.java
NUGGET~1 CLA           7,520  10-06-96  2:11p Nugget1.class


c:\JumpStrt\exercises\NewDirectory>java Nugget1

Nugget v1.0.1 by Noel Enete (options: 'java Nugget1 -?')

Extracting Nugget1 class...
expanding ./* 0 binary...
expanding ./x.bat 43 ascii...
expanding ./c.bat 72 ascii...
expanding ./r.bat 33 ascii...
expanding ./d.bat 75 ascii...
expanding ./p.bat 214 ascii...
expanding ./cdebug.bat 94 ascii...
expanding ./MyApplication.java 151 ascii...


c:\JumpStrt\exercises\MyApplication>java MakeNugget -?

  Format: java MakeNugget [BeginPath] [-n NuggetName] [-x] [-b] [-s]
```

```
    BeginPath      base path from which to pull files
    -n NuggetName  base name of the nugget classes, default = Nugget
    -x             skip OS specific (batch) files
    -b             treat all files as binary files
    -s             make small nuggets for marginal java systems

  Shareware $15

    noel@enete.com
    http://www.enete.com

  (c) Noel Enete, 1997
```

Dumpclass—A display of the constant pool

The quickest way to get a look at the inside of a class file is to run this utility. The utility accepts the name of the Java class file (with the .class extension) and dumps the contents of the Constant Pool to the standard output device. File offsets are included so each field can be identified in a raw dump of the class file.

`dumpclass` *`ClassFileNameWithDotClass`*

— or —

`java dumpclass` *`ClassFileNameWithDotClass`*

```
c:\JumpStrt\examples\Hello>dumpclass Hello.class

      - or -

c:\JumpStrt\examples\Hello>java dumpclass Hello.class

Java Class File================================
0x0001 Magic Number Record
          Java Magic Number
             0000:  0xCAFEBABE


0x0002 Java Class Version Record
          Java Class Version Number
             0004:  0x0003002D


0x0003 Constant Pool
          Const Pool Array Size (items go in [1] thru [Size-1], num = Size-1)
             0008:  0x0020
```

```
0x0001 String Item
          Item Tag
            000A:  0x08

          String Index
            000B:  0x001A

0x0002 Class Item
          Item Tag
            000D:  0x07

          Name Index
            000E:  0x001D

0x0003 Class Item
          Item Tag
            0010:  0x07

          Name Index
            0011:  0x001C

               .
               .
               .
```

APPENDIX F

Java Resources

Primary

Gamelan <http://www.gamelan.com/>

Gamelan (pronounced **Gah'** meh lonn) is the central repository for Java resources. This Web site contains thousands of links to Java programs that are arranged by categories. Some of the categories include *Arts and Entertainment, Business and Finance, JavaScript, Network and Communications, Programming in Java, Multimedia, Special Effects,* and *Web Sites.*

Roughly half of the Java programs include source code.

One reason the site is so helpful is that links to new Java resources are so easy to add. The site provides an HTML form for adding the links. Anyone can fill out the form and have their new Java program or Web site referenced in the repository. The new additions are appended to their category area after they have been hand-edited.

This is the Java resource to know the best.

Java World <http://www.javaworld.com>

This is a Web magazine published by IDG. It is free. There is no sign up or subscription required to read the articles. The articles are short with lots of examples. The articles are of interest to the Java programmer. It has the flavor of a popular systems journal for Java. It seems to have captured the pulse of the Java programming community. The applet reviews alone are worth the time reading the magazine.

JARS <http://www.jars.com>

This is an applet rating service. It examines Java applets and assigns them a rating. Then it displays a page of the top 1% of all applets, a page for the top 5% of all applets, etc. Since applets are becoming available from so many different locations on the Web, it is nice for Webmasters to have a place where they can shop for the most interesting behavior to add to their pages. It appears that source code is available on about one-third of the listed programs.

Cafe Au Lait <http://sunsite.unc.edu/javafaq/>

This is one person's digest of current events in the Java community. This is *not* an automated listing of somebody's product announcements. This is more of a knowledgable commentary on current Java events. The author of this site, Elliotte Harold, has also written a book on Java and lends a fresh style to his evaluations. He writes a short paragraph about each item and there are about three to five new items entered each week. The items are drawn from a wide variety of sources.

Elliotte also includes a *Resources* section in which he reviews the current Java books and categorizes them into books that should be *Bought*, *Browsed*, or *Recycled*.

The Java Developer <http://www.digitalfocus.com/faq>

The Java Developer site (*http://www.digitalfocus.com/faq*) is dedicated to the needs of the Java programmer. It includes a forum for matching Java employers with Java programmers.

It also includes an excellent resources section *<http://www.digitalfocus.com/faq/resources.html>*. What makes this section so good is the breadth of resources that are included. It identifies new Web sites, new FAQ's, new News Groups, new books, new software products, new courses, new periodicals, and new clubs.

Their most useful service is their "How Do I . . ." section *<http://www.digital focus.com/faq/howdoi.html>*. Answers to Java questions are organized in over twenty categories. Each of the questions begin with the phrase "How do I . . .". A wide range of questions are addressed in this section. The forum is dynamic and anyone from the Internet can post answers to problems they have encountered and solved. The open forum tends to slant the questions to a "tricks of the trade" focus. If one has a marginal issue that one can't figure out how to do in Java, this is a good place to look for a solution.

Secondary

Rapid Systems Solutions' Java Resource List <http://www.rssi.com/info/java-info.html>

This is a simple list of Web resources on Java. The layout of the links is very simple. But the breadth of links is what makes this so interesting. There are 15–20 links under each subject heading. The subject headings are as follows: *Sites of in-*

terest from Sun, Applet Collections / Indices, News / Message Exchange (news groups and lists), *Information Sources / Documentation* (bibliographies, FAQs, and tutorials), *Java Licensees / Wares* (the Java implementing vendors), *Java / CORBA / Persistence, Java Performance,* and *JavaScript.*

Performance Java <http://www.preemptive.com/lectures/Optimization.html>

This lecture from preEmptive Solutions is a knowledgeable discussion of the technical performance issues in Java. It is one of the few discussions that goes beyond the basic issues of native code and byte codes and provides a good conceptual view of the issues surrounding Java performance. It includes a discussion on Virtual Machines that perform "Just In Time" compilation. The format of the discussion is not heavy prose. It appears to be the visuals to the lecture.

Java Optimization <http://www.cs.cmu.edu/~jch/java/optimization.html>

Jonathan Hardwick has applied the general rules for program optimization systematically to the Java environment in this page. He discusses general rules for optimization and describes how to use the available Java tools, including the compiler for optimizing code. There is a section dedicated to optimizing for speed and one for optimizing for size. A table of the cost for common operations is also included.

Kaffe <http://web.soi.city.ac.uk/homes/tim/kaffe/kaffe.html>

This is a free "Just In Time" Virtual Machine for versions of Java that run on Intel Unix platforms like FreeBSD or Linux. If anyone has these systems, this could give them a significant performance boost.

Usenet <news:comp.lang.java>

The messages that go to the Java-interest mail list are placed onto this list. This is the intended forum for asking questions and getting help from other Java developers.

Borland's Internet Tools <http://www.borland.com>

This describes the Java tools that Borland is putting together. Borland seems to be taking an aggressive approach to supporting Java. With the low-level optimization approach that Borland gives most of its language products, programmers can expect some Java optimizations to come out of this work.

Symantec Cafe <http://cafe.symantec.com>

This site presents the current Java products and development environment for Symantec's Cafe. It is important to be aware of their "Just In Time" compiler for Windows 95NT.

Index

A

accept() method, 211, 215, 250
action() method, 108
ACTION_EVENT, 205
add() method, 131, 133, 138, 204
addItem() method, 145
alias, 320, 369
AliasMaint class, 320
animation, 89–103
append() method, 30
appendText() method, 142
applet, 5, 10–11, 13, 15, 79, 118, 308
  active, 98
  and Checkbox, 134
  and CheckboxGroup, 136
  client construction, 304
  compared with application, 10–12
  compared with browser, 329
  compared with independent window, 187
  as component, 194
  and controls, 131
  controls
    position, 152
    size, 152
  creation, 197
  and default Layout Manager, 152
  directory, 12
  and dripper pair, 329, 340
  and event, 132
  generation, 474
  inheritance, 18
  launching, 30
  links, 121
  and menu, 210
  methods, 18–23
  and mouse method, 71
  parameter, 31
  parameters, 420
  rating service, 481
  region, 12
  reloading, 434
  and Runnable object, 121
  security, 280
  and sound, 217–20
  standalone technique, 194–98
  testing, 12
  and text, 138, 142, 145, 147, 149–50
  and window, 195
  window surface, 36
  and World Wide Web, 280
  writing text, 422
Applet class, 23
APPLET tag, 453
appletviewer, 12, 19, 98, 280
application, 13, 15
  generation, 475
  initiation, 195
arg field, 140, 143, 145, 147, 150
arg variable, 111
args array, 336
argument vector array, 27
argv array, 27, 29
arithmetic coding, 404
array, 39, 44, 55, 232, 236, 254, 383–84
  applet, 48
  application, 44
  byte, 237–38
  compared with enumeration, 43–44
  compared with vector, 57–58
  conversion to string, 399
  dimension, 39–41
  index, 39
  length, 39
Array class, 40
AU format, 219
AudioClip interface, 219

B

BASIC, 1
bFlicker variable, 80, 87
BitSet object, 441
bitwise operator, 396
BorderLayout, 161, 167–70, 187
Borland, 483
Borland's Internet Tools, 483
bounds() rectangle, 136
bracket, square, 40
buffer, memory, 231, 233, 242
BufferedInputStream, 241
BufferedOutputStream, 241
button, 131, 308, 425
  creation, 131, 140
  radial, 136
Button class, 131
Button() constructor, 131
button control
  processing clicks, 133–135
  size, 162, 168
byte type, 54
ByteArrayInputStream, 237
ByteArrayInputStream class, 231
ByteArrayOutputStream, 384
ByteArrayOutputStream class, 231–32

C

C, 1, 6, 286
C++, 2, 6, 35
  pointers, 2

CAD tool, 98
Cafe Au Lait, 482
CaffeineCafe, 315, 317, 319, 322, 325
  documentation, 317, 344
  operation, 318, 349–50
  stopping, 319
CaffeineCafe class, 349, 373
CaffeineCafeDefaults, 373
CaffeineCafeDefaults object, 365, 369
CallMethod class, 414
capitalization, 25
CardLayout, 173
cascade, 30
cascading method send, 30
case logic, 394
catch block, 415
catch() method, 35
catch() section, 35
ceil() method, 405
CGI. *See* Common Gateway Interface.
character type, 54
Checkbox, 133
  and applet, 134
  creation, 133
Checkbox class, 131
Checkbox() constructor, 133
CheckboxGroup, 135
  appearance, 135
  and applet, 136
  creation, 135
CheckboxMenuItem class, 209
chip, computer, 3
Choice class, 147
class, 9–10, 16, 18, 53–54
  coding, 15
  as composite type, 54
  definition, 2
  extension, 24
  external, 11
  loading, automatic, 439
  name, 344, 364
  naming convention, 25
  storage, 11
class file, 478
  and error location, 469
  nugget, 476
  parsing, 463–69
class hierarchy, 443
class loading, 298–99
Class.forName() method, 299
CLASSPATH, 341–43
clear() method, 441
click and drag, 75
clickCount variable, 110
client, 308
client program, 249
Client/Server application, 247, 277, 286, 308, 340, 434
  coding, 329
  implementation, 304
COBOL, 1
code, 16
color, 31, 34–35
Color object, 34
color string, 34–35
command line, 27, 105, 419
Common Gateway Interface, 258, 275, 285–86, 300, 318
Component class, 23
  extensions, 131
composite type, 54, 400
connect() method, 242
constant, 52
Constant Pool, 52, 229, 463–65, 478
constructor, 18, 25
  naming, 18
  and return type, 18
Container class, 23
control
  visibility, 173
controls, 131
conversation, 248–49, 253, 275, 277, 353
  initiation, 249
Cool shareware, 219
copy, 419
copyArea() method, 427
cos function, 410
cursor
  type, 191
cut, 419

D

data
  access, 225, 229
    sequential, 231
  block movement, 241
  conversions, 397–402
  reading, 242, 255
  writing, 242, 255
data type
  read and write methods, 229
data variable, 237
database, 305
datagram, 447
DataInputStream, 106, 237–38
DataInputStream object, 241
DataOutputStream, 237
DataStream, 237
DebugLog class, 215
default document directory, 370
DefaultProperties file, 64
delete() method, 228
delItem() method, 145
destroy() method, 22
Dialog class, 199
dialog window, 198
directory tree, 226
displayQuietly() method, 22
documentation, 344
  generation, 443
domain name, 271
Doppelt, Adam, 150
double type, 54
do/while() loop, 387
drawImage() method, 87
drawing, 426, 429
drawSparkler() method, 75
drawString() function, 11, 36
drawString() method, 53, 422
dripper, 317–18
  as application, 322
  coding, 321–22
  creating application, 325, 329
  generation, 323
  and HTML form, 322
  purpose, 322
Dripper class. *See also* ServerExtension class.
  purpose, 364
Dripper object, 349, 354
Dripper program, 320
dumpclass, 478
Dynamic Link Library, 305

E

EchoDripper, 369
EchoDripper class, 319
elements() method, 44, 58, 61, 235
Enumeration, 41–42
  creation, 392
enumeration, 44, 55, 61, 235–36, 391
  compared with array, 43–44
  creation, 44
err, 105
Ethernet, 445
event, 105
  interception, 189
  passing, 119
  sent to applet, 132
  user-defined, 119
Event() constructor, 119
event id, 108, 140
Event object, 75, 105
  creation, 118

event triggering, 118–29
Event.ACTION_EVENT, 147
exception, 415
Exception class, 415
Exception object, 35
exit() method, 395
extend, 11
ExtendableWebServer, 286–87, 300, 312
  compared with SimpleWebServer, 297
extends clause, 24

F

Fielding, Roy, 354
file
  access, 231, 234
  coding file I/O, 402
  erase, 228
  maintenance, 330
File class, 225–26
file I/O, 225–45
File menu, 209
File object, 234
  instantiation, 225, 228
file request, 370
file stream, 105
File Transfer Protocol. *see* ftp.
FileDialog, 210
  displayed files, 211
FileDripper, 370
FileDripper object, 365
FileInputStream, 64–65, 236, 238, 402
FileInputStream class, 233–34
FileMaint application, 320
FilenameFilter interface, 211, 215
FileOutputStream, 64, 237, 274
FileOutputStream class, 233–34
FileServerExtension, 286
FileStream, 241
  instantiation, 234
fill variable, 179
FilterStream, 237
final keyword, 52
first() method, 173
flicker, 79–80, 87
float type, 54
floor() method, 405
FlowLayout class, 161–64
flush() method, 233–34, 242
font, 31, 35–36, 44, 47, 423
  default, 36, 53
  dimension, 36
  face name, 35–36, 48, 436
  name, 52
  selection, 52–53
  style, 35–36, 48, 52
Font class, 35
Font() constructor, 36
FontMetrics, 423
FontMetrics object, 36, 53
for() loop, 385
FormDripper class, 320
FormServerExtension, 300, 302
forName() method, 298, 439
frame, 187, 446
  window, 215
    as parent, 198
Frame class, 189
  extended, 189–91
Frame object
  compared with Applet object, 194
FreeBSD, 483
Friendly, Lisa, 344
fromConnection() method, 354, 364
ftp, 250, 450

G

Gamelan, 481
gateway, 447–48
GenApplet, 474
GenApplication, 475
GET, 267, 271, 275, 285, 300, 318, 324, 340, 353
get() method, 59, 61, 298–300, 302, 315, 324, 336–37, 354, 364
Get request, 331, 336–37, 340
getAddress() method, 435
getAliases(), 373
getAlias(String), 373
getAudioClip() method, 219
getBaseDocDir(), 373
getClassInstance() method, 298
getCursorType() method, 191
getDefaults(), 373
getDirectory() method, 211
getFile() method, 211
getFontMetrics() method, 423
getHeight() function, 36
getHeight() method, 53
getImage() method, 97
getInputStream() method, 254
getLength() method, 29
getLineNumber() method, 241
getMode() method, 211
getOutputStream() method, 254
getPackagePath(), 373
getParameter() method, 31, 420
getParent() method, 228
getPreloadClasses(), 373
getProperties() method, 42
getRequest() method, 266, 297
getSelectedText() method, 140
getState() method, 209
getText() method, 140
GoGetUrl class, 272
Gopher, 450
Gosling, James, 1
graphical environment, 131
Graphics class, 118
Graphics object, 36, 53, 93
grid cell, 180
GridBagConstraints class, 179
GridBagLayout, 175–81
  constraints, 179
gridheight, 179
GridLayout, 165
GridLayout class, 161
gridwidth, 179
group ID, 98
GUI event, 111

H

handleEvent() method, 107–8, 119–21, 132, 134, 136, 140, 145, 187, 189, 205, 209, 433
Hardwick, Jonathan, 483
Harold, Elliotte, 482
hash code, 61
Hashtable, 59, 61, 66, 108, 324, 336, 354
  addition of elements, 59
  data search, 61–62
  limitation, 62
  object use, 62
  removal of elements, 59
  retrieval of values, 59
header, 446–47
header field, 267, 354
header information, 370
Hello Application, 9
hexadecimal string, 34
hierarchy, class, 443
host, 446
host number, 446
HotJava, 1, 4–6, 452–53
  Internet address, 6
HTML, 286, 452
  form, 286, 300, 320
  link, 443
HTTP, 261, 297
  version, 353
HTTP communication, 353
HTTP rules, 354

Hyper Text Markup Language. *See* HTML.
Hyper Text Transfer Protocol. *See* HTTP.

I

IBM compatible PC, 4
IBM PC, 445
id field, 109
If/Then/Else logic, 393
image, 279, 439
  background drawing, 92, 96
  and loading, 97
  and memory, 96
  movement, 82–87
implementer, 471
import statement, 11
in, 105
index.html, 317
InetAddress object, 435
inheritance, 18
  functionality, 18, 24
init() method, 22, 25, 53, 80, 96, 108, 110, 198
input device, 75
input stream
  concatenation, 235
InputStream, 274
InputStream object, 106
insertText() method, 142
instance, 418
instance variable, 105
instanceof operator, 43, 418
int type, 54
integer
  and scrollbar, 149
Interface, 417
interface, 90
Internet, 1, 6, 9, 274, 445–53
  address, 4, 446–48
  history, 445–46
  Internet Engineering Task Force Draft, 354
  operation, 446–48
  program use of, 450
  software structure, 449
Internet application, 250
intValue() method, 397
I/O, 64
IP number, 435
isDirectory() method, 226

J

JARS, 481
Java, 1
  advantage, 278
  advantages, 259
  applet, 47
  application, 9–13, 44
    launching, 30
    running, 187
  array, 39
  case sensitive, 344
  choice class, 147
  class, 10–11, 15, 18
    specialization, 24
  class file, 12
  class hierarchy, 194
  classes, 57
  code, 16
  communication with computer chip, 3–4
  compared with C++, 2
  compiling, 10
  constructor, 40
  controls, 131, 140
  cursor control, 191
  database access, 305
  Enumeration, 41
  file, 225
  file access, 225–45
  file selection, 210
  functionality added, 279
  funding, 5
  GUI, 108
  helper functions, 108
  independent windows, 187
  I/O streams, 403
  methods, 54
  naming scheme, 344
  object-oriented, 13, 15
  origin, 1
  platform support, 75
  property, 41
  resources, 481–83
  socket, 253–54
    bug, 258, 266, 270
  source code, 25
  standalone programs, 215
  stream
    advantages, 241, 245
  Stream class, 229
  syntax, 6, 30
  types, 54–55
  and user input, 105, 118
  user interface, 170
Java component, 131
Java Developer, 482
Java Development Kit, 6
Java Interpreter, 3
Java Optimization, 483
Java World, 481
javadoc, 344–45
Java's DataBase Connectivity, 305
JDBC. *See* Java's DataBase Connectivity.
join() method, 438
JumpStrt directory, 318
Just In Time, 483
  compiler, 457

K

Kaffe, 483
key, 41, 59, 331
key field, 109
KEY_ACTION, 109
keyboard input, 419
keyDown(), 108
keyDown() method, 108
KEY_PRESS, 108–9
KEY_PRESS event, 140, 142, 145, 147
KEY_RELEASE event, 140, 142, 145, 147
keys() method, 61
key/value pair, 59, 331, 336, 354
Knuth, Donald, 344

L

Label, 150
  creation, 138
Label() constructor, 138
Label control, 199, 308
Label object, 138
language, script, 1
last() method, 173
lastModified() method, 228
Layout Manager
  BorderLayout Manager, 167–170
  CardLayout Manager, 173–175
  default, 161
  FlowLayout Manager, 161–165
  GridBagLayout Manager, 175–179
  GridLayout Manager, 165–167
Letters menu, 209
line
  count, 241
LineNumberInputStream, 241
LineNumberInputStream object, 241
link, 120
Linux, 483
List, 145
list
  creation, 145
  drop down control, 147
list, linked, 42
List class, 131
List control, 215
list() method, 64, 226

List request, 331, 336
listbox, 131
LIST_SELECT, 111
LIST_SELECT event, 145
literal pool, 52
literals, 411
load() method, 65
LoanApplet, 152
Local Area Network, 445–46
localhost, 268, 270
logic
  AND/OR, 396
  case, 394
  If/Then/Else, 393
long type, 54
loop, 231–32, 350, 385–88
  break, 388
  continue, 390
  exiting, 388
loop() method, 220

M

Macintosh, 6, 445
  PowerPC, 4
Magic Number, 463
mail, 250
mail, electronic, 451
main() function, 2, 10–11
main() method, 27, 194–95, 197, 349
maintenance class, 320
MakeNugget, 476
makeVisible() method, 145
math functions, 404–410
MediaTracker, 98
MediaTracker class, 97
memory, 279
  availability, 437
  buffer, 231
  current free, 44
  current total, 44
  dynamic, 6
menu, 204–5, 210
  item, 209
Menu class, 204
MenuBar class, 204
MenuItem
  selection, 205
MenuItem class, 204
META_MASK, 111
method, 16
  calling, 414–16
  constructor, 18
  definition, 53
  instance, 53
  naming convention, 25
  overriding, 18–19, 22–23
  sending, 53–54
  service, 22
  static, 53–54
method field, 353
Microsoft, 5–6, 305
  Internet Explorer, 6
MIME, 318, 370
minimumSize() method, 176, 178, 180
mkDir() method, 228
modal option, 198
modifier variable, 110
motion, effect of, 93
mouse, 23, 71
  button, 75, 142
  click and drag, 75–80
  double click, 110
  and list, 147
  picture, dragging, 82
  right button, 111
  and scrollbar, 150
mouse message, 71
mouse method, 23, 71, 75
mouseDown(), 108
MOUSE_DOWN, 108–10
mouseDown() method, 75, 82, 87, 98, 108
mouseDrag(), 108
mouseDrag() method, 75, 79, 82, 87
mouseEnter(), 108
mouseExit(), 108
mouseMove(), 108
MOUSE_MOVE, 108
mouseMove() method, 108
mouseUp(), 108
mouseUp() method, 75, 82, 87

N

naming, 9, 11
  convention, 25, 37
Netscape, 5, 98, 434
  Navigator, 5, 266
network number, 446
new operator, 2
newDripper() method, 365
newInstance() method, 439
next() method, 173
nextToken() method, 67, 69
null keyword, 31
number
  ceiling, 405
  constant e, 409
  division remainder, 407
  floor, 405
  Pi, 409
  power, 408
  rounding, 405
  trigonometry function, 410
  truncating, 406

O

Oak, 1
object, 15
  in array, 39
  chain, 42
  code association, 16
  creation, 15, 44
  data association, 16, 18
  definition, 37
  Enumeration, 41–42
  event sending, 121
  Graphics, 22
  interactions, 119
  naming convention, 25
  type, 43
  wiring, 119–20
object, Graphics, 11
Object class, 23
object maker, 15
object-oriented paradigm, 25
object-oriented programming, 6
  communication, 118
  and variable, 37
out, 105
OutputStream, 64

P

package, 11, 318, 341–44
  and directory, 341–42
  name, 341, 343–44
  package path, 365
  and .ZIP file, 341–42
PackageMaint class, 320, 365
paint() function, 11
paint() method, 18, 22, 52–53, 79–80, 93, 96, 187, 191, 422, 429
Panel class, 23
Panel object, 170–71
parameter data
  decoding, 337
passing to applet, 30–31
passer, 472
paste, 419
pattern
  repeating, 89
PCM. *See* Pulse Code Modulated technique.
performance
  and socket, 258–59

Performance Java, 483
PipedInputStream, 242
PipedOutputStream, 242
pixel, 11
  copying, 427
platform, computer, 2
play() method, 219–20
point, 136
point size, 35–36
port, 349
port number, 250
POST, 275, 285, 318, 324, 353–54
post() method, 324, 354, 364
pow() method, 408
preferredSize() method, 162, 176
PreloadMaint class, 320
previous() method, 173
print() method, 240, 255–56
printAString() method, 439
println() function, 10
println() method, 106, 215, 240, 269
PrintStream, 240
PrintStream class, 24
PrintStream object, 64, 254–55, 269
private attribute, 29
processFirstLine() method, 353
processing, distributed, 5
processNextLine() method, 354
processNode() method, 226
program
  exit, 395
program, remote
  communication with, 247–48
programming language, 1, 4, 6, 9
prop object, 64–65
properties, system, 42
Properties class, 41, 62, 64–66
  compared with Hashtable, 62
Properties file, 336
propertyNames() method, 42
protocol version, 353
public attribute, 22, 29
Pulse Code Modulated technique, 217–18
PushbackInputStream, 242
put() method, 59
Put request, 331, 336

R

RandomAccessFile class, 228
Rapid Systems Solutions' Java Resource List, 482–83
read() method, 229, 232, 235, 237, 254–56, 269–70, 274
readBoolean() method, 229, 237
readByte() method, 229, 237
readChar() method, 229, 237
readDouble() method, 229, 237
readFloat() method, 229, 237
readInt() method, 229, 237
readLine() method, 106, 229, 237–38, 241
receivePostParms() method, 354
receiveRequest() method, 354
registerEvent() method, 120
remove() method, 59
Remove request, 331, 337
repaint() method, 79
replaceText() method, 142
reply() method, 354
request line, 267, 364
reshape() method, 203, 432
resource field, 353
returner, 473
round() method, 405
router, 447
run() method, 90, 92, 253, 266, 354, 438
Runnable interface, 90, 92
Runnable object, 121
Runtime, 437

S

sArg variable, 300, 302
save() method, 64
saveDefaults() method, 373
SConnection, 353–54, 364
SConnection object, 300, 349–50
screen
  image, 82–87
  repainting, 89, 92–93
Scrollbar, 149–50
scrollbar, 131
  and events, 149
  orientation, 149
  page size, 149
  value, 149
Scrollbar() constructor, 149
Scrollbar event, 150
SCROLL_LINE_DOWN event, 150
security, 280, 369–70
seek() method, 229
select() method, 145
selectAll() method, 140
select(beginningOffset, endingOffset), 140
sendReply() method, 266
sendRepyly() method, 300
SequenceInputStream, 235–36
Server Connection object, 297
server extension, 258
server extension program, 249
server program, 249
ServerExtension, 308
  instantiated, 298
  server construction, 304
ServerExtension class, 286–87, 297, 299, 312. *See also* Java's Data-Base Connectivity.
ServerExtension object, 252–53
ServerSocket, 349–50
  instantiation, 253
ServerSocket class, 249
ServerSocket object, 250
set() method, 441
setConstraints() method, 179
setCursor() method, 191
setEchoCharacter() method, 140
setFont() method, 36
setLayout() method, 152
setMenuBar() method, 205
setState() method, 209
shift state, 110
short type, 54
show() method, 173
signature code, 466
simple type, 54, 400
  limitations, 55
SimpleDripper class, 320
sin function, 410
skipBytes() method, 229
Slider class, 150
Smalltalk, 6, 16, 25, 259
socket, 247–56, 353, 449
  bug, 258, 266, 270
  compared with URL class, 285
  creation, 253–254
  described, 247–48
  description, 253
  instantiation, 269
  read, 254
  write, 254
Socket class, 249, 280
Socket() method, 271
socketRequest() method, 280
Solaris, 6
sound, 217–22
  codes, 218
  file format, 219
  sample, 217–18
source file, 11
squaring a number, 408
SQL request, 305
SqlQuery, 305
sResource variable, 297
stack, 242
standard input devices, 105

standard output device, 105
start() method, 22–23, 92, 198, 253, 438
state change
  publishing of, 119
static attribute, 35, 106
stderr, 403
stdin, 403
stdout, 403
stop() method, 22, 220
stream, 231–25
Stream class, 231
string
  concatenation, 381
  conversion, 397–99
  expanding. *See* StringBuffer.
  parsing, 382
String object
  concatenation, 24, 30
StringBuffer, 30
StringBufferInputStream, 399
StringBufferInputStream class, 231–32
stringToColor() method, 34–35, 37
StringTokenizer, 66–69
  instantiation, 67
StringTokenizer class, 382
subdirectory
  creation, 228
Sun Computers, 6, 305
Sun workstation, 4
super class, 58, 79, 416
super object, 25
surfboard design, 98
SurfSpeak, 320
switch() method, 394
Symantec Cafe, 483
system
  default information, 62
  default property, 44
  information, 44
system information, 62
System.exit() method, 37
System.out object, 24, 240

T

tag, 4–5, 12, 285, 344–45, 451
tan function, 410
TCP/IP, 247–48, 445–46, 448
TCP/IP socket, 231
TCP/IP stack, 449
telnet, 250
terminal, 446
text, 138
  edit control, 140, 142
  formatting, 240
  justification, 138
  list, 145
  processing, 254
  selection, 140
  and user, 138, 140
  writing, 240
Text control, 138
TextArea, 142, 285, 419
  compared with TextField, 142
  initiate processing in, 143
TextField, 140, 419
  compared with TextArea, 142
thread, 92, 250
  creation, 92
  launching, 438
thread, execution
  sleep, 89–90
thread, independent, 90
Thread class, 90
time, 308
toByteArray() method, 232, 384
token, 67–69
token parsing. *See* StringTokenizer.
Token Ring, 445
Toolkit, 53, 436
toString() method, 435
triggerEvent() method, 120
try block, 415
try code, 35

U

Unicode String, 465
Uniform Resource Locator. *See* URL.
Unix, 483
unread() method, 242
update
  interval, 93
  time-oriented, 90, 92
update() method, 23, 25, 79–80
URL, 271–74, 354
URL class, 271
  compared with socket, 285
Usenet, 451, 483
user input, 105, 107, 118, 131
  single selection input technique, 135
User Interface, 419–33
utilities, 471–79

V

value, 41, 59, 331
valueOf() method, 53–54, 398
van Hoff, Arthur, 344
variable, 2, 16, 18, 29, 37, 39, 52
  creation, 412–13
  global, 35
  instance variable, 29
  static, 35
variable, bit coded
  creation, 441
variable pool, environmental, 41
vector, 59, 236
  allocation, 58
  compared with array, 57–58
  and diverse objects, 58
  iteration, 58
Vector class, 41, 44, 57
Vector object, 235
Virtual Machine, 3–6, 10, 40, 188, 197, 259, 272, 279, 285, 342, 455–61, 483
  documentation, 466
VM. *See* Virtual Machine.

W

walkTree() method, 226
WAV files. *See* AU format.
Web. *See* World Wide Web.
Web server, 261
weight value, 179
while() loop, 252, 386
window, 257, 318
  closing, 433
  dependent, 198, 204
  independent, 187
  placement, 432
  repainting, 79
Window class, 199
WINDOW_DESTROY event, 189, 203
Windows, 6
Windows95, 258–59, 419
Windows 95NT, 483
WindowsNT, 259
wipeout, 340
wire, 120
Wireable interface, 119
Wirer class, 120
Wirer object, 119
Wirer variable, 121
World Wide Web, 4, 10, 250, 445–53
  browser, 9, 12, 19, 98, 210, 261, 271, 365, 451–52
    compared with applet, 329
    extending, 278–85
    Java enabled, 4–6, 280, 452–53
  client, 261, 268, 279–80
  request, 261–62, 266, 269, 277–78, 280, 299–300, 318–19, 324, 353, 364

response, 261, 269, 277–78, 280
security, 369–70
server, 261–62, 268, 280, 285, 317–18
extending, 285–303
Web page, 4, 10–11, 30, 48, 68, 261–62, 271, 280, 297, 318–20, 322, 349, 452
applet region, 12
directory, 12
wrapper, 400
write() method, 384
writeLine() method, 24

X

x,y position, 11

LICENSE AGREEMENT AND LIMITED WARRANTY

READ THE FOLLOWING TERMS AND CONDITIONS CAREFULLY BEFORE OPENING THIS DISK PACKAGE. THIS LEGAL DOCUMENT IS AN AGREEMENT BETWEEN YOU AND PRENTICE-HALL, INC. (THE "COMPANY"). BY OPENING THIS SEALED DISK PACKAGE, YOU ARE AGREEING TO BE BOUND BY THESE TERMS AND CONDITIONS. IF YOU DO NOT AGREE WITH THESE TERMS AND CONDITIONS, DO NOT OPEN THE DISK PACKAGE. PROMPTLY RETURN THE UNOPENED DISK PACKAGE AND ALL ACCOMPANYING ITEMS TO THE PLACE YOU OBTAINED THEM FOR A FULL REFUND OF ANY SUMS YOU HAVE PAID.

1. **GRANT OF LICENSE:** In consideration of your payment of the license fee, which is part of the price you paid for this product, and your agreement to abide by the terms and conditions of this Agreement, the Company grants to you a nonexclusive right to use and display the copy of the enclosed software program (hereinafter the "SOFTWARE") on a single computer (i.e., with a single CPU) at a single location so long as you comply with the terms of this Agreement. The Company reserves all rights not expressly granted to you under this Agreement.

2. **OWNERSHIP OF SOFTWARE:** You own only the magnetic or physical media (the enclosed disks) on which the SOFTWARE is recorded or fixed, but the Company retains all the rights, title, and ownership to the SOFTWARE recorded on the original disk copy(ies) and all subsequent copies of the SOFTWARE, regardless of the form or media on which the original or other copies may exist. This license is not a sale of the original SOFTWARE or any copy to you.

3. **COPY RESTRICTIONS:** This SOFTWARE and the accompanying printed materials and user manual (the "Documentation") are the subject of copyright. You may not copy the Documentation or the SOFTWARE, except that you may make a single copy of the SOFTWARE for backup or archival purposes only. You may be held legally responsible for any copying or copyright infringement which is caused or encouraged by your failure to abide by the terms of this restriction.

4. **USE RESTRICTIONS:** You may not network the SOFTWARE or otherwise use it on more than one computer or computer terminal at the same time. You may physically transfer the SOFTWARE from one computer to another provided that the SOFTWARE is used on only one computer at a time. You may not distribute copies of the SOFTWARE or Documentation to others. You may not reverse engineer, disassemble, decompile, modify, adapt, translate, or create derivative works based on the SOFTWARE or the Documentation without the prior written consent of the Company.

5. **TRANSFER RESTRICTIONS:** The enclosed SOFTWARE is licensed only to you and may not be transferred to any one else without the prior written consent of the Company. Any unauthorized transfer of the SOFTWARE shall result in the immediate termination of this Agreement.

6. **TERMINATION:** This license is effective until terminated. This license will terminate automatically without notice from the Company and become null and void if you fail to comply with any provisions or limitations of this license. Upon termination, you shall destroy the Documentation and all copies of the SOFTWARE. All provisions of this Agreement as to warranties, limitation of liability, remedies or damages, and our ownership rights shall survive termination.

7. **MISCELLANEOUS:** This Agreement shall be construed in accordance with the laws of the United States of America and the State of New York and shall benefit the Company, its affiliates, and assignees.

8. **LIMITED WARRANTY AND DISCLAIMER OF WARRANTY:** The Company warrants that the SOFTWARE, when properly used in accordance with the Documentation, will operate in substantial conformity with the description of the SOFTWARE set forth in the Documentation. The Company does not warrant that the SOFTWARE will meet your requirements or that the operation of the SOFTWARE will be uninterrupted or error-free. The Company warrants that the media on which the SOFTWARE is

delivered shall be free from defects in materials and workmanship under normal use for a period of thirty (30) days from the date of your purchase. Your only remedy and the Company's only obligation under these limited warranties is, at the Company's option, return of the warranted item for a refund of any amounts paid by you or replacement of the item. Any replacement of SOFTWARE or media under the warranties shall not extend the original warranty period. The limited warranty set forth above shall not apply to any SOFTWARE which the Company determines in good faith has been subject to misuse, neglect, improper installation, repair, alteration, or damage by you. EXCEPT FOR THE EXPRESSED WARRANTIES SET FORTH ABOVE, THE COMPANY DISCLAIMS ALL WARRANTIES, EXPRESS OR IMPLIED, INCLUDING WITHOUT LIMITATION, THE IMPLIED WARRANTIES OF MERCHANTABILITY AND FITNESS FOR A PARTICULAR PURPOSE. EXCEPT FOR THE EXPRESS WARRANTY SET FORTH ABOVE, THE COMPANY DOES NOT WARRANT, GUARANTEE, OR MAKE ANY REPRESENTATION REGARDING THE USE OR THE RESULTS OF THE USE OF THE SOFTWARE IN TERMS OF ITS CORRECTNESS, ACCURACY, RELIABILITY, CURRENTNESS, OR OTHERWISE.

IN NO EVENT, SHALL THE COMPANY OR ITS EMPLOYEES, AGENTS, SUPPLIERS, OR CONTRACTORS BE LIABLE FOR ANY INCIDENTAL, INDIRECT, SPECIAL, OR CONSEQUENTIAL DAMAGES ARISING OUT OF OR IN CONNECTION WITH THE LICENSE GRANTED UNDER THIS AGREEMENT, OR FOR LOSS OF USE, LOSS OF DATA, LOSS OF INCOME OR PROFIT, OR OTHER LOSSES, SUSTAINED AS A RESULT OF INJURY TO ANY PERSON, OR LOSS OF OR DAMAGE TO PROPERTY, OR CLAIMS OF THIRD PARTIES, EVEN IF THE COMPANY OR AN AUTHORIZED REPRESENTATIVE OF THE COMPANY HAS BEEN ADVISED OF THE POSSIBILITY OF SUCH DAMAGES. IN NO EVENT SHALL LIABILITY OF THE COMPANY FOR DAMAGES WITH RESPECT TO THE SOFTWARE EXCEED THE AMOUNTS ACTUALLY PAID BY YOU, IF ANY, FOR THE SOFTWARE.

SOME JURISDICTIONS DO NOT ALLOW THE LIMITATION OF IMPLIED WARRANTIES OR LIABILITY FOR INCIDENTAL, INDIRECT, SPECIAL, OR CONSEQUENTIAL DAMAGES, SO THE ABOVE LIMITATIONS MAY NOT ALWAYS APPLY. THE WARRANTIES IN THIS AGREEMENT GIVE YOU SPECIFIC LEGAL RIGHTS AND YOU MAY ALSO HAVE OTHER RIGHTS WHICH VARY IN ACCORDANCE WITH LOCAL LAW.

ACKNOWLEDGMENT

YOU ACKNOWLEDGE THAT YOU HAVE READ THIS AGREEMENT, UNDERSTAND IT, AND AGREE TO BE BOUND BY ITS TERMS AND CONDITIONS. YOU ALSO AGREE THAT THIS AGREEMENT IS THE COMPLETE AND EXCLUSIVE STATEMENT OF THE AGREEMENT BETWEEN YOU AND THE COMPANY AND SUPERSEDES ALL PROPOSALS OR PRIOR AGREEMENTS, ORAL, OR WRITTEN, AND ANY OTHER COMMUNICATIONS BETWEEN YOU AND THE COMPANY OR ANY REPRESENTATIVE OF THE COMPANY RELATING TO THE SUBJECT MATTER OF THIS AGREEMENT.

Should you have any questions concerning this Agreement or if you wish to contact the Company for any reason, please contact in writing at the address below or call the at the telephone number provided.

PTR Customer Service
Prentice Hall PTR
One Lake Street
Upper Saddle River, New Jersey 07458

Telephone: 201-236-7105

Java^{TM} Developer's Kit
Version 1.0.2
Binary Code License

This binary code license ("License") contains rights and restrictions associated with use of the accompanying software and documentation ("Software"). Read the License carefully before installing Software. By installing Software you agree to the terms and conditions of this License.

1. LIMITED LICENSE GRANT. Sun grants to you ("Licensee") a non-exclusive, non-transferable limited license to use Software without fee. Licensee may re-distribute complete and unmodified Software to third parties provided that this License conspicuously appear with all copies of Software and that Licensee does not charge a fee for such re-distribution of Software.

2. JAVA PLATFORM INTERFACE. In the event that Licensee creates any Java-related API and distributes such API to others for applet or application development, Licensee must promptly publish an accurate specification for such API for free use by all developers of Java-based software. Licensee may not modify the Java Platform Interface ("JPI", identified as classes contained within the "java" package or any subpackages of the "java" package), by creating additional classes within the JPI or otherwise causing the addition to or modification of the classes in the JPI.

3. RESTRICTIONS. Software is confidential copyrighted information of Sun and title to all copies is retained by Sun and/or its licensors. Licensee shall not modify, decompile, disassemble, decrypt, extract, or otherwise reverse engineer Software. Software may not be leased, assigned, or sublicensed, in whole or in part. Software is not designed or intended for use in on-line control of aircraft, air traffic, aircraft navigation or aircraft communications; or in the design, construction, operation or maintenance of any nuclear facility. Licensee warrants that it will not use or redistribute the Software for such purposes.

4. TRADEMARKS AND LOGOS. Licensee acknowledges that Sun owns the Java trademark and all Java-related trademarks, logos and icons including the Coffee Cup and Duke ("Java Marks") and agrees to: (i) comply with the Java Trademark Guidelines at http://java.com/trademarks.html; (ii) not do anything harmful to or inconsistent with Sun's rights in the Java Marks; and (iii) assist Sun in protecting those rights, including assigning to Sun any rights acquired by Licensee in any Java Mark.

5. DISCLAIMER OF WARRANTY. Software is provided "AS IS," without a warranty of any kind. ALL EXPRESS OR IMPLIED REPRESENTATIONS AND WARRANTIES, INCLUDING ANY IMPLIED WARRANTY OF MERCHANTABILITY, FITNESS FOR A PARTICULAR PURPOSE OR NON-INFRINGEMENT, ARE HEREBY EXCLUDED.

6. LIMITATION OF LIABILITY. SUN AND ITS LICENSORS SHALL NOT BE LIABLE FOR ANY DAMAGES SUFFERED BY LICENSEE OR ANY THIRD PARTY AS A RESULT OF USING OR DISTRIBUTING SOFTWARE. IN NO EVENT WILL SUN OR ITS LICENSORS BE LIABLE FOR ANY LOST REVENUE, PROFIT OR DATA, OR FOR DIRECT, INDIRECT, SPECIAL, CONSEQUENTIAL, INCIDENTAL OR PUNITIVE DAMAGES. HOWEVER CAUSED AND REGARDLESS OF THE THEORY OF LIABILITY, ARISING OUT OF THE USE OF OR INABILITY TO USE SOFTWARE, EVEN IF SUN HAS BEEN ADVISED OF THE POSSIBILITY OF SUCH DAMAGES.

7. TERMINATION. Licensee may terminate this License at any time by destroying all copies of Software. This License will terminate immediately without notice from Sun if Licensee fails to comply with any provision of this License. Upon such termination, Licensee must destroy all copies of Software.

8. EXPORT REGULATIONS. Software, including technical data, is subject to U.S. export control laws, including the U.S. Export Administration Act and its associated regulations, and may be subject to export or import regulations in other countries. Licensee agrees to comply strictly with all such regulations and acknowledges that it has the responsibility to obtain licenses to export, re-export, or import Software. Software may not be downloaded, or otherwise exported or re-exported (i) into, or to a national or resident of, Cuba, Iraq, Iran, North Korea, Libya, Sudan, Syria, or any country to which the U.S. has embargoed goods; or (ii) to anyone on the U.S. Treasury Department's list of Specially Designated Nations or the U.S. Commerce Department's Table of Denial Orders.

9. RESTRICTED RIGHTS. Use, duplication or disclosure by the United States government is subject to the restrictions as set forth in the Rights in Technical Data and Computer Software Clauses in DFARS 252.227-7013(c) (1) (ii) and FAR 52.227-19(c) (2) as applicable.

10. GOVERNING LAW. Any action related to this License will be governed by California law and controlling U.S. federal law. No choice of law rules of any jurisdiction will apply.

11. SEVERABILITY. If any of the above provisions are held to be in violation of applicable law, void, or unenforceable in any jurisdiction, then such provisions are herewith waived to the extent necessary for the License to be otherwise enforceable ion such jurisdiction. However, if in Sun's opinion deletion of any provisions of the License by operation of this paragraph unreasonably compromises the rights or increase the liabilities of Sun or its licensors, Sun reserves the right to terminate the License and refund the fee paid by Licensee, if any, as Licensee's sole and exclusive remedy.